POPULATION STUDIES
OF
BIRDS

Above Great Tit bringing larva of Copper Underwing and a spider to its young. Photographed from back of nest by electronic flash operated by entering bird. (T. Royama)

Below Part of Marley wood, with nesting box on oak tree. (D. Kempson)

POPULATION STUDIES
OF
BIRDS

by

DAVID LACK

ILLUSTRATED BY
ROBERT GILLMOR

CLARENDON PRESS · OXFORD

Oxford University Press, Ely House, London W.1

GLASGOW NEW YORK TORONTO MELBOURNE WELLINGTON
CAPE TOWN IBADAN NAIROBI DAR ES SALAAM LUSAKA ADDIS ABABA
DELHI BOMBAY CALCUTTA MADRAS KARACHI LAHORE DACCA
KUALA LUMPUR SINGAPORE HONG KONG TOKYO

Casebound: ISBN 0 19 857335 0
Paperbound: ISBN 0 19 857341 3

FIRST PUBLISHED 1966
REPRINTED 1967, 1968 (WITH CORRECTIONS)
1973

Printed in Great Britain by
William Clowes & Sons, Limited, London, Beccles and Colchester

CONTENTS

v

1

INTRODUCTION

THERE has in the last thirty years been great controversy as to how animal populations are regulated. The very existence of regulation has been questioned, while those who hold that it exists have differed widely as to how it is brought about. Before 1954 there had been no general work on this theme, so my aim in *The Natural Regulation of Animal Numbers*, which appeared in that year, was a comprehensive survey, in which I tried to develop the argument progressively, completing each step with reference to the known examples before passing to the next. But as the examples had often to be taken from different kinds of animals, the reader could not see the picture as a whole for any one species. Since 1952, when the previous manuscript was completed, the chief advances have come from long-term studies, and these provide the best available means for testing the divergent theories that have been put forward, so I have in the present book concentrated on such studies, discussing each species in as many aspects as possible before passing to the next. After several changes of mind, I decided to limit the examples to birds, because my aim is to provide a critical assessment, which is possible only for animals of which one has had personal experience. That principles

Headpiece: Herons at the nest.

I

found in bird populations apply to other animals was, I hope, sufficiently shown in my earlier book.

Because I did not wish the studies selected here to be biased with respect to the views of the workers concerned, the principle on which I chose them was simply that each should have continued for at least four years and should consist of more than just an annual census. One study, on the Great Tit, *Parus major*, at Oxford, has been set out in three chapters instead of one, because it is fuller than the rest, and also to show the reader some of the practical difficulties in a field study. One other, on the Quelea, *Q. quelea*, covered less than four years, but is unusual in referring to a tropical species and in including detailed information on food throughout the year. In addition to the thirteen major species selected, I have added to several chapters another, studied for less than four years, if it shows important parallels, and in the chapter on shearwaters three species are included in the main discussion.

In evaluating these studies, the reader should keep in mind three divergent theories of population dynamics. The first, particularly associated with A. J. Nicholson (1933 and many later papers), is based on the assumption that animal populations are normally in a state of balance and that, though they fluctuate, they do so in a more or less stable and restricted manner. This situation can be brought about only through density-dependent factors, which tend to depress the population at high densities and to increase it at low densities, either at once or after delay. The chief factors influencing numbers which might vary in a density-dependent way are the reproductive rate, the mortality due to food shortage, predation or disease, and self-regulating behaviour such as territorial fighting. Due to a change in the environment, a few populations are at present increasing or decreasing rapidly, but both conditions are very temporary, the increase leading to a new and higher position of balance and the decrease to a lower position of balance or to extinction.

On the second theory, particularly associated with Andrewartha and Birch (1954), density-dependent control is held to be quite unimportant in nature, and most animal populations are considered to fluctuate irregularly in numbers from year to year through factors, notably those linked with climate, which act independently of density. On this view, many populations indeed become extinct, but many others persist through chance for a long time. In this latter connection, the ability of animals to move from one area to another, thus recolonizing areas of local extinction, is held to be of special importance.

On the third view, developed comprehensively by Wynne-Edwards (1962), the concept of density-dependent regulation is accepted, and food shortage is considered to be the ultimate factor limiting numbers;

but animals normally regulate their own density far below the potential upper limit set by food, because through group-selection they have evolved both dispersive behaviour and restraints on reproduction, by which means 'overfishing' is prevented and food supplies are conserved.

In my earlier book, I maintained the first theory, of density-dependent regulation. This was combined with the view, developed especially for birds, that the reproductive rate (in particular, the number of eggs in the clutch) has been evolved through natural selection to correspond with that number which, on average, gives rise to the greatest number of surviving offspring. Since clutch-size varies very little with population density, the main regulation of numbers must be brought about by density-dependent variations in mortality, and in wild birds the commonest density-dependent mortality factor is food shortage. I pointed out, however, that the effects of food shortage may be greatly modified by movements, not only by large-scale migrations and emigrations, but also by purely local movements, to which I gave the general name of dispersion.

In amplification of the above, when a bird is introduced to a new region and becomes established there, it at first increases rapidly, which shows that it is capable of rapid increase, but eventually its numbers level off, which shows that the capacity for increase has been checked, evidently by factors which operate more strongly at higher than lower densities of population. Thereafter the introduced species, like those native to the region, tends to fluctuate, in most cases irregularly, between limits that are small compared with what is theoretically possible. In my book of 1954 I illustrated this pattern of restricted fluctuations by, among others, the annual census of the Grey Heron, *Ardea cinerea*, in two areas in England; and as this is by now the longest census made of any British bird, I have in Fig. 1. extended the graph for another twelve years. During the thirty years in question, the Heron has decreased markedly after each hard winter; but it has then recovered quickly, showing that it is capable of rapid increase; in between, it has fluctuated much more slowly and rather irregularly, due to causes that are as yet unknown. Some of the bird populations discussed later in the present book have fluctuated more rapidly than that of the Heron, while others have shown slow, long-term changes, but all have agreed in fluctuating between limits that are extremely small compared with what is theoretically possible.

The idea that the clutch-size of each species of bird has been evolved through natural selection is critical to the later argument of this book, so it may be illustrated at the start by the species in which the point can be seen most clearly, the Swift, *Apus apus*. The figures in my earlier book (1954, p. 24) were extended later (Lack 1956a, b; Weitnauer and

INTRODUCTION

Lack, 1955). The normal clutch of the Swift at Oxford is 2 or 3 eggs. The number of young that the parents are able to raise varies with the weather, being greater in fine summers when airborne insects are abundant than in cold wet summers when they are sparse. In broods of 3 young, the proportion raised successfully was 100 per cent in the

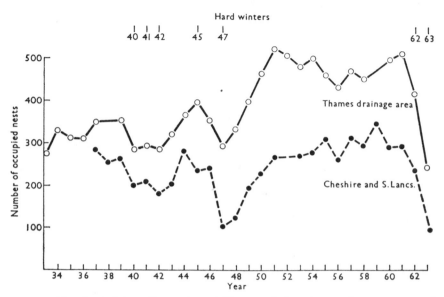

FIG. 1. Number of breeding pairs of Heron, *Ardea cinerea*, in two parts of England, 1933–63. Data from British Trust for Ornithology, analysed by J. Stafford (*pers. comm.*).

unusually fine summer of 1949, nine-tenths in the fine summers of 1951 and 1955, and three-quarters in the fairly fine summer of 1952; hence in each of these 4 years, more young were raised per brood of 3 than could have been raised per brood of 2. But in the moderately poor summers of 1953 and 1956, only three-fifths and one-half respectively of the young in broods of 3 survived, whereas all in broods of 2 did so, so that the average raised per brood was higher in broods of 2 (2·0) than in broods of 3 (1·8 and 1·5). This, I consider, is the main reason why the Swift has evolved a clutch of 3 or 2, 3 being advantageous in some years and 2 in others. Finally, in the extremely wet and cold summer of 1954, only 29 per cent of the young in broods of 2 survived, but all in broods of 1 did so, hence in that year the broods in which, by chance, only 1 egg hatched were the most productive, but this has happened too rarely for clutches of 1 to be selected. (There were, by chance, no broods of 3 in 1954.)

The most critical point is why the Swift has not evolved a clutch

4

of 4 eggs or more. On my view this must be because natural selection acts strongly against the laying of clutches larger than 3, presumably because any individuals doing so would raise fewer offspring per brood than those laying clutches of 3. To test this point, newly-hatched nestlings were transferred from one nest to another to make up broods of 4 (and also further broods of 3). The transfer itself took only a few seconds and, so far as observed, it did not harm the young, as the parents do not recognize their own offspring at this stage. The results for the years 1958–61 are shown in Table 1.

TABLE 1

Survival in relation to brood-size in the Swift, *Apus apus*, at Oxford

Year	Brood size	No. of broods	No. of young dying	Per cent lost	No. raised per brood
1958	2	21	2	5	1·9
	3	4	1	8	2·8
	4	2	4(+1)	50(+)	2·0(−)
1959	2	15	0	0	2·0
	3	4	0	0	3·0
	4	4	5	31	2·8
1960	2	18	2	6	1·9
	3	6	4	22	2·3
	4	5	14	70	1·2
1961	2	18	1	3	1·9
	3	6	4	22	2·3
	4	5	13	65	1·4

Notes. Based on Perrins (1964), but omiting broods of 1, as these were almost always successful and none died of starvation. The broods of 4 were not natural but due to the addition of nestlings from other broods. In 1957, another extremely fine summer, all 12 young in 4 broods of 3 were raised, but out of 8 young in two artificially supplemented broods of 4, 2 certainly died and 4 others which left the nest prematurely almost certainly died too, though this could not be proved. From two natural broods of 4 in Switzerland, 5, or 2·5 per brood, were raised, whereas nearly all the young in broods of 3 were raised there (Weitnauer and Lack, 1955).

In all 4 years, almost all the young were raised in broods of 1 and 2 and none of the few deaths was attributed to starvation. In the moderately fine summers of 1960 and 1961, just over three-quarters of the young from broods of 3 were raised, with an average of 2·3 per brood, whereas only-third of the young from broods of 4 were raised, with an average of 1·3 per brood, so that broods of 3 were much the more productive. There was a similar difference in the same direction in the rather fine summer of 1958. Moreover, even in the exceptionally fine summer of 1959, when all the young in broods of 3 were raised, only about two-thirds of those in broods of 4 were raised, with an average of 2·8 per brood, and no pair raised 4 young. The evidence is therefore clear that any hereditary tendency for an English Swift to lay a clutch of 4 will be eliminated by natural selection, because such birds will leave fewer offspring than those laying clutches of 3.

Not all the variations in the clutch-size of the Swift are due to hereditary differences. For instance, the pairs that start breeding later in the season usually lay 2 eggs, not 3, and this is probably adaptive to the later needs of the young, because it is harder, on the average, for a Swift to raise young successfully late than early in the season. Secondly, if there is unusually cold weather in what is normally the main laying period of the Swift in the second half of May, those individuals which have not yet started a clutch may postpone doing so, while those that have started tend to lay their second egg 3 instead of 2 days after the first, and to lay a full clutch of 2 instead of 3. These tendencies are not adapted to the later needs of the young, and they have presumably been evolved for a different reason, namely because, when food is sparse in the laying period, there is some risk to the adult female in using its food reserves to form eggs. Under these conditions it may, on balance, be more advantageous for a bird to produce 2 eggs instead of 3, even though this means that, on average, it will raise a slightly smaller brood than if it laid a clutch of 3. (The effect is similar whether it lays a clutch of 2 instead of 3 at the normal date, or whether it postpones laying altogether, because later in the season the normal clutch is 2 and the young will be raised under rather less favourable conditions.)

I did not appreciate when I wrote my book of 1954 that feeding conditions at the time of laying affected the number of eggs laid (except in poultry). But I have since found that this also holds in the Cuckoo, *Cuculus canorus*, though the latter is a special case because it is a brood-parasite. A young Cuckoo could presumably be raised at all seasons when the host species can raise its own young, but in England the Cuckoo starts laying several weeks after its main hosts, probably because it cannot earlier in the year find enough of its main food, large caterpillars, to form eggs (Lack, 1963).

Gallinaceous birds have active nidifugous young which seek food for themselves from hatching, so it is extremely unlikely that their clutch-size could have been evolved in relation to the number of young which the parents can raise, and when I wrote my earlier book, I could not suggest what the critical factor might be. But Siivonen (1954, 1956, 1957, 1958) has since provided circumstantial evidence that, in this group also, clutch-size is affected by the amount of food available to the female during or just before laying. For instance, in Finland the average clutch of the Partridge, *Perdix perdix*, was 17·4 eggs after mild winters, but only 15·2 after cold winters with much snow, which hinders the birds when feeding. Similarly the Capercaillie, *Tetrao urogallus*, and Blackgame, *Lyrurus tetrix*, weighed less, were in poorer physical condition and laid smaller clutches of less viable eggs in those years when April was cold than in those years when it was warmer; also two captive female Blackgame laid larger clutches than usual when given extra food. Similarly the availability of food evidently determines the interval between successive eggs, and hence the number of eggs laid in a season, by the Mallee Fowl, *Leipoa ocellata*, which like other megapodes lays a series of eggs in a large mound, the young being independent from hatching (Frith, 1959, modifying 1956). These findings do not mean that the food available to the hen birds at the time of laying is the sole factor affecting the clutch-size of gallinaceous birds. Hereditary factors must also be involved, at least in determining the size of the eggs, and hence the amount of food needed for each, and probably also in determining the limits between which the clutch-size of each species can be modified by the food supply at the time of laying.

The reproductive rate of a bird is influenced not only by its clutch-size but also by the number of broods in a year and the age at which it starts breeding. In my earlier book I provided circumstantial evidence for various species that the number of broods in a year is the largest that the environmental conditions permit. I similarly argued that each species starts breeding at the age at which it can first effectively raise young without risk to itself. Many species first breed when a year old, but others only after several years, the latter, I suggested, being species which have difficulty in finding enough food for their young and in which greater experience is needed before they can safely raise any. This view was strongly contested by Wynne-Edwards (1955, 1962) who argued instead that deferred maturity has been evolved by long-lived species in which breeding at an earlier age would lead to over-population.

Because most animal populations are neither increasing nor decreasing, except very temporarily, the reproductive and mortality rates must balance. In the past, this was usually explained by supposing that the reproductive rate of each species has been evolved to balance its mortality, and this view was recently revived by Wynne-Edwards (1962), who attributed such evolution to group-selection. But the balance is as readily explained through density-dependent variations in the mortality rate, and there are theoretical reasons for thinking that certain mortality factors, notably food shortage, predation, and disease, act in a density-dependent manner. When I wrote my earlier book of

7

1954, the existence of density-dependent mortality still rested largely on theoretical considerations, supplemented by data from laboratory populations of various insects which were, however, models rather than true experiments. The evidence from natural populations is not much stronger now, but nevertheless I believe that density-dependent mortality provides the best explanation of the balance between birth and death rates. Moreover, in birds, the high death rates necessary on this view have been demonstrated for many species through the capture and recapture of marked individuals, and there is circumstantial evidence that various populations are up against the limit set by food. This is not the whole story, however, because when numbers are limited by food shortage, natural selection will favour the evolution of movements away from areas of shortage, both large-scale migrations and small-scale dispersions, and, as argued in my earlier book, I consider that such movements have an extremely important modifying influence on bird numbers, though this influence is secondary to that of food.

Views contrary to those outlined in the previous paragraph have been advocated by various other workers. Divergent theories about animal populations have arisen partly because the available facts are as yet inadequate, but, much more importantly, because of fundamental differences between their advocates in regard to evolutionary theory. Thus Andrewartha and Birch did not bring evolutionary considerations into their basic analyses, while Wynne-Edwards advocated evolution by group-selection, and I regard natural selection as paramount. Controversies due to a fundamental cleavage of viewpoint combined with inadequate facts tend to be unprofitable, hence, while I owe it to the reader to explain why I reject these other views, and so far as birds are concerned the reasons need to be set out at length, I think it best to relegate this discussion to an appendix (pp. 281–312), and the points at issue will be treated in the main text only where they relate specifically to the populations selected for detailed discussion in this book.

Most of the species selected for detailed treatment here were studied by individual workers, a few by a team, while a few were studied independently by more than one person. The published papers or books by these main workers have been cited in the standard way, by surname and year of publication, near the start of the relevant chapter or section, but to avoid tiresome repetition later references to them in the same chapter have usually been omitted. Other workers have, however, been cited in the standard way whenever mentioned, while my own comments and interpretations have normally been preceded by the personal pronoun. I hope that in this way the reader will be clear as to whose findings or views are being reported.

Each chapter or section dealing with a particular species was sent for criticism in manuscript to the main author or authors whose work was reviewed, and several of them sent me papers in manuscript before publication. I am grateful to all these persons for the considerable trouble which they took in amending what I wrote, and as a result errors were removed and each chapter was substantially improved. I was happy, also, to find that this exchange was not all in one direction, as in several instances an author modified his own views before publication in the light of what I had written. Those to whom I am particularly indebted are: Dr. C. M. Perrins for the Great and Blue Tits, *Parus major* and *P. caeruleus*; Dr. J. A. Gibb for the Coal Tit, *P. ater*; Dr. B. Campbell and Professor L. von Haartman for the Pied Flycatcher, *Ficedula hypoleuca* (Dr. Campbell even lending me his raw data prior to his own analysis, while in addition Dr. E. Curio provided unpublished information supplementing what he had published); Dr. D. W. Snow for the Blackbird, *Turdus merula*, the manakins, *M. manacus* and *Pipra erythocephala*, and the Oil-bird, *Steatornis caripensis*; Mr. P. Walters Davies for the Song Thrush, *Turdus philomelos*; Mr. H. N. Southern for the Tawny Owl, *Strix aluco*; Dr. G. Orians for the Tricolored Redwing, *Agelaius tricolor*; Dr. P. Ward for the Quelea, *Q. quelea* (this chapter also being read by Mr. N. R. Fuggles-Couchman); Dr. R. K. Murton for the Wood Pigeon, *Columba palumbus*; Dr. I. Newton for the Bullfinch, *Pyrrhula pyrrhula*; Drs. D. J. Jenkins and A. Watson for the Red Grouse, *Lagopus scoticus*, and Ptarmigan, *L. mutus*; Drs. E. Schüz, J. Szijj, and G. Zink for the White Stork, *C. ciconia*; Dr. L. E. Richdale for the Yellow-eyed Penguin, *Megadyptes antipodes*; Dr. J. C. Coulson for the Kittiwake, *Rissa tridactyla*; Dr. B. Nelson for the Gannet, *Sula bassana*; and Drs. D. Serventy and M. P. Harris for respectively the Australian and British shearwaters, *Puffinus* (*Procellaria*) *tenuirostris* and *P. puffinus*. In addition, Mr. J. Stafford kindly provided me with the figures for the British Trust for Ornithology's annual census of the Heron, *Ardea cinerea*, Mr. R. E. Moreau and Dr. C. M. Perrins criticized the whole manuscript and Dr. J. Crook read Appendix, Chapter 3. Finally, Mrs. Perrins prepared nearly all the diagrams and maps and Mrs. Whittaker the rest, Messrs. D. Kempson and T. Royama took the photographs used for the frontispiece, and Mr. Robert Gillmor made the line drawings, the aim of which is to provide the reader with a picture of each main species and of some special techniques.

To save repetition, no population studies have been included in this book that were considered in *The Natural Regulation of Animal Numbers*, apart from brief mention of some of them in Appendix, section 1, where the earlier book is summarized. The five long-term studies which, but for this, would have found place here were those of Bump *et al.* (1947)

on the Ruffed Grouse, *Bonasa umbellus*, Errington (1945) on the Bobwhite Quail, *Colinus virginianus*, Kendeigh (1941) on the House Wren, *Troglodytes aedon*, Kluijver (1951) on the Great Tit, *Parus major*, and Nice (1937) on the Song Sparrow, *Melospiza melodia*.

Finally, though I myself have been actively engaged on one side of a three-cornered argument on population theory, I hope that my expositions and interpretations will not be considered partial. At the controversial stage which the subject has reached, it is easy to overlook good arguments brought forward by one's opponents, and mere awareness of this danger may not ensure its avoidance. Nevertheless an author has a double duty to his readers, first, unquestionably, to treat the views of other workers with fairness, but secondly, and of equal importance, to state clearly which he considers right and which wrong. In the end, of course, the test of this book will not be what is written here, but any new research which it may stimulate and, if I have been wise, may guide.

A brood of Swifts, the last to hatch being smaller than the others.

2

THE GREAT TIT IN WYTHAM
ANNUAL CENSUS AND LAYING PERIOD

THE value of the Great Tit, *Parus major*, for population research was first appreciated in Holland in 1912 by K. Wolda, whose work was continued by H. N. Kluijver (1951). This Dutch study, discussed in my previous book (1954), has now continued for just over fifty years, though the main wood worked by Kluijver, at Orange Nassau's Oord near Wageningen, had to be changed for one in the near-by Veluwe after 1944. The parallel study by members of the Edward Grey Institute (Oxford University) in Marley wood on the Wytham estate was begun in 1947 as a result of a visit to Dr. Kluijver, with whom I have since been in regular touch. From 1958 onward, this study was expanded by C. M. Perrins to include a further considerable area of woodland on th Wytham estate.

A special advantage of the Great Tit is that, particularly in woods where natural holes are scarce, virtually the whole population breeds in nesting boxes. Hence the number of pairs, the clutch-size, and the number of young raised are accurately known simply from a regular inspection of the boxes. In addition, the bird is common, conspicuous, diurnal in habits, easily trapped and marked in winter and, in the Oxford district, resident throughout the year. Not only do the birds not migrate

Headpiece: Great Tits at their nesting box.

but comparatively few ringed as young or adults in Wytham woods have been found off the area, except on a new housing estate in Botley-Cumnor a mile away, while hardly any have been found more than five miles away (Perrins, 1963; cf. Gibb, 1956b). Hence the Wytham population is virtually self-contained, in contrast to Dutch populations, in which a proportion of the birds move for a considerable distance in some years (Kluijver, 1951).

This study of the Great Tit is described at greater length than those of other species later in this book, mainly because it has been carried out in greater detail than the other long ones, and in particular the bird has been studied at all times of the year, not merely in the breeding season. Further, detailed treatment of one species may help to show the reader some of the difficulties inherent in any long-term population study. When I initiated this work, I considered that certain factors might have an important influence on the bird's numbers, and these were studied from the start, but some of my early ideas proved wrong and others needed modification, while various factors proved to be important which were not thought of at the start, so that they were measured only in later years. Another difficulty was that the first two years were in some important respects unusual, but one could not know this at the time, and as a result, I was misled in designing future work. The points on which most information has so far been obtained include the significance of the breeding season and of clutch-size, the mortality of the young after leaving the nest in relation to their time of hatching and brood-size, and the influence of this mortality on the annual fluctuations in the breeding population. The factors controlling the average level of population density are as yet more uncertain.

It is important to continue the study of a natural population for many years, and in this respect the Edward Grey Institute has had two special advantages. First, the Wytham estate is owned by Oxford University, and I knew in advance that Marley would be left undisturbed for so long as the study continued, while apparatus could be left there without fear of damage. Secondly, the Institute staff could always include an assistant to carry out the field work on tits. While in both respects the Institute has been fortunate, it may be stressed that long-term ecological studies are not so difficult as their paucity might suggest, and provided that the initiator feels that the work is worth while, ways can normally be found to continue it. The breeding study and winter trapping in Marley wood were started by J. A. Gibb in 1947 and continued by him until 1951, D. F. Owen took over from 1952 to 1957, and C. M. Perrins from 1958 up to the present time, Gibb and Perrins being themselves helped by field assistants in many of these years. In addition, R. A. Hinde studied the behaviour of the Great Tit in Marley wood from 1948 to 1950, while P. H. T. Hartley and Miss M. M. Betts worked on food and feeding behaviour from 1947 to 1951, and T. Royama made further studies on food in the breeding seasons of 1963 and 1964. I am extremely grateful to all these workers, whose publications on the subject will be found under their respective names in the bibliography. Some of the earlier work was included in my previous book (1954) and that described here and in the two following chapters has been based especially on the later work of Perrins (1963 and 1965), who has been responsible for many new findings and for the reinterpretation of former data (see also summary in Lack, 1964*b*).

The Blue Tit, *Parus caeruleus*, was studied in Wytham alongside the Great Tit, as it commonly breeds in the same type of nesting box, but it proved rather less suitable for a population study. First, young Blue Tits disperse over a wider area than Great Tits, and there are occasional irruptions into England from the Continent, so that the population is less self-contained. Secondly, even with far more nesting boxes than birds, some of the Blue Tits breed in small natural holes in trees, and these pairs could not be studied. Hence, while the number of Blue Tits in the boxes each year probably reflects the changes in the total population, it does not comprise the whole population. Thirdly, Blue Tits are harder to trap in winter than Great Tits. Nevertheless, the Blue Tit population in Marley has shown many instructive parallels with that of the Great Tit, so the two have been treated together here.

In England, the Great and Blue Tits are two of the commonest birds in broad-leaved woodland. The British forms differ in minor ways from the Continental races, and presumably evolved in the English primaeval oak forest. The latter must have looked rather different from modern managed woodland, but apart from the scarcity of old trees, and hence of natural holes, the broad-leaved woods in Wytham may well provide fairly similar conditions for the tits, especially for the Great Tit, which usually feeds on or near the ground. Moreover, the shortage of natural holes has been made good by the provision of nesting boxes much in excess of the number of tits. Wytham woods were planted only during the eighteenth century, but they consist chiefly of Oaks, *Quercus robur/sessiliflora*, and other native broad-leaved trees, with native secondary shrubs such as Hazel, *Corylus avellana*, and Elder, *Sambucus niger*, and Marley wood has been untended for fifty years. Marley consists of about 22 hectares of woodland with a closed canopy, another 3 hectares with scattered trees and just over a hectare of open marshy ground, and its vegetation was described by Gibb (1950). There are no conifers, but large oaks are sparser than in most broad-leaved woods, including Wytham Great Wood. Marley appears to provide highly favourable conditions for the Great Tit, but is less favourable for the Blue Tit than are woods with a higher proportion of oak trees.

Great and Blue Tits feed mainly on insects, especially in summer, but take certain seeds, especially beechmast, in winter. During most of the year they are ecologically separated, as the Great Tit feeds on or near the ground and the Blue Tit among the leaves and on the high twigs, and their feeding methods, and the size and shape of their legs and beaks, are adapted to this difference. Both species, however, feed their young chiefly on caterpillars on oak leaves, and both feed on beechmast on the ground in the winters when it is plentiful (Hartley, 1953; Gibb, 1954a; Betts, 1955; Gibb, 1958).

The number of pairs of Great and Blue Tits breeding in boxes in Marley wood each year, together with the mean date and mean clutch-size of first broods are set out in Table 2. The number of pairs is also plotted in Fig. 2, which shows that the two species have tended to fluctuate in parallel. In addition to these marked fluctuations, the Great

TABLE 2

Breeding of Great and Blue Tits in Marley Wood

Year	Number of pairs in boxes		Mean date of 1st egg (1st April=1)		Mean clutch	
	Great	Blue	Great	Blue	Great	Blue
1947	7	9	34	29	11·1	13·4
1948	21	19	10	10	12·3	13·2
1949	30	26	23	22	10·1	10·7
1950	c.31	c.34	29	22	9·1	10·8
1951	32	34	40	36	7·8	10·2
1952	20	17	23	24	9·9	10·2
1953	21	14	33	28	9·7	10·8
1954	31	18	25	22	9·7	11·3
1955	27	13	34	29	10·0	11·3
1956	24	15	34	32	10·0	11·3
1957	c.49	c.32	17	15	9·2	10·7
1958	27	17	35	34	9·2	9·5
1959	41	20	24	22	8·8	9·6
1960	51	25	27	20	8·3	10·2
1961	86	44	21	19	8·0	8·5
1962	43	21	34	32	8·8	9·9
1963	39	41	29	32	9·3	10·6
1964	54	46	34	30	9·1	11·0

Notes. Data from J. A. Gibb, D. F. Owen, and C. M. Perrins. The mean date of laying was reckoned from 1 April = 1, so, for instance, 35 = 5 May.

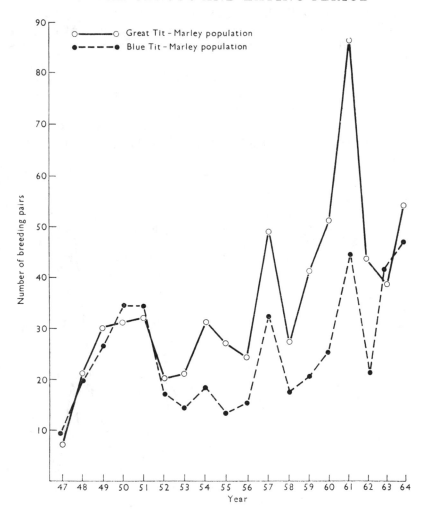

FIG. 2. Number of breeding pairs of Great and Blue Tits in Marley wood 1947–64 (from Perrins, 1965).

Tit has shown a gradual rise in numbers over the years. So far as known, there has been no corresponding change in the conditions in Marley wood in this time, apart from the gradual growth of the trees, but a large new housing estate has been built at Botley, about a mile from the wood, a number of the tits feed there in winter, and this has possibly meant that more survive in winter than formerly. This, however, is speculative. The importance of continuing a population study for long enough is shown by the fact that in the first fourteen years, the greatest number of Great Tits breeding in Marley wood was 51 pairs, from which it might reasonably have been concluded that this was about the greatest number which the wood could support. But in 1961 as many as 86 pairs bred there, an increase of nearly 70 per cent over the previous highest figure.

It is valuable to know whether the annual fluctuations in Marley wood were purely local, and hence due primarily to factors operating in the immediate vicinity, or whether they were widespread, in which case climatic factors might have been involved. In Fig. 3 are shown the population changes, in terms of pairs per hectare, (i) in mixed broad-

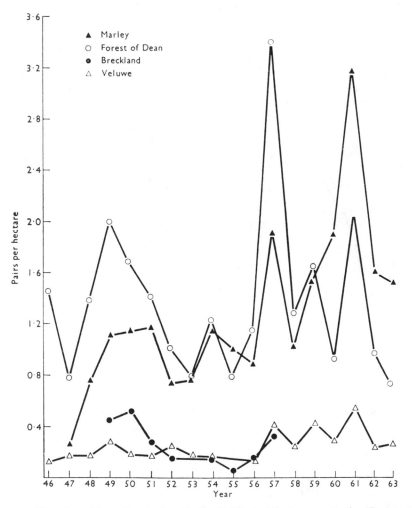

FIG. 3. Density of breeding pairs of Great Tit in Marley wood, the Forest of Dean, the Breckland, and the Veluwe (1946–62)

leaved woodland in Marley, (ii) in a mature plantation of pure oak in the Forest of Dean about 50 miles west of Oxford (B. Campbell, pers. comm.; also Lack 1955, 1958), (iii) in pine plantations in the Breckland about 90 miles north-east of Oxford (only up to 1957; Lack 1955, 1958), and (iv) in rather poor mixed coniferous and broad-leaved woodland in the Veluwe, near Arnhem in Holland, about 300 miles east of Oxford (H. N. Kluijver, pers. comm.). The positions of these woods, together with Wageningen, where Kluijver (1951) studied the Great Tit earlier, are shown in Fig. 4. It will be seen from Fig. 3 that the most marked

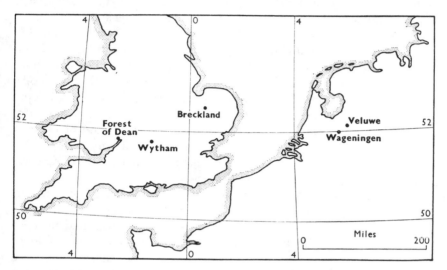

FIG. 4. Positions of the main woods where Great Tits were studied.

population fluctuations of the Great Tit occurred in the same years in all four woods, though the woods were of very different types and several hundred miles apart. All four populations increased from 1947 to 1949, also between 1956 and 1957, all decreased in 1958, increased again in 1959, markedly increased in 1961 and decreased in 1962. In the Veluwe and Marley, the breeding population in 1961 was the highest recorded, and though in the Dean it was lower than in 1957, the proportionate increase in 1961 over the previous year was even higher than in the other woods. By comparison, the differences between the woods were small and unimportant; in 1950 the population increased in two of the woods and decreased in the other two; in 1952 the population rose in the Veluwe but fell in the three English woods; in 1954 the marked rise in Marley and the Dean did not occur in the Breckland or the Veluwe; while in 1960 there was rise in Marley (though not the rest of Wytham) and a decline in both the Dean and the Veluwe. The Blue Tit tended

17

to fluctuate in parallel with the Great Tit in all these woods, though there were some exceptions.

The occurrence of parallel fluctuations in the numbers of the Great and Blue Tits in both broad-leaved and coniferous woods, and in woods up to several hundred miles apart, suggests that climatic factors are responsible, either directly or indirectly. This situation recalls the fluctuations correlated with climate in *Thrips imaginis* in Australia, on the basis of which Andrewartha and Birch (1954) decided that density-dependent control could be excluded, whereas Nicholson (1958*b*) and other authors claimed that it had to be included. (This example is further discussed in the Appendix, p. 294.) The same arguments apply to these populations of the Great and Blue Tits. It should be noted in particular that, though climatic factors may have been responsible for the parallel fluctuations in numbers, Fig. 3 shows that the fluctuations occurred around very different average levels in the different woods, and the average levels also require explanation. Further, the rapid increases in numbers between 1947 and 1949, between 1956 and 1957, and between 1960 and 1961, show that the potential rate of increase of the tits is high; yet such large increases occurred only occasionally, and one might have expected much greater fluctuations if density-dependent factors had not been operating.

On a different point, it should be kept in mind that graphs such as Figs. 2 and 3 are over-simplified, for while they suggest that between one year and the next the population in some cases rose and in other cases fell, what really happened every year was first a threefold to sixfold increase each spring due to breeding, then a marked decrease in late summer or autumn primarily due to juvenile mortality, and then a less marked decrease in winter due to mortality among both juveniles and adults (cf. Lack, 1954, p. 20). All that Figs. 2 and 3 show is the eventual difference in numbers between one spring and the next.[1]

Great and Blue Tits usually lay their eggs in late April, but the average date of the first broods has differed by up to five weeks in different years, the two species varying closely in parallel. The question of primary interest in a population study is the adaptive significance of the breeding season, but the proximate factors influencing the timing of breeding are of some relevance, so will be mentioned briefly first.

[1] In the censuses of Marley wood several times a year by Gibb (1956*b*), there was apparently a small rise in numbers each year in early spring just before breeding, but this may have been fallacious, as we did not at that time appreciate that in winter some Great Tits move from the woods to houses to feed by day, returning to the woods to roost each night; hence the counts by day in winter were probably a little too low, and the apparent rise in numbers in the early spring was probably due, at least partly, to the birds then staying in the woods for the whole day.

It has been known for over thirty years that, in several species of north temperate latitudes, the addition of extra hours of light during the winter causes the gonads to develop abnormally early, and one of the species for which this has been shown is the Great Tit in Finland (Suomalainen, 1937). Evidently the main proximate factor bringing wild birds of this type into breeding condition in spring is the increasing daylength. But since daylength increases at a constant rate each year while the average date of laying varies, in the Great Tit by up to five weeks, there must be at least one modifying factor. In Holland, the date of laying of the Great Tit each year was strongly correlated with the temperature in March and April, and to some extent with the temperature in February (Tollenaar, 1922; Kluijver, 1951, 1952). This was later confirmed for Marley wood (Lack, 1955, 1958; Perrins, 1965), as set out in Fig. 5. Either the temperature itself, or some factor linked with it, evidently modifies the date of laying in the Great Tit, and also in the Blue Tit, which varies in parallel. This factor evidently affects not merely breeding behaviour, but also the growth of the gonads, since on the same dates (13–15 March) in successive years the gonads of male Great and Blue Tits were much less well developed in

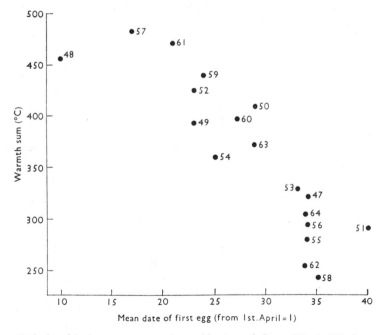

FIG. 5. Relationship between mean date of laying of Great Tit in Marley wood and the temperature in March and April in Oxford. The warmth sum is the sum of the degrees Centigrade above freezing point of the average temperature for each day 1 March to 20 April (from Perrins 1965).

the unusually cold season of 1947 than in the unusually warm season of 1948 (Marshall, 1949).

Further work is needed to determine whether temperature itself, or some factor linked with it, is responsible. After a cold spell in January, Great Tits often start singing and visiting nesting boxes on the first mild day, suggesting that temperature might have a direct influence. But Suomalainen (1937) showed that the winter temperature had no influence on the Great Tit's gonads, at least under the conditions of his experiments. Further, as discussed later (p. 101), in two other European passerine species, the Pied and Collared Flycatchers, *Ficedula hypoleuca* and *F. albicollis*, there is a correlation similar to that found in the Great Tit between the preceding spring temperatures and the average date of laying each year, but these flycatchers are migrants which arrive on their breeding grounds only in late April, so do not themselves experience most of the temperatures in question. Hence they presumably respond either to the appearance of fresh green vegetation or to their insect foods, both of which appear earlier in a mild than a cold spring; and the same may well apply to the Great and Blue Tits. Again, while the average date of laying of the Great Tit in any one year was usually similar in different English woods, in a few of the years studied it differed by a week or more, sometimes in one wood and sometimes in another, without consistency, except that every time that a difference occurred in the Great Tit, a similar difference occurred in the Blue Tit; and these occasional variations were not associated with any corresponding differences in temperature (Lack, 1958). There was also a minor variation due to temperature in those years when a cold spell occurred after some but not other pairs had started laying, the rest normally waiting until the return of warmer weather (Kluijver, 1951; confirmed by Lack, 1955, 1958). This could not be a response to green vegetation, and is presumably due to temperature itself or to the influence of temperature on the availability of insect foods. Kluijver showed that the response in question came four days after the change in temperature, presumably because the Great Tit takes four days to form an egg.

Considering now the adaptive significance of the breeding season, I postulated earlier (1954) that one would expect a single-brooded species to have evolved a breeding season such that its young are in the nest when food is most readily obtained for them. Nestling Great and Blue Tits, as already mentioned, are fed primarily on the caterpillars which occur in large numbers on the young leaves of oaks and other broad-leaved trees, especially in the second half of May and the first half of June. One of the commonest on oak leaves is the Winter Moth, *Operophthera brumata*, which in 1947, 1948, and 1949, when it was particularly abundant, was one of the main foods brought to young tits.

A later study by T. Royama has indicated, however, that in recent and more normal years, various other species have been more important than *O. brumata* in Marley wood, including *Allophyes oxyacanthae* which occurs primarily on Hawthorn, *Colotois pennaria* which occurs on a variety of trees but is scarce on oaks, and, after these have gone, the pupae of *Tortrix viridana* on oaks. These and the other species of caterpillars hatch around the time that the leaves of the trees emerge from their buds, and both leaves and caterpillars appear later in a cold than a mild spring, in which there is an obvious adaptive advantage to the caterpillars. The variations in the time of appearance of the caterpillars each year are most easily measured by the date of descent of those of the winter moth, which pupate on the ground, and Fig. 6 shows that the date of their descent each year has been strongly correlated with the time at which the young tits hatched.

Because this correlation has been so close, and because there is an obvious advantage to the Great Tit in having its nestlings at the time when caterpillars are most abundant, I formerly concluded (1954, 1955) that the date of laying of the Great Tit is adapted to the time of appearance of the caterpillars, and that this has led to the evolution in the Great Tit of an appropriate response to daylength modified by temperature. Certainly the response of the Great Tit has been such that every year the first broods have been in the nest at about the same stage in the caterpillar cycle, even though the date of appearance of the caterpillars varied by up to five weeks. It does not necessarily follow that this timing is the most efficient for raising young, but since most young Great Tits are in the nest when caterpillars are large and abundant, it is certainly near to the most efficient time. Further, the date of breeding of the Blue Tit has varied similarly to that of the Great Tit, so the same argument holds for this species.

Recently, Perrins (1963 and 1965) suggested that the above view must be modified, particularly because the spread in the dates of hatching of different broods in the same year has usually extended over two and often three weeks, so that certain pairs were well away from the date of 'half-fall' of the winter moth caterpillars and hence (*ex hypothese*) from the most favourable time for raising young.. There is, of course, a spread of variation in almost every biological character, with the individual measurements grouped round a mean which is, on average, the most advantageous for the population concerned. But Perrins showed that in the Great Tit the mean date of laying is definitely not the most advantageous for raising young. Instead, each year those pairs which laid early in the main period produced a higher proportion of surviving young than those which laid late in the main period. Between 1947 and 1957, for instance, the proportion of nestling Great Tits ringed in

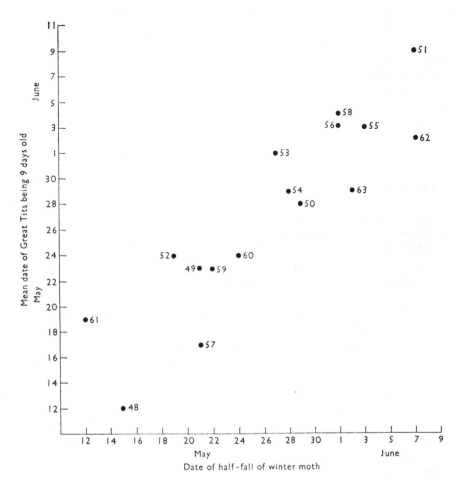

FIG. 6. Relationship between date of hatching of Great Tit in Marley wood and date by which half the Winter Moths, *Operophthera brumata*, under oaks in Wytham Great Wood pupated (except that the date in 1948 was for peak frass-fall in Marley wood, which was closely similar to that of 'half-fall' in Wytham in other years).

Wytham and later recovered after surviving at least three months was 9 per cent from those hatched in the first half of the main breeding period, as compared with only 6 per cent from those hatched in the second half, which in the years 1958, 1959, and 1960, when many more were trapped, the proportions were 24 and 14 per cent respectively. Moreover, since the clutches, and hence the broods, were slightly larger (on average by 0·5 nestling) in the first than the second half of the period, the average number of young raised per pair was somewhat greater than these figures suggest. It should be added that only genuine first broods were considered in this comparison, repeat clutches laid after the loss of a first attempt being excluded.

Since those Great Tits which lay their eggs early in the season raise more young than those which lay later, one would have expected the habit of laying later to be eliminated by natural selection, unless there were some further factor affecting the time of laying; and the only other factor which Perrins could suggest is the time needed by the female Great Tit to collect enough food to form a clutch of eggs. As the average weight of a hen Great Tit in March is 17·3 grams (Kluijver, 1952), as each egg weighs about 1·75 grams (Gibb, 1950), and as the commonest clutch is 9 or 10, the hen produces about her own weight in eggs in 9 or 10 days, so some individuals might well have difficulty in finding enough food for the purpose, particularly at the end of the time of year, in early spring, when food is probably scarcest for the birds. It also seems significant that the cock Great Tit regularly feeds the hen during laying (continuing during incubation). I earlier considered that such 'courtship-feeding' in birds is purely symbolic in function (Lack, 1940), but T. Royama (pers. comm.) has shown that in the related *P. major minor* of Japan, the rate of courtship-feeding is 5 times an hour, so that just prior to laying, the female receives some 70 meals a day from the male, and I would now suppose that such a habit would not have been evolved unless the food itself were of survival value. Hence this suggests that the female may be in critical need of food while forming her eggs. (It may be added that for the cock to feed the hen will also be of value during incubation, in shortening the periods when the hen needs to be off the eggs to get food, as demonstrated for a different species, the Pied Flycatcher, by von Haartman (1958, see also this book, p. 105).)

Yearling Great Tits breeding for the first time lay, on the average, a few days later than the older females (Kluijver, 1951, 1952; Perrins, 1965). This might well be because the yearlings, being less experienced in feeding, take somewhat longer to build up their food reserves. The food situation might also explain why, as discussed later, the Great Tit breeds rather earlier in gardens than woods, since householders provide food for tits in winter. Another point, shown in Table 2, is that the average date of laying was usually a few days earlier in the Blue than the Great Tit, though it varied in different years between seven days earlier and three days later. These differences seem more likely to be due to differences in the availability of food for the two species prior to laying than to adaptations in timing related to the future needs of their young. An as yet unexplained point is that each year in Marley wood the Great Tits started laying, on the average, one or two days earlier in bushy areas with lower trees than in areas with a high canopy of oaks and elms.

Summarizing these arguments, the close dependence of the average date of laying of the Great Tit each year on the preceding spring temperatures is probably not, as I once thought, an adaptation for timing breeding in relation to the appearance of the caterpillars needed later for the young, but results from a correlation between the spring temperatures and the time of appearance of the insect foods needed by the adult females to form their eggs. On this view, it is just a fortunate coincidence that woodland caterpillars are so abundant when the young tits require feeding; but the birds adapt their clutch-size to this situation, laying larger clutches than any other passerine species. As discussed later (p. 102), the Pied Flycatcher lays its eggs later than the Great and Blue Tits in the same wood, hence, though it also brings many caterpillars to its young, its young are in the nest after the time when caterpillars are most abundant. In the Pied Flycatcher, the earliest broods of all leave most survivors, and presumably breeding would be even more successful if they could lay their eggs at the same time as the Great Tits. These points fit the view that in the Pied Flycatcher, as in the Great Tit, the date of laying is correlated with the food requirements of the female prior to laying rather than with those of the nestlings later. The availability of food for the female prior to laying also influences the date of laying of the Common Swift, *Apus apus* (Lack, 1956), and the Cuckoo, *Cuculus canorus* (Lack, 1963), and at least in the latter species it appears to be the primary factor limiting the start of breeding.

When a clutch of the Great Tit is destroyed or deserted early in the season, the pair normally starts another after a few days, but when destruction occurs later in the season, for instance with well-grown nestlings, the birds by no means always lay again. The tendency for 'repeat' clutches late in the season was evidently stronger in some years than others, but this could not be assessed precisely because 'repeats' occur only after earlier losses, and the number of nests destroyed differed greatly in different years. As shown later, comparatively few young survived from late repeat nests, but more appeared to do so in those years when late broods were more numerous.

Occasionally, the Great Tit has a true second brood after a first has been successfully raised, the first egg being laid around the time that the young of the first brood leave the nest. Presumed second broods, in which the first egg was laid after the first young of the season had left the nest, were rare in Marley wood, there being 2 in 1948 (the exceptionally early year), 2 in 1950, 5 in 1960 (2 being ringed adults known to have raised first broods), 2 in 1962 and 2 in 1963. In addition, in plantations adjoining Marley wood studied in the first 3 years of this work, there was 1 second brood in 1947 and 3 more in 1948, but none in 1949. In all, rather under 2 per cent of the breeding pairs raised second broods, and this figure is probably representative for English broad-leaved woods (Lack, 1958). There is a shortage of insects suitable for the young of second broods, and caterpillars in particular are extremely sparse, so that the parents bring many adult insects, which seem less suitable. Further, many second-brood nestlings starved, and many others died soon after fledging (Gibb, 1950; Lack, Gibb, and Owen, 1957).

I postulated earlier (1954) that in nidicolous species the average clutch has been evolved by natural selection to correspond with that brood-size from which, on average, the parents can raise most surviving young. The critical test of this view for the Great Tit is deferred to the next chapter, and the ensuing discussion is concerned with the observed variations in clutch-size in relation to environmental factors, together with any circumstantial evidence as to whether or not these variations are adaptive.

The usual first clutch of the Great Tit in Marley wood is between 8 and 10 eggs. The largest was of 15 eggs, recorded 5 times in the exceptionally early year of 1948 but never since, while the smallest undisturbed laying was perhaps 5, a few yet smaller ones probably being due to disturbance during laying or to some other abnormality. The Blue Tit usually lays a rather larger clutch than the Great Tit, the lower limit being similar, while the largest recorded was of 18 eggs, again in 1948, and all 18 young successfully left the nest. The unusually large clutches of the Great and Blue Tits are advantageous for a population study, since the variations in clutch-size are easier to analyse than they are in the many passerine species which lay only 4 or 5 eggs. The range of variation in the tits, though seemingly great, is not proportionately greater than in many other species.

As first established in Holland (Kluijver, 1951) and later in Wytham, the average clutch of the Great Tit varies with the date of laying, the population density, the age of the parent, and the nature of the habitat. In Marley wood, the average size of the first layings varied in different years between 12·3 and 7·8, a marked difference. The progressive decline with the date, set out in Fig. 7, shows that the average clutch of the Great and Blue Tits declined respectively from 10·3 and 12·7 in the second week of April, to 7·6 in early June, and 8·5 in the third week of May respectively. The caterpillars available for nestling tits decline progressively in numbers from the start to the end of the time when there are young tits in the nest, and it is reasonable to postulate that the seasonal decline in clutch-size is an adaptive response to the

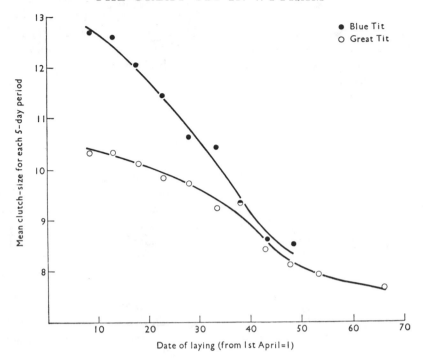

FIG. 7. Seasonal decline in average clutch of Great and Blue Tits in English broad-leaved woods. (Based on Lack, 1958, Table 10, except that a few clutches 1–5 April 1948 were excluded as abnormal, while new data for 6–15 April 1958–62 in Wytham were added to make the averages for this period more reliable.)

food situation for the young. But while this is presumably the ultimate factor involved, the eggs are laid some three weeks before the young hatch, and the proximate factor cannot be the availability of food for the laying female, since the caterpillars in question increase in size and abundance from the time that the first clutches are laid until about the time when the first broods fledge. Hence while the availability of food might significantly influence the time of laying, it appears to have no significant influence on clutch-size. The proximate factors involved in the seasonal decline in clutch-size are not known.

Figure 7 is based on the clutch records for twelve years combined. There is no reason to think that if, in any one year, Great Tits had laid clutches from early April to mid-June inclusive, their average size would not have declined in the same way. But in any one year, as already mentioned, most Great Tits start laying within two or three weeks of each other, and there are comparatively few late clutches, mainly repeats after earlier losses. The average seasonal decline is due only in part to the decline in the course of each season, and more to the fact that the mean size of first layings is larger in the years when breeding starts earlier and smaller in the years when it starts later, as can be seen from Table 2 and Fig. 8. Since, as mentioned later, the average clutch also varies inversely with population density, arrows have been added to the points on Fig. 8 for 1947 (population abnormally low,

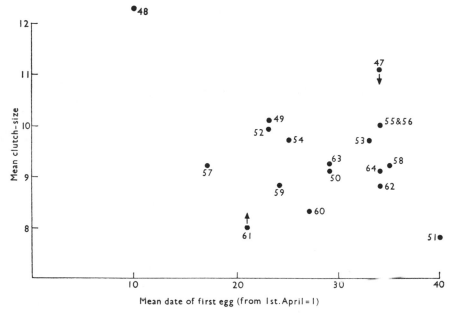

FIG. 8. Relation between mean clutch-size and mean date of laying each year of Great Tit in Marley wood (arrows indicate years of abnormal density).

hence mean clutch higher than expected from date alone) and 1961 (population abnormally high, hence mean clutch lower than expected from date alone). After making allowances for the population density in all years, a regression analysis showed that the mean clutch decreased by o·o9 egg (± o·o4) for each day later that it was laid. (This figure from Perrins, 1965, amends an earlier one in Lack, 1958.) The mean clutch of the Blue Tit in different years has varied in a closely similar way with the date of laying. It is interesting that, in the years already mentioned, in which breeding started a week or more earlier in one broad-leaved wood than another, the average clutch of the Great and Blue Tit was correspondingly larger in the wood where breeding was earlier, even though in other and more normal years it was similar in both woods (Lack, 1958).

While the decline in clutch-size during the course of each season

27

seems obviously adapted to the food situation for the young, the tendency for both Great and Blue Tits to lay smaller average clutches in years when all of them breed later is not easily explained. This could be an adaptation to the food supply for the young only if caterpillars tend to be more abundant in early mild springs than late cold ones, but G. C. Varley and G. R. Gradwell (pers. comm.) have found that there is no such correlation in Wytham (contrary to an impression in the first years of this study arising because caterpillars were exceptionally numerous in the exceptionally early season of 1948 and unusually sparse in the cold late spring of 1951).

Another possibility is that the difference in average clutch-size between one year and another correlated with the date of laying is not advantageous in itself, but is an incidental consequence of the (adaptive) decline in clutch-size in the course of each season. If, however, as on this view, it is disadvantageous for the Great Tit to lay a smaller clutch in years when breeding starts later, one would have expected the species to have evolved a means to avoid doing so, and to have laid clutches of the same average size at the start of every season, irrespective of variations in the date of starting. This problem needs further study, especially as the same type of variation occurs in the Pied and Collared Flycatchers (see p. 103).

The average clutch of the Great Tit also decreases with an increasing density of breeding pairs, as first demonstrated by Kluijver (1951) and shown for Marley wood in Fig. 9. In this figure I have added arrows to the points for the exceptionally early breeding season of 1948 (when the mean clutch was higher than would otherwise have been expected) and for the exceptionally late year of 1951 (when the mean clutch was lower than would otherwise have been expected). A regression analysis showed that, for a fixed date of laying, double the number of breeding pairs in Marley meant a reduction in the average clutch of 2·0 eggs (± 0·4); the relationship was probably not linear. This variation is presumably adapted to the food situation for the nestling tits because, other things being equal, it is harder for a parent to find food for its young when there are more than few other Great Tits searching for it.

A very small part of the annual variation in the clutch-size of the Great Tit with population density is due to the fact that, when the population is high, it includes a higher proportion of yearling birds, which have rather smaller clutches than older birds, on average 0·6 egg smaller at Wageningen (Kluijver, 1951); only a small part of this difference was attributable to the tendency of the yearlings to lay 2 or 3 days after the older birds. Similarly in Wytham, yearling Great Tits had an average clutch 0·6 egg smaller that that of the older birds in 1960, 1961, and 1962 and 0·4 egg smaller in 1963. These differences,

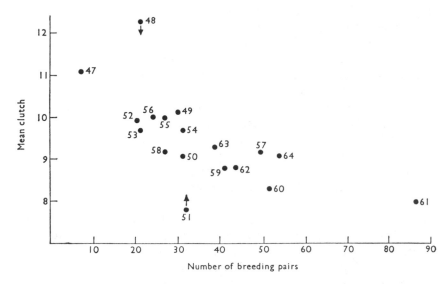

FIG. 9. Relation between mean clutch-size and number of breeding pairs each year of Great Tit in Marley wood (arrows indicate abnormally early or late seasons).

also, are too great to be explicable primarily through the yearlings laying, on the average, a few days later than the older birds (Perrins, 1963, 1965). There was no significant difference in clutch-size between the second-year and third-year birds. That in the Great Tit a smaller clutch has been evolved in the yearlings is due, I suggest, to the yearlings being rather less efficient parents than older birds, so that they cannot, on the average, raise quite such large broods, and evidence supporting this view will be given later.

The mean clutch in first broods of the Blue Tit each year in Marley wood is also shown in Table 2. Broadly speaking, the Blue Tit varied in parallel with the Great Tit, both, for instance, having unusually large clutches in 1947 and 1948 and unusually small ones in 1959 and 1961, but there have been minor differences. The parallel variations are readily explicable, first, through both species laying larger clutches in earlier years, and both breeding at about the same time as each other each year, and, secondly, through both species laying smaller clutches at higher densities and the numbers of both tending to fluctuate in parallel.

In Marley wood, the average clutch of the Great Tit has been consistently about 1 egg larger in the areas with tall oaks or elms and an extensive leaf canopy than in the areas with lower and at times denser trees, chiefly hazel, with a smaller canopy, averaging about ten eggs in the former and nine eggs in the latter. This has occurred despite the fact, noted earlier, that breeding starts slightly earlier in the areas with lower trees (Perrins, 1965). (Possibly the survival rate of the young Great Tits has also been higher in the canopy areas, but the 13 per cent difference in the recovery-rates of the young from the two areas was not statistically significant.) The clutch size of the Blue Tit also varies with the nature of the habitat, being on the average one egg larger in pure oak stands in Wytham Great Wood than it is in Marley wood where there are few oaks. The reasons for these differences are not known, but as the Blue Tit feeds especially in oak trees, the latter difference could well be adaptive. That the Blue Tit normally lays a rather larger clutch than the Great Tit suggests that, on the average, it is rather more efficient than the Great Tit in collecting caterpillars for its young in broad-leaved woods.[1]

Summarizing, the annual fluctuations in the breeding population of the Great Tit in Marley wood have been in parallel with those of the Blue Tit in the same wood and with those of both species in other woods, including woods of very different types up to several hundred miles apart. The average density of the birds has differed markedly in these woods. In Marley wood, the average date of laying each year has varied by up to five weeks, in parallel with the temperature in March and with the time of appearance of the caterpillars which comprise the main food of the young. This is now attributed to parallel variations in the time of appearance of the insect foods needed by the female bird to form her eggs, the correlation with the appearance of the caterpillars probably being incidental, though clutch-size is adapted to this abundant food for the young. Clutches are smaller later in the course of each

[1] At an early stage in this study it seemed possible that Great Tits laid larger clutches in the years when they had a greater chance than usual of raising larger broods. As discussed in the next chapter, the brood-size from which, on the average, most young were recovered per brood varied greatly in different years, and in the early years it was unusually large in 1947 and 1948, when clutches were unusually large, and unusually small in 1951, when clutches were unusually small. But this possible correlation was disproven by the data for later years. In particular, in 1959 and 1960 the most productive brood-size was above average but clutch-size was below average, while in 1961 the most productive brood-size was well below average in Marley and average, or a little above average, in Wytham Great Wood, but the average clutch-size was the same in both woods. The possibility that the Great Tits might lay larger clutches than usual in the years when caterpillars on oak leaves are more abundant than usual has also been disproven (Lack, 1958, correcting Lack, 1955), and anyway it is now known that the Great Tits also feed their young on many caterpillars from trees other than oaks. As already mentioned, Great Tits lay larger clutches in years when they breed earlier, but caterpillars are not more numerous in early than late years. Professor Varley suggested to me, however, that in a cold late spring the warm weather, when it eventually comes, often does so rapidly, to the caterpillars tend to develop faster in a late season, so are available to the sits for a shorter period, but it is not known whether this is at all important to the tits.

season, at higher population densities, and in yearling than older parents, these variations presumably being adaptively related to the number of young which the parents can successfully raise, which is probably smaller later in the season, at higher densities and in inexperienced parents. An unexplained variation is the tendency for clutches to be larger in the years when breeding starts earlier and smaller in the years when breeding starts later. In all the points discussed in this chapter, the Great and Blue Tit vary closely in parallel.

THE GREAT TIT IN WYTHAM
SURVIVAL OF THE YOUNG

A SMALL proportion of the eggs of tits, as of other birds, fail to hatch because they are infertile or addled. For instance, in Wytham in the years 1958–61 inclusive, just under 5 per cent of the Great Tits' eggs failed, and the proportion was similar in the Blue Tit. (Rather higher estimates for other woods given by Lack, 1955, were based on less satisfactory data.) In 1961 there were a few tiny yolkless eggs, not seen in any other year and possibly due to malnutrition at the time of laying. A further small proportion of nests with eggs were destroyed by predators, especially Weasels, *Mustela nivalis*, while a few others were deserted, either due to disturbance, or because the parent was killed when away from the nest. The total losses of eggs were so small, however, that they had no appreciable influence on the population, especially as whole clutches lost or destroyed were normally replaced.

In first broods of the Great and Blue Tits in broad-leaved woods, losses of part of the brood from starvation or accident were also small, in both species being about 4 per cent in Marley wood in the years from 1947 to 1957 and also in other parts of Wytham in the years from 1958 to 1961 (Lack, Gibb, and Owen, 1957; Lack, 1958; Perrins, 1965).

Headpiece: Blue Tit feeding fledgling.

But in Marley wood the losses were nearly 10 per cent in 1958 and 1960, and between 14 and 16 per cent in 1961, 1962, and 1963, though only 2 per cent in 1959. In 1962, but no other year, losses were heavy all over Wytham, due to unusually cold and wet weather when the earliest broods had hatched, and about one-quarter of these early young died. Kluijver (1951) observed similar heavy losses in Holland in wet cold weather, when the adults find it harder than usual to collect food and also have to brood young chicks for longer.

In 1961 caterpillars were scarcer on the oak leaves than in any other summer, and in Marley wood Great Tits bred in much larger numbers than in any other year. In Wytham Great Wood, where the breeding density was well under a half of that in Marley, only 3 per cent of the nestlings starved, but in Marley 16·4 per cent died. That this high figure was due to food shortage is suggested by the fact that losses were proportionately much heavier in the larger broods, being 3 per cent in broods of 2–4 young, 8 per cent in broods of 5–7 young, 17 per cent in broods of 8–10 young, and 24 per cent in broods of 11–13 young. The food shortage presumably arose through the unusual scarcity of caterpillars combined with the unusually large number of breeding Great Tits. Blue Tits were only slightly commoner than usual in 1961, and only 5 per cent of their nestlings died, an average figure, which suggests that they fed their young, at least partly, on different species of caterpillars from the Great Tits.

The figures so far discussed refer to first broods. Nestlings starve much more often in late repeat broods and second broods. For instance in the 17 latest broods in the years 1947–56 inclusive, 47 per cent of the nestlings died, as compared with only 4 per cent in the first broods (Lack, Gibb, and Owen, 1957). Likewise about half the nestlings died in the second broods in Wytham in 1962 and 1963, two years when they were unusually numerous. As mentioned earlier, the parents of late broods have difficulty in finding enough food for their young, and bring many adult insects and spiders in default of caterpillars. Further, whereas Great Tits normally start full incubation of their first clutches with the last, or sometimes the penultimate, egg, so that all the nestlings usually hatch within a few hours of each other, in late broods they start incubation when only part of the clutch has been laid. As a result, the later eggs to be laid hatch on successive days, so the young are at first of very different size, and if food is then short, the last to hatch, which are the smallest, quickly die (Gibb, 1950). Such asynchronous hatching presumably has the same function in the Great Tit as in raptorial birds, namely to reduce the brood-size quickly when food is sparse so that the parents can raise at least some of their young, without wasting food on those which would die anyway (see p. 223). It is interesting that the Great Tit has evolved this adaptation for its late broods, for which food is likely to be short.

Because they nest in holes, nestling tits are much less liable to predation than those passerine birds which build cup-shaped nests in bushes or on the ground. Great Spotted Woodpeckers, *Dryoscopus major*, occasionally bored through the wood of the nesting boxes and ate the nestling tits, and Grey Squirrels, *Sciurus carolinensis* (an introducted species to Britain), occasionally opened up the entrance holes and took some of the young. But the only enemy causing serious losses was the Weasel, *Mustela nivalis*, which is small enough to enter the holes, and in that way destroyed many broods, and occasionally took a parent bird as well. The extent of the losses from weasels differed greatly in different years, for reasons not yet established. Presumably it is due to variations in the density of the small rodents which comprise the normal diet of weasels, for which young tits are only incidental prey. However, individual weasels evidently learned to associate nesting boxes with food, since those clutches destroyed during incubation were often in small groups of adjacent boxes, each group probably corresponding with the hunting territory of a particular weasel. In this period the weasels presumably hunted by sight.

Unlike the eggs, the nestling tits taken by weasels were not necessarily in adjacent boxes and Perrins (1965) showed that at this stage a different factor influenced whether they were taken. Owing to marked variations in the predation by weasels in different years, comparisons should be made only within each year, and when this is done, as in Table 3, it is seen that each year more late than early broods, and more large than small broods, were destroyed. The young in later and larger broods tend to be hungrier than those in earlier and smaller broods respectively, and since it is primarily when they are hungry that young Great Tits call noisily in the nest, the weasels are presumably attracted by the sound of the young.

An indication of the amount of food supplied to nestling Great Tits is given by their weight on the fifteenth day (after which Gibb, 1950, found that their increase in weight levels off, and also that they are liable to leave the nest prematurely if handled). It is now established for many species, including the Great Tit (Gibb, 1955), that the parents pay more feeding visits to larger than smaller broods, but that the feeding rate does not rise proportionately to the number of young, so that each nestling receives, on the average, less food in a larger brood. In the Great Tit, in particular, Gibb found that the parents of larger broods slackened off in the latter part of the nestling period, as if they could not sustain their feeding effort, whereas parents of smaller broods did not do so. These findings are supported by the smaller average

TABLE 3

Rate of predation of Great Tit broods in relation to date and brood-size

Size of brood	Earlier broods		Later broods	
	no.	% taken	no.	% taken
		1959		
3–6	9	0	25	4
7–10	23	0	14	21
11–15	17	0	20	25
		1960		
2–5	13	8	20	15
6–8	24	8	34	15
9–14	28	18	21	29
		1961		
2–5	22	9	33	21
6–8	43	0	43	21
9–13	35	17	26	23
		1962		
2–7	31	3	42	12
8–10	30	10	26	15
11–14	20	15	19	21
		1963		
1–9	70	0	23	17
10–16	65	3	4	25

Notes. From Perrins (1963, extended in litt.). The brood-sizes were those on the last visit to the nest before predation, and were not always quite the same as at hatching. The broods of over 10 young were mainly artificially enlarged. The 'earlier' and 'later' broods were divided so that as nearly as possible half the broods in each year came in each category, except in 1963, when virtually all the predation came very late.

weight of nestling Great and Blue Tits in larger than smaller broods; there were also annual differences in weight, the two species tending to vary in parallel (Lack, Gibb, and Owen, 1957).

From 1958 onward, much more extensive weighings were made by Perrins (1963 and 1965) and the figures, omitting those for 1961 as they were abnormally low, have been plotted in relation to brood-size in Fig. 10. This shows a marked decline in the average weight of the nestlings in broods of larger size, from 19·6 grams in broods of 1 or 2 young to 17·6 grams in broods of 13 young. The true variation due to brood-size is actually rather greater than shown because, as discussed in the next paragraph, the nestlings in later broods weigh less than those in earlier broods, and most of the smaller broods come later in the season.

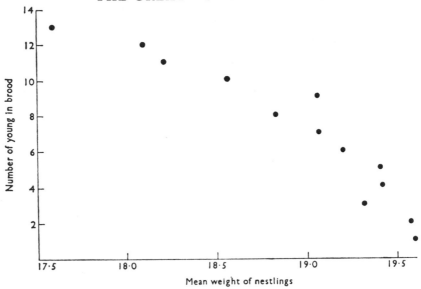

FIG. 10. Mean weight of nestling Great Tit in relation to brood-size (from Perrins, 1965).

Correlated with the marked decrease in the abundance of caterpillars later in the season, the nestlings also weighed less in late than early broods. This seasonal decline has been set out in Fig. 11 after allowing for the influence of brood-size, each calculation being based on the average brood-size in the year in question. The results had to be analysed separately for each year, because not only was the overall average weight rather different in different years but, which is much more important, the steepness of the decline in weight later in each season varied greatly. This decline was well marked in 1958, even though nearly all the broods hatched within nine days of each other, and it was definite, though much less steep, in 1959. But in 1960, when late broods were unusually common, the average weight of the nestlings was almost the same for those hatched around 18 May as for those hatched up to 18 June, though it probably declined after that. The decline with date was extremely marked in 1961, especially in Marley wood. A difference was not found between Marley and the rest of Wytham in other years, but in 1961 it was so striking that the two sets of data are shown separately in Fig. 11. In 1962, as already mentioned, there was unusually cold wet weather when the earliest broods hatched, and correlated with this the young in the early broods weighed less than those which hatched rather later. After this, the average weight declined very little until near the end of the unusually extended

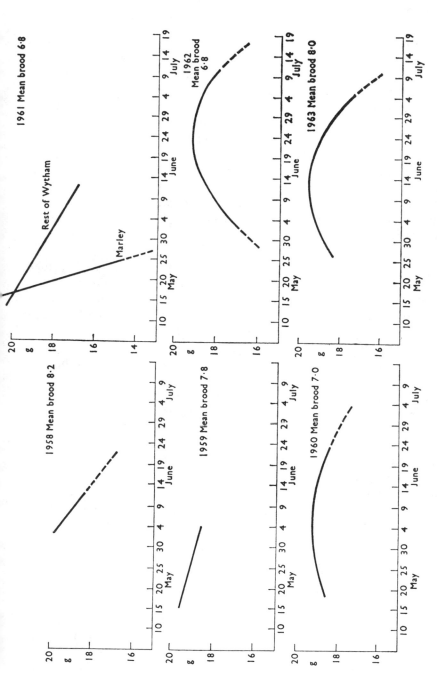

Fig. 11. Average weight of nestling Great Tits (for average brood-size in year in question) on 15th day in relation to date (ordinate = weight in grams, abscissa = date of weighing) (from Perrins, 1965).

breeding season. In 1963, the variation was of the same pattern as in 1962, but with a less steep rise at the start of the season and a steeper decline after about the middle of the period. It is interesting that the laying season was unusually extended, with more late repeat broods and even some second broods, only in those three of the six years studied, 1960, 1962, and 1963, when the young in later broods weighed almost as much as those in earlier broods and so presumably had enough food. In these respects 1964 was like 1958, 1959, and 1961. This suggests that in 1960, 1962, and 1963 the Great Tits responded to an unusual abundance of food late in the season. There were also several second broods in 1948, the season when caterpillars were far more abundant than in any other year, and one in 1947 (a high proportion of the few pairs), when caterpillars were numerous and Great Tits unusually sparse.

After the young Great Tits leave the nest, they are fed by their parents for another fortnight or so, during which they gradually come to feed themselves and to acquire independence. In this time, both the parents and their young usually feed high in the trees, so are hidden by the leaf canopy. Hence both direct observation and trapping are extremely difficult, though Goodbody (1952) showed that the young tend to stay near where they were hatched for about a month, after which many of them move further afield. In Marley wood, for instance, many young move out, while others move in, during the late summer, but few disperse for more than a mile, so that most of these movements occur within the Wytham estate.

Young Great Tits cannot be trapped in large numbers until the beginning of November. Between the time that they leave the nest and early November, there was in most years heavy mortality, and though the time at which this occurred could not be directly measured, most of it, as discussed later, almost certainly occurred in the first month after the young left the nest. Because some young dispersed beyond the trapping areas on the Wytham estate, while others that were present were not caught, the ringed young recovered during the winter were only a sample of those still alive, but there is no reason to suppose that this sample was biased with respect to the factors analysed here. It should be noted, however, that the proportion of the young present in winter that was trapped differed greatly in different years, partly because the trapping effort varied, being particularly low in the years 1952–7, and partly because differences in the availability of natural foods made the birds much easier to trap in some winters than others. Hence the figures for different years are not directly comparable with each other.

As already mentioned, the nestlings vary greatly in weight, and the recaptures of ringed young showed that far fewer of the light than of the moderately heavy nestlings survived to the winter (Lack, Gibb, and Owen, 1957). Further, the much greater number of ringing recoveries from 1958 onward has shown that the relation between the weight of the nestlings and their subsequent chance of survival has differed markedly in different years, as set out in Fig. 12 (Perrins, 1965). In 1958, for instance, the chances of subsequent recapture were about twice as great for nestlings weighing over 20 grams as for those weighing 18–20 grams, and twice as great for the latter as for young weighing only 14–17 grams. Hence the chances of survival were much lower for the lighter young. In 1960 on the other hand, the chances of survival were about equal for young weighing respectively 18 and 20–22 grams, while even young weighing only 16 grams had a relatively high chance of survival as compared with most other years. The results for 1961 were similar to those for 1958, while those for 1962 were similar to those for 1960. The results for 1959 and 1963 were intermediate.

The extra weight of the heavier young probably consists mainly of subcutaneous fat, which acts as a food reserve in the period just after they leave the nest, when it may be hard for them to obtain enough nourishment. Such a food reserve will obviously be more important in years when food is sparse than in years when it is plentiful, hence the results in Fig. 12 suggest that newly fledged young obtained food much less easily in 1958 and 1961 than in 1960 and 1962. These findings show that the chance that a young Great Tit will survive after leaving the nest depends both on the amount of food it receives when in the nest, which varies with brood-size and date of hatching, and also on the availability of food after it leaves the nest, which differs markedly in different years. The lightest nestling to survive for at least three months after fledging was one of only 11·8 grams in 1962. It was about half the weight of the heaviest nestling.

The chance of survival after leaving the nest also depends on the date, being greater for those young which fledge earlier in the season, as shown in Fig. 13. In every year, the chances of subsequent survival were highest for the earliest or almost the earliest broods to leave the nest. The decline later in the season was particularly marked in 1961, but was proportionately much less in 1960 and 1962, with the other years intermediate. In 1960 and 1962, even young fledging fairly late in the season had a good chance of survival, and some survived even from second broods, which had not previously been recorded in Wytham. This is a further indication that feeding conditions after the young left the nest were unusually favourable in those two years.

The survival rates in Figs. 12 and 13 were based on young Great Tits recovered when at least three months old, and almost all were at

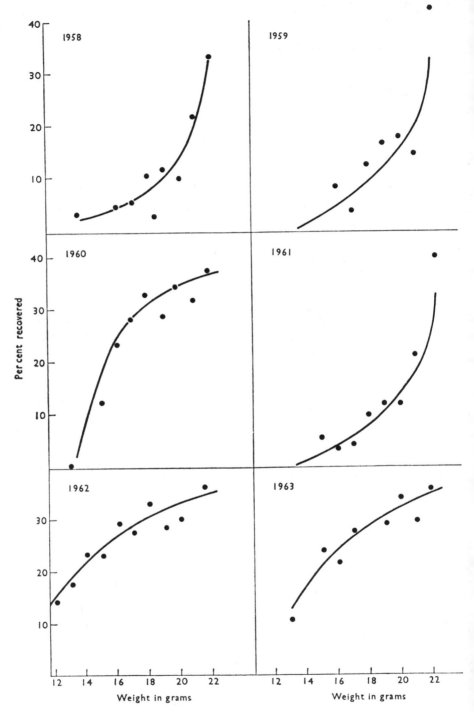

FIG. 12. Survival of young Great Tits after leaving nest in relation to nestling weight on fifteenth day (from Perrins 1965).

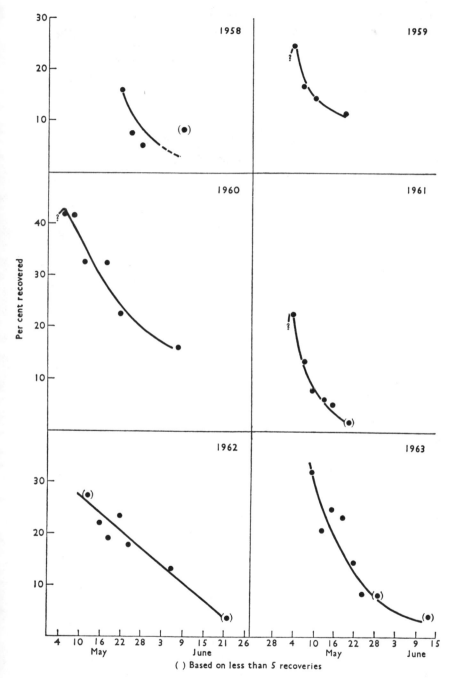

FIG. 13. Survival of young Great Tits after leaving nest in relation to date of hatching (from Perrins, 1965).

least five months old. One would expect that the weight of a young bird when it left the nest would influence its subsequent survival primarily in the next fortnight to a month, since probably within this period any that were undernourished would either succumb, or make up the deficit. This was tested in 1963 by placing on each nestling, in addition to its numbered ring, a coloured one indicating its weight, and in July observations were made through field-glasses on feeding Great Tits. As these birds were seen from a distance, not trapped, they were not distinguished individually, and some individuals were probably recorded more than once, but this is as likely to have happened for rings of one colour as of another. The results in Table 4 strongly suggest

TABLE 4

Proportion of marked young Great Tits seen alive in July 1963 in relation to their weight on 15th day in nest

Nestling weight in grams on 15th day	Number fledged and ringed	Colour rings seen in July	
		Number	Per cent
up to 15·9	39	0	0
16·0–17·9	182	5	3
18·0–18·9	269	13	5
19·0–19·9	405	33	8
20·0–20·9	268	30	11
21·0 or more	89	9	10

Note. From Perrins (1965). Observations were made up to 27 July. If observations had been included up to 7 August, there would have been another two records for each of the 18-, 19-, and 21-gram classes, and three more in the 20-gram class, thus further increasing the preponderance of heavier individuals.

that by late July more of the heavier than of the lighter young were still alive, and hence that at least much of the mortality due to under-nourishment in the nest occurred before mid-July, as one would expect.

In Marley wood in 1961, as already mentioned, the breeding density of Great Tits was unusually high, many nestlings starved and the decline in the weight of the nestlings later in the season was much steeper than in the rest of Wytham. In that year also, the chances of later recovery of nestlings of the same weight was much lower in Marley wood than the rest of Wytham, for which reason the figures for Marley wood in 1961 (but no other year) were excluded from the averages in Figs. 12 and 13. Other differences found in that year between Marley and Wytham Great Wood, which was the largest single other wood studied, are shown in Table 5. The breeding density was about 2½ times

TABLE 5

Comparisons of Great Tit's reproduction in Marley wood and Wytham
Great Wood in 1961

	Marley Wood	Great Wood Reserve
Density of breeding pairs per hectare	3·3	1·4
Mean clutch	8·0	7·9
Mean weight of nestling (15th day) in grams	18·0	19·0
Per cent nestlings dying in nest (excluding predation)	16·4	3·0
Per cent broods taken by predators	29·0	8·0
Fledged young recovered after 3 months		
Per cent of those fledged	6·6	12·4
Average no. per brood fledged	0·44	0·96
Most productive brood-size	6·0	10·0
Juveniles per adult at		
(i) fledging	2·1	2·5
(ii) winter and spring	0·25	0·7

Notes. The mean weight of the nestlings was of those that survived to the 15th day, and would have been lower in Marley if the starved young could have been added. There were too few figures to assess the juvenile : adult ratio in winter in Great Wood Reserve alone, and the figure given was that for all Wytham woods except Marley. The figures are slightly different from those in Lack, 1964, Table 3, first, because all of the latter (not solely those for the juvenile : adult ratio) referred to all other Wytham woods (loosely called Great Wood), and, secondly, because further ringed young were recovered later.

as high in Marley wood. The mean clutch was about the same (probably because, though the clutch-size of first broods is in general lower at higher densities, it rarely falls below 8 eggs). The average weight of nestlings surviving to the fifteenth day was a gram lighter in Marley, and the difference would have been much greater if the weights of the many young dying of starvation before the fifteenth day in Marley (but not in Great Wood), could have been included. The proportion of nestlings dying in the nest, nearly all of starvation, was more than five times as

43

great in Marley and the proportion taken by predators was more than three times as great (presumably because hungry young called more loudly). Moreover, the subsequent chances of survival of the young which successfully left the nest was also only about half as great for those raised in Marley as for those raised in the Great Wood, to judge from the proportion of each group recaptured in the following winter or later. Also, the brood-size which resulted in most surviving young, the significance of which will be discussed later, was normal in Great Wood but much lower than normal in Marley. Again, the juvenile : adult ratio at the time when the young left the nest was 16 per cent lower in Marley than in the rest of Wytham, and the subsequent reduction in the proportion of juveniles was also much heavier in Marley, so that by the winter, the ratio was nearly three times as low in Marley as in the rest of Wytham. The juvenile : adult ratio remained the same from the start of the winter to the next breeding season, so the intake of new breeding birds was smaller in Marley than the Great Wood in 1962; this may have been why, as compared with 1961, the breeding population in 1962 was 50 per cent lower in Marley but only 38 per cent lower in Great Wood.

It may be added that no corresponding differences between Marley and the other woods on the Wytham estate were found in 1958, 1959 or 1960, though in 1962 the young weighed $\frac{3}{4}$ gram less in Marley than the Great Wood and only half as many fledglings were recovered later. Data are needed for further years and other woods before the poor reproductive success in Marley in 1961 can certainly be attributed to the unusually high population density, presumably assisted by the unusual scarcity of caterpillars. The reasons for the unusually high population in Marley that year also need further investigation.

It was mentioned earlier that the yearling Great Tits had, on the average, rather smaller clutches than the older parents. If this difference is adaptive, it is presumably because the older parents are, on the average, more efficient in raising young than the yearlings, and so can, on the average, raise more young in a brood. As shown in Table 6, in three out of four seasons studied, the proportion of fledged young which survived was higher among those raised by older than by yearling parents (despite the older parents having slightly larger broods).

In studies of the Common Swift, *Apus apus*, discussed in Chapter 1, and the Starling, *Sturnus vulgaris* (Lack, 1948a), the commonest clutch-size was that which, on average, gave rise to the greatest number of surviving young. Earlier evidence (1954, p. 29) indicated that this did not apply directly to the Great Tit, and I suggested that this might be because, owing to adaptive modifications in clutch-size, larger clutches tend to be laid mainly when larger broods can be raised. Later

TABLE 6

Post-fledging survival of Great Tit in relation to age of female parent

Age of female parent	Mean brood-size at hatching	No. hatched	Recovered no.	%	Number per brood
		1960			
Older	8·1	234	75	32	2·6
Yearlings	6·9	160	40	25	1·7
		1961 (excluding Marley)			
Older	7·5	359	45	13	0·9
Yearlings	6·7	489	45	9	0·6
		1961 (Marley)			
Older	8·8	194	12	6	0·5
Yearlings	7·5	278	11	4	0·3
		1962			
Older	8·5	745	110	15	1·3
Yearlings	7·8	349	55	16	1·2
		1963			
Older	9·3	875	163	19	1·7
Yearlings	9·1	476	66	14	1·3

Notes. From Perrins (1965). The difference in the recovery rate of young raised by yearling and the older parents respectively was statistically significant in 1960, 1961, and 1963, but not 1962. In 1961, the survival rate was much lower in Marley wood than elsewhere, so for this year only, the figures for Marley were treated separately.

study has shown that such adaptive modifications exist, while in addition two mistakes were made in earlier analyses, the first being to group a few years of exceptional survival with more normal years, and the second being to omit taking into account the losses in the nest before fledging, which also vary with brood-size (Lack, Gibb, and Owen, 1957; Lack, 1958). All survival rates in the present chapter have been calculated in terms of the brood-size at hatching, while from 1958 onward, in order to get more data for large broods, Perrins (1965) sometimes transferred newly hatched young from one brood to another. Most such transfers were made early in the season, when broods are largest. Transfer as such did not appear to hurt the young in any way.

The data for all years have been set out in Table 7, the upper half showing the number of broods of each size at hatching, and the lower half the number of young from these broods (ringed shortly before they left the nest) which were recovered after surviving for at least three months. After three months, any influence of brood-size on

TABLE 7

Number of young Great Tits hatched and number recovered over 3 months old in relation to brood-size. In Wytham

Number of broods (size at hatching) in each year

Brood-size	1947	1948	1949	1950	1951	1952	1953	1954	1955	1956	1957	1958	1959	1960	1961(W)	1961(M)	1962	1963
1													1	1			1	1
2											1	1	3	5	2	3		1
3				1					1			1	11	6	8	4	1	5
4		2		2		1	1	1				2	13	10	16	3	3	9
5		2		2								7	18	11	15	10	9	
6	1	3	1	5		1		1		2	1	5	14	9	22	10	24	4
7	1	3	2	5		1	2	4	1	6	6	4	10	13	25	7	12	10
8	3	7	4	4		4	2	6	1	5	13	3	12	14	20	11	12	21
9	3	16	5	3		3	7	8	5	4	7	6	9	5	16	3	20	27
10	4	12	3	1		6	7	5	5	4	8	5	10	10	8	2	19	29
11	4	10	2			3	1	2	7	2		6	11	6	8	4	18	19
12		8	3				1	1	2	1		3	8	8	4	9	13	7
13	2	6							1			3	2	2	4	8	9	7
14		2								1				0			11	4
15		2												2			7	2
16																		2

Number of young recovered over 3 months old

1											1
2							2				
3											
4	1		8	2	3	1		1	6	2	
5	2	2	10	7	12	3	13	5	16	12	
6	1	3	1	19	13	11	13	6	14	3	
7	1	3	3	13	20	15	3	15	14		
8	3	3	2	4	3	5	33	12	3	21	39
9	1	14	4	6	5	16	11	19	2	28	38
10	3	8	9	1	6	4	12	26	12	24	36
11	3	7	5	1	4	14	22	9	11	40	
12	11	1	3	15	30	6	7	18			
13	3	8	3	2	5	6	2	13	11		
14	4	2	5	15	5						
15	4	5	13	15							
16	10	11									

Notes. From 1958 onward, a steadily increasing number of boxes were put up in other woods than Marley on the Wytham estate, so that the number of broods ringed has greatly increased. Also, up to 1957 inclusive, all broods were natural but after that year some were supplemented and others diminished, by the transfer of newly hatched nestlings. It should also be noted that the figures for 1949–56 inclusive differ somewhat from those published earlier (Lack, Gibb, and Owen, 1957, Lack, 1958) owing to (a) a slightly stricter exclusion of late nests, (b) the inclusion of broods destroyed by predators in the nest, (c) a few further recoveries of young ringed in 1954, 1955, and 1956. The results for 1961 have been separated for Marley (M) and the rest of Wytham (W).

survival would presumably have shown itself. As already mentioned, the overall proportion of ringed young later recovered differed greatly in different years, and the critical point is the recapture-rate of young in broods of different size in each year considered separately, as set out in Table 8. The summary in Table 8 shows that the survival rate from broods of 8–10 young was in many years similar to that from smaller broods, though it was lower in 3 years (1949, 1951, and 1961 in Marley) and possibly in two more. The more critical comparison is between

TABLE 8

The recoveries of young Great Tits at least 3 months old in relation to their brood-size at hatching

Year	Percentage of recoveries from broods of			Brood-size with most recoveries per brood
	7 or less	8–10	11 or more	
1947	8	9	9	13
1948	0	15	11	14, 15
1949	14	8	4	9
1950	3	6	0	9
1951	6	1	—	5
1952	0	10	0	9, 10
1953	7	7	9	(9–12)
1954	5	5	0	9
1955	0	6	0	8 (10)
1956	7	8	0	9
1957	2	4	—	8
1958	13	9	6	9 (14)
1959	16	12	9	9–12
1960	24	27	31	11, 12 (15)
1961(M)	8	4	2	6
1961(W)	9	11	9	10
1962	16	14	9	(9) 14
1963	19	16	16	12 (16)

Notes. Based on the data in Table 7. The brood-size with most recoveries per brood was not at all easy to assess owing to the small total number of recoveries from each brood-size in each year and to the chance irregular variations in the survival rate with respect to brood-size. Usually I took that brood-size from which most recoveries per brood were actually obtained, apart from grouping consecutive brood-sizes when the figure was closely similar for them, or adding another brood-size in brackets when the recovery-rate was only a little smaller. In 1958 and 1963, however, most recoveries per brood came from broods of 14 and 16 respectively, but as the next highest figures were from broods of 9 and 12 respectively, while the recovery rates decreased with increasing brood-size, 9 and 12 are the figures that I somewhat arbitrarily selected. As the full totals are set out in Table 7, the reader can see the grounds for my assessments.

broods of the same size as the average clutch (8–10) and larger broods. For 2 years, no figures were available for broods of more than 10 young. In half of the other 16 years (1949, 1950, 1952, 1954, 1955, 1956, 1961 in Marley, and 1962), the survival rate was decidedly higher from broods of 8–10 than from larger broods, while it was rather higher in 4 other years (1948, 1958, 1959, and 1961 in the rest of Wytham), though similar in the other 4 years (1947, 1960, 1963, and 1953; but for 1953 there were so few data that this might well have been due to chance, and in 1963, the survival rate was much lower from broods of 13 or more young than from broods of 11–12 young). Hence in nearly all the years for which there were enough data, the survival rate of the young after they left the nest was lower in those from larger than smaller broods, though the brood-size at which the difference occurred was different in different years.

The most productive brood-size is not, of course, that from which the greatest percentage of young survive, but that from which, on average, the greatest number survive per brood. In almost every year, the decrease in the survival rate with increasing brood-size was eventually sufficient to offset the greater initial number of young in larger broods, though the brood-size at which this happened was different in different years. Especially in the years 1952–7, the number of recoveries was small and subject to chance irregular variations with respect to brood-size, so the assessment of the most productive brood-size was not at all easy. For this reason, the data for the years 1949–57 were formerly grouped together (Lack, Gibb, and Owen, 1957; Lack, 1958), but as it is now known that the annual variations are greater than then supposed, it is probably better to keep the figures for each year separate, though this means that the totals for some years were too small to provide a reliable assessment. My estimates of the most productive brood-size in each year have been set out in Table 8, based on the data in Table 7.

The commonest clutch of the Great Tit in Wytham was usually 9, but in some years 10. Hence if the clutch-size of the Great Tit has been evolved to correspond with that brood-size from which, on the average, most young are raised, this should mean that 9, or perhaps 10, is the brood-size giving rise to most survivors per brood. In the earlier study just mentioned, the most productive brood-size was, in fact, 9 for the years 1949 to 1957 combined, thus according with expectation, though the figure was much higher than 9 in 1947 and 1948. The assessments for each year separately in Table 8 show that, excluding 1953 for which the data were too sparse for a clear answer, the most productive brood-size was 9 in 5 years, 8 in 1 year, 8 (but closely approached by 10) in another, 9 or 10 in another, 10 in another, while in another it was almost equal for broods of 9 to 12. Hence the results for 10 out of 17 seasons have been in reasonably close accord with what was to be expected on my theory of clutch-size.

There were, however, seven exceptional seasons. In two of them, 1951 and 1961 in Marley, the most productive brood-size was much lower than the normal clutch, being only 5 and 6 respectively, but this has been so uncommon that it would clearly be inefficient for the Great Tit to have a clutch of only 5 or 6 eggs. At the other extreme, the most productive brood-size was 11 or 12 in 1960, 12 in 1963, and yet higher in 1947, 1948, and 1962 (though in 1962 broods of 9 were almost as productive as those of 14). This might suggest that those pairs of Great Tits laying rather more than 10 eggs might, on the average, leave most surviving offspring. But the situation was really more complex than the figures suggest, and was not really so favourable for survival from the large broods, owing to the existence of adaptive modifications in clutch-size.

The most important modification was that with the date. As already mentioned, the survival rate was higher from earlier than later broods, and the earlier broods also tended to be larger. This applied not only to natural broods but also to those which, from 1958 onward, were artificially enlarged, as nearly all of these were made up from the earliest young to hatch, so that they were raised when their young had the greatest chance of survival. Strictly, one should have compared the survival rates only for broods hatched around the same date, but there were not enough figures to permit this. Secondly, as also noted earlier, there was a tendency for clutches to be one egg larger in some parts of Marley wood than others, and possibly the survival rate was rather higher from the areas where clutches were larger; in addition, clutches were rather larger in other parts of Wytham than Marley, and in some years survival was also rather higher in these other woods than in Marley. Thirdly, older birds lay rather larger clutches than yearlings and their young tend to survive better than those of yearlings. Fourthly, clutches were lower when the density of breeding pairs was higher and when it might therefore be harder to raise a brood. Hence the figures for survival in relation to brood-size in Tables 7 and 8 are biased in favour of the large broods, because the latter were more frequent when there was a better chance of raising them, while smaller broods were more frequent under less favourable circumstances. Particularly bearing this point in mind, the figures are in reasonable accord with my interpretation of clutch-size, as in most years those pairs with broods larger than 10 left fewer eventual offspring than those with broods of 9 or 10, i.e. with broods of the same size as the most frequent clutch.

The reason that young from broods of above the average size survived relatively better in five years than in the rest is not certainly known, It seems likely, however, that undernourished fledglings would either make up the deficit in their food reserves, or succumb, within one to three weeks after leaving the nest, so probably the food supply during the first three weeks after they leave the nest is critical. In this period Great Tits continue to eat caterpillars so long as they are available but, as already mentioned, caterpillars decline rapidly in numbers around this time. It is therefore highly suggestive that the five seasons when the most productive brood-size was unusually large were also the five when the breeding season was unusually prolonged and there were even second broods. Moreover, in 1947, caterpillars were numerous and Great Tits were exceptionally sparse; in 1948 caterpillars were far more numerous than in any other year, so that the oak trees were defoliated and stood as bare in midsummer as normally in midwinter, and in 1960, 1962, and to a lesser extent 1963, the nestlings in rather late broods were almost as heavy as those in early broods. All these points suggest that food supplies were maintained unusually late in these five seasons. It is also suggestive that, at the other end of the scale, the two seasons when the most productive brood-size was unusually low were 1951 and 1961 in Marley, when caterpillars were scarcer than in any other years, while in addition Great Tits were exceptionally abundant in Marley in 1961.

As shown in Table 2, the annual variations in the average clutch of the Blue Tit occurred more or less in parallel with those of the Great Tit, and it is therefore of interest to know whether survival in relation to brood-size also varied similarly in the Blue Tit. As already mentioned, Blue Tits ringed as nestlings are subsequently retrapped in much smaller numbers than young Great Tits, so that the figures cannot be analysed in such detail, but they have been summarized in Table 9, which shows a similar pattern to that in the Great Tit. For instance, in 1947 and 1948 the survival-rate was very similar from the largest and smallest broods, as it was in the Great Tit. In the years 1949–55, on the other hand, the recovery-rate was lower for the young in broods of larger size, and the brood-size which on average gave rise to the largest number of survivors per brood was 10, which was also the commonest clutch, much as in the Great Tit (Lack, Gibb, and Owen, 1957). Again, in the years from 1958 onward, the recovery-rate fell off with increasing brood-size more markedly in 1959 than in the other years, as it did in the Great Tit. As all these variations were in parallel with those in the Great Tit in the same years, the two species have presumably been influenced by similar factors. The only big difference occurred in 1961 in Marley wood, where young Great Tits, as already mentioned, survived unusually poorly in comparison with the rest of Wytham; but in the Blue Tit

TABLE 9

Post-fledging survival of first broods of Blue Tit in Wytham

Size of broods at hatching	Number of nestlings	Recovered no.	%
	1947–8		
8–12	281	11	4
13–14	201	10	5
15–18	78	3	4
	1949–55		
3–7	83	7	8
8	104	6	6
9–10	512	22	4
11–13	591	19	3
14	28	0	0
	1958		
2–9	185	14	8
10–12	250	21	8
13	26	1	4
	1959		
1–7	98	10	10
8–11	821	69	8
12–14	222	8	4
	1960		
2–7	94	10	11
8–12	1057	116	11
13–14	262	28	11
16	16	1	6
	1961		
1–7	224	10	4
8–11	1084	45	4
12	84	1	1
	1962		
3–10	512	32	6
11–12	505	36	7
13	130	3	2
14–15	43	0	0

Notes. Many fewer Blue than Great Tits were recovered, in 1956 and 1957 too few for analysis. The figures for 1958–62 are for the whole of Wytham, not Marley only. No broods of Blue Tits were artificially increased. Brood-sizes were grouped on the same principle as for the Great Tit in Table 8.

that year the recapture-rate of fledged young was only slightly and not significantly lower from Marley wood than from the rest of Wytham and the most productive brood-size was close to the average.

One further factor might possibly modify the presumed influence of natural selection on the clutch-size of the Great Tit, that the parents of large broods might have a smaller chance of subsequent survival than the parents of small broods. That feeding a brood involves a strain is indicated by the low weight of adult Great Tits in June and July (Kluijver, 1952), and that the strain is greater for parents of larger than smaller broods is indicated by the fact that the parents of larger broods do not maintain their higher rate of feeding late in the nestling period, presumably through accumulated fatigue (Gibb, 1950). This strain might reduce their chances of further survival. Also weasels took more large than small broods and sometimes killed the parent, so that at least in this respect, parents of larger broods were at a slightly greater risk.

As yet there are not enough data to test the survival rate of parent Great Tits in relation to the size of their broods. But caterpillars were unusually sparse in 1961, and Perrins (1965) recaptured in the following winter more of the parents that bred early than late, in all 6 out of 10 (60 per cent) of those with broods hatching between 29 April and 5 May, 51 out of 114 (45 per cent) of those with broods hatching 6–11 May, 22 out of 56 (39 per cent) of those with broods hatching 12–17 May, and 1 out of 9 (11 per cent) of those with broods hatching 18–29 May. Possibly, therefore, those parents which found it harder to feed their young, because food was sparser later in the season, survived less well afterwards than those which bred earlier. There was also a slight suggestion that those with larger broods survived rather less well than the others. But neither of these possible tendencies was proven, and both were absent in 1962, though since food supplies evidently held out unusually late in 1962, this might have been expected. This problem requires further study.

Summarizing, losses of eggs and nestlings in first broods of the Great and Blue Tit were negligible in nearly all years. But in one year when Great Tits were far more numerous than usual in Marley wood and caterpillars were unusually scarce, many first brood nestlings starved, especially in the larger broods. Also, about half the young in very late broods starved. In a few years, weasels destroyed many broods, chiefly the larger broods or those hatched later in the season, probably because the young in such broods were hungrier, and therefore noisier than others. The average weight of the nestlings was also lower in the larger broods and in those which hatched later in the season, the variations due to these factors being much more pronounced in some years than others, apparently correlated with variations in the availability of food shortly after the young left the nest. In many years the brood-size from which, on the average, most young survived per brood was the same as, or close to, the most frequent clutch-size of 9, suggesting that this is why the Great Tit has evolved a clutch of this size. But in two years the most productive brood-size was much lower than this and in five years higher, reasons for which could be suggested. Also the method of analysis probably biases the figures in favour of survival from the larger broods.

Appendix. Breeding in other habitats

Some notes may be added on the breeding of Great and Blue Tits in other habitats, various points being summarized in Table 10. Gardens differ from woods especially in the scarcity of native broad-leaved trees and hence of caterpillars. Confirming earlier conclusions (Lack, 1955, 1958), in the years 1958 to 1961 Great Tits started laying 4 to 5 days earlier in Oxford gardens than in Marley wood and had an average clutch about 1 egg smaller (but 2 eggs smaller than the average for all years in Marley); Blue Tits also had clutches 1 egg smaller in gardens than in Marley, but bred at about the same date (Perrins, 1965). Presumably owing to the paucity of caterpillars in Oxford gardens in the years 1958–60, 36 per cent of the young Great Tits died of starvation in the nest, while about 60 per cent died of starvation in 1961, as compared with only 5 per cent in Wytham Great Wood in the same years. Further, the average weight of those young that survived to the fifteenth day in gardens was 17·6 grams in broods of 2 and 3, 16·2 grams in brood of 4 and 5, 16·2 grams in broods of 6 and 7 and 15·2 in broods of 8 and 9, the young in broods of 8 and 9 weighing only four-fifths of those in broods of the same size in the woods. Similarly the nestling mortality of the Blue Tit in the years 1958–61 was 31 per cent in gardens as compared with only 4 per cent in Wytham Great Wood.

In plantations of Scots Pine, *Pinus sylvestris*, on the Breckland, caterpillars were far scarcer than in broad-leaved woods in late April and May, but increased in numbers to a peak in July (Gibb and Betts, 1963). Great Tits started breeding at the same average date in Scots pine as in broad-leaved woods and had a clutch of similar size (actually slightly larger in the pines, probably because of the lower breeding density), while the seasonal decline in clutch-size was similar to that in broad-leaved woods, although in pines caterpillars were more, not less, abundant for the late than the early broods (Lack, 1955, 1958). Clearly, the Great Tits breeding in Scots pines retained their adaptations to broad-leaved woods. This was to be expected, since pine plantations have become common in England only during the last 100

TABLE 10

Breeding of Great and Blue Tits in different habitats in southern England

Habitat	Mean density per 10 hectares	Mean date of laying (d = mean for Great Tit)	Mean clutch	Nestling weight	% Nestlings dying (excluding predation)
	GREAT TIT 1st broods				
Pure oak and Marley	10–20	d	9·8	18·9	5
Scots pine	2·5	d	10·0	14·6	38
Corsican pine	1·3	d + 8	9·1	14·0	40
Gardens	c.6–12	d − 4½	7·6	16·0	44
	BLUE TIT 1st broods				
Pure oak	20 +	d − 3	11·5	—	4
Marley	9 +	d − 3	10·7	10·6	8
Scots pine	1·2	d − 3	10·4	10·4	29
Corsican pine	0·6	d + ?	9·3	9·5	38
Gardens	—	d − 3	8·8	—	31

Habitat	% Pairs starting	Mean clutch	Mean nestling weight (g)	% Nestlings dying (excluding predation)
	GREAT TIT 2nd broods			
Broad-leaved	2	7·3	15·9	41
Scots pine	28	7·6	17·4	13
Corsican pine	11	8·4	18·1	22

Notes. The basic information is derived from Lack, 1958 (modifying Lack, 1955) but the nestling weights are from Gibb and Betts (1963) and the figures for gardens are from Oxford 1958–61 (Perrins, 1965). As the date of laying differs in different years, dates are expressed in terms of the mean date of laying of the Great Tit in broad-leaved woods. The density of the Blue Tit in broad-leaved woods was higher than that in boxes because other pairs use natural holes. This did not apply to the pine plantations. The pure oak plantations were in the Forest of Dean, Gloucestershire, and Alice Holt, Surrey, and the pine plantations were on the Breckland, close to the Norfolk-Suffolk boundary. The average density in some Oxford gardens 1959–61 was 1·3 per hectare when Marley wood held 2·2 per hectare, but as the latter figure was exceptionally high, the average density for gardens was scaled down proportionately in Table 10.

years, and especially in the last 40 years, while they have usually been near broad-leaved woods, so there has been neither sufficient time nor sufficient isolation for the Great Tits breeding in pines to evolve special adaptations to this habitat in England. Blue Tits also bred at about the same date in Scots pines as in Marley wood, and had a similar average clutch. But in plantations of Corsican Pine, *P. nigra*, which supports fewer insects than Scots pine, both Great and Blue Tits started breeding several days later than in adjacent Scots pine plantations and, perhaps for this reason, they also had smaller clutches.

The first broods of both Great and Blue Tits fared extremely badly in the pine plantations. In those of Scots pine for instance, 38 per cent of the nestling Great Tits and 29 per cent of the nestling Blue Tits died of starvation, while the nestling Great Tits that survived weighed about three-quarters of those in broad-leaved woods, and some broods were so retarded that they fledged after 25–27 days instead of the usual 19 days (Gibb and Betts, 1963). The losses would probably have been heavier if there had not been some broad-leaved trees at the edge of the plantations, where both Great and Blue Tits obtained many cater-pillars. This meant, however, that the parents made unusually long journeys for food, and some of them even flew across open fields, which may have been why several were killed by Sparrowhawks. In the Scots pines, about a quarter of the Great Tits started second broods as compared with 11 per cent in Corsican pines and only 2 per cent in broad-leaved woods. Late broods were more successful in the pines than in broad-leaved woods, as measured by both the weight and the survival rate of the nestlings, and this accords with the increase in cater-pillars in the pines in late June and July already mentioned.

The important findings of Kluijver (1951) on the Great Tits breeding in a rather poor mixed coniferous and broad-leaved wood at Oranje Nassau's Oord near Wageningen in Holland were included in my earlier book (1954), so it must suffice to say here that many of the aspects of breeding biology described in this and the previous chapter for Marley wood were first established by Kluijver in Holland. The chief difference from England, not yet explained, is the much higher proportion of pairs with second broods in Holland. For instance, over the same period of years about 36 per cent of the pairs raised second broods in a broad-leaved wood at Liesbosch but about 76 per cent did so in a pine wood at Hoenderlo, whereas the corresponding proportions in English woods were respectively 2 and 28 per cent. In Holland, second broods were more frequent in pines than broad-leaved woods, in sparse than dense populations, in older than yearling females, and in earlier than later years for breeding, while when they were commoner, clutches tended to be larger, and probably they were more successful.

To test the survival of young Great Tits in relation to brood-size in Holland, Kluijver kindly lent me his data on the recoveries of ringed young at Oranje Nassau's Oord. As many nestlings starved, it was essential to analyse survival from the time of hatching, not fledging, but as the number of young hatching was not recorded, the analysis had to be based on the initial clutch-size (Lack, Gibb, and Owen, 1957). Large numbers of young were recovered from clutches of 7, 8, 9, and 10, and the rates of recovery were respectively 7·7, 7·1, 4·3, and 4·2 per cent. Hence the average number of recoveries per clutch was highest from clutches of 8 (0·57), and about the same from clutches of 7 (0·54), but lower from clutches of 9 (0·39) and 10 (0·42). On the theory advanced earlier, one might therefore have argued that the commonest clutch in this wood should have been 8, but in fact 9 was the commonest, presumably because this population has not been isolated from that in Continental broad-leaved woods (where, as in England, 9 might be the most productive brood-size). Kluijver (1963) later reported a seeming contradiction to this result, that those females which raised most fledglings in a year contributed most surviving young to the subsequent population. But this was based on an analysis of survival after fledging, not from the time of hatching, and the recoveries from first and second broods of the same pair were added together, so that the results are not comparable with those cited above. Kluijver also showed that the subsequent survival of the adult females was independent of the size of their broods. But the size of the first broods affected the proportion of pairs raising second broods, which decreased progressively from 48 per cent of those which had previously raised 1–4 young to 31 per cent of those which had previously raised 9–11 young.

Summarizing, in gardens, as compared with Marley wood, the Great Tit starts breeding four to five days earlier and lays a clutch one egg smaller, while many more nestlings starve and the survivors weigh less. In Scots pine plantations as compared with Marley wood, Great Tits start breeding at the same date, have the same average first clutch and the same seasonal decline in clutch-size, but these adaptations do not fit with the poorer food supplies in pines, where many young starved, the survivors weighed less than in broad-leaved woods and some broods stayed for a week longer than usual in the nest. The birds have presumably retained their adaptations to broad-leaved woods because the populations in pines are not genetically isolated. Probably it was for the same reason that at Oranje Nassau's Oord the commonest clutch was 9 but that giving rise to most young was only 8. Second broods are much commoner in Holland than England, and more are raised by pairs with small than large first broods. Kluijver also found that the subsequent survival of the adult females was independent of the size of brood which they had raised.

57

4
THE GREAT TIT IN WYTHAM
MORTALITY AT DIFFERENT TIMES
OF YEAR

THE two previous chapters were primarily concerned with the
factors affecting the reproductive rate of the Great Tit. The
mortality at different times of year must now be considered, and the
basic information available for each year has been set out in Table 11.
In most years, the heaviest mortality was that of the juveniles between
the summer and the ensuing winter, as can be seen most readily from a
comparison of the ratio of juveniles to adults in the population in the
summer as compared with the winter. The ratio in summer is approximately given by the number of young which leave the nest compared
with the number of breeding adults. The figure is not exact because,
before some of the later young leave the nest, some of the earliest to do
so have already died, but this is unimportant. The figures in column (v)
of Table 11, being expressed per pair, have to be divided by two for the
proportion of juveniles per adult at the time when the young leave
the nest. This ratio varied in different years between 2·1 (in 1961)
and 5·0 (in 1948), due to variations in the average clutch or the nestling
mortality.

Headpiece: Great and Blue Tits feeding on beechmast.

In 1958, Perrins (1963) discovered that in winter a juvenile Great Tit can reliably be distinguished from an adult by its greenish instead of greyish primary coverts, and from then on, all Great Tits trapped in Wytham in winter were aged by examination in the hand, which provided many records each year. There was, however, some bias with respect to age in the trapped samples, depending on where the birds were caught. For instance, in the good beechmast winter of 1960–1, the juvenile : adult ratio was 3·4 : 1 among the birds trapped under beech trees, but only 2·0 : 1 among those trapped at bait in Marley wood. The ratio in Marley wood was probably unbiased, as the same ratio was found there in the nesting boxes in the following spring. Under beech trees there were proportionately more juveniles, probably because the juveniles wander to a much greater extent than the older birds in winter, and particularly frequent areas where food is plentiful. In contrast, in 1961–2 when there was no beechmast, the proportion of juveniles trapped in Marley wood and other parts of Wytham was slightly lower in the winter than in the following spring, presumably because, without the attraction of beechmast, some of the juveniles wandered out of the woods to a near-by housing estate in search of food, but they returned to breed there, and at least some of them probably returned each night to the woods, as mentioned earlier. It is reasonably certain, however, that the biases with respect to age in the trapped samples were small compared with genuine large differences in the juvenile : adult ratio in different winters.

The situation in 1962–3 was unusually complex. Starting near the end of December, England experienced the most prolonged spell of extremely cold weather for over a century. There was a rich crop of beechmast, and under beech trees in Wytham in November and December, before the cold spell, the juvenile : adult ratio was 3·8 : 1, the highest recorded. Although, as in 1960, the sample under beech trees was probably biased in favour of juvenile birds, the juveniles evidently survived unusually well that year up to December. Then, however, the ground was covered by snow for many weeks. During and just after this cold period, a number of the juveniles (but none of the adults) trapped earlier under beech trees in Wytham were recovered up to several miles away, presumably having left Wytham because the snow made it hard for them to find food there. The juvenile : adult ratio in most of the Wytham woods in the next breeding season was only 0·6 : 1, so the death rate of the juvenile birds during the cold weather must have been far higher than that of the adults. In none of the other years studied in detail from 1958 onward was there a change in the juvenile : adult ratio between the start and the end of the winter, but there was no other really cold winter, and it is understandable that in severe

59

TABLE 11

Population changes of the Great Tit in Marley wood

Year	No. of breeding adults	% Change in nos. breeding in next year	No. of young flying Total	Per pair	Total summer population	% Loss summer–spring	Juv.:adult ratio, winter	Estimated maximum winter population	% Estimated loss winter–spring	Beech-mast	Winter cold
(i)	(ii)	(iii)	(iv)	(v)	(vi)	(vii)	(viii)	(ix)	(x)	(xi)	(xii)
1947	14	+200	65	9·2	79	47	—	—	—	2	13
1948	42	+48	209	9·9	251	76	(0·9)	—	—	8	3
1949	60	+3	260	8·7	320	81	0·9	115	46	1	13
1950	62	+3	190	6·1	252	75	—	—	—	8	10
1951	64	−38	157	4·9	221	82	0·3	83	52	0	6
1952	40	+5	150	7·5	190	78	—	—	—	3	16
1953	42	+48	184	8·8	226	73	1·3	97	36	5	35
1954	62	−13	262	8·5	324	83	0·5	93	42	0	25
1955	54	−11	183	6·8	237	80	—	—	—	0	58

1956	48	+104	189	7·9	237	59	—	—	—	6	5
1957	98	−45	225	4·6	323	83	0·2	118	54	0	14
1958	54	+54	150	5·6	204	60	1·5	135	39	4	14
1959	82	+24	277	6·8	359	72	1·0	164	38	0	6
1960	102	+69	274	5·4	376	53	2·0	306	43	5	1
1961	172	−50	365	4·2	537	83	0·2	206	58	0	47
1962	86	−9	226	5·3	312	75	2·6−0·4	312	75	4	165
1963	78	+38	253	6·5	331	67	1·0	156	31	0	15

Notes. To clarify the procedure adopted, the calculations of the percentages are here set out for 1949. In that year, 60 adults (30 pairs) bred in the following year 2 more, meaning an annual change of +3 per cent (column iii). The total summer population was 60 adults and 260 young, in all 320 birds (column vi), but only 62 adults bred in the following year, so the loss between the summer and the following spring was 258 birds or 81 per cent (column vii). The juvenile:adult ratio in the summer was 4·3 (half the figure in column v) and 0·9 in the following winter, a reduction of 79 per cent. Hence if no adults died before the winter, the maximum winter population was 60 adults and 55 (21 per cent of 260) juveniles, in all 115 birds (column ix). These 115 birds were reduced to 62 by the following spring, so 53 or 46 per cent were lost (column x). The figures for the beechmast crop are on an arbitrary scale in which o means crop failure, 2 a poor, 4 a moderate, 6 a good, and 8 an abundant crop, with the odd numbers intermediate in each case. Winter cold was calculated by adding together the number of degrees Centigrade below freezing-point for all those days in each winter at Oxford on which the average temperature was below zero. Only one winter, 1962–3, was really cold, but that of 1946–7, just before the study started, had a score of 113 and was also very cold. The juvenile:adult ratio in winter was doubtful (probably higher than shown) in 1948, while in 1962 it was high at the start of the winter and low at the end. The number of breeding adults in 1964 was 108.

weather the experienced adults, living on familiar ground, would find food more easily than the inexperienced juveniles.[1]

For the winters prior to 1958, the juvenile : adult ratio could be assessed only from those trapped birds which had been ringed previously as nestlings or adults, and so were of known age. The totals were very small and may have been biased as to age, since in these years all the nestlings, but only a proportion of the adults, in Marley wood bore rings. Hence the figures for these earlier years are unreliable, but they in general bear out the conclusions of the later years, presumably because genuine differences in the juvenile : adult ratio were large compared with the possible errors in the samples. The figures for these years refer, on average, to the middle of each winter, and all were obtained in Marley wood itself, not under beech trees.

A further indication of juvenile survival, and hence of the juvenile : adult ratio each winter, is given by the change in the breeding population from one year to the next, a marked increase probably meaning good recruitment and hence that the juveniles survived well, and a decrease meaning poor recruitment and hence that the juveniles survived poorly. These figures support those for the juvenile : adult ratio in the small trapped samples in the years before 1958. Thus, the marked increase in the breeding population between 1953 and 1954 suggests that the juvenile : adult ratio in the intervening winter was high, the absence of change between 1949 and 1950 suggests that in that winter the ratio was average, and the decreases between 1951 and 1952, 1954 and 1955, and 1957 and 1958 suggest that the ratios in these winters were low; the ratios in the trapped samples varied conformably.[2]

As shown in Table 11, there were large differences in the juvenile : adult ratio in different winters, the juveniles being in some years more than twice as common as the adults, but in others only one-fifth as

[1] It is puzzling, however, that in Marley wood the juvenile : adult ratio in November and December 1962 was only 0·4 : 1, and though it was based on only 16 trapped individuals, the ratio was the same in the following spring. It is impossible to believe that many juvenile birds had already died in Marley wood before the cold period, so presumably nearly all had left in November to feed under the beech trees, some of which were only one or two hundred yards from Marley wood. In view of these uncertainties, the juvenile : adult ratio in Marley wood that winter has been scored in Table 11 as 2·6–0·4 : 1 (2·6 : 1 being the figure at the time when the young left the nest, which was presumably maintained until the start of the cold period).

[2] The only exception was in 1948–9, in which the proportion of juveniles to adults trapped was only about average (0·9 : 1), whereas the subsequent increase in the breeding population suggested that it should have been high; since two other conditions usually associated with a high juvenile ratio, namely a large most productive brood-size and abundant beechmast, also held in 1948, it is almost certain that the juvenile : adult ratio was really high, not average, in that season, and that the small trapped sample was misleading; hence the figure for 1948 was excluded from Table 11.

frequent. These differences were not due primarily to variations in the number of fledglings produced in the previous summer. Obviously, if extremely few fledglings are produced, the ensuing winter ratio must be low, but the important point is whether the variations in the production of young that actually occurred had an appreciable influence on the winter ratios. The figures in Table 11 provide little or no evidence for this. It is true that the three summers in which the production rate of young was lowest, 1951, 1957, and 1961, were followed by the three winters in which the juvenile : adult ratio was lowest, but after three other summers with low production rates, the ensuing winter ratio was rather high in 1958–9, extremely high in 1960–1, and extremely high at the start of the winter in 1962–3. Again, the three summers with the highest rate of production were 1949, 1953, and 1954, after which the ensuing winter ratios were respectively near average, rather high, and low. Hence the rate of production has probably had no important influence on the winter ratio in the years studied.

It follows that the winter ratio has been influenced primarily by variations in the loss of juveniles between the summer and the ensuing winter. As discussed in the last chapter, young Great Tits from large broods suffered a proportionately higher mortality in some years than others, as most readily shown by the figures for the most productive brood-size each year in Table 8, and comparison of these figures with the winter ratios in Table 11 suggests that the two have been correlated, i.e. the young from larger broods tended to survive proportionately better than usual in the years when all young survived well. One or the other figure is missing for several years, but among those which can be compared, the three summers in which the most productive brood-size in Marley was smallest (1951, 1957, and 1961) were those in which the the juvenile : adult ratio in the following winter was lowest, while the three summers in which the most productive brood-size was largest (1960, 1962, and 1963) included the two in which the juvenile : adult ratio at the start of the winter was highest, and the ratio was on the high side in 1963. Moreover in two other summers, 1947 and 1948, when the most productive brood-size was extremely high, all juveniles almost certainly survived unusually well, as there was after both years a big increase in the breeding population in the following year.

As discussed in the previous chapter, the differences in the mortality of the young with respect to brood-size are almost certainly determined during the first one to three weeks after the young leave the nest. Hence the correlation between the most productive brood-size and the juvenile : adult ratio in winter suggests that the latter also has been determined mainly by the mortality of the young in their first one to three weeks after leaving the nest. In 1962–3, however, the juveniles survived unusually well from the time of leaving the nest up to late December, but then suffered heavy losses in the ensuing cold period. But except in this year the heaviest juvenile mortality evidently occurred soon after the young left the nest, at a time when caterpillars become scarce and there has just been a threefold to sixfold increase in the tit population due to breeding. Hence there may well be a serious food shortage at this time, in which the juveniles would almost certainly fare badly in competition with the adults. It is also suggestive that the years for which there is other evidence that food was unusually plentiful after the earliest broods left the nest, notably 1947, 1948, 1960, and 1962, and to a lesser extent 1963, were also the years in which the juveniles survived unusually well.

As mentioned in the previous chapter, the survival of young Blue Tits after leaving the nest tended to vary similarly to that of young Great Tits and it is therefore interesting to find that the juvenile : adult ratios of the two species in winter have also varied in parallel in the years for which they can be compared. The figures in Tables 11 and 13 (p. 71) show that this ratio was highest in both species in 1960 and 1962 and lowest in both in 1961, while in most of the other years for which comparison is possible, the figure was intermediate in both species. The tendency shown in Fig. 2 for the breeding populations of the Blue and Great Tit in Marley to fluctuate in parallel also indicates that the annual recruitment, and hence the juvenile mortality, of the two species has varied in parallel. If this mortality occurs primarily in the first few weeks after the young leave the nest, it suggests either that the Blue Tit takes the same types of food as the Great Tit, or that its food supplies are affected by the same factors as those which affect the food supplies of the Great Tit in June and early July.

In view of this last conclusion, it was unexpected to find a strong correlation between the juvenile : adult ratio at the start of each winter and the beechmast crop. The latter varies greatly from year to year, usually in parallel throughout England and much of continental Europe, so that though it was not precisely measured in Wytham in most years, the figures for England as a whole can be used. These have been set out on an arbitrary scale in Table 11, and summarized in relation to the juvenile : adult ratio of the Great Tit in the upper part of Table 12. This shows that, out of the thirteen winters in which the juvenile : adult ratio was measured, the four with the lowest ratio were all seasons with no beechmast, and the four with the highest ratio were all seasons with a rich or moderate crop, so the correlation could hardly have been closer. Comparison with Table 13 shows that the juvenile : adult ratio of the Blue Tit in winter was similarly correlated with the beechmast crop.

As both the Great Tit and the Blue Tit feed extensively on beechmast when it is present, the obvious explanation of this correlation is that the crop itself has a marked influence on juvenile survival. This seems unlikely to be the explanation, however, because at least in the winters from 1958–9 onward, in which the juvenile : adult ratio was measured repeatedly, the main change in this ratio (after the breeding season) had already occurred each year before early November; but the beechmast does not fall to the ground until about this time, the Great Tits do not feed on it until it has fallen, and though the Blue Tits also take it from the trees, they do so only when the fruits have opened and are almost ripe. Further, strong reasons were given earlier for thinking that in most years the main juvenile mortality occurs within a month or so of the young leaving the nest. This suggests the possibility that the availability of the foods eaten by Great and Blue Tits soon after leaving the nest might be influenced by whatever factors influence the formation of

TABLE 12

Relation of juvenile : adult ratio of Great Tit in winter to beechmast, and of population fluctuations to beechmast and winter cold. The figures show the number of years in each category

| Beechmast crop | Juveniles per adult in winter | | |
	0·2–0·5	0·9–1·3	1·5 or more
0	4	2	0
Small (1–3)	0	1	0
Moderate or Large (4–8)	0	1	3

| Beechmast crop | Breeding population in following year | | |
	Decreased by over 10%	Changed little (−9 to +24%)	Increased by by over 37%
0	5	1	1
Small (1–3)	0	2	1
Moderate or large (4–8)	0	2	5
Winter cold			
Mild (less than 17)	2	4	6
Fairly cold (25–58)	3	0	1
Very cold (165)	0	1	0

Notes. Based on data in Table 11. The season of 1946–7 was omitted because the breeding population was not know in 1946, but since that in 1947 was much the lowest recorded, there was almost certainly a big decrease, after a good beechmast crop but a very cold winter.

beechmast. The latter is known to be favoured by three weather factors. But the first of these, a fine spring in the year before the crop is formed, could hardly influence the survival of tits nearly eighteen months later, while the second, the absence of frost during the flowering period in April and May, lasts only a very few days, and also precedes the fledging of the tits. Thirdly, the ripening of the nuts is favoured by warm dry weather in late summer, but the critical period apparently comes somewhat later than the first month after the young tits leave the nest in June and early July. In view of this, however, I compared various weather factors in June and early July each year, such as sunshine, temperature and rainfall, with the ensuing juvenile : adult ratio of the Great Tit, but found no correlations.

Another point suggesting that the correlation between the beechmast crop and the survival of juvenile Great Tits is not due to a weather factor with a parallel influence on both is that a beech tree does not produce mast in two successive years, however favourable the weather in the second year, owing to the drain on its food reserves in producing the first crop. Hence if the survival of juvenile Great Tits depends on a weather factor influencing the beechmast crop, one would expect to find some years with a high survival of juvenile Great Tits but no beech-mast, namely those in which the weather conditions were favourable for a rich crop but the trees did not produce it because they had fruited in the previous year. There is as yet no evidence that such years exist. Further, the fluctuations in Dutch populations of the Great Tit have also been closely correlated with the beechmast crop, as discussed later.

If the correlation with the beechmast crop is not due either to the crop itself or to a weather factor which also affects the survival of the juvenile tits, it is presumably due to some other factor which varies in parallel with the beechmast. In fact, the fruiting of quite a number of other trees including the oak and Ash, *Fraxinus excelsior*, has fluctuated in parallel with the beech in Wytham in the last twelve years, so there are various other possibilities, but none of them has yet been investigated.

At this inconclusive stage, the discussion has to be broken off for lack of further evidence. It may, however, have helped to show some of the difficulties in a population study. In particular, observations have to be continued for many years to distinguish between causative and coincidental variations in the environment. Also, it would have been almost impossible to have measured from the first year onward all those factors which might conceivably have influenced the Great Tit population, and there was at the start no reason to think that the survival of the juveniles in the first month after they left the nest would be so important, or that it might be correlated with the size of the beechmast crop several months later.

In Table 11 are set out the main facts known about the changes in the Great Tit population in Marley wood, and the way in which the various percentages have been calculated is explained in the footnote. To analyse the annual fluctuations in the number of breeding pairs, it is probably best not to use the actual numbers involved, but to express the change from one year to the next as a percentage of the initial population, as in column (iii). To interpret the changes, it is desirable to measure the population several times each year, but while the breeding population and the number of young raised were accurately known for each year, no direct counts were made at other times of year. However, the juvenile : adult ratio was recorded in most winters, and provided that the main mortality after breeding and before the winter is of juveniles, as seems likely, then the change in the ratio between the summer and the winter indicates the mortality in this period. If no adults died before the winter, the number of Great Tits alive at the start of the winter would be the number of adults which bred in the previous summer together with the surviving juveniles as assessed from the change in the juvenile : adult ratio, and these figures have been set out in column (ix). They are very unreliable before 1958, as it was only from that year onward that the juvenile : adult ratios were based on large samples. On the basis of these estimated winter populations, it is then possible to assess the loss between each winter and the following spring, set out in column (x), but these figures, of course, are as doubtful as those in column (ix).

A comparison of column (iii) with column (ii) in Table 11 shows that the number of breeding pairs each year has not itself had any important influence on the change in numbers by the following year. In particular the population has not tended to increase after being small or to decrease after being large, and it is striking that the second highest population recorded, that of 1960, was followed by an increase which, when measured in terms of the number of pairs, instead of as a percentage change, was the biggest recorded.

The number of young raised per pair (in column v) has in Fig. 14 been plotted against the subsequent change in the breeding population, and this shows that variations in the production of young have also had little if any influence on the population changes. Obviously, if no young were produced, the breeding population in the following year would almost certainly be lower than before, but the important question is whether the variations that actually occurred had an influence. The three years with the lowest average production of young, 1951, 1957 and 1961, were each followed by a big decrease in the breeding population as compared with the previous year, but on the other hand the production rate was also low in 1958 and 1960, after which there was a

67

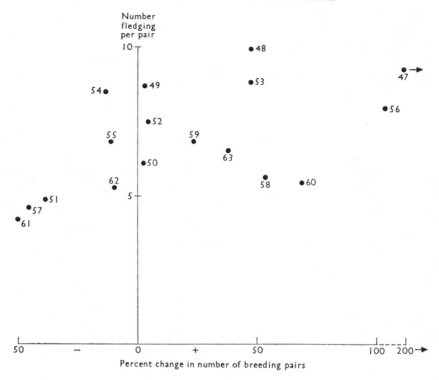

FIG. 14. Number of young Great Tits raised per pair per year in Marley wood in relation to change in breeding population in following year.

big increase, and in 1962, after which there was only a small decrease. Again, while the three years with the highest average production, 1947, 1948, and 1953, were each followed by a big increase, the high production rate in 1954 was followed by a decrease and that of 1949 by a negligible change in numbers. From this it follows that the annual fluctuations have been due, at least mainly, to variations in the mortality rate, and this is borne out by a comparison of the figures in column (vii) with those in column (iii). The six years with a mortality of at least 80 per cent between the summer and the following spring included all five in which the breeding population in the ensuing year decreased by at least 10 per cent, while the four years with a mortality of only 60 per cent or less between the summer and the following spring were the four with the biggest proportionate increase in the subsequent breeding population.

It is next of interest to determine in what part of the year the critical mortality occurs. The existence of a strong correlation between the juvenile : adult ratio at the start of the winter and the change in the subsequent breeding population, discovered by Perrins (1963) and set out in Fig. 15, indicates that in most years it was the juvenile mortality before the winter that was critical. The main exception was in 1962–3, when, as explained earlier (p. 61), the juvenile : adult ratio was high at the start of the winter but low at the end as a result of losses during the exceptionally severe winter, and the subsequent breeding population showed a decrease. (Both figures for the ratio in 1962–3 have been plotted in Fig. 15, but it is clearly that at the end of the winter which mattered.)

Since the juvenile : adult ratio in winter has been correlated with the beechmast crop, so, therefore, have the annual fluctuations in the breeding population, as shown in the middle section of Table 12. Points are available for more years than in the uppermost section, and the correlation is nearly, though not quite, as close. There were, however, a few exceptional years. A big proportionate increase in numbers after a small beechmast crop in 1947–8 is readily explicable, as the Great Tit

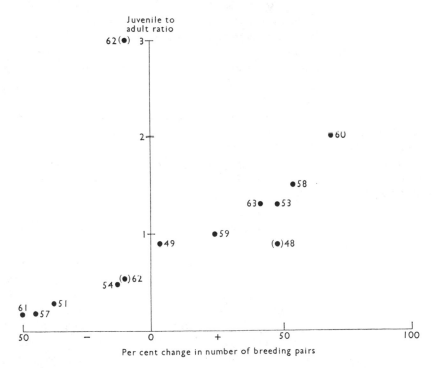

FIG. 15. Ratio of juvenile to adult Great Tits in winter in Marley wood in relation to change in breeding population in following year. In 1962–3, unlike other years, the ratio was high at the start but low at the end of the winter (presumably due to juvenile mortality during the exceptional cold weather), so both points are shown in brackets (from Perrins, 1965).

population at the start of this winter was far smaller than in any other, so that there was presumably less competition than usual for food, enabling an unusually high proportion of the birds to survive. There were also two seasons with little change in numbers after a big crop of beechmast; but that of 1962–3 is readily explained since the juvenile tits survived extremely well up to the start of the long cold spell and then suffered heavy losses, as already noted; that of 1950–1 has not been explained. Another unexplained exception was 1963–4, when there was no beechmast, a moderately high juvenile : adult ratio at the start of the winter, and a big increase in the next breeding population, due partly to an unusually light mortality during the winter itself. (In 1959–60, likewise, there was no beechmast, a moderate juvenile : adult ratio and a moderately large increase in the breeding population in Marley; but this increase was exceptional, as there was no increase in numbers in Wytham Great Wood, while in the other woods shown in Fig. 3 the population decreased; hence in these other woods, unlike Marley, the correlation with the beechmast crop held in that year.) While, however, there have been these few exceptions, the correlation between the beechmast crop and the population changes was in general close. Yet, as discussed earlier, variations in the beechmast crop itself could not have been responsible, as in most years the critical juvenile mortality occurred before the beechmast was ripe. Since, however, the tits feed extensively on beechmast after it has fallen, it presumably assists their subsequent survival during the winter (though the estimates for the winter mortality in Table 11 do not lend support to this idea).

It is widely believed that the Great Tit has a higher mortality than usual in severe winters (Ticehurst and Witherby, 1940; Ticehurst and Hartley, 1948). However, winter cold appeared to have little if any influence on the population fluctuations in Marley wood in the years studied, as indicated by the bottom section of Table 12 (see note to Table 11 for method of measurement). But in this period only one winter, that of 1962–3, was really cold, and in that year, though snow lay for a long time, there were no prolonged glazed frosts, and it is the latter which seem particularly dangerous to birds such as tits. Perhaps this was why the breeding population in 1963 was only 9 per cent smaller than in the previous summer. Glazed frosts were frequent in the cold winter of 1946–7, but unfortunately the Great Tit was not studied in 1946, so that, while the breeding population was much lower in 1947 than in any other year studied, the reduction from the previous year, though presumably heavy, was not measured. There were, in addition, four other winters with some cold weather. That of 1953–4 was followed by a big increase in the Great Tit population, and while those of 1954–5, 1955–6, and 1961–2 were each followed by a decrease, these are sufficiently explained by there being no beechmast. It may be added that the second largest decrease recorded, that of 1957–8, followed a fairly mild winter, and that there was also a marked decrease after the very mild winter of 1951–2. The picture is much the same if, instead of the change in the breeding population from one year to the next, one uses the rough estimates of winter mortality. The estimated winter mortality was heaviest, perhaps 75 per cent, in 1962–3, which might well have been due to the prolonged cold spell. But of the three other winters in which the estimated mortality exceeded 50 per cent, only one was rather cold (1961–2) and the others mild (1951–2, 1957–8). Hence winter cold probably had no appreciable influence on the numbers of the Great Tit breeding in Wytham, except in 1946–7 and 1962–3.

The figures for the Blue Tit in Table 13 are based on smaller totals than those for the Great Tit, while part of the population, as mentioned earlier, breeds in natural holes and so escapes record. These figures

TABLE 13

The Blue Tit population in nesting boxes in Marley wood

Year	No. of breeding pairs	% Change in nos. breeding in next year	No. of young flying Total	Per pair	Juvenile : adult ratio in winter
1947	9	+111	107	11·9	—
1948	19	+37	200	10·5	—
1949	26	+31	204	7·8	—
1950	34	0	238	7·0	—
1951	34	−50	223	6·6	—
1952	17	−18	163	9·6	—
1953	14	+29	80	5·7	—
1954	18	−28	165	9·2	—
1955	13	+15	120	9·2	—
1956	15	+113	135	9·0	—
1957	32	−47	155	4·8	—
1958	17	+18	82	4·8	1·3
1959	20	+25	153	7·7	1·0
1960	25	+76	172	6·9	3·5
1961	44	−52	314	7·1	0·7
1962	21	+95	162	7·7	2·8
1963	41	+12	341	8·3	1·6

Notes. Forty-six pairs bred in 1964. The unusually low production of young in 1953 was based on a small sample in which many nests were deserted. The juvenile : adult ratio in 1960 was presumably too high as all were caught under beech trees.

suggest that, as in the Great Tit, there was no correlation between the production of young and the change in the numbers of breeding pairs from one year to the next. Also, if there was any correlation between the population changes and the juvenile : adult ratio in winter, it was less marked than in the Great Tit (and there was a temporarily inflated ratio in 1957 due to an irruption of juvenile Blue Tits from the Continent, mentioned earlier). As in the Great Tit, the correlation with the beechmast crop was close, the chief exception being 1959–60, when the population increased although there was no beechmast, as it did in the Great Tit. Finally, there was no correlation with winter cold and it is particularly noteworthy that the breeding population almost doubled between 1962 and 1963, despite the exceptionally prolonged winter. Hence though further data are desirable, it would seem that the fluctuations in the breeding population of the Blue Tit, which have usually been in parallel with those of the Great Tit, have been affected by similar factors.

As shown in Fig. 3 (p. 16), the fluctuations of the Great Tit in other woods in England and Holland have been in parallel with those in Marley wood, suggesting that these populations have been affected by similar factors. In Holland Kluijver (1951) considered that the marked fluctuations in the breeding population of the Great Tit at Oranje Nassau's Oord between 1912 and 1943 were positively correlated with the annual variations in the production rate of fledged young, especially at low densities, and negatively correlated with the coldness of the winter, especially at high densities, and this population also showed a strong tendency to rise after being low and to fall after being high. Later Perrins (1965) found that the fluctuations there, as elsewhere, were correlated with the beechmast crop, as summarized in the upper part of Table 14, which showed that there was a marked decrease in the Great Tit population after six of the seven years with no beechmast and a marked increase after seven of the nine years with a good crop, the only marked exception being a 35 per cent decrease after a good crop in 1934–5 (which was not, it may be noted, a hard winter). The possible relationship with winter cold, also summarized in Table 14, is suggestive, though less strong than that with the beechmast, perhaps due to the tendency reported by Kluijver for winter cold to cause a decrease mainly in the years when numbers were high at the start of the winter.

A fresh analysis of Kluijver's published data by J. F. Scott (of the Unit of Biometry, Oxford, pers. comm.) showed that the positive correlation with the beechmast crop was statistically significant irrespective of other factors, while there was no significant correlation with the production rate of young, and the negative correlation with winter cold

TABLE 14

Influence of beechmast crop and winter cold on fluctuations in the breeding population of the Great Tit 1912–43 at Orangje Nassau's Oord, Holland

	Number of years in which the breeding population of the following year		
	Decreased by over 9%	Changed little (−9% to +20%)	Increased by over 20%
BEECHMAST CROP			
None	6	1	0
Small (1–3)	5	4	4
Moderate or Large (4–8)	1	1	9
WINTER WEATHER			
Mild	5	3	11
Cold	7	3	2

Notes. The data for the beechmast crop have been published by Perrins (1965). The other data are from Kluijver (1951), the winter being considered cold when the 'cold figure' on his basis of calculation was at least 85°C.

was doubtfully significant as it could not certainly be separated from a possible negative correlation with population density. But since in Marley there was no correlation with population density, whereas the two really cold winters evidently reduced the population, the fluctuations in the Dutch population were probably influenced by winter cold rather than by population density. In Holland, as in England, the cause of the correlation with the beechmast crop was certainly not the crop itself, since between 1956 and 1963 inclusive, an isolated population of Great Tits on the island of Vlieland has fluctuated in parallel with those in the Veluwe and Marley, and hence with the beechmast crop, but there are no beech trees on Vlieland (Kluijver, pers. comm.). There are places, however, where the beech crop has a direct influence on numbers, notably in southern Sweden, where many Great and Blue Tits stay the winter and feed on beechmast when it is plentiful, but emigrate in winters when it is sparse or absent (Ulfstrand, 1962). This, however, refers to the numbers in winter, not the breeding season.

While the critical factor influencing the annual fluctuations in the breeding population of the Great Tit in Marley wood has been the juvenile mortality, particularly between the summer and the start of the winter, there is no evidence that this mortality has varied significantly with population density. But as Morris (1959), also Varley

73

and Gradwell (1960), pointed out, 'key factors' affecting annual fluctuations are not normally density-dependent. Hence the density-dependent regulation of the Great Tit population has evidently been brought about by some different factor.

Conceivably this density-dependent factor could be the production rate of the young, since the number of young raised per pair to fledging has shown a clear inverse relationship with density, as set out in Fig. 16

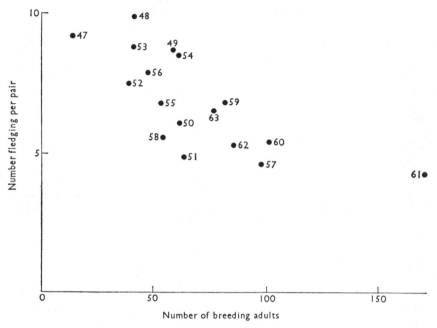

FIG. 16. Number of young Great Tits raised per pair per year in Marley wood in relation to density of breeding pairs.

for the Great Tit, while a similar correlation holds in the Blue Tit (cf. Table 13). For instance, the middle part of Fig. 16 shows that an increase in the number of breeding Great Tits from 40 to 100 adults was accompanied by a decline in the average production rate from 9 to 5 young per pair, a fairly marked difference. But it does not, in my view, account for the regulation of the population. This is because, as discussed earlier, the annual variations in the mortality of the young Great Tits soon after they leave the nest have been so great that the number of young leaving the nest has borne no relation to the number of juveniles surviving to the start of each winter. In Holland likewise, Kluijver (1951) found a marked inverse correlation between the density of breeding pairs and the number of young raised per pair. Indeed the effect was more marked than in England, as the proportion of second broods varied strongly with density. But he likewise concluded that this factor did not account for the regulation of the Great Tit population.

If variations in the production rate are not critical, then presumably those in the mortality rate are critical at some stage. As already mentioned, the change in the breeding population from one year to the next, and also the total mortality of both adults and juveniles between each summer and the following spring, have not varied significantly with population density. But much the largest part of this mortality is that of the juveniles between the summer and the start of the winter, which is independent of density.

On the present inadequate data, probably the best figure for the mortality excluding that of the juveniles between the summer and the start of the winter is that of the breeding birds each year between one spring and the next. In recent years Perrins (1965) caught and aged the breeding females in spring, and the proportion of yearling to older individuals in the nesting boxes in Marley was 1·8:1 in 1961, 0·25:1 in 1962, 0·35:1 in 1963, and 0·71:1 in 1964. The number of females breeding in these four years was respectively 86, 43, 39, and 54, hence the number of breeding females older than one year was respectively 31, 34, 29, and 32, and these older birds were the survivors from respectively 51, 86, 43, and 39 females breeding in 1960, 1961, 1962, and 1963. Hence the mortality of the adult females between one spring and the next was in these years 39, 60, 36, and 18 per cent respectively.

Unfortunately, the breeding birds were not aged before 1961. But the ratio of juvenile to adult birds was approximately known for most previous winters, and at least in recent years, this ratio did not change appreciably between the start of the winter and the spring, except in the unusually cold winter of 1962–3. Hence in default of better information, the annual mortality of the adults between one spring and the next has, for the years prior to 1960, been based on the winter ratios, the calculation being in other respects the same as in the previous paragraph. The figures for these earlier years need not be set out here, as they are the same as the estimates for the winter mortality in column (x) of Table 11.[1]

[1] This is because the estimates in column (x) were based on the assumption that no breeding adults died before the start of the winter. They might, indeed, reflect the annual mortality of the adults between one spring and the next more truly than the winter mortality of the adults and juveniles combined, since the assumption (used for the estimates of the annual adult mortality) that the juvenile : adult ratio changed negligibly between the winter and spring is probably more nearly correct than the assumption (used for the estimates of the overall winter mortality) that the breeding adults suffered no mortality before the start of the winter. The unusually cold winter of 1962–3 was exceptional in that the juvenile : adult ratio changed markedly between the winter and spring, and in this year the estimated loss of birds of all ages between the

Omitting the years for which neither the spring nor winter ratio of juveniles to adults was measured, the estimated annual survival of adults between one spring and the next has been plotted against the initial number of breeding adults in Fig. 17. This does not suggest that the mortality rate was higher at higher densities, but if the critical

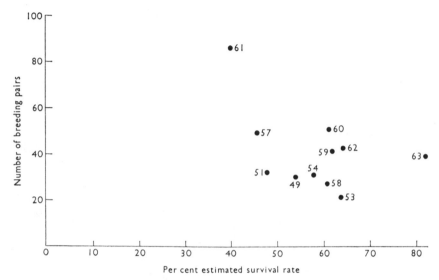

FIG. 17. Estimated survival rate of adult Great Tits from one breeding season to the next, as a percentage of number present in first season.

mortality was due to food shortage, as seems most likely, any effect of population density on survival was presumably modified by annual variations in the food supply, which may well have been large, as they certainly were for beechmast. (It should perhaps be added that these annual variations in the adult or winter mortality were not correlated with the annual fluctuations in the breeding population.)

If the population density of the Great Tit is critically regulated by the mortality that takes place each year after the main period of juvenile losses in the summer and autumn, there are four factors which, on theoretical grounds, are capable of providing the necessary density-dependent control, namely predation, disease, food shortage, and the birds' own territorial behaviour. Of these, the first two can reasonably be excluded. The occasional severe raiding of nesting boxes by Weasels, *Mustela nivalis*, has been highly irregular, and there has been hardly

winter and the spring (75 per cent) was much higher than that of the adult females between one spring and the next (36 per cent), providing a further indication that the juveniles suffered disproportionately heavy losses in the cold weather that year.

76

any predation on the adult tits at other times of year. There has likewise been no evidence that the birds died in appreciable numbers from disease. Hence the food supply might be critical at some time of the year, and there is nothing pointing against this idea, but the foods taken by the Great Tit in the very mixed woodland of Marley are so varied that it has not been possible to measure the density of any of them except beechmast. It is suggestive, however, that the Great Tit spends a very high proportion of its time each winter day in searching for food (Gibb, 1954b). Further, as shown in Fig. 3, it breeds at a much higher density in broad-leaved woods than conifers and, except perhaps in late summer, much more insect and vegetable food is available for Great Tits in broad-leaved woods than conifers. More cannot be said on this point until measurements have been made of the availability of food for the tits in winter, and this seems almost impossibly difficult in Marley.

Turning now to the fourth possible controlling factor, territorial behaviour, there are two critical questions. First, does such behaviour actually limit the number of pairs (as distinct from merely spacing out the pairs that are present as a result of the operation of some other factor)? Secondly, if so, is this limit related to the food resources? In Holland, Kluijver and Tinbergen (1953) found that, in strips of broad-leaved woodland, Great Tits took up breeding territories earlier in the spring, occupied much smaller territories, and were much more stable in numbers from year to year, than in nearby coniferous woodland. They concluded that territorial behaviour is important in adjusting the density of breeding pairs to the nature of the habitat, and that the population in the highly favourable broad-leaved areas was 'buffered', birds occupying the conifers chiefly after the territories in the broad-leaved areas had been filled.

This conclusion has been widely quoted and accepted, including by Gibb (1956b, 1962c), while Wynne-Edwards (1962) used it to corroborate his general theory, discussed in Appendix, section 3, that birds regulate their own numbers to prevent over-exploitation of food supplies. There are, however, some puzzling features. First, the broad-leaved areas were only 100–200 metres wide, hence the effect was very local. Secondly, very similar variations were found in the Coal Tit, but this species, unlike the Great Tit, is primarily adapted to conifers, so might not have been expected to vary in the same way. Thirdly, while the figures for English woods confirm that the Great Tit is much denser in broad-leaved woods than pine plantations, the fluctuations were similar in extent in both types of wood, instead of being greater in the pines (Lack, 1958). Finally Marley wood, as already mentioned, includes areas with tall canopy trees and others with smaller trees and bushes, and the Great Tit lays, on average, a larger clutch in the

77

canopy areas than the others. Perrins (pers. comm.) analysed the population fluctuations in these two types of habitat, which interdigitate with each other in Marley, and found that, while the breeding density was similar in both habitats when the overall numbers were low, it was proportionately higher in the canopy areas in years of high numbers. Hence here the population fluctuated more strongly in the more favourable, not the less favourable, habitat; though it should be added that the criterion of favourability was rather different from that used by Kluijver and Tinbergen. I therefore consider that judgement on Kluijver and Tinbergen's conclusion should be suspended until further data are available.

There are several views as to how territorial behaviour might limit population density in birds, but the prevailing one today is that of Huxley (1934), supported for instance by Tinbergen (1957), who compared territories to rubber discs; the more they are compressed, the greater becomes the resistance to further compression. On this view, though territorial behaviour does not set a rigid upper limit to numbers, one would expect that at higher densities the population would fluctuate between very restricted limits. Moreover, if territorial behaviour is at all important, there should be many years in which numbers are near to this upper limit. This, in fact, was the picture described by Kluijver and Tinbergen (1953) for the Great Tit in the strips of broad-leaved woodland. But the population changes in Marley wood in Fig. 2 and in the Forest of Dean in Fig. 3 do not at all conform with this picture. Before 1961 one might perhaps have argued that territorial behaviour set an upper limit to the number of Great Tits breeding in Marley wood at around 50 pairs, even though, in the course of 14 years, this level was reached only twice, in 1957 and 1960. But in 1961, 86 pairs bred there. This is so far above the number in any other year that, if the analogy of the partly compressible disc is valid, effective pressure from territorial behaviour can have been exerted only in this one year; and there is, of course, no critical evidence for thinking that it was exerted then. Moreover, if territorial behaviour limited the number of breeding pairs at most only once in 17 years, it has clearly been of little importance.

There is, however, an alternative view of territorial behaviour, that birds modify the size of their territories in accordance with the food situation, especially with the food situation for their young. On this view, one would expect more pairs of Great Tits to have settled in Marley wood in the years when caterpillars for their young were numerous than in the years when caterpillars were sparse. But the number of breeding pairs of Great Tits in Marley wood has definitely not been correlated with the density of caterpillars on oak leaves (Lack, 1958, confirmed by Perrins, 1965, from 1958 to 1964). It may be added that, on this view, it should have followed that in 1961 the Great Tits in Marley wood defended much smaller territories than usual because of an unusually favourable food situation, but in fact caterpillars were sparser on the oak leaves in 1961 than in any other summer, and the Great Tits raised a smaller number of young per pair than in any other year. Yet as discussed earlier, they raised an average number of young per pair in Wytham Great Wood that year, very possibly because the breeding density there was much lower than in Marley. This suggests that, if the Great Tits in Marley had been able to restrict their density through territorial behaviour to that in Great Wood, each pair would have raised more young. Hence restriction of the breeding density by territorial behaviour would probably have been advantageous for the reason usually claimed for it, but in fact it did not occur. For these reasons, I conclude that territorial behaviour did not limit the number of pairs of Great Tits breeding in Marley wood. It should perhaps be added that the Great Tit is not a typical territorial passerine species, as at least part of its aggressive behaviour is centred round its nesting hole, so my conclusion that its numbers have not been limited by territorial behaviour need not be applicable to other species.

Summarizing, the annual fluctuations in the breeding population of the Great Tit in Marley wood were due primarily to corresponding variations in the juvenile mortality before the winter, most of which probably occurred in the first one to three weeks after the young left the nest. Circumstantial evidence suggests that the marked annual variations in this mortality were correlated with the availability of food soon after the young left the nest. Yet there was a strong correlation with the beechmast crop, for reasons not understood, since Great and Blue Tits feed on beechmast only when it is ripe, and hence after the critical period of juvenile mortality. Moreover, the same correlation held on Vlieland, where there are no beech trees. However, various other species of trees have tended to produce seeds in the same years as the beech. Winter cold had no appreciable influence on the population fluctuations in Marley except in the unusually severe winter of 1962–3 and probably also in 1946–7, but it evidently had an influence on a Dutch population between 1912 and 1943. The average number of fledged young produced per pair varied inversely with population density, but it probably had no influence in population regulation, as this variation was swamped by the much greater variations in juvenile mortality after the young fledged, which were not density-dependent. The critical density-dependent mortality was not brought about by disease, predation or territorial behaviour; very possibly the winter numbers in relation to food supply were important, but this problem would be extremely difficult to study in Marley wood.

5

THE COAL TIT IN PINE PLANTATIONS

A STUDY of the Coal Tit, *Parus ater*, is placed next because it was an extension of the work of members of the Edward Grey Institute on the Great Tit, described in the previous three chapters. The main purpose of this work was to investigate the influence of the food supply both on breeding success and on adult survival outside the breeding season. The most important finding was that, in winter, insectivorous birds at times remove a substantial proportion of the available prey; hence in winter they may be limited in numbers by their food and may have a marked influence on the density of their prey.

As already mentioned, a quantitative analysis of the food supply of adult Great Tits in relation to their numbers proved impossibly difficult in the mixed broad-leaved woodland of Marley. Even a pure oak plantation in the Forest of Dean proved to be too complex a habitat for this purpose, though a qualitative survey of the foods of the Great and Blue Tits throughout the year was undertaken there (Betts, 1955). For this reason, the studies on the food of tits at the Edward Grey Institute were transferred to the much simpler and more uniform conditions provided by pure pine plantations on the Breckland. This sandy area on the border between Norfolk and Suffolk formerly consisted mainly of dry heathland, but between the wars it was extensively planted by the Forestry Commission with Scots Pine, *Pinus sylvestris*,

Headpiece: Coal Tit feeding artificial nestling gape operated from hide beside nesting box.

and some Corsican Pine, *P. nigra*. The change of study area also involved transferring the main work from the Great Tit to the Coal Tit, *Parus ater*. As mentioned in the appendix to Chapter 3, both Great and Blue Tits breed in the Breckland pine plantations, but they are scarce there and are also badly adapted to them. On the other hand the Coal Tit is common, and as it is primarily a species of coniferous forest, it fares well there.

The chief habitat of most European populations of the Coal Tit is Spruce, *Picea abies*, a tree not native to Britain, where the bird's ancestral habitat was presumably Scots pine, which it still inhabits in the remnants of the ancient Scottish forest. Virgin pine forest disappeared from England about 3000 years ago. Some Coal Tits doubtless persisted in the broad-leaved forest which replaced it, as the bird breeds in small numbers in pure oak woods at the present day, but the species was evidently rare in England in historic times until the extensive planting of Scots pine in the nineteenth century (Newton, 1874). The woods where the bird was studied on the Breckland were planted in 1926, and the close, uniform stands of tall slender trees obviously provide very different conditions in certain respects from the mature, more varied, and presumably more open, primaeval pine forest.

A breeding study of all tits in nesting boxes in a plantation of Scots pine and another of Corsican pine was carried out under my direction from 1949 to 1957 by students of Lynford Hall Forester Training School (Lack, 1955, 1958). In parallel, a detailed study of the birds' food and of the numbers of insects throughout the year in these and other plantations was made from April 1952 to August 1957 by Gibb (1957, 1958, 1960, 1962*a*, *b*) Betts (1956, 1958) and Gibb and Betts (1963). See also Grimshaw *et al.* (1958). Their work, which forms the basis of the present chapter, was financed by the Nature Conservancy. Close touch was maintained with a Dutch group which had earlier started a study of tits in relation to the numbers of caterpillars in pine woods in the breeding season (Tinbergen, 1949; *et al.*, 1960).

The density of Coal Tits breeding each year in the nesting boxes is shown in Fig. 18; probably these comprised the whole population. Comparison with Figs. 2 and 3 shows that the fluctuations were not in parallel either with those of the Great Tit in the same plantations, or with those of the Great and Blue Tits in Marley wood, except that all three species increased markedly after the unusually mild winter of 1956–7. The average breeding density of the Coal Tit in these pine plantations was about 0·3 pair per hectare, roughly six times what it was in Marley and other broad-leaved woods.

In the Scots pine plantations, first clutches of the Coal Tit were laid, on the average, ten days earlier than those of the Great Tit, which breed

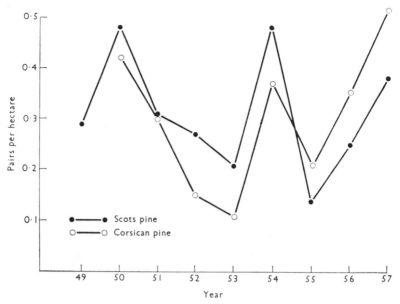

FIG. 18. Annual fluctuations in population density of Coal Tit, *Parus ater*, in Breckland pine plantations.

there at the same time as in oakwoods. The Coal Tit also breeds earlier than the Great Tit in Holland. The reason is not known. It is also not known why the Coal Tit, like the Great and Blue Tits, laid later, on the average by five days, in Corsican than Scots pine, even when the plantations were adjacent to each other, but insects were in general sparser in Corsican than Scots pines. The proportion of pairs of Coal Tits which started second broods was 9 per cent in the Scots pine and 4 per cent in the Corsican pine, lower than for the Great Tit in the same plantations (see p. 55), although the Coal Tit is adapted to conifers, and its second broods were much more successful than those of the Great Tit. This difference is understandable, however, if as suggested earlier for the Great Tit, most second broods were laid by birds which had lost their first broods, as in these plantations first broods were usually successful in the Coal Tit but usually failed in the Great Tit.

The average first clutch of the Coal Tit in the pine plantations was just under 10 eggs, but it varied in different years between 9·1 and 10·5 eggs, these variations, as shown in Fig. 19, being correlated inversely with population density, as in the Great Tit. The average clutch was somewhat over 10 eggs in the few pairs which nested each year in Wytham and other broad-leaved woods, but this is readily explicable through the low population density in broad-leaved woods. It will be recalled that, presumably for the same reason, the Great Tit had a

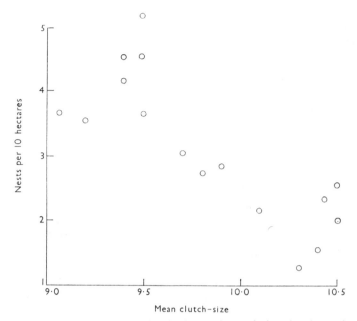

FIG. 19. Relation between mean clutch-size and population density each year of Coal Tit, *Parus ater*, on Breckland (based on Lack, 1958, Table 9, p. 111, combining data for two plantations).

somewhat larger average clutch in Scots pine (to which it is not well adapted) than in broad-leaved woods (see p. 54). The average clutch of of the Coal Tit did not vary at all between 1 April and 10 May, this constancy presumably being an adaptation to the fact that in pines the supply of caterpillars did not diminish between April and June; it is in contrast to the marked seasonal decline in broad-leaved woods of both caterpillars and the clutch-size of the Great Tit. After mid-May, the average clutch of the Coal Tit was one egg smaller than in April. At first sight this seems surprising because, in the Breckland pines, the supply of caterpillars available for the young continued to increase until mid-July. However, at the time when the second broods of nestlings were being fed, the Coal Tit population was much higher than earlier in the spring owing to the presence of many first-brood young out of the nest. Further, these late layings were by birds which had already raised or attempted to raise a brood, so they may have been in a weakened state. Unlike what happened in the Great Tit, annual variations in the mean date of laying had no effect on the clutch-size of the Coal Tit, but this was to be expected from the fact that the average clutch did not decrease in the course of each season between the beginning of April and mid-May.

Nearly all the eggs hatched successfully. Excluding a few losses of complete broods through predation by weasels, the proportion of the hatched young which flew from the nest was 98 per cent for first brood and 99 per cent for second broods in Scots pine, and 92 and 100 per cent respectively in Corsican pine. This high rate of success is in marked contrast to the poor success of the Great and Blue Tits in the same plantations (cf. Table 10), presumably because the Coal Tit, unlike the other two species, is adapted to conifers. On the other hand the Coal Tit is presumably not adapted to broad-leaved woods, yet the few pairs breeding there raised 99 per cent of their young. In view of this, one might have thought that the species would breed commonly in broad-leaved woods. In explanation, Gibb suggested that in winter any Coal Tits in broad-leaved woods might have to compete for food with Great, Blue, or Marsh Tits, *Parus palustris*, and might well be less efficient in this habitat than the other species, which also displace them in interspecific encounters for food. In 1963 for the first time, three second broods of Coal Tits were raised in broad-leaved woods in Wytham, but only three-fifths of the hatched young were raised, so that they fared about as badly there as second broods of the Great Tit (C. M. Perrins, pers. comm.).

The density of caterpillars and of the other main foods brought by Coal Tits to their young in the Breckland pine plantations has been summarized in Table 15. This shows the marked increase, already referred to, in the numbers of caterpillars available between April and July, and also that many fewer caterpillars were available in Corsican than Scots pine. The commonest prey taken to first broods, comprising half the items brought in 1952 and 1956, though few in other years, were larvae of two species of the moth *Evetria*. In addition, the larvae of another moth, *Thera*, and spiders and their cocoons were also common Spiders comprised about half the prey brought to second broods, in which period the commonest caterpillars were those of the moth *Panolis*.

Systematic observations were made from a hide only a few inches from the entrance to certain nesting boxes, the approach of the parent birds being temporarily blocked by a stick across the nest, which allowed the observer to see and identify the foods brought. In addition, the parent birds could often be induced to feed an artificial nestling gape placed by the nest entrance (Betts, 1956), as illustrated in the chapter head. By these means it was found that, on the average, each young Coal Tit received each day from its parents an average of 69 prey items in first broods and 50 items in second broods. At both seasons caterpillars predominated, but the individual items tended to be larger for second broods. As a result, the young in late broods

TABLE 15

Numbers of lepidopterous larvae per 10 m² in Breckland pine plantations

	Scots pine					Corsican pine
	Thera	Ellopia	Panolis	Bupalus	All species	All species
1955						
16–31 May	9·7	1·8	3·5	0	15·9	2·7
1–15 June	1·6	0	18·0	0	19·6	7·6
16–30 June	1·7	0	16·7	0	18·4	6·1
1–15 July	14·5	0	29·1	0	45·3	6·8
16–31 July	46·0	0	18·5	33·1	103·2	36·3
1956						
16–30 April	14·7	1·1	0	0	19·4	—
1–15 May	7·8	2·0	3·4	0	14·5	—
16–31 May	5·7	1·4	16·5	0	24·9	—
1–15 June	1·6	0	38·4	0	43·8	—
16–30 June	15·8	0	36·5	0	65·6	—
1–15 July	24·8	0	31·1	3·8	89·0	—
16–30 July	27·8	1·3	23·0	6·2	79·1	—

Notes. From Gibb and Betts (1963, Tables 4, 5), who also gave the confidence limits for each figure and the area of needles examined in each sample. The totals for 'all species' exclude *Evetria*, which was not sampled except from 16 May to 30 July 1956, when the figure for larvae and pupae combined was in successive fortnights, 19·2, 8·2, 6·4, 2·4, and 1·1 per 10 m² respectively. No other species than those in the genera listed were at all important except in the second half of July 1955 and from mid-June to the end of July 1956. In addition, diprionid (sawfly) larvae were counted in 1956, those over 10 mm long being present, only from 1 June onward, at densities of 19·3, 10·0, 9·8 and 8·9 per 10 m² respectively in successive fortnights.

received nearly twice as much fresh weight of food each day as those in early broods (4·5 cf. 2·8 grams per older nestling per day, to judge from Gibb and Betts, Table 17), and even though the calorific value of the food was rather higher for the early than the late broods, this compensated for only a small part of the difference. Nevertheless, the nestlings in second broods were only 5 per cent heavier than those in first broods, a point which deserves further study.

These observations also showed that Coal Tits did not take caterpillars from the pine needles at random. The geometrid larvae which they brought to their young in May 1955 and May 1956 were respectively 14 and 24 per·cent longer, and 43 and 62 per cent heavier, than those present on the pine needles at the time, and those taken by Great Tits were proportionately larger still. Again, for second broods in

85

July 1955, the *Panolis* larvae taken by Coal Tits were on the average 58 per cent longer and over three times heavier than those present on the needles at the time. Similar results were obtained earlier in Holland by Tinbergen (1949; *et al.*, 1960), who showed that the tits were highly selective in their feeding, and perhaps adopt specific search images when hunting.

The density of Coal Tits per hectare was known, and assuming that each adult ate the same amount as a large nestling, Gibb and Betts estimated that in some fortnightly periods the breeding Coal Tits removed from each hectare more than a hundred larvae of each of the moths *Evetria*, *Thera*, *Ellopia* and *Panolis*. Much bigger numbers were recorded occasionally, including more than 900 *Panolis* larvae per hectare in the first half of July 1956 and more than 2500 per hectare of the small *Evetria* larvae in the second half of May 1956. Indeed, in the six weeks between the beginning of May and the middle of June 1956, Coal Tits probably removed about 4800 *Evetria* larvae per hectare, which was about one-fifth of the whole population. But in no other instance did the birds remove more than about 3 per cent of the available caterpillars, so that, with one possible exception, their influence on potential pests of the pine trees was negligible. This is because, in spring and summer, the caterpillars on the pine needles grow fast and pupate quickly, so that they are open to attack by birds for a relatively short time, during which they are extremely abundant relative to the birds.[1] This is in marked contrast to the winter, when most of the species preyed upon by the Coal Tit are present on the needles throughout the period from September to March, in which time, except for aphids in a mild winter, they do not normally increase through breeding. Nearly all the prey taken in winter are extremely small compared with the caterpillars taken in summer and, as discussed later, Coal Tits probably had a marked influence on their density, while their density, in turn, probably influenced that of the Coal Tits.

In the Coal Tits on the Breckland, as in the Great Tits in Marley wood, the annual variations in reproductive success appeared to have no influence on the annual fluctuations in the breeding population. After breeding, the number of Coal Tits present in the plantations fell each autumn by about a half, and as this reduction was similar each year, it likewise was not the main cause of the population fluctuations. Also, since the stocks of food in the conifers when the autumn reduction occurred could at that time have supported many more Coal Tits, Gibb (1962a, b), concluded that dispersal to other habitats was due, not to food shortage but to territorial behaviour, but the latter was not

[1] Tinbergen (1949; *et al.*, 1960) estimated that tits took a higher proportion of the available caterpillars in Dutch pine woods in the breeding season.

studied. As the Coal Tit population did not increase again before breeding, the birds which dispersed in autumn evidently did not return.

After the autumn reduction, the population of the Coal Tit decreased gradually each year between the end of September and the following breeding season, but to a very different extent in different winters. Gibb concluded that this reduction was the most important factor regulating the size of the ensuing breeding population and he attributed it primarily to mortality, not emigration. In any case, since there was no later increase in numbers before the birds bred, any individuals that moved away during the winter evidently did not return, so that any emigration can be equated with mortality.

There was no evidence for disease, and predation was thought to have been negligible in winter. On the other hand, each Coal Tit spent about nine-tenths of each winter day in feeding, and the remaining tenth on other essential activities such as preening; this suggests that food might well be critical. Observations showed that a Coal Tit spent, on the average, 24 seconds searching a tree for food before flying on to the next. This means that it searched about 1100 trees in a 9-hour winter day. From each tree it took, on the average, 10 food items, finding one about every 2½ seconds, but the dry weight of the 10 items was only just over 2 milligrams, equivalent to one of the smaller larvae brought to the nestlings in spring. Between July and October, Coal Tits found about one-third of their food on the needles and the rest on the boles and lower branches. From November to February inclusive, they spent about two-thirds of each day on the needles, but also some time on the cones, and it was in this period that their food tended to be short. In March and April, they spent about half their time on the needles, but they also took pine seeds from opened cones and searched the swelling buds for *Evetria* larvae. During the winter, Coal Tits had only two important competitors for food in the plantations, Goldcrests, *Regulus regulus*, taking the same species of extremely small insects from the needles and Blue Tits the same species of larvae from the cones. Both Goldcrests and Blue Tits were mainly winter visitors to the plantations, though a few pairs of each species bred there.

The foods available to the Coal Tit during the winter on branches and boles could not be sampled quantitatively, but it was possible to measure the density of insects and spiders on the pine needles, though the work was extremely laborious. From observations on captive birds, it was also possible to estimate how much food a Coal Tit needs each each day. The dry weight of invertebrates per unit area of ground in each month is shown in Table 16, and the number of Coal Tits and Goldcrests present in Table 17.

In the fairly mild winter of 1953–4, the stock of invertebrates on the

TABLE 16

Stock of invertebrate food in Scots pine foliage in winter, expressed
as dry-weight in mg/m²

Month	1953–4	1954–5	1955–6	1956–7
Sept.		114	204	} 190
Oct.		81	203	
Nov.	560	33	193	} 143
Dec.	560	29	150	
Jan.	278	11	84	} 133
Feb.	201	20	72	
Mar.		17	95	} 217
April			120	

Note. From Gibb (1960), Table 11. In his Table 13, he gave the stock in March 1954
as 111 mg/m², but this was omitted from his Table 11.

TABLE 17

Numbers of Coal Tits, *P. ater*, and Goldcrests, *R. regulus*, in a
pine plantation of 86 hectares on the Breckland

Month	Coal Tit				Goldcrest			
	1953–4	1954–5	1955–6	1956–7	1953–4	1954–5	1955–6	1956–7
Sept.	97	188	121	185	58	62	47	110
Oct.	93	136	119	109	95	86	92	105
Nov.	79	145	100	131	91	81	104	126
Dec.	97	149	92	120	108	53	56	121
Jan.	72	106	111	111	82	54	97	157
Feb.	80	63	54	141	89	51	47	154
Mar.	77	54	58	110	65	40	51	96
Apr.	58	54	61	112	21	(48)	22	56

Note. From Gibb (1960), Table 12. The Coal Tit was resident and the seasonal decrease
was attributed to mortality. The Goldcrest was primarily a winter visitor, the increase
in early winter being due to arrivals, the decrease in spring to departures, but some
mortality presumably occurred during the winter as well. Counts were not made in
April 1955 and the figures in the table were obtained in May.

pine needles at the start of the winter was much larger than in the other three years studied, and though it decreased rapidly after December, it remained fairly large until February, after which measurements were not made. The number of Coal Tits present at the start of the winter was the lowest recorded and there was only a small reduction in numbers by March, as was to be expected from the food situation.

Preceding the cold winter of 1954–5, the stock of invertebrates was the smallest recorded in the four years, and it decreased much faster than in any other year, to the lowest level recorded. The number of Coal Tits present at the start of the winter was the highest in the four years studied, and it decreased faster than in any other year. As a result, the invertebrate stock estimated to have been removed by birds decreased from 35 mg/m² in September to about 8 mg/m² in April. However, in each of the five months from November to March inclusive, the stock of invertebrates remained almost constant relative to the density of birds, at around 0·1 kg per bird. It is unlikely that this could have been a coincidence, and it suggests that the density of the birds was limited by the density of the food supply. The percentage of the invertebrates taken by birds could not be adequately assessed because some growth and reproduction took place among some of the insects that winter, as shown particularly by the fact that despite predation by birds, the average stock was rather higher in February than January.

The winter of 1955–6 was nearly as cold as that of the previous year. The stock of invertebrates available at the start of the winter was intermediate between those of the two previous winters, its rate of decrease was intermediate, and so were both the initial density of Coal Tits and their subsequent rate of decline. The stock of invertebrates in mg/m² was about 100 at the beginning of January and 75 at the end of February, and since in this time the birds were estimated to have taken 27·5, there was little if any reproduction. Since the birds took about a quarter of the available invertebrates, they probably had an important influence on their numbers, though less than in the previous winter.

In contrast, the winter of 1956–7 was extremely mild. The stock of invertebrates which, at the start, was intermediate between those in 1953–4 and 1954–5, declined only slightly between October and March inclusive. This was because the amount taken by birds was replaced by reproduction, especially by aphids, in the mild winter weather. Coal Tits did not decline in numbers between October and April that year.

Goldcrests were chiefly winter visitors to the pine plantations, and most of them disappeared in the early spring to breed elsewhere. It is therefore hard to know how much of any decline in their numbers between the late winter and the early spring should be attributed to mortality and how much to the normal spring emigration. The figures in Table 17 suggest, however, that between mid-November and mid-February, when migration does not ordinarily occur, Goldcrests decreased markedly in 1954–5 and 1955–6, when food was short, but not in the other two years, when food was more plentiful. Also, the average number of Goldcrests present was lower in the two winters when food was sparse than in the two when it was more plentiful.

These relationships between the numbers of Coal Tits, Goldcrests, and invertebrates are summarized in Table 18. Figures for only four seasons are not enough for firm conclusions but, so far as they go, they strongly suggest that the availability of food had a marked influence on the numbers of both species of birds. Moreover, in the winters of 1954–5 and 1955–6 the birds appeared to have a marked influence on the density of their prey. These two latter winters were also colder than the other two, which perhaps increased the effect of food shortage. The other

TABLE 18

Survival of Coal Tit and numbers of Goldcrest in relation to invertebrate stocks on pine needles in winter on the Breckland

	1953–4	1954–5	1955–6	1956–7
Percentage of Coal Tits surviving Oct.–March	83	40	49	100
Number of Coal Tits present in March	77	54	58	110
Mean number of Goldcrests present Dec.–Feb.	93	53	67	144
Lowest level of invertebrate stock on needles (mg/m^2)	111	16	72	133
Mean air temperature (°C) in January	3·3	1·4	1·9	5·2

Notes. From Gibb (1960), his Table 13 and my Tables 16 and 17. For the survival of the Coal Tit, Gibb in his Fig. 13 used the decrease in numbers between the end of September (average of September and October figures) and April, but as he stated that the decline between September and October (which was marked in 1954–5 and 1956–7 but negligible in the other two years) was independent of the food supplies, it is better excluded, while in 1953–4, but no other year, there was a marked drop between March and April, after the period when the food supply was last measured. Hence I have used the decline over a rather shorter period, from mid-October to mid-March each year. The counts for the Goldcrest showed more irregular variations than those for the Coal Tit, perhaps due partly to movements during the winter, but the figures in Table 17 indicate that the population present between mid-November and mid-February, outside the main periods of migration, stayed fairly constant in 1953–4 and 1956–7 but decreased markedly in 1954–5 and 1955–6.

common bird in the pine plantations in winter, the Blue Tit, did not depend on the invertebrates on the needles, and its numbers did not fluctuate in parallel with those of the Coal Tit and Goldcrest.

In the Coal Tit, unlike the Goldcrest, there was no change in the numbers present in the plantations between the end of the winter and the breeding season, and the number of pairs breeding each year was evidently the number which survived the winter, which, in turn, was determined by the winter food supply. On general grounds one might expect such a relationship to be density-dependent, but observations for only four seasons are too few to test this, especially as there were also variations in the size of the invertebrate stocks each year and in the coldness of the winter. Further, the density of the Coal Tit at the start of each winter was greatly affected by the 50 per cent decrease in the autumn. This, as already mentioned, was attributed by Gibb to territorial behaviour, but in that case I would have expected either a similar density at the start of each winter, or variations in parallel with the autumn food stocks, neither of which applied, as can be seen from Tables 16 and 17. Until the causes and significance of the decrease each autumn are understood, it is hard to be certain how the size of the breeding population of the Coal Tit was regulated, but the amount of food available in winter was certainly important and probably critical.

The only other common bird in the pine plantations in winter, the Blue Tit, was especially studied in relation to its predation on the larvae of the eucosmid moth, *Ernarmonia conicolana*, which were also taken by Coal Tits. *E. conicolana* lays its eggs singly on one-year-old pine cones in June, the larvae hatch early in July and burrow to the seeds, of which each larva eats about seven by the end of September, when it eats its way back close to the surface, where it excavates a chamber with a thin outside wall, rests for the winter, pupates in March, and the moth emerges in late May or June (Betts, 1958). Usually only one or two larvae are found on one cone, but at times up to eight, though if three or more larvae are present, they tend to be undernourished and to emerge late. The ichneumonid *Ephialtes laticeps* parasitizes the larvae and Red Squirrels, *Sciurus vulgaris*, destroy many cones for their seeds and in the process destroy any *E. conicolana* present. However, the chief cause of larval mortality, once they have entered their pupal chambers, is predation by tits. As the larvae are hidden, the birds find them mainly by tapping, and the Blue Tit, with its shorter and stouter beak, extracts them more quickly than the Coal Tit with its longer and thinner beak. Blue Tits also spend proportionately more of their time than Coal Tits in searching the cones for food.

The predation on *E. conicolana* could be measured precisely. This is because *E. conicolana* emerges from a smooth round hole, the parasite

E. laticeps from a much smaller hole, tits that have taken a larva leave a large irregular hole, and red squirrels that have eaten the seeds from the cones strip off the bracts. Hence an accurate record of events is left on each fallen cone (see tailpiece p. 96). The discovery and interpretation of this record have been described by Gibb (1958; see also 1962a) in a paper which has become an ecological classic.

The size of the cone crop varied markedly from year to year, while the proportion of cones containing *E. conicolana* larvae varied greatly from year to year, from plantation to plantation in the same year, and even from tree to tree. Two measurements of availability were needed, the density of larvae per unit area, and their 'intensity,' i.e. the number per 100 cones. The proportion taken by tits was 'intensity-dependent', as shown in Table 19. In the winter of 1955–6, with a heavy crop of cones, the tits ate 20–30 per cent of the larvae in plantations with 10–15 larvae per 100 cones, 50 per cent in plantations with 30–40 larvae per

TABLE 19

Relationship between intensity of *E. conicolana* larvae and proportion eaten by tits in Breckland pine plantations

Percentage of larvae eaten by tits

Intensity (larvae per 100 cones	1 larva per cone	2–3 larvae per cone	4–5 larvae per cone
	1955–6 (rich cone crop)		
1–16	22	14	—
17–30	35	45	—
31–49	50	57	62
50–70	61	68	85
	1956–7 (poor cone crop)		
15–18	6	14	—
25–50	54	54	61
51–75	53	54	67
95–110	38	53	63
183	48	66	78
256	50		28

Notes. From Gibb (1958, Table 8). Note the marked difference in the intensity-dependent relationship when cones were abundant (in 1955–6) and sparse (in 1956–7). Note also that, at equal intensities, the proportion taken was normally higher with more larvae per cone; of the two exceptions, the difference in the first line for 1955–6 was not statistically significant, while in the last line for 1956–7 it was based on only 45 cones from a single tree with a much higher intensity than on adjacent trees.

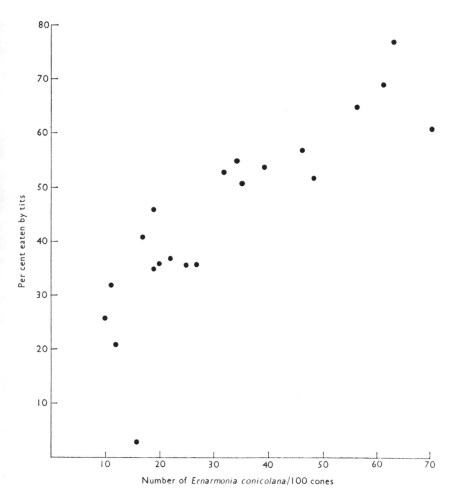

Fig. 20. Percentage of *Ernarmonia conicolana* larvae eaten by tits in different localities in winter of 1955–6 in relation to number initially present per 100 cones (from Gibb, 1958, Table 5).

100 cones, and 70 per cent in a plantation with 65 larvae per 100 cones. This disproportionate attack, combined with the large numbers taken, flattened out the marked variations in the intensity of the larvae in different plantations, which at the start of the winter varied between 10 and 70 larvae per 100 cones, but at the end only between 7 and 25 larvae per 100 cones. These points are shown in Figs. 20 and 21.

The predation by tits was found to be intensity-dependent not only in comparisons between different plantations, but also between different small patches of trees in the same plantation. In a later analysis, Gibb

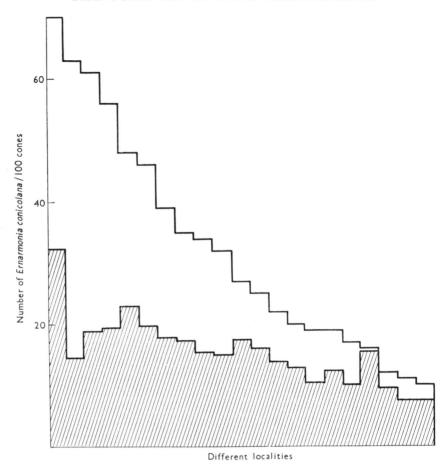

FIG. 21. Numbers of *E. conicolana* larvae per 100 cones before (full columns) and after (shaded) predation by tits in winter 1955–6. Each column represents one locality and they are arranged in descending order of initial intensity of larvae (from Gibb, 1958, Fig. 3).

(1962*b*) showed that, within one plantation studied in detail, the rate of predation increased linearly up to intensities of about 50 larvae per 100 cones, but unexpectedly declined for intensities of 50 to 90 larvae per 100 cones. Patches with such a high intensity of larvae were rare, and Gibb postulated that the birds had become used to lower intensities, so did not prolong their search in these areas. However, with yet higher intensities, the rate of predation rose again, to 81 per cent with an intensity of 160 larvae per 100 cones. 'Hunting by expectation' is an interesting concept which should be studied further. In this connection it should be noted that, since the larvae of *E. conicolana* are hidden, they are not encountered by chance, and the tits have always to seek actively for them.

In the winter of 1956–7 cones were scarce, and though the intensity of the larvae per 100 cones was, if anything, higher than in the previous year, it did not by any means compensate for the low density of cones. The tits took only about 10 per cent of the larvae when there were between 10 and 15 per 100 cones and about 50 per cent at all higher intensities up to 256 per 100 cones. This is also shown in Table 19, which shows further that in both years the proportion of larvae taken was greater (at the same intensity) when there were more larvae per cone.

In November and December of the last three winters studied by Gibb, the density of the Blue and Coal Tits combined was respectively 1·8, 1·8, and 2·1 per hectare, while the density of *E. conicolana* larvae was respectively 2200, 15200, and 3200 per hectare, of which the tits took respectively 55 per cent, 54 per cent, and 60 per cent. Especially considering that the larvae are hidden, this is a considerable achievement on the part of the birds. Hence one of the important facts shown by this study is that insectivorous birds can remove a substantial proportion of their prey in winter. This also emerged from the study of the Coal Tit and Goldcrest in relation to the invertebrates in the pine needles in winter described earlier, but the evidence for the latter depended on sampling, whereas the predation on *E. conicolana* is recorded visibly and precisely in the fallen pine cones, and so is much more convincing.

It does not necessarily follow that, because Blue and Coal Tits remove a large proportion of *E. conicolana* larvae, they are important in controlling its numbers. This could not be determined without a full study of the moth, including the other mortality factors, such as losses of larvae through starvation, parasitism by *E. laticeps* (in all, 6 per cent in 1957), and the removal of unparasitized and parasitized larvae alike when red squirrels destroyed the cones. In three seasons studied, red squirrels destroyed respectively 22 per cent, 16 per cent, and 65 per cent of the cones, so their influence might be important, particularly in seasons like the last when cones were scarce. A further complication is that the rate of predation by tits probably varied with the availability of other foods; for instance, when other foods were unusually plentiful in the winter of 1953–4, tits took only 23 per cent of the *E. conicolana* larvae, less than half of the proportion removed in the other four seasons studied.

It may be added that, when my earlier book was written in 1954, I could find extremely few published estimates of the proportion of their prey eaten by insectivorous birds, and nearly all of these referred to the breeding season, when the proportion taken was extremely small. But if I am right in thinking that many bird populations are limited in a density-dependent way by food shortage outside the breeding season, birds should at times destroy a substantial proportion of their prey, and the evidence reviewed in this chapter shows that this was indeed so for the Coal and Blue Tits on the Breckland. The same was found in certain woodpeckers in North America, as discussed, with various other observations, in Appendix, section 1 (p. 289).

Summarizing, the population density of the Coal Tit was measured in pine plantations throughout the year, and so were the available prey on the pine needles. In the summer of 1956, Coal Tits took about one-fifth of the *Evetria* larvae, but in no other instance in summer did they consume more than 3 per cent of any prey species. The numbers of the Coal Tit fell to about one-half after breeding and before the winter (apparently due to movements out of the area, but without subsequent return). The size of the breeding population each year depended on the winter losses, which differed greatly in different years in accordance with the availability of insect food on the needles, while in some winters the birds caused a marked reduction in the density of the insects on the needles. Blue (and Coal) Tits also took a high proportion of the larvae of the moth *Ernarmonia conicolana* from pine cones in winter, the proportion taken varying strongly with the proportion of cones containing larvae.

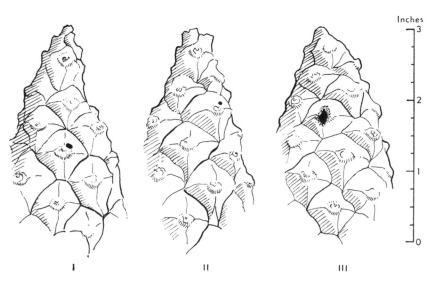

Inches

I   II   III

Pine cones after parasitism by *Ernarmonia conicolana* (i) a normal emergence hole, (ii) the smaller hole left by the ichneumonid parasite *Ephialtes laticeps*, (iii) the larger tear left by a predatory Blue Tit.

6

THE BREEDING OF THE PIED FLYCATCHER

T HE Pied Flycatcher, *Ficedula* (or *Muscicapa*) *hypoleuca*, is a summer visitor to Europe, though there are gaps in its breeding range in most of France and parts of Britain. In south-eastern Europe it is replaced by the closely similar Collared Flycatcher, *F. albicollis*, while the two species have a fairly extensive area of overlap, notably in Germany, where they occasionally interbreed. Both species spend the winter in tropical Africa, so the studies discussed in this chapter refer solely to the breeding season, and this means a serious and unavoidable gap in existing knowledge of the factors influencing their numbers. The special value of these studies lies in the close similarities in breeding ecology with the Great and Blue Tits. In addition, both the adult mortality and the age of first breeding have been claimed to present unusual features, but this is somewhat uncertain, being complicated by the fact that some of the adult flycatchers change their breeding site in successive years, and the extent of such movements is not fully known. To save confusion, the main discussion of the Collared Flycatcher is deferred to the end of the chapter.

In primaeval Europe the Pied Flycatcher presumably frequented broad-leaved forest, and broad-leaved woods still constitute its favourite

Headpiece: Cock Pied Flycatcher feeding artificial nestling-gape operated from back of nesting box.

habitat provided that there are suitable holes for nesting. In Fenno-Scandia, however, and to a lesser extent farther south, the Pied Fly-catcher also nests regularly in coniferous forest, though it is commonest where there are at least a few broad-leaved trees (Merikallio, 1946). Like other hole-nesting species, it has also taken readily to nesting boxes, and where boxes have been put up, it breeds abundantly in planted woods, both broad-leaved and coniferous, as well as in orchards, city parks and gardens. As a result, it has during the present century recolonized much of central Europe (Voous, 1960), from which it evidently disappeared after the clearance of the forest.

In summer the Pied Flycatcher feeds on both caterpillars and adult insects. The only other British breeding flycatcher, the Spotted Fly-catcher, *Muscicapa striata*, catches insects almost entirely in the air, but the Pied Flycatcher, though doing this at times, often hunts for cater-pillars in the foliage or drops on insects on the ground from a perch above. In England, caterpillars on oak leaves form a high proportion of the food brought to the nestlings. For instance, they comprised about half the diet at one nest in the Forest of Dean, where the birds were induced to feed an artificial nestling gape operated by the observer from a hide on which this nestbox was placed, as shown in the chapter head (Betts, 1954). Despite their dependence on caterpillars when available, Pied Flycatchers usually breed two or three weeks after the Great Tits, so they miss the time when caterpillars are most abundant. Adult insects form a higher proportion of the diet of late broods in England, and of all broods in Fenno-Scandia (Meidell, 1961; von Haartman, 1954).

Because of the ease with which nesting boxes can be examined, the Pied Flycatcher was one of the earliest subjects of population studies in birds, and it has two advantages over the Great Tit, in that it can freely be caught at the nest without deserting, and in that the black-and-white cock is readily distinguishable at a distance from the much browner hen. The present chapter is based primarily on the work of Dr. Bruce Camp-bell (1954-5, 1955, 1959, and pers. comm.), who with great kindness allowed me to analyse all his data prior to his own final publication. Another important study has been that of Professor Lars von Haart-man (1949, 1951*a*, *b*, 1954, 1956*a*, *b*, 1957, 1958, 1960), but most of his observations for later years had not been analysed at the time when this book was completed. Campbell's study was carried out on 24 hectares of rich oak plantation in the Forest of Dean, Gloucestershire, probably an extremely favourable environment for the species, and von Haartman's on 390 hectares, of which 300 consisted of open mixed woodland with many conifers, and the rest on open ground at Lems-jöholm in south-western Finland. Two other detailed studies were by Creutz (1955) in a park of 5 hectares, a garden of 8 hectares and an orchard of 50 hectares near Dresden in Germany, and by Curio (1958, 1959a, b, 1960) in 24 hectares of mixed broad-leaved woodland, chiefly Birch, *Betula*, and Alder, *Alnus*, surrounded by much larger Scots Pine, *Pinus sylvestris*, plantations near Berlin, Germany. These four studies are mentioned so often in this chapter that they will be referred to as in the Forest of Dean, at Lemsjöholm, near Dresden and near Berlin respectively, usually without detailed citation of the authors or papers just listed. Further German studies were carried out in Silesia by Trettau and Merkel (1943), near Frankfurt-am-Main by Trettau (1952), and in various birch woods in north Germany by Berndt (1960) and Berndt and Sternberg (1963). There was also an important study near Moscow, U.S.S.R., by Lichatschev (1955).

The density of breeding Pied Flycatchers differed greatly in the various areas studied, being highest, with 4·9 and 4·5 nests to the hectare respectively, in the garden and park near Dresden, but both these areas were small, so the birds perhaps depended for food partly on surrounding land. In the rich oak wood in the Forest of Dean there were up to 4 nests on each hectare, and near Berlin up to 2, but there was only 0·9 in the orchard near Dresden and 0·2 at Lemsjöholm. The density is far lower than any of these figures in woods with few natural holes and without nesting boxes (Merikallio, 1946; Creutz, 1955, who cited other studies).

The number of occupied nesting boxes each year in the Forest of Dean, together with the average date of laying, the average clutch and the total number of young which left the nest each year, are shown in Table 20. The number of breeding pairs fluctuated irregularly, rising from 1948 to 1952, then declining till 1957, showing a marked rise in 1958 and then a decline until 1962. The fluctuations were much smaller than those of the Great Tit in the same wood (see p. 16), the largest number of pairs, in 1951, being not quite double the smallest, in 1957. The fluctuations were also independent of those of the Great and Blue Tits in the same wood. At Lemsjöholm there was a sixfold to sevenfold increase in numbers between 1941 and 1955, due primarily to an increase in the number of nesting boxes, after which numbers stayed fairly constant until 1964, the greatest number of occupied boxes being 74 in 1961 (von Haartman 1956a and pers. comm., partly correcting Lack, 1954, p. 277, see also footnote to Table 20). In the garden near Dresden, the number of nests varied irregularly between 10 and 22 between 1935 and 1952. At Drömling in Braunschweig, there was an increase from 82 in 1954 to 400 in 1960 and then a decrease to 298 in 1961 (Berndt and Sternberg, 1963). Unlike what happened in the Great Tit, the fluctuations in these different areas were not in

THE BREEDING OF THE PIED FLYCATCHER

TABLE 20

Breeding of Pied Flycatcher, *Ficedula hypoleuca*, in Forest of Dean

| Year | Approx. number of pairs | First layings | | All broods young raised |
		Mean date (in May)	Mean clutch	
1948	58	5	7·4	399
1949	67	5	7·5	369
1950	87	10	7·3	475
1951	100	19	6·9	461
1952	98	13	6·9	485
1953	85	15	6·6	445
1954	76	15	7·2	479
1955	67	22	6·4	346
1956	60	17	6·9	355
1957	54	11	7·2	289
1958	71	10	7·1	434
1959	71	13	6·8	355
1960	58	12	7·1	293
1961	62	7	6·7	263
1962	59	11	7·0	326
1963	58	20	6·5	336

Notes. Based on data loaned by B. Campbell. Each year nearly all clutches were started during about a fortnight, after which a few further clutches were begun during the next month. Many of these late layings were probably repeats after loss of an earlier attempt and a few near the end were second broods, but some were probably first attempts. The end of the main laying period each year was determined rather arbitrarily by inspection, as the date after which the number of new clutches started became very intermittent, and the mean date of laying and mean clutch-size were calculated for this group. The total involved was in most years a little smaller than the total number of breeding pairs as estimated by Dr. Campbell, in the second column. In 1958 and 1959, but no other years, the boxes were blocked up until the Pied Flycatchers arrived, in order to prevent their prior use by Great and Blue Tits; it is doubtful if this caused any increase in the number of Pied Flycatchers, though in view of the large increase in 1958 over 1957, Campbell thought that it did so. At Lemsjöholm, the number of occupied boxes each year from 1941 to 1955 inclusive was given by von Haartman (1956a). The number of occupied boxes in 1956–64 inclusive was 59, 64, 53 (perhaps somewhat too few), 70, 71, 74, 60, 70, and 64 respectively (von Haartman, pers. comm.).

parallel, but the areas were much farther apart than those where the Great Tit was studied.

In England and Germany, Pied Flycatchers usually arrive in late April and lay their eggs in the first half of May, but they are rather later in Finland. As mentioned at the end of this chapter, in the Collared

Flycatcher Löhrl (1957) found that annual variations in the average date of laying were correlated with the average temperature in April before the birds returned from the south, so that they did not experience the temperatures in question. As shown earlier (Fig. 5, p. 19,) there is likewise a correlation between the average date of laying of the Great Tit and the temperature during March and early April. The same correlation is found in the Pied Flycatcher in the Forest of Dean, and here, as a result, the mean date of laying each year has been strongly correlated with that of the Great Tit, as shown in Fig. 22. Since Pied Flycatchers have not returned to England in March and early April, the cause of this correlation is clearly not the temperature itself. In the Great Tit, as discussed earlier, the time of appearance of the caterpillars which form the main food of the young was also correlated with the temperature in March and early April, so that the birds bred at about the same time each year in relation to the appearance of the caterpillars. Since, however, the earlier broods are the more successful, the correlation with the time of appearance of the caterpillars is not now thought to be an adaptation of the date of laying to the food requirements of the young. Instead, it seems likely to be due to the fact that the female Great Tits can get enough insects to form their eggs earlier in a mild early spring than a cold late one, and that it is advantageous

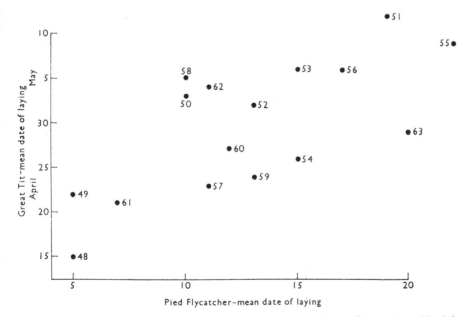

FIG. 22. Correlation between mean date of first layings of Pied Flycatcher, *Ficedula hypoleuca*, in Forest of Dean and first layings of Great Tit, *Parus major*, in Forest of Dean (1948–57) or Marley (1958–63). (Dates closely similar for both areas.)

for them to breed as early as possible. Similar conditions apply even more strongly to the Pied Flycatcher which, as already mentioned, usually breeds two or three weeks after the Great Tit in the Forest of Dean, and in which, as shown later, the earliest broods of all are the most successful. Particularly as caterpillars are a favourite food for their young, it seems possible that the Pied Flycatchers could raise young even more successfully if they could lay their eggs two or three weeks earlier than they do. These considerations suggest that the date of breeding in the Pied Flycatcher, like that of the Great Tit, is determined by the date at which the hens can get enough insects to form eggs, and that they are able to get enough insects earlier in a warm than a cold spring.

In addition to the general correlation between the average date of laying of the Pied Flycatcher and the average temperature in March and early April, there is a tendency for laying to occur five days after the first day of warm weather in spring (von Haartman, 1956b). Similarly cold inhibits and warmth stimulates the start of laying four days later in the Great Tit (Kluijver, 1951), the interval needed to form an egg evidently being a day less than in the Pied Flycatcher. In Finland, von Haartman also found a tendency for laying to occur earlier in those years in which the Pied Flycatchers arrived earlier from the south, an earlier arrival being correlated both with warmer spring weather and with the earlier appearance of leaves on the birch trees.

In most years in the Forest of Dean, most first clutches were started during a period of ten to fourteen days, occasionally of only seven days, but the laying period was more extended in early seasons and also when laying was interrupted by unseasonable cold after the earliest pairs had started. After the main laying period, there were each year a few late clutches, most of which were probably second attempts after loss of a first clutch. In the Forest of Dean, and also near Moscow (Lichatschev, 1955), there were also a very few second broods after successful first broods.

The average clutch of the Pied Flycatcher, like that of the Great Tit, is smaller later in the season. This was noted by all the workers mentioned earlier, and is set out for the Forest of Dean, and also for the Collared Flycatcher near Stuttgart, in Fig. 23. As in the Great Tit, this decline occurs despite the fact that food is more plentiful for the laying hens late than early in the season. But by the time that the young in these late layings have hatched, caterpillars are much scarcer than before, and presumably the smaller clutch-size is an adaptation to the fact that the birds cannot raise such large broods late in the season.

The averages plotted in Fig. 23 are those for all nests in all years and they combine two different points, first the decline in clutch-size

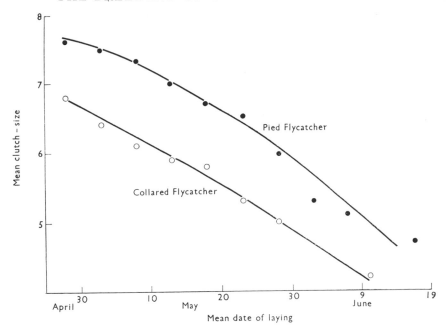

FIG. 23. Seasonal decline in average clutch of Pied Flycatcher, *F. hypoleuca,* in Forest of Dean and Collared Flycatcher, *F. collaris,* near Stuttgart.

later in the course of each season, just mentioned, and secondly a tendency for the Pied Flycatcher, like the Great Tit, to lay a larger average clutch in the years when breeding starts earlier than in the late years, as shown in Fig. 24. Each year, as already mentioned, the Pied Flycatcher (like the Great Tit) bred at about the same time in relation to the appearance of the caterpillars, and there is no reason to think that more caterpillars were available for either species in the early than the late years. So far as known, therefore, this annual variation in clutch-size with date of laying has no adaptive signifiance. I suggested earlier for the Great Tit that it might be an incidental consequence of the (adaptive) decline in clutch-size in the course of each season but, if so, it is curious that neither the Great and Blue Tits on the one hand, nor the Pied and Collared Flycatchers on the other hand, should have evolved a way of overcoming it. Hence I am extremely uneasy about this explanation, but can think of no better one (see p. 28).

The average size of first layings varied in different years between 6·4 and 7·5 in the Forest of Dean, between 6·3 and 6·7 at Lemsjöholm, between 6·0 and 6·8 near Berlin, and between 5·8 and 6·9 near Dresden. Nearly all these variations were correlated with the annual variations in the date of laying, as shown in Fig. 24 for the Forest of Dean, which

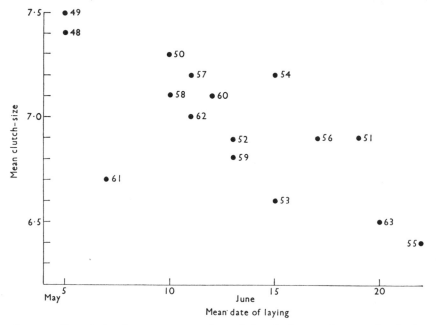

FIG. 24. Correlation between mean date of first layings and mean clutch-size each year of Pied Flycatcher in Forest of Dean.

presents a close parallel with Fig. 8 (p. 27) for the Great Tit in Marley wood. At Lemsjöholm likewise, the years when a high proportion of pairs bred early, before 26 May, were those with a high proportion of large clutches, of 8 or 9 eggs (von Haartman, 1956b). Near Dresden, again, the average size of the first clutches was between 6·5 and 6·9 in the years in which laying started in the first half of May and between 6·1 and 6·3 when laying did not start until the second half of May.

In the Great Tit, as already discussed, the average clutch also varied with population density (see p. 28). In the Forest of Dean, the years in which Pied Flycatchers were most numerous were 1951, 1952, and 1953, while the years of lowest density were 1948, 1957, 1960, and 1963. As shown in Fig. 24, the clutch-size in these years was close to what would be expected from the date of laying alone, so variations in population density evidently had no appreciable effect in the years studied. However, the population fluctuated between much narrower limits than that of the Great Tit in Marley wood, so further data are desirable. The only exceptional year for clutch-size in Fig. 24 was 1961, when the average was much lower than would have been expected from the average date of laying. The reason is not known. The average clutch was also unusually small in the Great Tit in 1961, but in this species (though not in the Pied Flycatcher) it was correlated with an extremely high density of breeding pairs.

The average clutch also differed somewhat in the different study areas, being 7·0 in the Forest of Dean, 6·7 near Moscow, 6·5 in the garden area near Dresden, 6·4 at Lemsjöholm, 6·3 near Berlin and in the park near Dresden, and 6·1 in the orchard near Dresden. The factors responsible for these differences have not been studied. There was no difference in clutch-size between adjacent areas of broad-leaved and coniferous trees at Lemsjöholm. The possible influence of age on clutch-size also requires further study, as the average difference between year-old and older females was recorded as 0·9 egg near Dresden and 1·0 egg near Moscow, but absent near Berlin, and negligible (0·1 egg) in the Collared Flycatcher near Stuttgart; presumably some of these figures were wrong. The studies of Creutz, von Haartman, and Curio, also those of Löhrl on the Collared Flycatcher, showed that the clutch-size of individual hens in successive years was less variable than that of the whole population, a result which might well be due to hereditary differences influencing clutch-size.

In the Pied Flycatcher, only the hen incubates the eggs, but the cock, like the male Great Tit, feeds the hen on the nest. As in the Great Tit, the food brought by the cock seems of real value. For instance, von Haartman (1958) found that two cocks fed their mates assiduously whereas a third did not, and the hen of the third pair incubated for shorter periods than the other two because it needed to seek food more often. That this depended on the food brought by the cock was shown when von Haartman temporarily removed the cock of one of the other pairs, after which its mate incubated for only 58 per cent instead of 79 per cent of the day, while her weight fell from 16·0 to 14·2 grams. Again, Curio found that a cock fed his mate up to 7 times an hour (average 2·7 feeds per hour) providing about half of her food.

As in other hole-nesting species, a high proportion of the eggs laid give rise to fledged young. In the Forest of Dean between 1953 and 1956, for instance, 88 per cent of the eggs hatched and 95 per cent of the hatched young flew, so that 84 per cent of the eggs produced fledglings, these figures taking losses from all causes into account. Similarly near Berlin, 78 per cent of the eggs hatched; and in the years 1951–4, 92·5 per cent of the hatched young flew, so that 72 per cent of the eggs gave rise to fledglings, but the proportion was lower in 1955; broods laid in the main period were about 10 per cent more successful than late broods. Near Dresden, 71 per cent of the eggs hatched and 88 per cent of the hatched young flew, so that 62 per cent of the eggs gave rise to fledglings, the proportion being 63 per cent in 540 broods started during the main laying period and 54 per cent in 66 late broods.

At Lemsjöholm in the years 1941–7, 17 per cent of the clutches failed completely and from the rest 86 per cent of the eggs gave rise to fledglings. In the Forest of Dean, the average number of young raised per pair varied between just over four in 1961 to nearly seven in 1948. These were likewise the years of lowest and highest production of young in the Great Tit (see Table 10), but except for these extreme cases, the production of young did not vary in parallel in the two species.

On my interpretation of clutch-size, and in line with the findings for the Great Tit, one would expect the proportion of young Pied Flycatchers surviving to be larger from broods of average size than from broods of above average size, to such an extent that broods of average size gave rise to most survivors per brood. However, both Curio (1958) near Berlin and Löhrl (1957) for the Collared Flycatcher found that the survival-rate after the young left the nest was similar from broods of all sizes, including the largest, so that more young survived per brood from the largest broods than from those of average size. In their analyses they grouped all broods together, irrespective of their date, and this could give a misleading result if, as shown previously for the Great Tit, large broods occur only in the early part of the nesting season and early broods have a higher rate of survival than the rest. To test this point I analysed Dr. Campbell's data on survival in relation to brood-size in the Forest of Dean, as set out in Table 21. This shows that the chances of survival varied markedly with the date of laying, hence it is not legitimate to group together broods begun at different dates when analysing survival in relation to brood-size.

For this analysis, all clutches laid two days on either side of the mean date of laying were classified as in the 'middle period', those before this date as 'early' and those after it but still within the main laying period as 'second period', while the late clutches, mainly repeat layings, have been treated separately again. A few broods that were total failures, due to desertion or other causes, were excluded. The birds ringed as young that were recovered later were nearly all trapped when breeding in the Forest of Dean, but a few were found on migration; any recovered within three months of ringing were ignored. Only a small proportion of the young which survived were recaptured later, but there is no reason to think that they were not a representative sample in relation to the date of laying or the size of brood from which they came.

Few young survived from the late broods, only 1·6 per cent being recaptured later as compared with 4·8 per cent, or three times as many, from all broods started in the main laying period. Hence late broods are relatively unsuccessful, which is presumably why the extremely late second broods are so rare. Even within the main laying period, the chances of survival were greater for the young from earlier than later

TABLE 21

Survival of young Pied Flycatchers in relation to date of laying
and brood-size in Forest of Dean

| | Number of young | | |
| | Hatched | Recovered | Per cent recovered |
Brood-size			
	Early		
2–5	144	8	5·6
6	246	15	6·1
7	280	14	5·0
8	168	9	5·4
9	18	0	0
All	856	46	5·4
	Middle Period (± 2 days from mean date)		
1–5	426	26	6·1
6	654	27	4·1
7	910	39	4·3
8	280	18	6·4
9	18	0	0
All	2288	107	4·7
	2nd Period		
1–4	111	4	3·6
5	165	6	3·6
6	162	7	4·3
7	217	12	5·5
8	40	0	0
All	695	29	4·2
	Late		
1–4	84	1	1·2
5	115	3	2·6
6	60	0	0
All	256	4	1·6

Note. Data from Dr. B. Campbell based on all nestlings ringed in the Forest of Dean
1952–62 inclusive and later recovered when at least three months old.

broods, the proportion recaptured being 5·4 per cent from the early
period, 4·7 per cent from the five days comprising the middle period,
and 4·2 per cent from the second period. As in the Great Tit, therefore,
the earliest broods were the most successful, and it is remarkable that a
difference in the time of laying of only a few days should have so big an
influence on survival. This reinforces the view advanced earlier that
the breeding season of the Pied Flycatcher is not timed in relation to the

food supply for the young, and that, instead, the birds lay their eggs so soon as they have enough food reserves to form them. These figures further indicate that it would be advantageous for at least most individuals if they could breed earlier than they do.

While the picture for survival in relation to the date of laying is clear-cut, that for survival in relation to brood-size is confused and hard to interpret, even when the earlier and later broods are analysed separately. In the main laying period the commonest clutch was 7 eggs, so on my view of clutch-size, one might have expected survival to be poorer from broods of 8 and 9 than from broods of 7. For clutches laid in the early part of this period, the recapture rate was higher from broods of 6 than 7, but if anything higher from broods of 8 than 7, while there were no recoveries from the 2 broods of 9. For clutches laid in the middle period, the recovery rate was much higher from broods of 1–5 and also from broods of 8 than from broods of either 6 or 7, while there were again no recoveries from the 2 broods of 9. For clutches laid in the second period, the recovery rate was highest from broods of 7, and there were none from the 5 broods of 8. In the late period most recoveries were from the commonest brood-size of 5 and there were none from broods of 6, but there were in all so few recoveries from late broods that this means little.

It is hard to know how to interpret such irregular variations. As the figures stand, they provide no support for my interpretation of clutch-size, but on the other hand they are not sufficiently clear-cut to exclude it. In each of the four periods analysed, there were no recoveries from the largest broods represented, but in the first two periods, though not the others, a higher proportion of young was recovered from broods one larger than the average size than from broods of average size (with, of course, a corresponding but rather larger difference in the average number of recoveries per brood). It seems possible that the study area in the Forest of Dean, consisting of a pure stand of mature oaks, provides unnaturally favourable conditions for a high density of caterpillars, and therefore of food for the young, so that the Pied Flycatchers can there raise unusually large broods, but there is no reason to think that this held in the areas studied by Curio or Löhrl. I think it more likely that there are in the Pied Flycatcher other phenotypic and adaptive modifications in clutch-size in addition to that with date allowed for (at least partially) in Table 21. It will be recalled that, in the Great Tit, there are further modifications in clutch-size adapted to the age of the parent, the population density and the habitat, and as I earlier pointed out (p. 44), if larger clutches tend to be laid chiefly when there is a greater chance of larger broods being raised, the average clutch will probably not be that from which, on the average, most young are raised per brood. Hence a more refined analysis, with greater allowance for possible adaptive modifications, is needed before a proper evaluation can be made of survival in relation to brood-size in the Pied Flycatcher.

A further possibility was raised for the Great Tit (p. 53), of whether the rearing of a brood of above average size might impose an additional strain on the parents, so that their own chances of survival were reduced. This point could be tested for the hen Pied Flycatchers nesting in the Forest of Dean, but as the overall rate of recapture varied markedly in different years, each year had to be treated separately, and as in most years hens breeding in the area for the first time were later recaptured in greater numbers than the older hens, it was for these years necessary to restrict the analysis to hens breeding for the first time in the area. The figures in Table 22 show that the proportion of breeding hens recaptured in a later year was lower for those successfully raising broods of 7 or 8 than for other hens in three years (1953, 1959, 1962), about the same in three other years (1951, 1952, 1960), and higher in one year (1961). This does not support the idea that the hens raising large broods had a substantially smaller chance of subsequent survival than the others. The same conclusion was reached earlier by Kluijver (1963) for the Great Tit (see p. 57).

As established by von Haartman and later confirmed by other

TABLE 22

Survival of adult female Pied Flycatchers in relation to the size of brood which they raised (Forest of Dean)

Year of breeding	Breeding groups included	Those with b/7 or b/8		All others	
		Number ringed	Recovered number %	Number ringed	Recovered number %
1951	1st and 2nd	25	10 40	70	32 46
1952	1st	11	5 45	39	15 38
1953	1st	10	2 20	33	15 45
1959	1st	8	2 25	30	12 40
1960	1st and 2nd	20	9 45	25	14 56
1961	all	13	8 62	45	18 40
1962	1st	16	4 25	16	13 81
Total		103	40 39	258	119 46

Notes. Data from Dr. B. Campbell. In those years (see Table 24) in which the previously unringed breeding birds (called 1st above) survived better than those which had bred before, it was necessary to exclude the others. But second-time breeders could be included in 1951 and 1960 because their overall survival rate was the same, and this held for all age-groups in 1961.

workers, a proportion of the cock Pied Flycatchers hold more than one breeding territory, and a few of these birds obtain two mates. Of 237 males at Lemsjöholm one-third had a single territory, nearly one-half had 2, one-sixth had 3, and 3 per cent had more than 3 territories. Different territories of the same individual were often separated from each other by intervening land held by another bird. However, the territory of the Pied Flycatcher is centred on a nesting hole, and is not defended chiefly at its periphery, like that of most small passerine species. Hence one should perhaps speak of cocks defending nesting holes rather than territories.

At Lemsjöholm, 7 per cent of the cocks and 13 per cent of the hens were involved in bigamous relations, nearly all the cocks in question being at least two years old. Normally, each of these cocks paired first with one hen and took another only after the lapse of at least five days, this being termed 'successive polygyny' by von Haartman. The cock usually helped to feed the brood of his first but not his second mate, and in large broods the nestlings fed by both parents were heavier than those in broods of the same size fed by the hen alone. Near Dresden, likewise, about 10 per cent of the cocks studied had two mates. Near Berlin, however, the proportion was only 3 per cent, and it was also very low in the Forest of Dean.

As von Haartman pointed out, because many cocks with one mate also held another territory without a second mate, careful observations are needed to be sure that an individual is unmated. On the basis of figures which he stressed were approximate, he found that, of the cocks known to have bred in his area at least once before, about one-tenth were unmated, whereas of those caught for the first time in the year in question, about one-third were unmated; and as about one-third of those caught for the first time were older than one year, he considered that about half the one-year-old cocks were unmated.[1]

[1] Near Berlin, similarly, about 30 per cent of the cocks were unmated, but on the basis of plumage differences identified in the field, Curio concluded that only about half of these unmated individuals were one year old, and hence that the proportion of unmated cocks was similar among yearling and older birds. It seems to me unlikely, however, that older males would not be more successful than yearlings in obtaining mates. Further, the possibility of determining the age of the cock Pied Flycatcher by its plumage in the field has been questioned (von Haartman, 1949, p. 76; B. Campbell, pers. comm.). Also Curio found that many of the unmated cocks had nesting holes that were unusually broad or unusually high off the ground which suggests either inexperience or a result of competition, and both explanations favour the view that yearling cocks were involved. Finally, of the cocks ringed as nestlings in Curio's area, 17 bred as yearlings, 9 were unmated as yearlings and were not seen again, 11 first bred when 2 years old and two not until older than 2 years. If, as discussed later, about half the cocks died each year, the 11 which first bred when 2 years old were presumably the survivors from 22 yearlings. Hence these figures suggest that about two-thirds rather than 30 per cent of the yearling cocks were

THE BREEDING OF THE PIED FLYCATCHER

Cock Pied Flycatchers usually change their mate and often change their nesting hole in successive years, the average distance between successive nests of the same bird being 188 metres near Berlin (and 114 metres in the Forest of Dean where the area searched was smaller). Of the cocks breeding in one year near the centre of the study area at Lemsjöholm, 42 out of a possible 83 were recaptured in a later year, and as a few that returned may have been missed, this means that rather less than half of them died each year. (Over the whole area, only 38 per cent were recaptured in a later year, due to some birds which bred near the periphery in one year moving outside the area in another year.) Similarly 45 per cent out of a possible 121 cocks near Berlin were recaptured in a following year, and as Curio estimated that another 5 per cent were missed, this means that, as at Lemsjöholm, about half of them died each year. The recapture rate of 39 per cent in the Forest of Dean, shown in Table 23, was certainly smaller than the survival rate, as some cocks were known to have been missed; the unusually high recapture rate of 60 per cent in 1961 presumably means that the birds survived unusually well between 1960 and 1961 (but other annual differences in Table 23 are attributable to the differences in catching efficiency in different years).

The return of breeding hens in later years is harder to evaluate than that of the cocks owing to the greater tendency of the hens to shift their nesting areas in successive years. At Lemsjöholm, only 13 per cent of the hens breeding for the first time returned in the following year, whereas of those which bred a second or third time, 20 out of a possible 42 returned. The latter figures suggest that about half of them died each year. Von Haartman concluded that at Lemsjöholm the hens were of two types, those which shifted their breeding area in successive years and those which returned to the same area. (If half of those breeding for the first time were alive in the following year but only 13 per cent returned, roughly three-quarters of those still alive returned to a different breeding area.) Von Haartman cited figures from another worker in Finland, and also from a Swedish worker, that the same held in their study areas, but pointed out that the situation was very different

unmated. But care is needed in interpretation owing to the possibility that some cocks shifted their breeding areas, and so escaped capture in some years. In the Forest of Dean, of 78 cocks ringed as nestlings between 1952 and 1961 which were later recaptured when breeding in the area, 54 per cent were caught as yearlings, but another 37 per cent not until 2 years old, 8 per cent when 3 years old and one aged 4, and though not all the breeding cocks were caught each year, this also suggests that over half the yearlings did not breed (assuming that those first caught when two years old were the survivors from twice as many yearlings). Creutz likewise recorded a low proportion of recaptured cocks breeding as yearlings near Dresden, but he certainly missed an important fraction of those present.

TABLE 23

Recapture of breeding adult Pied Flycatchers in later years in the
Forest of Dean

Breeding year	*Birds breeding one year and recaptured in next (or a later year)*					
	Males			Females		
	Number ringed	*Recovered Number*	*%*	*Number ringed*	*Recovered Number*	*%*
1951	—	—	—	99	42	43
1952	91	31	34	98	34	35
1953	66	17	26	81	26	32
1959	—	—	—	67	21	31
1960	50	21	42	53	25	47
1961	50	30	60	58	26	45
1962	56	22	39	59	25	42
Total	313	121	39	515	199	39

Note. Data from Dr. B. Campbell.

in England and much of Germany, where the recapture rate of hens
was much higher than in Finland and about equal to that of cocks in
the same area, as shown for the Forest of Dean in Table 23, in Silesia
by Trettau and Merkel (1943), in Frankfurt-am-Main by Trettau
(1952), and near Dresden by Creutz (1955). In these areas von Haartman presumed that the hens normally bred in the same area in successive years. The situation was apparently intermediate near Berlin,
where Curio recaptured 45 per cent of the cocks but only 30 per cent
of the hens.[1]

In all wild birds previously investigated, the annual adult mortality

[1] Curio (1958) attributed this difference to a higher mortality among the
hens than the cocks, but I think it most likely to be due mainly to a proportion of
the hens shifting their breeding area, though this proportion was evidently
smaller than at Lemsjöholm. In this connection it is relevant that out of 90
ringed hens which nested in two different years near Braunschweig (Brunswick),
at nearly the same latitude as Curio's area near Berlin, only 72 per cent nested
less than a kilometre apart, 12 per cent between 1 and 2 km, 3 per cent at 2–4
km, 4 per cent at 8–16 km, 4 per cent at 23–33 km, and 3 per cent at 55–60 km
(Berndt, 1960). The area studied by Curio was of such a size and shape that
he would probably not have recaptured hens settling over 2 km away, nor
about half of those nesting between 1 and 2 km away; and if the hens in this
area moved to the same extent as near Brunswick, and if about half of them died
each year, he would have recaptured about 30 per cent of the hens, as in fact he
did. The average distance between nests of the same hen in different years in
Curio's area was 291 metres, rather farther than for the cocks; this figure of
course takes no account of any hens that shifted outside his study area.

was the same for all ages up to an age at which so few individuals remained alive that figures could not be given (Lack, 1954). The hen Pied Flycatcher is an apparent exception in Lower Saxony, where Berndt and Sternberg (1963) estimated the annual mortality at 26 per cent between the first and second years, 35 per cent between the second and third years, 59 per cent between the third and fourth years, 70 per cent between the fourth and fifth years and then 100 per cent. These estimates were based, not on the recapture of marked individuals in successive years, but on the ages of all hens caught when breeding which had earlier been ringed as nestlings, and so were of known age. The latter figures, adjusted for the fact that different numbers of nestlings were ringed in different years, were used to calculate the age distribution of the breeding population, from which the annual mortality is readily calculated. The method is sound provided that the chances of recapture are the same for all age-groups, and it is difficult to see why they should not be. Nevertheless, a loss of only one-quarter of the hens between their first and second years seems improbably small, while the rise in mortality with increasing age seems improbably steep.

In the Forest of Dean, the catching efficiency varied too much in different years for the recapture rates of members of the same year-class in successive years to be comparable, but the rates of recapture of different year-classes in the same year can be compared, as in Table 24. These year-classes had to be determined by the year in which the birds were first caught as breeding adults in the area, as most of them were not previously ringed as nestlings. Hence the year-classes were not precise as to age and only most, not all, of those caught breeding in the area for the first time were a year old, and only most, not all, of those caught breeding in the area for the second successive year were two years old, and so on. The results, however, support those of Berndt and Sternberg, since in seven of the eight years studied, the rate of recapture in the next year was lower for hens that had bred twice in the area (most of which were two years old) than for those previously unringed (most of which were a year old), and there was probably a tendency for those that had bred more than twice to return in smaller numbers than those that had bred twice before. This suggests that the mortality rate of the hen Pied Flycatcher increases with increasing age, and a similar result was obtained near Dresden (Creutz, 1955). But at Lemsjöholm, as already mentioned, hens that had bred twice or more returned to the area in greater numbers than those that had bred only once, owing to more of the latter birds shifting their breeding territories in a later year. Possibly, therefore, the results for the Forest of Dean and Dresden were also due to movements, but in these areas it would be necessary to suppose that more older than younger hens

TABLE 24

Recapture in next year of breeding female Pied Flycatchers in
relation to whether they had bred before (Forest of Dean)

Breeding year-class	Previously unringed			Ringed as adults in year before			Ringed as adults at least 2 years before		
	Ringed	Rec.	% Rec.	Ringed	Rec.	% Rec.	Ringed	Rec.	% Rec.
1951	60	27	45	35	15	43	4	0	0
1952	50	20	40	32	11	34	16	3	19
1953	43	17	40	26	6	23	12	3	25
1954	41	9	22	11	2	18	21	4	19
1959	38	14	37	20	4	20	9	3	33
1960	31	16	52	14	7	50	8	2	25
1961	33	14	42	15	7	47	10	5	50
1962	32	17	53	14	3	21	13	5	38
Total	328	134	41	167	55	33	103	25	24

Notes. Data from Dr. B. Campbell. In each group the recapture of all ringed individuals
breeding in the year shown in the left-hand column is given for the following year.
Birds earlier ringed as young, and so of known age, were scored for the first year in
which they were recorded breeding, irrespective of their known age, which was one
year in two-thirds of them but older in the rest. Probably, therefore, about two-thirds
of those breeding when unringed were then a year old, and similarly about two-thirds
of those ringed as breeding adults in the year before were then two years old.

shifted their breeding areas. Until the movements of hen Pied Flycatchers have been fully worked out, I think that judgement should be
suspended on the apparent rise in mortality with age, especially as
such a rise has not been found in any other species of bird.

Von Haartman and Curio estimated the mortality of juvenile Pied
Flycatchers between leaving the nest and their first summer at about
70 per cent. If each pair produces four young, and if half the adults
die each year, the population will be stable if about three-quarters of
the fledged young die in their first year, except for the complication
introduced by the existence of non-breeding birds. However, the
above estimates for the adult mortality are as yet very rough. Moreover,
while the figures in Table 23 suggest that the cock and the hen have an
equal mortality, the existence of a sizeable fraction of unmated cocks
indicates that the cocks survive rather better than the hens, a point
requiring further study.[1]

[1] Of 88 hens ringed as nestlings in the Forest of Dean between 1952 and 1961
and later recaptured there when breeding, just over two-thirds were caught
when 1 year old, but 17 not until 2 years old, 8 not until 3 years old and 3 not

THE BREEDING OF THE PIED FLYCATCHER

In the study area near Berlin, the average distance from its birthplace at which a Pied Flycatcher ringed as a nestling later settled to breed was 665 metres for cocks and 962 metres for hens, hence in the young birds, as in the adults, hens tend to move farther than cocks. (These averages do not allow for any individuals which escaped recapture through breeding right outside the area.) More extensive figures are available for Lower Saxony where, of 168 hens ringed as nestlings, nearly half bred within a kilometre of their birthplace, two-thirds within 2 km and three-quarters within 5 km; but 11 settled at 5–10 km, 18 at 10–20 km, 8 at 20–26 km, and 4 at over 40 km (Berndt, 1960). As most recaptures were made in areas with nesting boxes, these figures probably exaggerate the proportion of hens which bred near where they were born. In view of these findings, it is not surprising that the proportion of Pied Flycatchers ringed as nestlings which later bred in the various study areas was small, being only 2·5 per cent for cocks and 1·1 per cent for hens at Lemsjöholm, but 12·4 and 8·5 per cent respectively near Berlin. Both figures confirm the tendency for cocks to return to a greater extent than hens.[1]

Little can yet be said about the factors influencing the annual fluctuations in numbers or the average breeding density of the Pied Flycatcher. The figures in Table 20 show that, as in other species discussed in this book, the annual variations in the output of young had no obvious influence on the subsequent changes in the number of breeding pairs. Presumably, therefore, the survival of the young after they left the nest, including during the time when they were in their winter quarters in Africa, was important. Curiously, the unusually high recapture rate in 1961 of cocks that had bred before in the Forest of Dean was not

until 4 years old. Similarly, near Berlin, 16 were found breeding when 1 year old but 9 not until 2 years old despite careful search. (Many of the hens which returned to breed near Dresden were likewise not recaptured until 2 or 3 years old, but probably a number of them were missed, so these figures are less critical.) In explanation of his findings, Curio postulated that a substantial proportion of the yearling hens do not breed. But as 30 per cent of the cocks are unmated, I think it unlikely either that hens could not normally find mates, or that there exist immature hens which do not return to the breeding grounds. It seems more likely that some hens bred outside the area of their birthplace as yearlings but returned to it when 2 years old or older, but this is speculative. This is another point which cannot be established with certainty until the tendency for hen Pied Flycatchers to shift their breeding areas is precisely known.

[1] The percentage of ringed nestlings later recaptured breeding was also low elsewhere, 2·5 per cent of the cocks and 2·7 per cent of the hens near Dresden (Creutz, 1955), 4·4 and 6·7 per cent respectively in Silesia (Trettau and Merkel, 1943) and 3·3 and 4·4 per cent in the early years of Campbell's study in the Forest of Dean. The sex ratio should not be judged from these figures, as these observers caught a higher proportion of hens than cocks in the years in question.

associated with an increase in the number of nests there in that year. The number of pairs breeding at Lemsjöholm, and also in various areas in Germany, increased markedly after the erection of nesting boxes, showing that, especially where old trees have been removed, the numbers of the Pied Flycatcher may be held down by a shortage of of suitable nesting sites. The figures given earlier also show that, with nesting boxes in excess, the breeding population was more than twice as dense in a rich oak plantation in the Forest of Dean as in a birch and alder wood near Berlin, about twice as dense in the latter as in an orchard near Dresden, and four to five times as dense in the Dresden orchard as in mainly coniferous forest at Lemsjöholm. The density of insect foods very possibly varied in parallel, so the Pied Flycatcher, like other birds, probably settles more densely in those habitats which are richer in food than in those which are poorer, but the availability of its food has not been precisely measured. As the Pied Flycatcher defends a nesting hole rather than a breeding territory with a definite perimeter (von Haartman, 1956a), it is unlikely that its numbers are limited by territorial behaviour in the sense of defence of a specific area. But more cannot be said on these problems at the present time.

The Collared Flycatcher is closely similar both in appearance and in all aspects of breeding ecology to the Pied Flycatcher. It was studied on 11 hectares of orchard country near Stuttgart, Germany, by Löhrl (1949, 1957, 1959). There were on the average 10 pairs per hectare, a much higher density than any recorded for the Pied Flycatcher, but the area was small and its shape was not mentioned, so the birds perhaps depended in part on surrounding land. In the seven years studied, laying occurred earliest in 1949 and latest in 1955, with 1953 intermediate. As already mentioned, this was not correlated with the temperatures in late April and early May, after the birds arrived, but with the temperatures in April as a whole, most of which the birds did not experience. Hence the cause, as in the Pied Flycatcher, was probably that insects emerge earlier in a warm than a cold April. About one-third of the diet of the early broods of young consisted of caterpillars, but the proportion might presumably have been lower in this orchard than in natural woodland. The average clutch varied in different years between 5·5 and 6·2 eggs, being smaller in the years when breeding started later, while it was also smaller later in each season. Yearling hens probably bred rather later than older hens, but their average clutch was apparently only 0·1 egg smaller. Excluding total failures, 90 per cent of the eggs hatched and 85 per cent of the hatched young left the nest. The latter proportion was 96 or 97 per cent in 3 years and 92 per cent in 2 other years, but only 72 and 54 per cent respectively in 2 other years in which the weather was unseasonally cold. Nestling losses did not vary with brood-size, and the survival rate of the young after they left the nest was similar from broods of all sizes, including those of above average size, as already discussed.

A small proportion of the cocks had two mates. The cocks were not ringed, but on the basis of plumage Löhrl concluded that 37 per cent were 1 year old; it may be wondered, however, whether plumage distinctions are reliable. Of the breeding hens, only 31 per cent of those breeding for the first time were recaptured in the next year, as compared with 45 per cent of those which had bred before. This presumably means that about one-third of the hens (14 out of 45) changed their breeding area in successive years, and that about half the hens died each year. Of the nestlings ringed in the area, 4 per cent of the cocks and 3 per cent of the hens bred there later, but the proportion of cocks recaptured was higher than this in the 2 years in which special search was made for them. Of the hens, 15 bred as yearlings while 14 were first recaptured when 2 years old. Hence Löhrl suggested, like Curio for the Pied Flycatcher, that a proportion of the yearling hens are unmated. But pending a fuller analysis of movements, I think it possible that they may have bred elsewhere as yearlings and returned to the area of their birth when 2 years old. During 5 years in which the whole population was counted, the number of nests was respectively 109, 101, 115, 113, and 82, the drop in the last year following the unsuccessful season in which only half the hatched young left the nest; but the latter might, I suppose, have been a coincidence.

Summing up, the breeding ecology of the Collared Flycatcher is almost identical with that of the Pied Flycatcher, and both species show striking similarities with the Great and Blue Tits. All four species breed earlier in a warm than a cold spring, even though the two Fly-catchers have not themselves experienced the temperatures in question; the most likely explanation is that the hens start laying when they have acquired enough food reserves to form eggs, and that food becomes sufficiently plentiful for this earlier in a warm than a cold spring. Clutch-size declines later in each season, so does the availability of caterpillars for the young, and since the proportion of surviving young is higher from earlier than later broods, the seasonal decline in clutch-size is presumably adaptive, as in the Great Tit. The reason that clutches tend to be smaller in years when breeding starts later than earlier is as obscure as it is in the Great Tit. The survival of the young in relation to brood-size shows irregular variations which do not fit well with my view that clutch-size has been selected with respect to the most productive brood-size, but which do not exclude this interpretation. Probably more allowance must be made for phenotypic variations in clutch-size. It seems unlikely that the size of brood raised affected the subsequent chances of survival of the adult hens. Roughly half the adults die each year. A proportion of the cocks, most of them probably a year old, are unmated. In northern Europe many hens shift their breeding area in successive years, and the existence of this and other movements greatly complicates the analysis of mortality rates and of the age of first breeding in this species. I consider that, pending a more detailed analysis of movements, judgement should be suspended on two postulates of German workers, that the mortality of th e hens increases steeply with increasing age, and that a high proporti on of the yearling hens are unmated.

Collared Flycatcher.

7
THE EUROPEAN BLACKBIRD IN GARDENS AND WOODS

THE European Blackbird, *Turdus merula*, a thrush which is not related to the American blackbirds (Icteridae), frequents woods with secondary growth, finding most of its food among the leaf litter, and nesting mainly in bushes. It occurs in both broad-leaved and coniferous woods, but rich broad-leaved forest is probably the natural habitat in which it is, or rather was, most abundant. During about the last 150 years in England and the last century elsewhere in Europe, the Blackbird has also spread into gardens, city parks, and cultivated fields bordered by hedges or copses, and these provide its main habitats in Europe at the present day (Snow, 1958*a*; Havlin, 1962*a*; Heyder, 1955, and general works). More unusually, the bird has during the last hundred years become established in treeless country, chiefly cultivated fields but also moorland, in the Orkney and Shetland Isles, where it nests on banks or, where available, in farm buildings (Lack, 1942-3; Venables, 1952). After its introduction by man to New Zealand, the Blackbird has also become common there, and has spread to outlying islands (Gurr, 1954). The species feeds chiefly on the ground

Headpiece: Cock Blackbirds displaying in Botanic Garden. (The Edward Grey Institute occupies that part of the building immediately in front of Magdalen tower.)

on invertebrates, including earthworms and fallen caterpillars, but it takes many fruits in season and also household scraps.

The present chapter is based primarily on a small population of Blackbirds studied for 4½ years in the 2·4 hectares of the Oxford Botanic Garden, just outside the Edward Grey Institute, by D. W. Snow (1955a, b, 1956b, 1958a, b), the breeding census being continued for a fifth summer by C. M. Perrins and M. J. Ashmole (pers. comm.). Snow also made a breeding study of the Blackbird in Wytham woods, and further valuable comparisons between woodland and garden populations have been made in Czechoslovakia (Havlin, 1962a, b, c, 1963a, b) and Poland (Graczyk, 1959, 1961). The two points of most interest for the present book are, first, the comparison of breeding in two dissimilar habitats, one (planted woodland) nearly natural and the other (town gardens) unnatural, and, secondly, the possible influence of territorial behaviour on population density. These same problems are then discussed in the Song Thrush, *Turdus philomelos*, in the same areas, and also in two classical territorial species, the Robin, *Erithacus rubecula*, and Song Sparrow, *Melospiza melodia*.

Both the Blackbird and the closely related Song Thrush, *Turdus philomelos*, raise a succession of broods from March to June or July (Myres, 1955), and they therefore have more extended breeding seasons than any other European birds which feed primarily on invertebrates, being surpassed only by a few seed-eating species, notably pigeons. Most pairs in the Oxford Botanic Garden raised two or three broods each year, while in the nearby garden of the Queen's College, a pair once raised five broods successfully in a year, their first clutch being started in mild weather in late January and their last at the beginning of July (Mayer-Gross and Perrins, 1962). In general, both Blackbird and Song Thrush start breeding earlier in a mild than a cold spring, many pairs starting to lay five days after the temperature rises above 40°F (cf. the Great Tit, p. 20), while a cold spell during the normal laying period temporarily inhibits laying (Myres, 1955). Cold dry weather in April one year checked the expected second layings in the Botanic Garden, but it had a less marked effect in Wytham woods, probably because frost and drought are more pronounced and have a more adverse effect on the bird's food on open grass lawns than in the leaf litter below trees in a wood. This suggests that food shortage, rather than cold or drought as such, might be the critical factor influencing laying, but this is not certain. At the other end of the season, breeding is prolonged in a wet summer, at least in gardens, perhaps because rain increases the availability of earthworms or other foods.

In the Blackbird, as in the Great Tit, laying starts later in year-old than older birds and later in woods than gardens. In 3 successive years in the Botanic Garden, the earliest 1-year-old hen laid respectively 25, 6, and 14 days after the earliest hen that was at least 2 years old. Probably, also, the first-year birds stopped breeding a little sooner than the older birds at the end of the summer. Further, the average interval between the fledging of one brood and the start of the next was $10\frac{1}{2}$ days in year-old hens as compared with $7\frac{1}{2}$ days in older hens. As a result, the average number of clutches laid each year in the Garden was 2·3 among year-old hens and 3·1 among older birds. Also, breeding started later in Wytham woods than the Botanic Garden, the average date of the first 15 clutches in each of 3 successive years being respectively 8, 13, and 7 days later in the woods than the garden. This difference was much longer than the corresponding difference in the Great Tit (see p. 54).

The Blackbird usually lays a clutch of 3 to 5 eggs, occasionally 2 or 6, and the average, like that of the related Song Thrush, rises from March to May, in all by about one egg, and then declines again (Snow, 1955). This is a common type of variation in birds which regularly raise more than one brood each year (Lack, 1954). The increase in the first part of the spring is not completely regular, since in both Blackbird and Song Thrush, clutches tend to be smaller than usual in a cold dry spell in April. In gardens, including the Botanic Garden, the main food brought by Blackbirds to their young consists of earthworms, which are abundant on the surface in March and in a wet April, but are scarce from May onward, and also in a dry April. In woods, earthworms are often brought to first broods; but especially in the second half of May and in early June, caterpillars which have just descended from the leaves of the trees to pupate on the ground are the main source of food, and are far more abundant than any food available to Blackbirds breeding in gardens. Hence the seasonal rise and fall in clutch-size fit well with the seasonal rise and fall in the availability of food for young Blackbirds in broad-leaved woods (the natural habitat), but not in gardens. In addition, there is longer each day in which to collect food around midsummer than in the early spring or late summer, and this of course applies to gardens as well as woods.

The seasonal variations in clutch-size must be allowed for when examining the possible influence of other factors. When this is done, as in Table 25, it is seen that in the Blackbird, as in the Great Tit, the average clutch is larger in woods than gardens and larger in older than yearling hens. The reasons for the difference in habitat require more study and might, partly at least, be linked with the fact that the population density is much lower in woods than gardens. The difference due to age is, I suggest, adaptive and due, as in the Great Tit, to older parents being able, on the average, to raise rather larger broods than

TABLE 25
Variations in the average clutch of the Blackbird, *Turdus merula*

| | | Botanic Garden | | | Wytham |
		Older	Yearlings	All	woods
March	(2)	3·2	(3·0)	3·2	3·8
April	(1)	3·5	3·2	3·5	3·8
April	(2)			3·9	3·9
May	(1)	4·5	3·9	4·3	4·6
May	(2)			4·3	4·7
June	(1)	3·7	2·7	3·8	4·6
June	(2)			2·9	(3·0)

Notes. From Snow 1958*b*. (1) and (2) after the month mean the first half and second half respectively. The mean brood-size in April was 2·8 in the Garden and 3·2 in the woods and in May was 3·4 in the Garden and 4·1 in the woods.

those breeding for the first time. On the other hand Wynne-Edwards (1962, p. 566) attributed it to his idea that fertility is governed by the interplay of social rank and economic conditions, with the result that newcomers to the breeding caste are liable to be handicapped by their inferior social position. He provided no evidence for this, nor is any to be found in the studies of Snow on the Blackbird or Perrins on the Great Tit, but both these latter authors had evidence that older parents could raise more young than one-year-old parents, fitting my simpler explanation.

Omitting nests destroyed by predators, 90 per cent of the eggs hatched in the Botanic Garden and 92–95 per cent in Wytham woods. In the Garden, there were sufficient data for age differences to be discerned, the proportion of eggs which hatched being 95 per cent where both parents were more than a year old, 89 per cent where one but not the other was a year old, and 82 per cent where both were a year old. Failure to hatch was nearly always due to infertility.

The average weight of 8-day-old nestlings was, in the Botanic Garden, 53 grams in broods laid in March or June and 59 grams in broods laid in April or May, while in the April and May nests the young were, on the average, 3 grams heavier in Wytham woods than in the

Botanic Garden. These differences held despite the fact that the average brood-size was larger in those laid in April and May than in those laid in March or June, and larger in Wytham woods than in the Botanic Garden. Moreover, the difference in weight between Wytham woods and the Botanic Garden was really greater than shown, because some young in the Garden starved before they were eight days old, and these birds, which were the lightest, could not be included in the averages.

Especially in large clutches, incubation usually began before the last egg was laid, so that the young did not hatch together, and if any of the brood starved, it was normally the last young to hatch. Young sometimes starved in the Botanic Garden, mainly in dry weather in April, when worms became unavailable, but they survived a drought one year in May, because caterpillars were abundant on a line of elm trees just beyond the Garden. Drought, as already mentioned, is much less important in woods than gardens, as it does not affect the supply of caterpillars, while leaf litter dries out much less quickly than open lawns. Considering all broods which consisted of 3, 4, or 5 young at hatching and which survived predation, in the Botanic Garden 35 out of 296 nestlings (12 per cent) died of starvation before they were 9 days old, whereas in Wytham woods only 1 out of 85 (1·2 per cent) did so.

While a slightly smaller proportion of the eggs were infertile, and a much smaller proportion of the young starved in woods than gardens, predation was much higher in the woods, only 14 per cent of all the clutches found in Wytham giving rise to fledged young, as compared with half of those in the Botanic Garden. The chief predator was the Jay, *Garrulus glandarius*. Similarly in the Long-tailed Tit, *Aegithalos caudatus*, and the Bullfinch, *Pyrrhula pyrrhula*, a far higher proportion of the nests in Wytham woods than in hedgerows were taken by predators (D. and E. Lack, 1958, I. Newton, see p. 190). It seems possible that the clearance of much of the scrub and secondary growth in Wytham by foresters has made the nests of birds which breed low down easier for avian predators to find, and that such high rates of predation would not be typical of primaeval forest, but this is not certain.

In 4 years in the Botanic Garden, each pair of Blackbirds raised an average of 4·1 young per year to the fledging stage. Year-old parents, with an average of 3·4 per pair, were markedly less successful than older parents, with an average of 6·3 per pair. In 13 instances, a pair produced no young in a year, while on the other hand some pairs produced 10, 11, or 12 young in a year. The Queen's College pair mentioned earlier raised 16 young in a year from 5 broods, and another pair (not in Oxford) raised 17 young in a year from 4 broods (Mayer-Gross and Perrins, 1962). No comparable figures could be obtained for Wytham woods, as the birds were not marked, but here the later start to breeding, and hence the shorter season, together with the much higher rate of predation, mean that far fewer young were raised per pair. Hence the Blackbird breeds much more successfully in gardens than woods, though its natural habitat must have been much more like modern woods than gardens.

Similarly in Poland, the Blackbirds in a city park raised 3 broods a year, but those in woods only 2 (Graczyk, 1961). Again, in Czechoslovakia, in a town as compared with woods, breeding started on the average 10 days earlier, the average clutch was 3·94 as compared with 4·14 eggs (with a more marked increase in May in woods) and the proportion of nests lost was 31 per cent as compared with 38 per cent (Havlin, 1963b). Hence the differences between the town and the woods were in the same direction in Czechoslovakia as at Oxford, but the predation, especially in woods, was much lower, so that the average number of young raised was similar in both habitats (2½ per nest and twice that number per pair per year).

After the young leave the nest, they are normally cared for by one or both parents for a further two to three weeks. In the Botanic Garden, about one-third of them died in this period, more than half the deaths occurring in the first five days after the young left the nest. It is interesting that of 41 fledglings attended by year-old cocks, only 56 per cent survived to independence, as compared with 70 per cent of 99 fledglings attended by older cocks, but the difference was not statistically significant.

Out of 26 ringed young Blackbirds in the Garden which survived to independence, 16 (62 per cent) were found still alive in the following breeding season, and there might, presumably, have been some others which had wandered too far from the Garden to be seen. If, as mentioned earlier, each pair in the Garden produced 4·1 fledglings, of which two-thirds survived to independence, of which 62 per cent survived to breed, the recruitment rate was 1·7 per pair per year. This was much more than was needed to replace the average loss of adults, of which only about one-third died each year. This suggests that a proportion of the young moved out of the Garden to settle elsewhere, perhaps in less favourable habitats where the annual loss of adults exceeded the replacement ratio, but this point requires further study.

In the Botanic Garden, on average, 40 per cent of the resident cocks and 37 per cent of the resident hens were 1 year old, but the proportion varied in different years, from 56 per cent of the cocks and 47 per cent of the hens in 1954 to 23 per cent and 17 per cent respectively in the following year. In Wytham woods, only about 13 per cent of the breeding cocks were a year old; it is not known why the proportion should have been so much lower there than in the Garden, but the number of young fledged per pair was also much lower in the woods.

In a stable population in which the individuals breed when a year old, the proportion of year-old birds, i.e. the new recruits to the population, should equal the annual adult mortality. Among the ringed Blackbirds resident in the Botanic Garden between 1953 and 1956, the annual mortality was 33 per cent, similar in both sexes, and this figure did not differ significantly from the observed proportion of 38 per cent of year-old birds (the totals on which both estimates were based being small). Ringing recoveries for Britain as a whole showed an annual adult mortality of 44 per cent, equal in both sexes, but it varied in different years between 34 and 69 per cent (Coulson, 1961). This suggests that the annual loss of adults in the Botanic Garden might have been lower than in Britain as a whole.

The adult mortality was not spread equally throughout the year. As many as 62 per cent of the deaths in the Botanic Garden, and 55 per cent of those in the national ringing scheme, occurred in the four months of the breeding season from March to June inclusive. In the Botanic Garden, only 4 per cent of those alive at the end of June disappeared before the end of November, and only 13 per cent of those alive at the end of November disappeared before the end of February, despite some periods of very cold weather. The proportionately heavier loss during the breeding season was attributed by Snow to the increased strain due to breeding. Beven (1963) considered that the Blackbirds breeding in a Surrey oak wood decreased after hard winters, but his evidence does not, in my view, suggest this, and in particular, as he pointed out, there was no decrease in the breeding population after the extremely cold winter of 1962–3. The number of breeding pairs each year in this wood and in the Botanic Garden have been set out in Table 26.

The breeding density of the Blackbird was about ten times as high in the Botanic Garden as in Wytham woods. The highest density recorded in the Garden, which is, indeed, the highest so far recorded anywhere, was 7·5 pairs per hectare in 1957. The highest recorded in woodland was 0·8 per hectare in 1954 in the Surrey oak wood studied by Beven (1963). Similarly in Poland, the breeding density was up to 1 pair per hectare in a city park but only 0·06 and 0·03 per hectare respectively in two woods (Graczyk, 1961), while in Czechoslovakia it was up to 4 pairs per hectare in town gardens, but only about a quarter of this figure in two small woods surrounded by fields (Havlin, 1962a, 1963a). Figures for other areas in continental Europe summarized by Snow (1958a) support this general difference between gardens and woods, with minima of 0·2 per hectare in urban areas and of 0·015 per hectare

TABLE 26

Numbers of Blackbird and Song Thrush breeding in Oxford Botanic Garden (2·4 hectares) and a Surrey oak wood (16·2 hectares)

| | Pairs in Botanic Garden | | Singing males in oak wood | |
	Blackbird	Song Thrush	Blackbird	Song Thrush
1946	—	—	4	—
1949	—	—	5	1
1950	—	—	9	1
1951	—	—	$9\frac{1}{2}$	7
1952	—	—	$11\frac{1}{2}$	5
1953	11	5	8	3
1954	16	6	$12\frac{1}{2}$	5
1955	13	6	8	4
1956	13	$6\frac{1}{2}$	$7\frac{1}{2}$	5
1957	18	—	—	—
1958	—	—	$11\frac{1}{2}$	4
1959	—	—	9	2
1960	—	—	7	3
1961	—	—	9	4
1962	—	—	8	5
1963	—	—	8	4

Notes. From Snow (1958*a*) and Beven (1963) respectively, but the count of Blackbirds in the Botanic Garden for 1957 was made by C. M. Perrins and M. J. Ashmole. — means no count in the year in question, ½ means a second mate for one cock in the Botanic Garden or a territory partly outside the area studied in the Surrey oak wood. Another long census, from 1951 to 1964, was carried out in a London suburb by Simms (1965). This showed a remarkably constant number of singing males, apart from a reduction to under a half after the cold winter of 1962–3 and a larger number than ever before in 1964, due to many yearling males reoccupying the empty ground.

in woodland. Hence the Blackbird breeds at a much higher density in the artificial habitat of town gardens than in its natural habitat of woodland, and even though all the woods studied were planted, some of them, notably Wytham and the Surrey oak wood, probably do not differ greatly in suitability for the Blackbird from the vanished primaeval forest. (For some recent figures for Germany, see also Erz, 1964.)

In central and eastern Europe the Blackbird is a partial migrant, some individuals moving south for the winter but others staying. In Poland, two-thirds of the woodland Blackbirds left for the winter, whereas those in the city park were resident throughout the year. In Czechoslovakia likewise, many more of the urban than the woodland birds stayed throughout the year, and Havlin attributed the much higher breeding density in town gardens than woods to conditions being much more favourable in the gardens than the woods for survival in winter, which seems reasonable. It implies, incidentally, that the birds did not move locally from woods to towns in autumn and the reverse in spring. In southern England, unlike central Europe, almost the whole breeding population is resident (Lack, 1943-4), and in particular Blackbirds normally stay in the woods, even in severe weather, though some evidently moved out of the Surrey oak wood in the exceptionally prolonged cold weather of 1962-3 (Beven, 1963).

The territories of the cock Blackbirds in the Botanic Garden each year at the start of the breeding season are shown in Fig. 25. The birds held territories almost throughout the year. After breeding, the adults moulted in their territories but rarely attacked intruders, and they resumed their territorial defence in the autumn. At this time many Blackbirds came in from outside to feed on exotic fruits, sometimes up to fifty individuals being present, but these birds left after the fruit had gone. Thereafter, until February, the Garden was occupied mainly by resident territorial adults from the previous year, together with a few juveniles, which often held small and very temporary territories. In severe cold weather with snow, however, when food was not available in many of the territories, their owners wandered rather far from the Garden in search of food.

Each year in the early spring, usually when the weather became milder some time in February, there was a big influx of juvenile Blackbirds of both sexes into the Botanic Garden, the cocks seeking territories and the hens mates. In November, only about one-sixth of the Blackbirds in the Garden were juveniles, as compared with two-fifths by March. The new arrivals were evidently not migrants from afar, but birds that had spent the winter close by, chiefly in open grassy areas suitable for feeding but not for breeding. In two such grassy areas, the University Parks and Christchurch Meadow, the latter immediately adjoining the Botanic Garden, rather over half the Blackbirds present in December were juveniles, but the proportion fell to less than a quarter by the breeding season, those that stayed breeding in the comparatively small areas of shrubberies and hedgerows at the edge of these open spaces.

With an unusually small population in the Botanic Garden in the early spring of 1953, all the juveniles observed seeking territories there were successful, whereas with an unusually high population in 1954, though some juveniles became established, others failed, often after repeated attempts. Some of the latter birds settled in less suitable habitats near the Garden, one was found 700 yards away, and others presumably wandered farther. Of the juvenile cocks which settled in the Garden in spring, 26 did so before the end of March and 7 later, 2 of the latter carving out territories between existing occupants and the

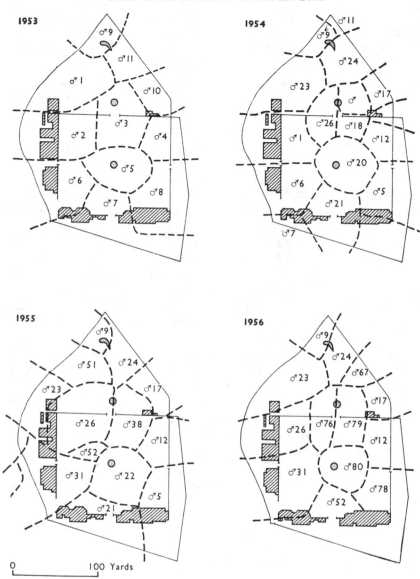

FIG. 25. Territories of male Blackbirds, *Turdus merula*, in Oxford Botanic Garden at start of breeding season (from Snow, 1958a).

other 5 replacing cocks that died. One further cock stayed all the summer without obtaining a territory.

The strong pressure on breeding territories was well illustrated in 1955, when a gardener left some rat poison exposed in one territory. As a result, the owning cock Blackbird, an old bird, died on 20 March.

128

His territory was quickly taken over by an old cock which had been in the vicinity for some time, but this bird was poisoned on 27 March. Its place was filled by an old cock from a very urban (and presumably unsatisfactory) territory 40 yards outside the Garden. This bird was poisoned in turn, and was replaced by an unringed yearling cock which appeared suddenly in the area, but which died of the poison on 2 April. The territory was then annexed by the old cock of one of the adjacent territories, but he succumbed on the following day and a yearling cock took over which had been trying to establish itself in the Garden since January. The poison was then discovered and removed, but there was one more change of ownership, since the yearling just mentioned was attacked and displaced by another yearling cock which had been resident in the Garden during the autumn and winter without acquiring a territory.

With such pressure on the Garden territories, it is not surprising that of 8 hens which lost their mates there during the breeding season, 4 obtained new mates almost at once and 2 more after 3 or 4 weeks; 3 of these 6 birds stayed in their old territories and the other 3 moved nearby. The other 2 hens vanished, and may well have obtained mates outside the Garden. In contrast, of 7 cocks which lost their mates, 5 did not find new mates that year and the other 2 did so only after a considerable interval, in one case of 27 days and in the other of up to 17 days. If, as these observations suggest, there is a surplus of cocks, one would expect the annual adult mortality to be higher in hens than cocks, but as already mentioned, it was apparently similar in both sexes, both for Garden residents and for all Blackbirds ringed under the national scheme, so this point requires further study.

Blackbirds spend much time patrolling and defending their territories, there are several published records of one killing another, and Snow concluded that territorial behaviour was the critical factor limiting the number of breeding pairs in the Botanic Garden. He further considered that the primary function of territory is to enable the male to obtain and retain a mate, while secondarily it provides each bird with an area which it comes to know intimately, which assists it both in finding food and in avoiding predators. With these latter conclusions I agree, but they imply that any effect of territory in limiting the breeding density at a particular level is incidental or, at most, secondary (though Snow himself did not state this). Snow added, however, that he was very doubtful whether the Blackbird's territory could have a function in relation to food, for though the birds obtained much food in their territories, they often fed outside them, notably during the two times of year when food is scarcest, during cold weather in winter and during dry weather in summer. I would add that, though there was a more dependable and, at least in May and June, a much larger food supply for the young in Wytham woods than in the Botanic Garden, the territories in the wood were about ten times as large as those in the Garden, so the marked difference in the size of the territories in the two habitats was not related to the availability of food for the young. Further, since in the Garden 12 per cent of the nestlings starved, while those that survived weighed less than those in the woods, each pair in the Garden might perhaps have raised more young if it had held a larger territory.

Snow pointed out that it is extremely hard to prove the survival value of territorial behaviour to the Blackbird because virtually all individuals are territorial. Hence one cannot compare territorial with non-territorial Blackbirds in regard to their breeding success or survival. To this difficulty I would add another: that territorial behaviour was studied in a habitat greatly modified by man, in which Blackbirds were at least ten times as dense as in their natural woodland habitat. It may be doubted whether an assessment of the ecological advantages of terri-torial behaviour would be likely to be valid under circumstances so different from those in which the behaviour in question was evolved.

That the territorial behaviour of the Blackbird and many other passerine species is of value for the acquiring and retention of a mate may, I think, be accepted. Further, the fact that many resident juvenile Blackbirds survive the winter in Oxford without territories, as do the many continental Blackbirds which spend the winter in England, indicates that the possession of a territory in autumn and winter is not at all essential for their survival at this season. The main advantage to the resident cocks in the Botanic Garden of retaining their territories in autumn and winter may therefore, I suggest, be that this increases their chances of possessing territories, and hence mates, in the following breeding season. In addition, I agree with Snow that intimate knowledge of an area is likely to improve a bird's chances of finding food and avoiding enemies, though non-resident Blackbirds have a compensating advantage in being able to move more readily to places where food is temporarily abundant.

The critical question from the viewpoint of population dynamics is whether, at the time of the influx of juvenile Blackbirds into the Garden in early spring, territorial behaviour sets a limit to the number of cocks that settle there to breed. Snow's observations indicated that it did set a limit, and that, as a result, unsuccessful individuals were forced to occupy other, and probably less satisfactory, breeding areas near by. However, the available evidence does not show whether the resulting dispersion of pairs was more than very local. Further, terri-torial behaviour did not set by any means a fixed limit, since the number of pairs in the Garden varied between 11 and 18 in the five years studied (and between 4 and 12½ pairs in different years in a Surrey oak wood; see Table 26).

If, as seems possible, the Botanic Garden was not fully occupied in the year with 11 pairs, a variation of between 13 and 18 pairs might just possibly accord with the concept of territory as a 'partly compressible disc' (see p. 78). The same might hold for the Surrey oak wood if the years with 4 and 5 pairs are omitted, since otherwise the population fluctuated between 7 and 12½ pairs. But the model of the partly compressible disc cannot possibly account for the great difference in breeding density between gardens and woods. If the Blackbird had been studied only in its natural woodland habitat, one might well have concluded that territorial behaviour set an upper limit to its breeding density of around 0·8 pair per hectare, and that this was about the limit of compressibility, but in gardens the density reached almost ten times this figure. The alternative theory, that the variation in the size of the breeding territories is adaptive, and adjusted to the food requirements of the young, can also be ruled out, since on this view food for the young should have been more plentiful in gardens than woods, instead of the other way about. I agree with Havlin, already cited, that the most likely explanation of the difference in breeding density between gardens and woods is that gardens provide much more favourable conditions than woods for the survival of Blackbirds in winter, presumably because food is much more abundant in gardens than woods at this season. As already mentioned, this implies that there is no appreciable movement of Blackbirds between gardens and woods in autumn or spring, and from this it might perhaps follow that the spacing out of pairs and limitation of density through territorial behaviour is very local. Hence despite appearances to the contrary, and in opposition to what I first thought on reading Snow's work, I am doubtful whether territorial behaviour can be the factor primarily responsible for limiting the breeding density of the Blackbird, and suggest instead that the most important factor may be the food supply in winter. Even so, territorial behaviour evidently forces some individuals into rather unfavourable places for breeding, and the critical question, as yet unanswered, is how far they may be forced to move.

In parallel with Snow's study of the Blackbird, Davies and Snow (1965) studied the related Song Thrush, both in the Botanic Garden and in Wytham. Both species often feed their young on earthworms from garden lawns, and on caterpillars from oaks and other trees when breeding in woods. Hence their breeding ecology is very similar, and so are the factors that influence both their breeding seasons and their clutch-size (Myres, 1955; Snow, 1955). But in England a much higher proportion of Song Thrushes than Blackbirds migrate away for the winter, which is readily understandable, as the resident Song Thrushes suffer proportionately much heavier losses than Blackbirds in the periodic hard winters (Ticehurst and Hartley, 1948). The proportion of the population which migrates is, as might be expected, higher in the north than the south of Britain (Lack, 1943–4). In general, Blackbirds seem to find food more easily than Song Thrushes in winter, but the Song Thrush has one important reserve food, namely land snails, to which it turns in times of drought in summer or winter, and which the Blackbird does not normally exploit, presumably because it has not evolved the special behaviour needed for breaking snail shells on stones (Morris, 1954).

The annual cycle of the Song Thrush is rather different from that of the Blackbird. In the Botanic Garden, the resident cocks surviving from the previous year reoccupied their former territories with song in November and early December. They stayed in their territories and defended them when they could find food there, but often left them for long periods in winter, especially when snow covered their food supplies, including snails, and they then foraged widely for food. New cocks started to take up territories in the Garden from December onwards until March, chiefly in mild weather after the winter cold. There was no evidence that any cocks migrated. Hens arrived to form pairs chiefly in March, presumably after migration, though a few had earlier held individual territories, like cocks. Song Thrushes are much scarcer in woods than gardens in winter and in Marley wood, nearly all the birds first took up territories in March, but occasionally in November.

The number of pairs of Song Thrushes breeding each year in the Botanic Garden, and also the number of singing cocks in the Surrey oak wood censused for Blackbirds, have been shown in Table 26. In the Garden, as shown also in Fig. 26, 5 or 6 cocks held territories in each of the 4 years studied, one having 2 hens in one year. The average breeding density was 2·4 pairs per hectare, rather less than half that of the Blackbird in the same area. In Marley wood in one year, there were 6 singing cocks on some 26 hectares, and both here and in the Surrey oak wood the density was about 0·23 pair per hectare, one-tenth of that in the Botanic Garden, the difference between the two habitats being proportionately about the same as in the Blackbird. In the Garden, the territories of the Song Thrush, unlike those of the Blackbird, had indefinite boundaries, but Snow (1958a) suggested that this might be merely an effect of the lower population density, since at a lower density of pairs the territories of Blackbirds were also ill-defined (Steinbacher, 1953), as were those of the related American Robin, *Turdus migratorius*, at a similar density (Young, 1951, 1956).

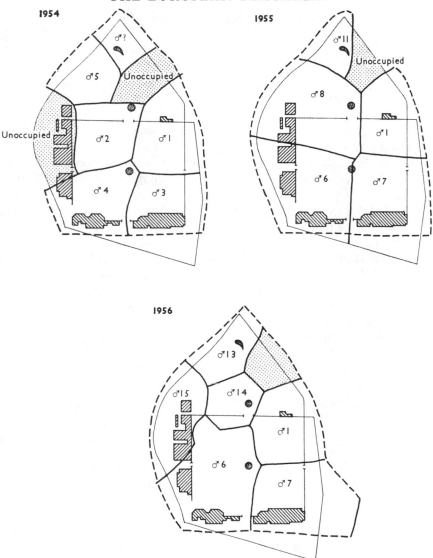

FIG. 26. Territories of male Song Thrushes, *Turdus philomelos*, in Oxford Botanic Garden at start of breeding season (from Davies and Snow, 1965).

Davies and Snow attributed the stability of the breeding population of the Song Thrush in the Botanic Garden to territorial behaviour. Certainly territorial behaviour must have played some role, as in the Blackbird, but the difficulties in this interpretation are the same as for the Blackbird (so need not be repeated). Also, the Song Thrushes had such similar breeding ecology to the Blackbirds that it is hard to know why they should have defended territories of over twice the size, from which, it may be added, Blackbirds were not in any way excluded. These points suggest that the difference in the size of the territories of the two species was not adaptive. Furthermore, in the Song Thrush, like the Blackbird, there is no reason to think that the marked difference in the size of the territories in gardens and woods respectively is adaptive; and if this difference is not adaptive, it may be wondered whether territorial behaviour is of value in limiting the number of breeding pairs.

The problem of whether, and if so how, territorial behaviour limits population density is raised in similar form again in the Robin, *Erithacus rubecula*, a classical territorial species. In the 27 hectares of Marley wood, the number of singing males each April from 1945 to 1953 inclusive was 12 (after a hard winter), 22, 16 (after a very hard winter), 16, 16, 27, 31, 24, and 20 respectively (Lack, 1954*b*). Omitting the reductions after hard winters, the number fluctuated between 16 and 31, and there is nothing to suggest that territorial behaviour acted like a partly compressible rubber disc, setting a nearly constant upper limit to numbers. Counts in some adjoining plantations in the same years showed similar fluctuations, but may have been a little less accurate, as the plantations were narrow and some territories may have been only partly in the area counted. Likewise in the Surrey oak wood of 16 hectares counted for Blackbirds, the number of Robin territories each year between 1946 and 1963 varied between 19 and 33, or, if the summers after cold winters are omitted, between 22½ and 33, again with no suggestion of a nearly constant upper limit set by territory (Beven, 1963).

The average density of Robin territories per hectare was 0·75 in Marley wood and 1·7 in the Surrey oak wood, while it was 1·4 in a Devon copse and 2·5 in an adjoining area of orchard and scrub (Lack, 1954*b* and 1965). Each of the Devon areas consisted of only 1·3 hectares, but the difference in density held good in each of four years. Probably, therefore, the Robin resembles the Blackbird and Song Thrush in breeding at a lower density in near-natural woodland than in a rural habitat much modified by man, though the difference was proportionately smaller than in the two thrushes. In winter, Robins survive better in cultivated land than in woods, but whether this suffices to explain the higher breeding density in cultivated land, or whether territorial behaviour also plays a part, is not known. The Robin further resembles the Blackbird in that its average clutch is higher in May than in either April or June, especially in woods, in that it feeds its young on caterpillars when available, and in that more nests are destroyed by predators in woods than most rural habitats, though the latter difference is smaller than in the Blackbird.

Another classical territorial species is the Song Sparrow, *Melospiza melodia*, owing to the pioneer study of Nice (1937) in Ohio, where the birds bred and fed within their territories, which averaged 2700 square metres. On Mandarte Island in British Columbia, thick scrub, a mild winter climate, and the absence of other common passerine species, evidently offered highly favourable conditions, and here the average size of the territories was about one-tenth of that found by Nice in Ohio, and the birds frequently fed outside their territories in undefended areas common to a number of individuals (Tompa, 1962, 1963, 1964). The birds raised a succession of broods from the beginning of April to the end of June, the average clutch rising from 3·3 in April to 3·9 between 6 May and 10 June, recalling the similar rise in the clutch-size of the Blackbird and Song Thrush in the first half of the breeding season. As nest predators were rare, 85 per cent of the eggs gave rise to fledged young, a very high figure for this type of bird (cf. Lack, 1954). By mid-August, after the last young had become independent of their parents, more than 4 young survived per breeding pair in 3 of the years studied and an average of 2·8 per pair in the other. About half of these surviving young disappeared during the next part of the autumn, with the onset of territorial behaviour among the residents, but how many died and how many dispersed to other places could not be determined. In all, between 10 and 20 per cent of the fledged young survived on Mandarte to the following spring, as compared with 46, 53, and 81 per cent respectively of the adults in three successive years.

As each cock excluded others from its breeding territory, as many juveniles disappeared at the time when, and presumably as a result of, the resumption of territorial behaviour in autumn, and as the number of breeding pairs on Mandarte was nearly constant in the first three years of his study, Tompa not unreasonably concluded that the breeding density was regulated by territorial behaviour. In my view, however, there are considerable difficulties in this view, and they are much the same difficulties as those found in the Blackbird and Song Thrush. First, territorial behaviour presumably assists the cocks to obtain mates (a function of territory that has never been questioned), and since it has this function, there is no need to postulate another. The fact that territories are staked out in the autumn, long before breeding, might be merely because, in the mild climate of Mandarte, individuals that acquire territories in autumn have a greater chance of possessing them in spring than any individuals which start only in the spring; the same argument applies to the staking out of territories by Blackbirds in autumn in the Oxford Botanic Garden. Secondly, the birds feed freely outside their territories, and the territory does not conserve a food supply either for the owner in winter or for the young in summer.

Thirdly, if territorial behaviour provides the primary limit to numbers, why (and how) should it have done so at a density ten times as high on Mandarte as in Ohio? Fourthly, on the view that territorial behaviour operates like a partly compressible rubber disc, one would have expected the upper limit of numbers on Mandarte to be nearly constant. This appeared to be so in the first three years of Tompa's study, when the number of breeding pairs was respectively about 47, 47, and 44, and it was after this that he concluded that territorial behaviour regulated numbers. But in the final season 69 pairs bred, an increase of 50 per cent over the average for the three previous years, and this cannot be reconciled with the concept of a partly compressible rubber disc. (There was no reason to think that feeding conditions for the young were unusually favourable in this last year.) It should be added that the number of unmated cocks present in the four seasons was respectively about 5, 7, 25, and 12, so their number also varied greatly. In the Song Sparrow, therefore, as in the Blackbird, territorial behaviour apparently plays some part in dispersion, and it could be an important part, but the precise nature of this part is highly obscure, and territory does not appear to be an adaptation for regulating breeding density, at least in the ways in which it has previously been thought of as doing so.

Summarizing, in the unnatural habitat of town gardens, as compared with the nearly natural habitat of mature planted woods, the Blackbird starts breeding earlier, has a somewhat smaller clutch, less plentiful food for its nestlings, so that more starve, but less predation, so that more young survive, while its breeding density is about ten times as high. Year-old birds raised rather fewer young than older parents. At least in gardens, territorial behaviour evidently excludes individuals that would otherwise settle to breed, but it is possible that the excluded birds move only locally. In the Botanic Garden, parents often collected food for their young from outside their territories, and as 12 per cent of the young starved, it would presumably have been advantageous for the parents to have held larger territories. Both in the Garden and in an oak wood, the number of breeding pairs each year was rather variable, so that territory did not set a fixed upper limit to numbers, and territories were about ten times as small in the Garden as in the wood, though food is more plentiful for young Blackbirds in woods than gardens. Hence it is doubtful whether the breeding territories have an ecological function; in any case, this might not be revealed by study in a habitat where the bird is ten times as dense as in the natural habitat where its territorial behaviour was presumably evolved. The high breeding density in gardens is perhaps due to unnaturally favourable conditions for survival in winter. The main advantage of retaining territories in autumn and winter is probably to ensure possession of a territory, and hence a mate, in the following spring. These points also hold in the related Song Thrush in the same two habitats, except that it is rather less than half as dense as the Blackbird in both gardens and woods, suffers heavier losses in hard winters, and is a partial migrant. The Robin also shows many parallels in clutch-size, nesting success and breeding density in relation to territory. In the Song Sparrow, likewise, there is similar difficulty in seeing just how territorial behaviour might regulate numbers, the breeding density being ten times as high on Mandarte Island as in Ohio, while after three years of nearly steady numbers on Mandarte, it increased by half as much again in the final year studied.

Song Thrush in Botanic Garden.

8

TAWNY OWLS AND OTHER PREDATORS
ON RODENTS

IN several important respects, the relationships between a predator and its prey can be studied much more easily in a large raptorial bird than in an insectivorous small passerine species. This is because raptors often depend on only a few main species of prey, while the remains of small mammals or birds can be more easily identified in the prey, and the living animals can be more easily sampled for density in the wild, than most insects. Against this, most raptors are so scarce and hunt over such wide areas that a human observer finds it hard to study more than two or three pairs, which is, of course, too few for a population study. Fortunately there is one European bird which preys on vertebrates but lives at a sufficiently high density for one observer to study many pairs, and that was why the Tawny Owl, *Strix aluco*, was selected by H. N. Southern (1954, 1959, and in prep.), on whose work the following account is based. He made this study on the 400 hectares of woodland on the Wytham estate also worked for the Great Tit. This rather open broad-leaved woodland probably represents a highly favourable habitat for the Tawny Owl, and one which closely resembles that which the species frequented in primaeval England. The bird is highly territorial, and though it is nocturnal, it can be censused by ear, as the territorial hoot of the male, the breeding call of the female and the food call of the fledged young are characteristic. Up to thirty

Headpiece: Tawny Owl feeding young in flood-lit nest-box.

pairs bred in the area, the adults are strictly resident, and the young move for at most a few miles, so the population was virtually self-contained.

The Tawny Owl normally nests in large and rather open holes in trees. A nesting box, illustrated in the chapter head, was designed to simulate the hole at the end of a broken branch and each year about one-third of the Wytham pairs bred in these boxes, while a number of nests in natural holes were accessible, so that an adequate sample could be studied for breeding success. A mirror was fixed at an angle near the entrance to each box, so that the observer could see from the ground whether it was occupied, without having to climb the tree and put off the bird. Further, the owls were not disturbed when the nests were floodlit at night by red light, so that their behaviour could be watched from a hide, and the types of prey brought to the young could be identified by direct observation.

The diet throughout the year was studied by an analysis of the bones in pellets, which are ejected by the owls after feeding, particularly at set perching posts, many of which Southern (1954) found and cleared on regular visits. The chief prey in Wytham were the Wood Mouse, *Apodemus sylvaticus*, and Bank Vole, *Clethrionomys glareolus*, which together comprised nearly 60 per cent, in about equal proportions, of all identified items, and were taken especially in winter. Also included were 13 per cent of Short-tailed Voles, *Microtus agrestis*, 12 per cent of Common Shrews, *Sorex araneus*, which being light are of little importance, and 4 per cent of Moles, *Talpa europaea*, which are much heavier than small rodents and comprised an important fraction of the food in summer. A variety of other foods were taken occasionally, especially when mice and voles were scarce or hard to catch, including small birds, beetles, and even earthworms. The birds hunt mainly by perching quietly a few feet above the ground, and flying down when they detect prey, which they locate by sound.

Southern estimated the relative density of the wood mouse and bank vole each year by trapping. Both species of rodents breed mainly between April and September, but continue up to December or even later in years with a good crop of beechmast or acorns. Their density varied greatly, between about five and fifty per acre, but the relationship between the numbers trapped and the true density has not yet been worked out in detail, and the figures for each summer in the right-hand column of Table 28 are on a relative scale. In 1954, the natural economy of the woods was greatly disturbed by the outbreak of myxomatosis, which killed nearly all the Rabbits, *Oryctolagus cuniculus*, in England. As a result, Foxes, *Vulpes vulpes*, Stoats, *Mustela erminea*, and other predators of rabbits turned to mice and voles, which decreased heavily,

and since then the numbers of woodland mice in Wytham have fluctuated violently. Many of the mice were marked with metal leg-rings
and a proportion of these was recovered later from the pellets of Tawny
Owls. As the mice are sedentary, this provided an ingenious way of
mapping the hunting territories of the owls, and showed in particular
that each pair normally kept to a restricted and exclusive area.

Tawny Owls are single-brooded and lay their eggs about the middle
of March, earlier than most other British birds, though at the same
time as the Long-eared Owl, *Asio otus*, which also preys mainly on
small rodents, but in more open country; it is absent from Wytham.
The young owls normally leave the nest about the middle of May, but,
unlike most other birds, they then stay for three further months in
the care of their parents (Southern *et al.*, 1954). This fact does not
appear to have been recorded by any previous biologist, though it was
known to T. H. White, author of *The Sword in the Stone* (1938, Chapter

TABLE 27

Breeding history of Tawny Owl, *Strix aluco*, in Wytham woods, Oxford

Year	Number of pairs	% Pairs breeding	Mean clutch	Number of young fledged	Young fledged per pair	Abundance of rodents on arbitrary scale
1947	16	69	(2·5)	20	1·3	?
1948	20	65	(2·0)	19	1·0	?
1949	20	90	2·8	25	1·3	5
1950	21	81	2·7	27	1·3	6
1951	22	50	2·0	6	0·3	3
1952	24	70	2·6	20	0·8	5
1953	25	60	2·1	19	0·8	4
1954	26	69	2·4	16	0·6	5
1955	27	15	(2·0)	4	0·1	2
1956	29	79	2·2	23	0·8	6
1957	30	60	3·0	20	0·7	7
1958	30	0	—	0	0	1
1959	30	—	—	29	1·0	8

Notes. Based on Southern (1959). The mean clutch was based on only a sample of the
nests (at least 11 each year, except for only 2 in each year where the average has been
placed in brackets). The density of rodents, *Apodemus sylvaticus* and *Clethrionomys
glareolus*, is scored on a relative scale from 8 (extremely abundant) to 1 (extremely
scarce), but the intervals between successive numbers do not necessarily correspond
to equal differences in density. Myxomatosis destroyed the rabbits in 1954.

11). Fledged young hardly ever died in summer while still with their parents, but a number were picked up starving, and others wandered a few miles off the estate, soon after they became independent.

As shown in Tables 27 and 28 and Fig. 27, the breeding success of the Tawny Owl varied greatly with the density of wood mice and bank voles. First, by no means every pair of owls attempted to breed each year, and the proportion which bred was higher in years when mice

TABLE 28

Influence on breeding success of Tawny Owl of the density of
(a) rodents, (b) Tawny Owls

Tawny Owls	(a) Density of Rodents (scale 1–8)	
	At least moderate (5–8) (7 years)	Scarce (1–4) (4 years)
Number of pairs	26	26
Per cent of pairs breeding	75	31
Mean clutch-size	2·6	2·0
Young fledged per pair	0·9	0·3
	(b) Density of Tawny Owls	
	16–24 pairs (5 years)	25–30 pairs (5 years)
Young fledged per pair	1·1	0·8

Notes. Based on the figures in Table 27. The averages in part (a) are the averages of the figures for each year 1949–59 inclusive, except that clutch-size was not recorded in 1958 or 1959, and the percentage of breeding pairs was also not recorded in 1959. The averages in part (b) are for the years 1947–59 inclusive, but omitting the bad mouse years of 1951, 1955, and 1958.

were abundant than in years when they were scarce. No pairs bred at all in 1958, when mice were extremely scarce, whereas in three other years when mice were abundant, over three-quarters of the pairs bred. The average clutch was also affected, being 2·0 in the bad mouse year of 1951 and 3·0 in the good mouse year of 1957, with other years intermediate. In all years combined, only 50 per cent of the eggs hatched, a much lower proportion than in other birds, most failures being due to the desertion of complete clutches by incubating females. The male feeds the incubating female assiduously on the nest, and desertion seems usually to have been due to his failure to bring her enough food. Fitting with this view is the two bad mouse years of 1951 and 1955, only a quarter (7 out of 26) of the eggs hatched, a much lower proportion

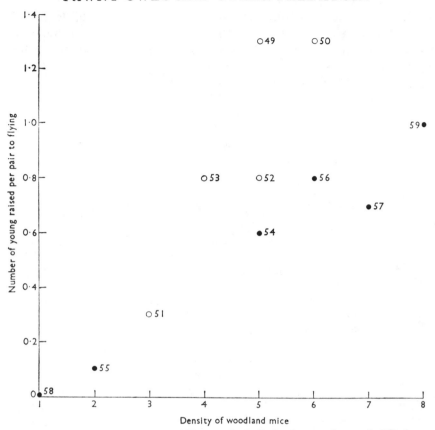

FIG. 27. Reproductive success of Tawny Owl, *Strix aluco*, each year in Wytham in relation to density of woodland mice. ○ years with less than twenty-six pairs of Tawny Owls. ● years with more than twenty-five pairs of Tawny Owls. Density of mice, *Apodemus sylvaticus* and *Clethrionomys glareolus*, scored on arbitrary increasing scale 1–8.

than in any other year. In all, 79 per cent of the hatched young were raised to fledging (the proportion apparently being similar in good and bad mouse years, but the broods tended to be larger in good mouse years, which complicates the issue, and there were not enough figures to analyse the survival-rate in different years solely for large broods, which is the critical point). If a clutch was lost, the owls did not usually lay again in the same year, but some pairs did so in 1950, 1953, 1954, 1956, and 1957, in all of which mice were at least moderately abundant; hence the tendency to lay again after failure was probably greater when mice were more abundant.

The most important measure of breeding success, as it takes all the others into account, is the average number of young raised per pair, and this could be accurately measured each year for the whole population because, as already mentioned, newly fledged young are noisy and easily located. Table 28 shows that the average number raised was three times as high in the years when mice were at least moderately abundant as in the years when they were scarce, while Fig. 27 shows the same point graphically in more detail.

The figures also suggest the possibility that breeding success might have varied inversely with the population density of the owls. In the first 4 years, when the number of resident pairs was lowest, the number of young raised per pair was in three years 1·3, the highest figure recorded, and in the other year was 1·0, reached later only in one year when mice were exceptionally abundant. In contrast, the number of young raised per pair in the good mouse years of 1956, 1957, and 1959, when owls were most abundant, was less than might have been expected on the basis of earlier years. This apparent variation with population density can be seen from Fig. 27, but Table 28 shows that, if present, its influence was small. However, the available figures do not provide a good test, first because the number of breeding pairs varied only between rather small limits, secondly because this variation took the form of a steady increase, during which time there might perhaps have been other progressive changes in the wood affecting reproduction, and thirdly because, after exclusion of the bad mouse years of 1951, 1955, and 1958, figures were available for only 10 years. Hence this point needs further study.

The number of resident pairs of Tawny Owls in Wytham increased by one quarter, from 16 to 20 pairs, between 1947 and 1948, this presumably being a return towards the number present before heavy mortality in the unusually cold winter of 1946–7. During the next 10 years, up to 1957 inclusive, the number rose slowly and steadily, in all by half as much again, and it stayed at 30 pairs for the last 3 years of the study. Southern thought that part of this increase might have been caused by the clearing of undergrowth in forestry operations, which probably made it easier for the owls to hunt, and therefore to obtain their food in smaller territories than before. It was certainly not due to the marked variations each year in the number of young raised to fledging, which varied between 0 and 29 without any corresponding fluctuations in the subsequent breeding population. In the Great Tit, likewise, the production of fledged young had no appreciable influence on the population fluctuations (see p. 67), and in this species the key factor was the mortality of the young after they left the nest and before the start of the winter. Probably, as already mentioned, there was heavy mortality among young Tawny Owls soon after they became independent of their parents, and ringing recoveries, both of young raised in Wytham and of those ringed in Britain as a whole, suggested that some 60 per cent of them died in their first year. There were not enough figures, however, to compare the extent of the juvenile mortality in different years, and anyway it could not have had any important effect on the size of the resident population.

For the striking feature of the adult population of the Tawny Owl, in marked contrast to that of the Great Tit in the same woods, was its stability. This is what one would expect if the density of resident pairs was determined by territorial behaviour, and it is hard to conceive of any other explanation. As discussed earlier (pp. 78), there are two main views as to how territorial behaviour might limit numbers. On one view (the partly compressible rubber disc analogy), the lower limit of territory-size is nearly constant, and so, therefore, is the upper limit of numbers; hence, except after unusual mortality such as that due to a hard winter, the number of breeding pairs remains similar each year. On the other view, the size of the territories is adjusted to the food supply, so that if the food supply fluctuates, the number of breeding pairs fluctuates in parallel. As shown in Table 27, the number of resident pairs of Tawny Owls was fairly constant, and in particular it did not fluctuate with the density of wood mice and bank voles. Hence territorial limitation was evidently of the first type. Southern suggested that a strictly resident habit is of advantage to the Tawny Owl because each adult can then become extremely familiar with its own hunting area. Hence even when food is very scarce, this familiarity may well enable it to find food more easily on its own ground than if it moved out in search of another wood, where mice might anyway be as scarce as in its home wood, and where it might have to compete against established residents. That the resident population in Wytham did not decrease at all after the bad mouse years of 1951, 1955, and 1958 shows that the adult owls were able to survive on their own territories. Under these conditions, however, they did not breed successfully, and when mice were extremely scarce, they did not even attempt to breed. The survival of Tawny Owls when mice are scarce is presumably assisted by their turning in part to other prey, and perhaps also by their fat stores, which are larger than in those species of owls, discussed later, which are nomadic when food is short (Piechocki, 1960).

Finally, Southern considered that Wytham is probably a favourable habitat for the Tawny Owl, and he suggested that the numbers of the resident population might perhaps be 'buffered' by territorial behaviour, as Kluijver and Tinbergen (1953) phrased it. On this view, the juveniles seeking territories fill any gaps due to the death of residents, and the rest are forced out into less favourable or marginal habitats, where the population presumably fluctuates. The numbers of the Tawny Owl have not been studied in a less favourable habitat, but it is suggestive that, on the basis of ringing recoveries, Southern found the annual mortality of the adults to be much lower in Wytham than in the country as a whole, but since both samples were small, this point needs checking. That the Tawny Owl may have a very different economy in different habitats is shown by the fact that, whereas the proportion of small birds in the prey was only 5 per cent in Wytham, it was 96 per cent, mainly House Sparrows, *Passer domesticus,* in the London area (Harrison 1960). Since, where both small rodents and small birds are available, as in Wytham, the Tawny Owl takes mainly rodents, it may well survive better in woods than suburban areas, where wood mice and bank voles are very scarce.

Some studies of the Tawny Owl in other European countries may be briefly mentioned. In three territories in a Danish wood studied for 3 years, the average number of young still alive in July each year was 3·5 young per successful pair and 2·3 young per resident pair, both figures being much higher than in Wytham; the resident owls were evidently at a density of about three-quarters of that in Wytham, but the density of small rodents was not measured (Andersen, 1961). In a forest near Berlin studied for 5 years, 16 or 17 pairs were resident on 3138 hectares, which is about one-tenth of the density in Wytham, though the author considered it to be high. From a possible 70 pairings, 30 resulted in 61 young being raised, an average per year of 2 per successful pair and 0·9 per resident pair, both figures being slightly higher than in Wytham (Wendland, 1963). In parts of Germany, clutches are much higher than in England, at times consisting of 5, 6, or even 7 eggs, during plagues of the vole *Microtus arvalis*, which does not occur in Britain (Schmaus, 1938).

As regards the adult mortality, in Switzerland, on the basis of all the recoveries of Tawny Owls ringed as young, the annual mortality was 47 per cent in the first year of life, 45 per cent in the second year, and 24 per cent in subsequent years (Schifferli, 1957). The corresponding figures in Sweden were much higher, 67 per cent in the first year and 43 per cent in each later year (Olsson, 1958). As the reproductive rate is also higher in Sweden than Switzerland, this is what one would expect with stable populations. In Switzerland, most young birds were found dead either in June or in the following March, but most adults in April and May. In Sweden, on the other hand, most juveniles were found starved in autumn, and most adults were found starved in severe winters, after which there was a marked reduction in the breeding population (Ollson, 1958; Edberg, 1958).

The Short-eared Owl, *Asio flammeus*, unlike the Tawny Owl, frequents open treeless country, especially grassland and moors.

Correlated with this, it has much longer wings, and it catches most of its prey by quartering the ground in flight, often hunting by day, and using its eyes. Its main food in Britain is the Short-tailed Vole, *Microtus agrestis*, while in the rest of Europe it preys mainly on the related *M. arvalis* and, in the far north, on Lemmings, *Lemmus lemmus*. It differs from the Tawny Owl in being a seasonal migrant and also highly nomadic, both in summer and winter, for which there are probably two main reasons. First, the numbers of voles and lemmings fluctuate

Short-eared Owl.

more violently, probably much more violently, than those of woodland mice, and these fluctuations are often local. Secondly, knowledge of the ground probably makes a much bigger difference to hunting efficiency in closed woodland than open grassland. Hence, when food is sparse, Short-eared Owls probably have a higher chance of survival if they move out in search of better hunting grounds than if they stay, whereas the reverse holds for the Tawny Owl.

When voles are particularly abundant, the Short-eared Owl may lay a clutch of double the usual size (references in Lack, 1954, p. 208). In a recent plague of voles in rough moorland planted with young conifers in the Carron valley in Scotland, the numbers of both voles and Short-eared Owls were probably greatest in 1953, but were not measured. They were still high in the following April, when between 30 and 40 pairs of the owls settled to breed on 1400 hectares. Each pair defended a territory of about 16 hectares, in which it nested, over which it hunted, and from which it drove away other individuals. But by June, the voles had declined steeply in numbers, nearly all the owls departed, and the two remaining breeding pairs held territories of nearly 120 and 160 hectares respectively (Lockie, 1955*b*).

Hence, in contrast to the Tawny Owl in Wytham, the breeding density of the Short-eared Owl in the Carron valley fluctuated markedly with its food supply. If this was due to territorial behaviour, the latter was of the second type referred to above, in which the size of the territories is adjusted to the food supply. Observations have not made it clear, however, whether the territorial behaviour of the Short-eared Owl merely spaced out the available pairs (which seems undoubted), or whether it also determined the number of pairs which settled. In particular, were the original 30 to 40 pairs all that found and tried to settle in the Carron valley in 1954, or did other pairs arrive, only to be driven out by the territory owners? Also, were the many pairs that departed in May or June that year driven out by increased aggressiveness on the part of the pairs that remained, or did they simply respond to a shortage of food? Without experiments, for instance by removing resident birds and seeing whether gaps are filled, it is impossible to be sure which alternative is correct. It seems unlikely, however, that the departures in June were due to territorial expulsion, as only two pairs remained and these occupied only a small fraction of the previous area. In that case, the initial number of 30–40 pairs may likewise not have been limited by territorial behaviour.[1]

The Short-eared Owl was one of the predatory species that bred at Point Barrow, Alaska, in 1953, a year when Brown Lemmings, *Lemmus trimucronatus*, were particularly abundant (Pitelka *et al.*, 1955*a*, *b*). Over the whole area there were 3–4 pairs to the square mile and locally up to 7 pairs, roughly 1 pair to each 40 hectares, while the smallest territories were only about 20 hectares: in the two preceding years none bred. The Snowy Owl, *Nyctea scandiaca*, which in its nomadic

---

[1] Of the other native British owls, the Long-eared *Asio otus* breeds in more open woodland than the Tawny and feeds in more open country, while the Barn Owl, *Tyto alba*, nests primarily in agricultural country and hunts along banks, at the edge of woods and over fields. These two species have longer wings than the Tawny Owl and take a much higher proportion of short-tailed voles, both are somewhat nomadic and both lay larger clutches than usual when rodents are abundant. Hence they are evidently intermediate in their adaptations and ecology between the Tawny and Short-eared Owls respectively, but they have not been studied in detail. (For earlier references, primarily to the Long-eared Owl, see Lack, 1954; and for later work on the food, nomadism, and mortality of the Barn Owl see Becker, 1958; Honer, 1963; Sauter, 1956; and Schifferli, 1957.) In Europe, the Barn Owl succumbs much more often than the Tawny Owl in cold winters, which Piechocki (1960) attributed to its having a lower percentage of fat reserves, but presumably the difference in feeding habits might be partly responsible, while since the Barn Owl frequents fields and the Tawny Owl woods, dead Barn Owls are probably more often found than dead Tawny Owls. Piechocki (1961) later discovered that, while the moult of the Tawny Owl follows the normal pattern, that of the Barn Owl is slower and somewhat unusual. Perhaps, as in boobies (cf. p. 249), this is connected with the greater dependence of the Barn Owl on flight when hunting.

habits and variable clutch-size closely resembles the Short-eared Owl, was rather commoner at Point Barrow (and for another study of its habits see Watson, 1957). However, the most abundant predator was not an owl, but the Pomarine Jaeger (or Skua), *Stercorarius pomarinus*, of which none bred in 1951 when lemmings were scarce, while there was a pair to about each 65 hectares in 1952, when lemmings were commoner, and a pair to about each 14 hectares in the peak lemming year of 1953.

While the Pomarine Skua belongs to a very different family of birds, its ecology when breeding so closely resembles that of the Short-eared Owl that it is worth considering the significance of its territorial behaviour in the present chapter. Like the Short-eared Owl it is highly nomadic, moving to breed in areas where lemmings are abundant, and it is also strongly territorial, nesting in its territory, hunting for food primarily within it, and defending it from other individuals of its species throughout the breeding season. Further, the territories at Point Barrow varied greatly in size in accordance with the food supply, in the densest areas averaging about 45 hectares in 1952 and roughly 7 hectares in 1953. The same doubt remains, however, as in the Short-eared Owl, namely whether territorial behaviour merely spaced out the available pairs, or whether it also determined the number present, and there seem to be no critical observations on this point. It is also interesting that, though the main prey of the Snowy Owl was likewise the brown lemming, and though Pomerine Skuas chased Snowy Owls, the latter nested among the skuas, so the latter did not exclude from their territories their chief potential competitor for food.

In the related Arctic Skua, *S. parasiticus*, different individuals first breed when three, four or five years old (Williamson, 1959). This point has not been investigated in the Pomarine Skua, but it is interesting that in the year when brown lemmings were abundant at Point Barrow, several birds bred in sub-adult plumage, lacking the long twisted central tail feathers of the adult, which was not observed in the other years. This suggests that Pomarine Skuas may breed a year younger than usual when it is particulary easy for them to raise young. Similarly, Spanish Imperial Eagles, *Aquila heliaca*, rarely breed in sub-adult plumage at the present day, when their numbers are up to strength, but frequently did so when their numbers were greatly reduced by human persecution at the end of the nineteenth century (Valverde, 1960). Presumably this was because, when adult eagles were sparse, their prey was relatively more abundant, and/or it was easier for sub-adults to establish breeding stations in the absence of competition from adults.

Finally it may be added that, though Pomarine Skuas, Snowy Owls, and other predators were the chief cause of mortality among brown lemmings at Point Barrow during their decline in numbers in the summer of 1953, the lemmings were doomed anyway, because they had earlier destroyed most of the vegetation which composed their food and cover (Pitelka, 1959). This fits with the view of Errington (1946) that predators of vertebrates remove a 'doomed surplus'.

Summarizing, the reproductive output of the Tawny, Short-eared and other owls discussed in this chapter varies greatly from year to year, correlated with the marked variations in the density of their rodent prey. The Tawny Owl hunts by ear at night on woodland mice, and in its hunting, it is probably helped greatly by familiarity with the ground, hence it is strictly resident, with an exclusive territory; territorial behaviour evidently limits the density of resident pairs at a nearly constant figure, irrespective of the density of mice. In contrast, the Short-eared Owl hunts by sight, often by day, on voles in open country, familiarity with the ground is probably less important, while voles probably fluctuate much more strongly in numbers than woodland mice. Hence the Short-eared Owl is nomadic, and while it is strongly territorial, the size of the breeding territories varies greatly with the density of voles. Whether, however, its territorial behaviour merely spaces out the available pairs, or also limits the number of pairs that settle, is not known, and the same applies to the territorial behaviour of the Pomarine Skua.

Pomarine Skua.

9

QUELEA IN TROPICAL AFRICA

IN the tropics the ecology of only two passerine species has been
studied in sufficient detail for inclusion in this book, and their ways
of life could hardly be more different. The African weaver-finch
considered in the present chapter lives in semi-arid grassland, where it
experiences a short rainy season and prolonged dry season, while the
American manakin discussed in the next chapter frequents humid
evergreen forest with a prolonged wet season and relatively uniform
conditions throughout the year. The special interest of the present
species lies first in its enormous colonies, secondly in the clear evidence
for food shortage at one particular season of the year, and thirdly in
its remarkable convergent resemblance to a North American species of
icterid discussed at the end of the chapter.

The Red-billed or Black-faced Quelea or Dioch, *Quelea quelea*, will
for simplicity be referred to in this chapter as the Quelea, although
there are two other congeneric species about which little is known.
The present species is widespread in Africa south of the Sahara, especially on rich alluvial soils where a regular rainy season allows the growth
of annual grasses with a huge crop of seeds, as, for instance, in the
Senegal river valley, the bend of the Niger, Lake Chad, and the head-
waters of the Nile. It is the chief species feeding on the seeds of annual
grasses, being replaced by other weaver-finches in perennial grassland.

Headpiece: Minute fraction of a Quelea colony.

As it normally breeds in thorn trees, it occurs especially in the thornbush belt and savanna close to areas liable to flooding. Here it breeds in denser masses than any other living species of land bird, since individual colonies typically consist of over a hundred thousand pairs, and not infrequently of a million pairs, while a colony of ten million pairs has been recorded. Such numbers were evidently exceeded by the extinct Passenger Pigeon, *Ectopistes migratorius* (Bent, 1932), but are otherwise without parallel among land birds.

In recent years the Quelea has attracted much attention, and has given rise to three international conferences, because of its depredations on grain crops, including those of rice, millet, and wheat (see Wilson, 1947 for the Sudan; Williams, 1954; Disney and Haylock, 1956; and Haylock, 1959 for Kenya and Tanganyika, Morel and Bourlière, 1955, 1956, and 1957 for Mauretania and Senegal; Ward, 1963, 1965 for Nigeria; and the references cited by these authors for these and other areas). Past records indicate that immense numbers of Queleas were present in the drier parts of central Africa before the recent increase in grain crops sown by man, and in both East and West Africa the birds still live primarily in uncultivated areas (Williams, 1954; Ward, 1963, 1965). Whether their numbers have been appreciably increased through human cultivation is in doubt, Williams and Ward considering not, but Haylock (1959) and R. Fuggles-Couchman (pers. comm.) stating that in East Africa the widespread cultivation of wheat on the fringes of the range has probably helped larger numbers than before to survive the dry season when natural foods become relatively sparse. The present chapter is based primarily on the recent quantitative study in Nigeria by Ward (1963, 1965), and if no reference is specified, the statement in question is from his study.

While most of the reported breeding colonies have consisted of between a few hundred thousand and about two million pairs, much smaller colonies, for instance of only ten thousand pairs, have been found, and they may be more frequent than the records suggest, since economic ornithologists tend to concentrate their attention on the large ones. The relation of the size of the colonies to food supplies, nesting sites or other factors has not been investigated. It is known, however, that the birds normally settle to breed near water and close to extensive areas of fresh green grass, which supply their nesting material and later the small insects and soft green seeds needed for their nestlings. Hence the birds at times fly only an extremely short way to collect food for their young (Ward, 1963), though longer journeys have been reported by others, of up to 25 kilometres in Mauretania (Morel and Bourlière, 1957) and in East Africa (Haylock, 1959). The nests are usually on dry land in thorny bushes of various species of *Acacia*, or occasionally *Balanites*, but at times in thorns or rushes over water, and the latter may be more frequent than is at present realized, because most such sites are inaccessible. Hence the Quelea, like other colonial land birds, usually nests where it obtains protection from ground predators, in this case either among dense thorns or over water. In East Africa, however, the birds at times nest in ten-foot grass on dry land (Vesey-Fitzgerald, 1958).

Over nearly the whole of the Quelea's range there is a long dry season and a shorter but fairly dependable rainy season, the latter occurring in different months in different parts of Africa. The birds normally breed in the latter half of the rains, this timing presumably having been evolved because it is only in this period that the small insects and especially the soft green grass seeds needed for the nestlings are available in large quantities. The proximate factors evolved to achieve the timing include a response by the birds to the presence of green grass, and perhaps also to the falling of rain (Marshall and Disney, 1957). At times, colonies are deserted during building, or with eggs, or with young, the reasons for which have not been studied.

Often, all the pairs in a colony start breeding within a day or two of each other, so that all are at the same stage of the breeding cycle, but in other colonies different sections start on different days (Wilson, 1947; Disney and Marshall, 1956; Haylock, 1959; Crook, 1960; Ward, 1963). Synchronization might merely be an incidental result of all the pairs that are ready settling in the same area, but probably it has adaptive value in 'swamping' predators, as discussed for another weaver-bird, *Ploceus nigerrimus*, by Elgood and Ward (1963). Potential predation might also be the reason for the unusually rapid rate of development in the Quelea. At least at times, incubation lasts only 9 or 10 days, a shorter period than in any other known bird (cf. Nice, 1953), while the young stay in the nest only 10 to 12 days (Ward, 1963; also summarizing and qualifying the comments of others).

Normally the species raises only one brood a year. Unusually late breeding was recorded in Nigeria in a year in which the rains continued later than usual (Ward, 1963), while in parts of Kenya with two rainy seasons a year, the birds normally breed in the long rains but sometimes also start breeding, though rarely finishing successfully, during the short rains (Disney and Haylock, 1956). As breeding extended over two months in Tanganyika, Vesey-Fitzgerald (1958) suggested that the birds there raised two successive broods, but this needs confirmation.

The Quelea differs from nearly all other colonial and graminivorous weaver-birds in being monogamous (Crook, 1962, 1963, 1964), and Ward (1963) has produced evidence that this is because two parents are needed to feed the brood. The commonest clutch is 3 eggs, this occurring in 84 per cent of the nests in a colony studied by Ward, while nearly all the others consisted of 2 eggs. But clutches of 2 and 4 were commoner in colonies studied by others, including Morel and Bourlière (1957). The latter authors also found a lower average clutch in 1956, when the rains came later and were less abundant, than in 1955, when the rains came earlier and were more abundant. This difference (2·85 cf. 3·06 eggs) may have been adaptive and related to the number of young which the parents could rear, since the number of nestlings averaged only 2·2 per nest in 1956 but 2·7 per nest in 1955, presumably because, in the year of sparser rains, many parents could not bring enough food to raise a third nestling. Similar variations in clutch-size in relation to the rains have been found in other tropical passerine species in dry regions, for instance by Marchant (1960) in Ecuador.

At the colony studied by Ward, 95 per cent of the eggs hatched and 83 per cent of them gave rise to young which left the nest, while if deserted nests with eggs were excluded, 87 per cent of the eggs gave rise to young which left the nest. This is an extremely high rate of success for a small passerine bird (cf. Lack, 1954). It is attributable primarily to the comparative safety from predators. A few Marabou Storks, *Leptoptilos crumeniferus*, and Tawny Eagles, *Aquila rapax*, took some of the young, but the proportion taken was negligible. Losses of eggs and young were also negligible at some of the colonies in Mauretania studied by Morel and Bourlière (1955), though in 1956, as just mentioned, some young apparently starved (Morel and Bourlière, 1957). Predators recorded by Morel and Bourlière included Marabou Storks, Tawny Eagles, Red-beaked Hornbills, *Tockus erythrorhynchus*, and snakes, but their effect was extremely small. Again, at a colony of two and a half million pairs studied by Vesey-Fitzgerald (1958) no predators were recorded, though at another colony many nests were destroyed by flocks of Cattle Egrets, *Bubulcus ibis*. This last appears to be the only published instance of large-scale predation. It shows that predation is a potential threat, but presumably it is normally kept in check by the safe nesting sites and synchronized breeding.

In 1956, Morel and Bourlière (1957) found that the average weight of a nestling was lower in a brood of 4 than 3, and lower in a brood of 3 than 2, and they inferred that this probably affected the chances of subsequent survival of the young concerned. Ward (1963) did not find similar differences in weight, but there were suggestive differences in survival in relation to brood-size. Out of 157 broods in which 3 young hatched, only 8 per cent died before they left the nest, whereas in 4 broods starting with 4 young 19 per cent died, and in 1 brood of 5 young 2 died. Ward could not follow the survival of the young after they left the nest, which they do before they are fully grown, and since they probably depend on their parents for food for at least another 10 days, further mortality from starvation probably occurred, and this might presumably have been heavier in larger than smaller broods. Ward also found that parents feeding young lost much weight. He therefore concluded that three is probably the largest brood that a pair of Queleas can normally rear without significantly diminishing their own chances of survival, and that this is why the species is monogamous and has evolved a normal clutch of 3. In this connection he considered that it was not the quantity of available food that was critical, but the time needed by the parents to fly back and forth collecting it in the available hours of daylight. This sets a premium on the birds breeding close to abundant food, as they usually do.

While few young Queleas die in the nest, there is suggestive evidence that many do so soon after they become independent of their parents, though the losses in this period have not actually been measured. While the young birds are being fed by their parents, they lay up fat reserves, which eventually form about 10 per cent of their body-weight, but as shown in Table 29, nearly two-thirds of this is lost within a few days of independence. Probably many young die of starvation in this period,

TABLE 29

Fat content of young Queleas as a percentage of their wet body-weight

Age	Number studied	Percentage of fat Mean	Range
Late nestlings (8–12 days)	23	8·3	1–12
Early fledglings (10–14 days)	9	9·5	5–12
Late fledglings (2–3 weeks)	5	9·9	5–15
Independent juveniles (over 3 weeks)	10	3·5	1–7

Note. Late nestlings were young still in the nest 8–12 days after hatching, fledglings were birds which had left the nest but were still fed by their parents, independent juveniles were those that were no longer fed by their parents but were still in the colony. The specimens were collected after an explosion in the colony by the Control Unit. Data from Ward (1963).

while others are killed by the Lanner Falcons, *Falco biarmicus*, and Gabar Goshawks, *Micronisus gabar*, which enter the colonies at this time, but predation is evidently of little importance compared with starvation.

At an East African colony, many insects were brought to the nestlings from the first to the fifth day of life (but not later), including Orthoptera, Coleoptera, Hemiptera, lepidopterous larvae, and especially the workers of a diurnal termite, *Hodotermes mossambicus* (Disney and Marshall,

1956). At a Nigerian colony studied by Ward, well over half of the diet of the two-day-old nestlings (as measured by dry weight) consisted of small insects, mainly orthopterous nymphs and lepidopterous larvae, with some coleopterous larvae, but thereafter the proportion of insects steadily declined, and none were observed in the diet from the seventh day onward. Soft green seeds were given from the first day onward, by regurgitation, and they formed the whole of the nestlings' diet after the first five days. In Ward's colony the seeds were almost entirely of the grass *Echinochloa pyramidalis*, but at other colonies they have been of other sweet grasses, such as *Setaria*, *Panicum*, or *Sorghum*. The parents also brought water to their young, particularly in the heat of the day. So soon as the young fed for themselves, they took the same foods as the adults.

In Nigeria, the Queleas took insects in three periods of the year. First, as just noted, they brought them to their nestlings until they were about five days old. Secondly, they ate many termites when these were swarming for a few days at the start of the rains. Thirdly, both sexes, especially the females, ate insects just before breeding, which presumably helps to bring them into breeding condition. Otherwise, their food consisted almost entirely of seeds, primarily of ten species of grasses, five with small seeds (*Echinochloa* spp., *Panicum*, *Pennisetum*, and *Ischaemum*) and five with large seeds (two wild *Sorghum* species, a wild rice *Oryza*, cultivated millet, and cultivated rice). Hence the diet was easy to analyse and it has been summarized in Fig. 28. In the wet season, which lasts from August to October, it consisted almost entirely of the small seeds of *Echinochloa* and *Panicum*. In the dry season, which

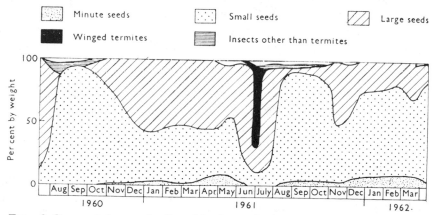

FIG. 28. Seasonal changes in diet of *Quelea quelea* in Nigeria (from Ward, 1963). Note that a much higher proportion of large seeds (mainly cultivated) was taken in the dry season of 1960–1 than in that of 1961–2 when the preferred small seeds held out much longer.

lasts from November to late June, it at first consisted of these same small seeds, but to an increasing but variable extent of large seeds. In the first dry season studied, wild rice was prominent in the diet from January onward and became the chief food in April, May and June. In April and May many minute seeds (of *Digitaria*, *Dactyloctenium*, and *Schoenfeldia*) were also taken, but being so small, they did not comprise much of the diet by weight and they were presumably not very rewarding to collect. In the second dry season studied, the supply of small seeds of *Echinochloa* and *Panicum* held out much longer, and these formed the bulk of the Queleas' diet throughout. Crops of dry-season Guinea corn, which had been severely damaged in the first year, were virtually untouched in the second, even by birds roosting alongside the fields in question. In East Africa, likewise, crops were damaged only in some seasons, primarily those when there was a drought in the normal areas frequented by the Queleas (Williams, 1954; Disney and Haylock, 1956).

In the dry season, when Queleas feed primarily on seeds that have been shed on the ground, they occur in flocks, which vary greatly in size according to the feeding conditions. In open country, a small flock that is successful in finding food is quickly seen and joined by others, until a huge number may be present. Conversely, if a large flock fails to find further food, the groups quickly break up and disperse. Such 'feeding by enhancement' (Hinde, 1961) is common in birds which feed in the open in flocks or groups, but it is not so prevalent in Queleas in wooded country, where the birds see each other less easily. A similar method of finding food by observing other individuals and joining them occurs not only in other seed-eating species but in many sea-birds and also in vultures, being particularly characteristic of birds of open country whose food is very locally distributed.

Early in the dry season, when food is plentiful, the individual Queleas hunt over the ground in a rather random fashion. Once food becomes scarcer, they tend to feed in closely-knit groups, all the individuals hopping forward in the same direction. A bird which finds a seed usually gets left behind while it eats it, and since virtually no seeds are left by the advancing flock, it then flies over the flock and alights at its front. This process continues all the time, so that the whole flock, which often comprises thousands of birds, 'rolls' steadily forward.

In the dry season the birds feed in the morning and late afternoon, but rest during the hottest hours of the day, often in thorn trees. At night they assemble in immense roosts, often in thorns, but in East Africa also in rushes or reeds over water, in tall grass, hill scrub or other dense and rather low vegetation (Disney and Haylock, 1956). The value of big roosts has been questioned, and Ward suggested that protection from predators does not provide a sufficient reason for them. I suggest, however, that those individuals which have been undisturbed by predators during the night will tend to return to the same place to sleep on the following night, hence the presence of roosting birds will be a valuable indication to others seeking a roost that the area in question is safe from predators, and in this way big numbers could quickly build up. In addition, the large numbers present may help to swamp potential predators, as already mentioned under nesting. Alternatively, or in addition, Ward suggested that one of the main functions of communal roosting, in this and perhaps other species, is in helping individuals to find food. This is because the individuals which had found a good source of food on the previous afternoon but had not exhausted it before dark would normally fly straight back to it next morning, and it would therefore be advantageous for undecided birds to follow those taking a definite course. Ward pointed out that this is an extension of the principle of feeding by enhancement already mentioned.

In the dry season, in certain types of annual grassland, the Quelea is the most important species of bird dependent on grass seed. There are many other seed-eating weaver-finches in tropical Africa, but they frequent other habitats, suggesting that Gause's principle is in operation (see p. 284). This in turn indicates that there is potential competition for food among these species, that the Quelea is the most efficient in its particular habitat, and that it may be limited in numbers by its food supply. It need not, of course, be so limited throughout the year, and during much of the year the small seeds of wild grasses which it prefers are abundant. As already mentioned, it is primarily when these small seeds become sparse in the latter part of the dry season that the Queleas turn to larger seeds, including human crops. But the time when food becomes really scarce for them, at least in Nigeria, is in the early rains, at the end of June and through July, since in this period all the wild seeds that are left on the ground start germinating. Just prior to this period, as already mentioned, the birds put on fat, presumably as an adaptation to the impending food shortage. Near its start, also, temporary alleviation is provided by the huge swarms of flying termites, but these fly only in the afternoons and soon disappear, and then the Queleas eat germinating seeds, others that are broken or non-viable, and also such unusual items at the pulp of fruits.

Apart from the nature of the foods taken, there are several other indications that food may be very hard to find in the early rains. First, the feeding and flocking behaviour was often abnormal, movements tending to be disorganized, and birds hunting for food in unusual and unlikely habitats. Secondly, birds often disputed with each other for food, which was not normally seen when food was plentiful. (I earlier (1954) argued that this is in general an indication that food is short.) Thirdly, many birds were on one occasion observed still feeding five kilometres away from their roost when darkness fell, though normally all would have entered their roost at least fifteen minutes earlier. Fourthly, whereas during the dry season the birds coming in to their roosts for the night normally carried between 0·3 and 0·4 gram of seeds in their crops, during the early rains, after the termites had gone, the birds carried on the average only 0·2 gram, and occasionally even 0·1 gram of seed. Since a bird first eats its fill and then stores any surplus in its crop, the crop content is a good indication of the availability of food, as it also is in the Wood Pigeon (see p. 186). Fifthly, a series of measurements showed that the males lost weight at a rate of 0·5 per cent per day between 5 and 10 July and 0·9 per cent per day in the next three days, and females at about double these rates. Sixthly, while it was rare during the dry season to find more than a very few individuals dead under a roost after the morning exodus, on two visits to a roost during the early rains hundreds were found dead there, and many others had probably been removed already by scavengers; these birds had presumably died of starvation.

The changes in average weight of the Quelea in Nigeria are shown in Fig. 29. Twice each year the birds increased in weight by about 10 per cent as an adaptation to an impending period of difficulty, first at the start of the rains and secondly just before they started feeding their young. After each of these increases they rapidly lost the extra weight, during the early rains because, after the termites disappear, food is very

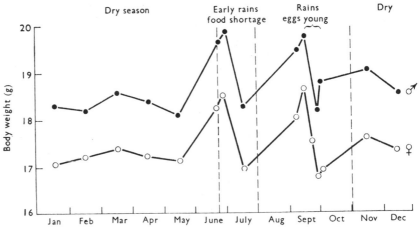

FIG. 29. Seasonal changes in weight of *Quelea quelea* in Nigeria (from Ward, 1963).

sparse, and when feeding young because they are evidently strained to raise their broods. While, however, the average weight of birds which had just raised young was as low as that of birds at the end of the early rains, the spread of measurements was very different in the two periods, all birds which had just raised young being close to a low average, whereas in the early rains many individuals were heavy with much fat and many other extremely light. I argued earlier (1954, see also p. 284) that the latter type of weight-distribution was to be expected where birds were competing with each other for food, particularly because individuals successful in disputes for food would tend to win each time and so would maintain their weight, while those which failed would quickly go under and die. Hence this provides further evidence that the birds were up against a limit set by food shortage in the early rains.

At the start of the early rains, which are at first extremely local in their incidence, the Queleas often moved locally to areas where rain had not yet fallen and dry seeds were still available. Later, in early August, most of them left Ward's study area altogether for about a fortnight. A small proportion went north to districts where the rains had not yet started, and one roost here was thought to have included well over ten million birds, while most went south, to districts where the rains had been established some weeks and fresh green seeds were available, and it was then that they damaged the millet crops. Later, the birds returned in large numbers to breed. Although these movements took place each year, they occurred over so short a period that they seem best classified as nomadic rather than migratory, and similar nomadism also occurs in the Sudan (P. J. Dare, pers. comm.). But in East Africa there are evidently big and fairly regular migrations over great distances between Tanganyika and Kenya (see especially Haylock, 1959).

Finally Ward obtained some interesting information on the sex ratio. The Quelea, as already mentioned, is monogamous, and the sex ratio of breeding adults in the colonies is about equal. It is also about equal in both newly hatched and newly fledged young. But in the course of the dry season, at least in two years, there was a progressive shift in favour of males. The proportion of males found among large numbers of Queleas shot at random from feeding or drinking flocks was 50 per cent early in the dry season (October and November), 57 per cent in the middle of the dry season (December to February), 68 per cent late in the dry season (March to May), and 81 per cent at its end (in June and July). As there is no reason to think that the females (or indeed any Queleas) dispersed from the study area during the dry season, Ward concluded that in this period females died in greater numbers than males, which could well have been due to competition for food in which the females tended to come off worse than the males. The problem of how the sex ratio returns to normal by the start of the following dry season has not yet been resolved.

Two seasons' work in Nigeria, combined with a general knowledge of the ecology in other areas, is obviously not enough to establish how the huge numbers of the Quelea may be regulated, but there are some highly suggestive pointers. The reproductive output of about three young per pair per year is evidently determined by the feeding capacity of the parents. Of the factors which might possibly limit adult numbers, disease has not been recorded, while predators evidently take a negligible toll, mainly of fledged young in the colonies and of adults when food is short in the early rains, the latter presumably being birds that would otherwise have died of starvation. Hence the size of the population may well be determined by food shortage. In the second half of one, but not the other, dry season studied in Nigeria, a change in the diet from small to large seeds indicated that the supply of the preferred small seeds was being exhausted, but whether large seeds in turn became sufficiently sparse for birds to starve is not known. The ecological situation is simple in that all the seeds on which the birds depend during the dry season have been formed by the end of the preceding rainy season. Hence from November to the end of June the amount of available food steadily declines, mainly through consumption by Queleas and other animals. Under these circumstances, the availability of food depends initially on the size of the seed crops, and thereafter on the density of the Queleas and other animals which eat it, so that the situation is one in which a density-dependent limitation of numbers by food shortage is likely to occur. Finally, the dry season is succeeded by a few weeks in which food becomes extremely sparse and many birds probably die of starvation, but in this period the situation is complicated by movements to other areas, so that details are not known. To conclude, there is suggestive evidence that the Quelea population is limited in a density-dependent manner by food shortage around the end of the dry season, and nothing points against this view, but quantitative observations are needed to prove it.

Before ending this chapter, mention should be made of the many remarkable similarities in habits and adaptations between the Quelea in Africa and the Tricolored Blackbird or Redwing, *Agelaius tricolor* in California, studied by Orians (1960, 1961*a*, *b*). The Quelea, as already mentioned, belongs to the Ploceinae, a group restricted to Africa save for a few species in Asia. The Tricolor belongs to an unrelated New World family, the Icteridae, which includes the oropendolas, American orioles, grackles, meadow-larks, and other diverse species. Since, in the ways to be discussed, the Quelea and the Tricolor are more like each other than is either to the other members of its family, it seems safe to say that the resemblances between them are convergent adaptations to a similar way of life.

The Tricolor occurs primarily in California in the Great Valley formed by the Sacramento and San Joaquin rivers, an area now so highly cultivated that the natural habitat of the bird up to a century ago has virtually vanished, and one cannot tell what its ecology then was. Formerly, there were big marshes and extensive winter and spring floods. There were also huge swarms of locusts, which may well have been the main food of the Tricolor when breeding, as they still bring chiefly members of this family of insects to their young. Most areas were later drained, but there has been an artificial return to something approaching former conditions with the introduction of rice grown by irrigation in spring.

The Tricolor is nomadic outside the breeding season. Feeding flocks often 'roll' forward like Quelea flocks. In general, the Tricolor seems more insectivorous than the Quelea, particularly when feeding its young, though it has been recorded bringing soft green seeds to its nestlings, and after breeding it feeds extensively on the seeds of the grass *Echinochloa* and on cultivated rice, which are two of the favourite foods of the Quelea. The nesting colonies have at times included two hundred thousand pairs, and though this is only one-fiftieth of the size of the largest recorded Quelea colony, one does not know what happened before the Great Valley was cultivated, and even as it is, no other passerine bird except the Quelea has colonies approaching this size. The usual nesting site is in cattails, *Typha*, over water, and though the Quelea usually breeds in thorn trees, it at times uses rushes over water. As in the Quelea, all the birds in one section of a colony usually start laying within a day or two of each other, while often the members of a whole colony do so.

In the Tricolor the commonest clutch is 3, while 4 is proportionately rather commoner than in the Quelea. The third nestling in a brood sometimes starves, which suggests, as in the Quelea, that the average clutch may correspond with the greatest number of young that the parents can normally raise. The Tricolor differs from the Quelea in being polygynous, correlated with which the males do not assume breeding plumage or breed until they are two years old, whereas the females evidently breed when a year old. The latter also holds in the closely related Redwing, *Agelaius phoeniceus*, which nests solitarily, and in which each male has two to four females, whereas there are only two females or less to each male in the colonies of the Tricolor. Further, the Tricolor resembles the Quelea in that both parents regularly feed the brood, whereas in the related Redwing the male takes only a small share. Hence, as in the Quelea, the trend of evolution has been away from polygyny and towards monogamy, with both parents feeding the brood, but this trend has not been carried so far in the Tricolor. The Quelea has an accelerated incubation period, but in the Tricolor it usually lasts eleven or twelve days and is at most only slightly shorter than that of the related Redwing and Yellow-headed Blackbird, *Xanthocephalus xanthocephalus*, in both of which it is normally twelve days (G. H. Orians and R. B. Payne, pers. comm.). Tricolor colonies, like Quelea colonies, are deserted at times, for reasons not fully understood. In some deserted colonies all the eggs were destroyed, which Orians attributed to an unidentified predator, but the possibility that the Tricolors themselves might have been responsible before deserting does not seem to be excluded, a suggestion with which Orians (pers. comm.) agreed.

Finally, Orians was able to study a problem not yet investigated in the Quelea, namely the relation between the size of the colonies and the food supplies. As shown in Table 30, most of the colonies alongside the poorest feeding areas, in grazing and dry farming land in the foothills, consisted of under a thousand birds. At the opposite extreme, most of the colonies adjacent to flooded rice fields with abundant food consisted of over ten thousand birds. The average size of the colonies

TABLE 30

Relation of habitat to size of colony and date of laying in the Tricolored Blackbird, *Agelaius tricolor*

Habitat	Number of colonies of			Mean date of laying	
	<1000	*1000–10000*	*>10000*	*1959*	*1960*
1. Grazing and dry farming in foothills	7	2	1	21 April	4 May
2. Irrigated valley crops excluding rice areas	3	2	3	1 May	6 May
3. Irrigated rice areas	0	3	7	8 May	17 May

Note. From Orians (1961*b*).

in irrigated valley land not used for rice was intermediate, and so, presumably, was the food supply. It may be added that, owing to the date when the rice fields are irrigated, suitable food for the Tricolors is not available there so early as in the foothills. Correspondingly, breeding started about a fortnight later alongside the rice fields than in the foothills, the birds in irrigated valley land not used for rice again being intermediate.

Hence, within a comparatively small area over which the birds roam freely outside the breeding season, both the size of the colonies and the date of laying in each varied markedly, in close adjustment with the feeding conditions. How the timing of laying is regulated is not known. It might presumably be due to visual inspection, perhaps of some factor linked with the subsequent appearance of suitable food. Evidently it is not a response to rain in spring, though the irregular autumnal breeding of this species followed a fortnight after heavy rains (Orians, 1960).

The adjustment of the size of the colonies to the food supplies is harder to understand. Orians found that, before a colony settled to breed, it might consist of twice or even four times the number of birds that eventually bred. Further, the flocks took repeated flights over the surrounding country, the number of flights seeming very excessive if their object were merely to find food for present consumption. He therefore concluded that these flights were 'a special case of the general phenomenon of environmental evaluation among birds', and that the size of the colonies was regulated by this means. But how, after an 'evaluation' had been made, each colony was reduced to the ecologically appropriate size, and how it was determined which individuals should breed and which leave, is not known. Whatever means are used, the evaluation and response apparently take only a few days, whereas in other colonial birds, such as the Heron, as discussed elsewhere (1954; see also p. 287), newcomers to a colony wait a year or more before actually breeding. The problem of dispersion is evidently of a specialized type in the Quelea and Tricolor, and would repay further study.

Tricolored Blackbirds

Summarizing, the Quelea, an African weaver-bird, breeds in colonies which at times exceed a million pairs. Breeding is normally very successful, because the immense numbers 'swamp' the few predators, while the birds breed in the second half of the rainy season alongside abundant insects and grass seeds. However, there was some evidence for starvation in large broods, the parents lose weight while feeding young, and the species is monogamous, both sexes raising the brood, whereas other graminivorous weavers are polygynous and only the female raises the brood. The main food in the dry season consists of the small seeds of five species of wild grasses, and larger seeds, including human crops, are taken primarily when small seeds become scarce. The size of the population is almost certainly limited by the availability of foot at the start of the rainy season, when the seeds that are left start germinating, feeding behaviour then becomes abnormal, the birds may lose weight and emigration occurs. The Tricolored Blackbird, a Californian icterid, presents close parallels to the Quelea in breeding ecology, presumably due to convergent evolution. The size of its colonies and the date of laying in each colony are adjusted in some unknown way to the availability of food.

10

MANAKINS IN TRINIDAD

AS mentioned in the last chapter, most tropical land-birds live under one of two very different climatic systems, the one, experienced by the Quelea, with a short rainy season and abundant food followed by a dry season in which food becomes scarce, and the other, experienced by the birds discussed in the present chapter, in which rain falls during most months, so that conditions are humid and fairly similar throughout the year. The dominant vegetation also differs, in the former areas being grassland with deciduous trees and in the latter evergreen forest. While conditions in tropical evergreen forest vary much less in the course of the year than in most other habitats, they are not completely uniform, as there are differences in the amount of rain in each month, in the fruiting seasons of different trees and bushes, in the time of swarming of termites, and in the breeding seasons of birds, many though not all of which have restricted seasons, as shown, for instance, for Africa by Moreau (1950).

Manakins, which comprise the family Pipridae, are small fruit-eating birds of the tropical American forests renowned for their bizarre communal displays. (They should not be confused with mannikins, the name given to some of the Old World estrildine finches.) Together with the closely related Cotingidae (Bell-birds, Cock of the Rock, *etc.*)

Headpiece: Male Black and White Manakins on their courts.

165

and Tyrannidae (tyrant flycatchers), which are also confined to the New World, they are placed in the primitive (sub-oscine) section of the passerine order. The first detailed ecological study of a member of this group, on which the present chapter is based, was that of D. W. Snow (1962*a*) on the Black and White Manakin, *Manacus manacus*, which he carried out over 4½ years at the New York Zoological Society's field station in the Arima valley, Trinidad, West Indies. He also studied more briefly the ecology of the Golden-headed Manakin, *Pipra erythro-cephala*, in the same area (Snow, 1962*b*). As yet these are the only long-term population studies of any birds of tropical forest and their chief interest is in demonstrating a low adult mortality, correlated with a low reproductive rate.

M. manacus is a bird of secondary forest rich in berry-bearing trees and shrubs, those of the Melastomaceae, and to a lesser extent of the Rubiaceae, providing most of its food throughout the year as a succession of species come into fruit. Manakins also eat insects, for instance follow-ing driver ants for the insects that they flush, and they bring insects as well as fruit to their nestlings. The females and juveniles have dull plumage, while the adult males are brightly coloured and take no part in building, incubation or raising the young, but spend most of their time on communal display grounds, where each has an individual court, and where they are visited by the females for copulation. The birds are promiscuous, some males copulating with several females, and some females being observed to visit several males. This behaviour was first described by Chapman (1935) for the closely related *M. vitellinus* on Barro Colorado in the Panama Canal, Chapman being, incidentally, the first man to elucidate the significance of display by the use of stuffed specimens in the wild.

In the Arima valley, the males of *M. manacus* occupied their display courts almost throughout the year except when moulting. In an area of about 180 hectares, there were seven main display grounds, which between them included the courts of 205 individual males. Field observations suggested that about one-quarter of the males in the population were not established on courts, while trapping with mist-nets suggested that the sex ratio was equal. Hence the density was probably about three birds to the hectare, much higher than Snow found it for the same species on the American mainland, which he attributed to two factors. First, islands in general differ from the nearest mainland in having many fewer species, but some of those present may be much more abundant than on the mainland, and this evidently applies to *M. manacus* on Trinidad. Secondly, as the bird prefers open secondary forest, and as the species of Melastomaceae and Rubiaceae which provide its main diet are not used for timber, lumbering has produced unusually favourable conditions for the bird in the Trinidad forests.

In the Arima valley, the year is divided into a dry season from January to May and a wet season for the rest of the year, with sometimes a short dry spell in part of September and October. There is a succession of fruits suitable for manakins throughout the year, but the number of species of Melastomaceae in fruit is lowest between August and October and increases markedly from January to May, in which period the supply of insects also increases. In the five years studied, the time at which *M. manacus* started breeding was extremely variable. In the first season, apart from one nest in March, breeding began in late May and reached its peak in early June, in the next two seasons it started abruptly in mid-April, in the next there was one nest at the end of December and the main start was in early January, while in the last it started in late February. These marked variations were not correlated with the only conspicuous environmental change, the start of the rains, which varied only between late April and late May in the years in question. As the males normally occupied their courts from October through to June each year, the date of breeding was evidently determined primarily by the behaviour of the females. But the reason why the females should have started to visit the courts much earlier in some years than others is not known; possibly their food supply was involved, but there was no obvious parallel variation in the supply of fruits. It may be added that breeding started earlier, in one year by several weeks, in a more humid valley ten miles east of the Arima valley than at Arima itself.

In contrast to the start of breeding, its termination was relatively constant, occurring each year between late August and late September, and being followed immediately by the moult. Snow considered that this regularity must be primarily due, not to some factor influencing breeding, but to the need for the moult to occur at a particular season, and this conclusion was reinforced by the regularity in the timing of the moult of males in their second year, before their first breeding season. Most adults moulted between August and October, the outside limits being July and December, and each individual took about eighty days. Particular ringed males varied by up to two months in the time at which they started in different years, for unknown reasons. Young males retained the dull colouring characteristic of the juveniles and adult females until their second year, moulting into their bright plumage for the first time between June and September, a little earlier than the adults moulted. The second-year moult took place in these months irrespective of when the birds concerned left the nest, which might have been at any time between one and two years earlier, so that they got into phase with the adults before they bred for the first time. Clearly, the moult must be timed by some factor in the external environment, though Snow did not discover what this was, nor did he discover the adaptive significance of this timing.

The birds nested solitarily, each female having a small nesting territory. The inconspicuous nest, a thinly woven shallow cup, was normally slung in fine branches a few feet above the ground over or close to a stream, presumably to reduce the chance of its being seen and reached by a predator. The usual clutch was 2 eggs, laid 2 days apart, but 22 out of 244 clutches contained only 1 egg. Incubation lasted 18 or 19 days, which is longer than in most small passerine birds. The young left the nest after between 13 and 15 days and were attended by the female for about another 3 to 4 weeks. When in the nest, the young were fed, by regurgitation, on fruit with some insects, the rate of feeding increasing from once every 28 minutes on the first day to once every 18 minutes shortly before the young left the nest.

Despite the relative inaccessibility of the nests, only 40 per cent of the clutches hatched, and only 19 per cent produced fledged young, nearly all (at least 86 per cent) of the heavy losses being due to predation, mainly by snakes. On average, each nest gave rise to only 0·33 fledgling, those between January and April being particularly unsuccessful (0·13 per nest), those in May and June intermediate (0·35 per nest) and those in July and August the most successful (0·55 per nest). The reason for this seasonal variation is not known.

The female normally laid a succession of clutches, the interval between one brood leaving the nest and the start of the next clutch usually being 3 to 6 weeks. If a brood was lost, the next clutch followed any time from a few days to over 6 weeks later. The new clutch was often laid in the same nest, or one that was closely adjacent. One female had 5 successive clutches in a season, 2 others had 4, many others 3, and some only 2. The average number in any particular year depended on the date at which breeding started, which as already mentioned differed greatly, so that in different years the length of the breeding season varied between 4 and 8 months. In general, a female probably attempted about 3 broods a year, and if each brood produced an average of 0·33 young, this means that each female raised about one fledged young a year, a much lower rate than in the small passerine species of north temperate regions. Of 15 marked fledglings at least 5 were still alive a year later, and if this rate is representative, each female raised each year an average of 0·33 young which became yearlings.

If a population is stable, a low rate of reproduction must result in a low annual mortality. With the help of mist-nets, 38 adult males of *M.*

manacus which had display courts were caught and ringed, and of those alive one year, 89 per cent were still alive in the next year. As males with courts are strictly resident, this is probably the true rate of survival. An annual adult mortality of 11 per cent is far lower than that of any other passerine bird so far recorded (cf. Lack, 1954), but no species of tropical forest has previously been studied. Adult females also lived a long time, since of the first eight which were trapped, one vanished at once but at least five were still alive when the study finished. Also, since trapping indicated that the sex ratio was equal, the mortality rate of adult females was presumably similar to that of adult males.

The males of *M. manacus*, like those of other Pipridae, visit the communal display grounds as yearlings in juvenile-type plumage, but evidently do not breed. There would presumably be selection against breeding at a year old if display and bright colouring were dangerous, for instance increasing the risk of predation, and if at the same time one-year-old males were unlikely to obtain females, as might well hold with the intense competition of a promiscuous mating system. In contrast, the juvenile females visit the courts and probably breed when a year old, though this has not been proved with marked individuals. If the females first breed when a year old, if the sex ratio is equal, and if each female produces, on average, 0·33 yearling per year, a stable population of 100 birds should include 16·5 yearlings, and the annual mortality should likewise be 16·5 per cent. The recorded figure, as already mentioned, was 11 per cent. But the estimate of 16·5 per cent of yearlings depends on two very rough approximations, that one-third of the fledglings survived to be yearlings (based on only 15 birds), and that each female attempted three broods a year, and bearing this in mind, the agreement was as close as could be expected.

Snow postulated that the remarkably prolonged courtship displays of male manakins have been made possible by two ecological factors, first an abundance of food, and secondly the emancipation of the male from helping at the nest, which is itself a consequence of the abundance of food, as it enables the female to build, incubate and feed the young unaided. In support of this view, though the adult males did not feed in their courts, they left them for, on the average, only 10 per cent of the day, so presumably they needed at most only 10 per cent of their time for collecting food. Further, there was normally a succession of suitable fruiting trees throughout the year. Only twice during the study was fruit extremely scarce, in the second half of March in one season and from December to January in another, in both of which the males deserted their courts and in the first of them even visited cultivated guava trees in gardens to feed. Since only two such periods were observed in 4½ years, they are evidently rare, and even in these, at least most of the adult males evidently survived, as all 38 of the ringed males at courts returned afterwards.

Skutch (1949, see also 1961) considered that tropical passerine species, most of which have a clutch of two, could find enough food for more than this number of young, and the same *leitmotiv* has recurred in the works of Wagner (1957, 1961). Similarly Snow argued that, since the male Black and White Manakin can obtain all its food in under 10 per cent of the day, the female should in the course of the whole day be able to find much more food than is needed for herself and two nestlings. He therefore agreed with Skutch that the reason that such species have evolved a clutch of two cannot be because two is the greatest number of young which they can feed. Instead Skutch suggested, and Snow agreed, that if there were more than two young, the parent would have to bring food more frequently and would therefore be in greater danger of revealing the nest to predators. This view, as Snow pointed out, depends on a quantitative relationship, namely on whether the advantage of one or more additional nestlings would more than offset the postulated increase in predation, and this has not been tested. He added in conversation that the experimental addition of further nestlings would be difficult in manakins as the nest is very small, presumably to assist its concealment; and the nestlings, unlike those of temperate regions, are almost completely silent, presumably to reduce further their conspicuousness to predators.

While I agree that in tropical passerine species with open nests, the high rate of predation probably makes for a different balance between selection pressures from that found in north temperate regions, I am extremely doubtful whether Skutch's explanation constitutes the basic reason for their low clutch-size. The argument depends partly on the way in which predators find nests. All experienced egg-collectors whom I have consulted find nests 'by looking in likely places', not by watching the parent birds, and their consummate craft shows what can be achieved by this means. Admittedly, the human parallel is dangerous. However, it was found that as many nests of the Long-tailed Tit, *Aegithalos caudatus*, in Wytham were destroyed by predators in periods when the parents paid few visits, during laying and incubation, as in periods when the parents paid many visits, during building and feeding the young (D. and E. Lack, 1958). Hence the predators in question, chiefly Jays, *Garrulus glandarius*, did not find most nests by watching the parent birds. It does not follow, of course, that the same holds for snakes and other predators in tropical forest, but this becomes clear from Snow's figures for *M. manacus*, since the percentage of the available nests lost was 60 per cent with eggs and 52·5 per cent with young (because 19 per cent in all survived). Hence, as incubation lasted about four days longer than the nestling period, the rate of predation was extremely similar in both periods. But the female left her eggs during incubation only about once an hour, whereas she brought food to her nestlings up to nearly four times an hour. Presumably, therefore, the predators paid little if any attention to the visits of the parent bird, as otherwise the rate of predation should have been three or four times as high with nestlings as with eggs. Probably, visits by the parents somewhat increase the chance that a nest will be found by predators, as if it were not so, passerine birds would hardly have evolved such surreptitious means of approach, but this is evidently of minor importance.

I therefore think it likely that predation is not the main factor which has led to the evolution of a clutch of two in manakins, and that further study should be made to determine whether two might be the largest number of young for which the parent can find enough food. Admittedly fruits are abundant during the breeding season, but they are not a satisfactory diet from which to form proteins. That is perhaps why, despite the high nest predation, the female manakin differs from most other passerine birds in laying her second egg two days, instead of one, after the first egg; and if she has difficulty in getting enough protein to form an egg, she might have even more difficulty in collecting enough for two growing young. Snow found many more remains of fruit than insects below nests with young, but fruit is more likely to leave remains than insects, so insects perhaps comprise more of the nestlings' diet than he thought. Hence the critical factor limiting brood-size might be the time taken by the female to find insects, but this needs testing, if possible by the experimental addition of young. Should two prove to be the greatest number of young that a female can raise at one time, the further point remains of why, from the long-term evolutionary standpoint, natural selection should not, instead, have resulted in a clutch and brood of four, with the male parent helping to feed the young.

Snow also thought that the population density of the adult manakins was not limited by the food supply since, as already mentioned, fruits were abundant almost the whole time, while the males apparently survived even the two observed periods of shortage. Further, *M. manacus* does not at any time of the year lay up fat reserves. The latter are a normal adaptation in small passerine and other birds which experience a regular seasonal food shortage, as in many British resident species in winter and in the Quelea at the start of the rains (see p. 158). The absence of such reserves in *M. manacus* implies that in Trinidad these birds experience no regular season of food shortage. It does not, however, rule out the possibility of irregular shortages, or of the population being close to the limit set by food for much of the time. Evidently the numbers of the manakin were not normally near the limit set by the availability of fruits. However, the marked differences in the time at which breeding started each year were apparently not connected with the fruit supply, so the availability of insects might possibly have been critical, and this would also help to explain the two-day instead of one-day interval between the eggs in the clutch, already mentioned. Also, in the period of fruit shortage in December and January when Black and White Manakins deserted their courts, all Golden-headed Manakins did so too, but this was in a locality six miles from the Arima valley where fruit was plentiful, which again suggests that the insect diet would repay further study.

In discussion, Snow attributed at least most of the 11 per cent mortality among the adult males to predation. As the sex ratio is nearly equal, such predation presumably falls equally on both sexes, and though females probably incur an extra risk through predation on the nest, males perhaps do so on their display courts. In the latter connection Gilliard (1959) pointed out that manakins, like other tropical passerine species which display near the ground, spend much time keeping their courts clear of leaves, which might well be an adaptation to reduce the chance of a predator approaching unobserved. While, however, predation on adult manakins may be important, it seems unlikely that it could be density-dependent. It is also impossible that *M. manacus* could provide the main food for any predator, since their density is only about 3 to the hectare, while only about 11 per cent of them, or 1 per 3 hectares, die each year. Further, there are no hawks which prey primarily on small birds in the Trinidad forests, *Spizaetus* eating large birds and *Harpagus* mainly lizards. There is also no evidence for disease in manakins.

Finally, there is no reason to think that the number of resident male *M. manacus* was limited through their communal displays, as postulated by Wynne-Edwards (1962, p. 208), who wrote of the courts of the closely related *M. vitellinus* that they 'serve all the purposes of property, and it seems fairly safe to conclude that the number of courts tends to remain very constant, placing a ceiling on the number of males that are candidates for mating within a particular area'. Wynne-Edwards provided no evidence whatever for this statement, nor was it based on the observations of Chapman (1935), whose descriptions of the display he relied on. It is true that each male manakin owns an exclusive court or territory, from which it excludes other males. But there appears to be room at the display grounds for many more courts, and no observer has witnessed the males in occupation attempting to restrict the number of courts, or has provided any indirect evidence that this might happen. Wynne-Edwards continued that 'the number of females coming in for fertilization must be known to all members of the display group whether they are performers or onlookers, and the regulation (i.e. the giving or withholding) of this essential office could thus presumably reside with them'. Snow (pers. comm.) commented that there is no reason to think that the latter holds, and he thought it likely that a male would copulate with any female that offered itself. As mentioned later (p. 306), Wynne-Edwards similarly postulated that a function of the leks of the Blackcock, *Lyrurus tetrix*, is to regulate the number of females fecundated, and for this likewise there is no evidence, though many observers, including myself (1939), have studied this species. Moreover, mutual advertisement and sexual selection in the wide sense provide a sufficient explanation of these communal displays.

Summing up, I consider that the population density of the Black and White Manakin is not regulated by social behaviour, or by disease, and probably not by predation, though the last requires further study, and that while Snow's work shows that the supply of fruits could not normally be limiting, the possibility of limitation by food, particularly insects, remains open and should be investigated further.

Snow (1962b) made briefer observations on a second and smaller species, the Golden-headed Manakin, *Pipra eythrocephala*, which has very similar feeding and breeding habits. Its food consists mainly of the fruits of Melastomaceaea and Rubiaceae, though it does not take such large fruits as *M. manacus*. Also, it feeds higher in the trees and takes a higher proportion of insects. The males have a similar elaborate communal display, they assume their bright plumage in their second year, and the pattern of the moult is also the same as in *M. manacus*. As in *M. manacus* also, the females undertake the whole of nest-building, incubation and the care of the young.

P. erythrocephala was even more abundant than *M. manacus*, with certainly more than three, and perhaps two or three times as many, individuals to the hectare. The breeding season was similar, between January and August, mainly in the latter part of this period. Only 15 nests were found, probably because this species usually nests higher off the ground than *M. manacus*. These nests included 4 clutches of 2 eggs and 1 of 1 egg, the second egg in clutches of 2 being laid after an interval of 2 days, as in *M. manacus*. All 15 nests were destroyed, so predation is evidently as high as in *M. manacus*. The annual mortality could not be estimated from the recapture of marked individuals, but was probably similar to that of *M. manacus*. Of the first 200 adult birds trapped, 89 were in adult male plumage. If the sex ratio was equal, and if those caught were an unbiased sample with respect to age and sex, this means that there were 11 yearling males, and this proportion should, in a stable population, be equal to the adult mortality.

The reproductive rate and adult mortality have recently been measured in one other tropical passerine species the estrildine firefinch, *Lagonosticta senegala*, in Senegal (Morel, 1964). This is a widespread species in semi-arid country in tropical Africa and has also spread into villages and towns. It eats mainly grass seed. The average clutch in 112 nests found by Morel was 3·4 eggs, 45 per cent of the eggs hatched and 28 per cent of them gave rise to fledged young. Many losses of nestlings were due to the viduine brood-parasite *Hypochera chalybeata*, which laid in 44 per cent of the observed nests; of the young firefinches which hatched successfully, three-quarters were raised in unparasitized nests but only about half in parasitized nests. Despite these losses, the reproductive rate was high, because breeding took place during nine months of the year, and one ringed male was observed to raise four successive broods. If the latter was typical, each pair raised about 3½ young per year. Further, irrespective of the date of hatching, the young birds started to breed at the beginning of the next breeding season, when some of them were only three or four months old. The annual mortality of the adult male was estimated by two different methods at about 70 per cent, the highest figure recorded for any bird population. While the habitat, gardens and a park near the Senegal River, had been greatly modified by man, a high mortality is an inevitable consequence of a high reproductive rate, and there is therefore no reason to think that the figure would have been substantially different in the natural habitat of the species.

Since so little has been recorded of the ecology of frugivorous birds, mention may be made of another, but quite unrelated, species studied in Trinidad by Snow (1961, 1962c), namely the Oil-bird, *Steatornis caripensis*. This remarkable species, usually classified with the nightjars in the family Caprimulgidae, resembles them in general coloration and in being nocturnal, but differs in being much larger, in eating fruit not insects, and in nesting in large groups in dark caves, through which it finds its way by echo-location (sonar). Both sexes share in nesting activities, indeed they probably pair for life. In Trinidad, the laying season extends from December to September inclusive, with a peak between March and May, and most young are in the nest when the greatest variety of fruits is available. The normal clutch consists of 1 to 4 eggs, successive eggs being laid several days apart, and sometimes a week apart. The average clutch is 2·7 eggs, and it is larger earlier than later in the season, probably correlated with the food supply. Incubation lasts 33 to 34 days and the nestling period is unusually long and unusually variable, between 90 and 125 days. Just under half of the observed nestings were successful, and of the young which hatched, just under 60 per cent were known to have left the nest. Dark caves presumably provide safety from nest predators. The cause of most losses was uncertain, and starvation was thought to be unimportant, except possibly in the first few days after hatching. When 70 days old, the young weighed 1½ times as much as the adults, owing to fat deposits which Snow considered might be an adaptation to conserve heat losses in cool caves. Later, however, he suggested (pers. comm.) that, if the young are to obtain enough proteins, they must eat large quantities of fruit, and since the fruit is rich in oil, there is little they can do with the fat except to deposit it. In most nestlings which have big fat deposits, such as shearwaters, the fat acts as a reserve for periods

Oil-birds in their nesting cave.

of starvation, but there is no reason to think that young Oil-birds have periods of food shortage. A full breeding cycle took about five months, and many pairs made only one attempt to breed in a year. But a few pairs raised two broods in a year, while others started a second attempt after loss of a first; the second clutch was laid after an interval of 19 to 65 days. Most birds moulted between June and November, when not engaged in breeding, but some of them must have undertaken part of their moult while breeding. The moult was not precisely timed in any one individual but evidently lasted several months.

Their nocturnal feeding habits, their nesting in dark caves and their cryptic plumage would not have been evolved by Oil-birds except against predators, but predation does not seem an important cause of mortality under present conditions in Trinidad (excluding human predation on the nestlings for fat). Also no evidence was found for food shortage, though the long interval between successive eggs in a clutch, and between the end of one brood and the next clutch, also the prolonged and variable nesting period, suggest that it is hard for the birds to make proteins from fruit pericarps. Hence the factors which might regulate the Oil-bird population are not known. The main interest of this study in relation to that on manakins is to show that a fruit diet does not necessarily lead to the female raising the family alone, and hence to elaborate male displays.

Summarizing, the Black and White Manakin feeds mainly on fruit, with some insects. The birds are promiscuous, the cocks having elaborate displays and taking no part in raising the young. The clutch is two, and each hen raises a succession of broods, but owing to heavy nesting losses through predation, the number of young raised was normally small, about one fledgling per hen per year. Correspondingly, the annual mortality of the adults was only about 11 per cent, lower than in any other passerine species so far investigated. While Snow, who made this study, considered that predation was probably the main factor both restricting brood-size and regulating adult numbers, I consider that in both contexts the insect foods deserve further investigation. The Golden-headed Manakin has closely similar breeding ecology to the Black and White Manakin. The Senegal Firefinch, a grassland species, has a much higher reproductive rate and an annual adult mortality of about 70 per cent. The unusual breeding ecology is described of another frugivorous species in Trinidad, the Oil-bird.

11

THE WOOD PIGEON IN RURAL ENGLAND

IN primaeval Europe the Wood Pigeon, *Columba palumbus*, was presumably a forest species, eating during at least much of the year foods found in forests, such as the seeds and leaves of ground vegetation, tree flowers, and such seeds as acorns and beechmast, and being preyed upon by large raptors such as the Goshawk, *Accipiter gentilis*. In modern England, however, it lives primarily in the artificial habitat of farmland, feeding especially on grain and the leaves of clover and brassicas, nesting in hedges and copses, and roosting in winter in copses; the raptors have largely gone but the Wood Pigeon is itself shot by man in winter. It still enters woods to eat acorns or beechmast where these are available, but it is plentiful in many areas without them. It is not possible to say what factors may have regulated its numbers in primaeval times, and its present habitat is so artificial and disturbed that it might have been thought that the English population would be too unstable to reveal principles relevant to this book. However, work by a team under R. K. Murton of the Infestation Control Laboratory of the Ministry of Agriculture, Fisheries, and Food has shown that the population attains a balance in this environment, due primarily to inter-action with its main food in late winter the clover. The present chapter is based on successive papers by Murton (1958, 1961), Murton and Isaacson (1962, 1964), Murton, Isaacson, and Westwood (1963*a*, *b*) and Murton, Westwood, and Isaacson (1964 and 1965).

Headpiece: Wood Pigeons.

177

The study was made in open farmland at Carlton in south Cambridge-shire, at first on just over 700 hectares, later extended to just under 1000 hectares, while comparative nesting studies were made at Spikehall Wood, a few miles distant. Parent Wood Pigeons feed their young on seeds, mainly grain, supplemented particularly in the early stages by 'pigeon milk', a secretion from the crop rich in proteins. Cereal grains, are much the most important food for both adults and juveniles in late summer and autumn, first on the standing crops and later, as soon as it becomes available, on the stubble. In winter, after the grain has gone, the birds depend primarily on clover leaves, and when these are covered with snow, on brassicas. At Carlton, between 50 and 60 per cent of the land is sown with wheat or barley, with a very little oats, and about 15 per cent of these fields are undersown with clover. Some of the latter are left for four or five years as leys, so that nearly 30 per cent of the cultivated fields provide clover, to which must be added 10 per cent of permanent grass pasture which includes clover. The remaining land, being used for root crops and beans, is little utilized by the Wood Pigeon. Few brassicas are grown. In addition to the fields, there are some 40 hectares of woodland, where the birds nest and roost in the trees, but these copses do not provide any appreciable quantity of food as they contain very few oaks or beeches. On the whole area there were about 700 breeding pairs of Wood Pigeons, and rather over 3000 birds were present in October, which decreased from then until the summer. Probably a small proportion of the juveniles moved out of the area in the autumn, and in some years there was a correspond-ing small immigration in spring. During the winter, other birds moved out very temporarily while snow was lying but returned when it melted. Except for a virtually complete exodus during the cold weather of 1962–3, such movements had little influence on the numbers present.

The breeding season was extended, eggs being laid between mid-March and late October, with a decided peak between mid-July and mid-September, so that most young were in the nest when food was most plentiful, around the time of the grain harvest. In some years, but not others, there were two peaks in laying activity, the second being due to the start of second broods, but this tendency was always blurred, and in some years concealed, because many of the first broods were destroyed by predators at irregular intervals during incubation and the birds concerned laid again soon afterwards. Since incubation takes eighteen days and the young stay in the nest about twenty days, it would be possible for a pair of Wood Pigeons to raise three broods between late June and late October each year, but nesting losses were so high that it is doubtful if any did so. The main laying period is later than that of any other British bird, while only one other species, the related Rock Dove, *Columba livia*, has a more extended season, laying in every month (Lees, 1946).

Murton found that the gonads of the Wood Pigeon are in breeding condition for longer each year than the period in which laying actually takes place, and he concluded that the main proximate factor inducing laying was the food supply. Between November and the spring, when they depend on clover, they need to feed throughout the day to get enough for themselves, and this suffices to explain why breeding did not occur then. Each year a few pairs laid eggs in the spring, but nestlings in May were fed chiefly on the seeds of weeds such as *Ranunculus* and *Cerastium* and fared badly, and it was only when cereal grains became available in late July that the young grew well. In 1958, for instance, omitting a few nestlings taken by predators, the parents raised only 9 out of 21 young hatched in late June and early July as compared with 32 out of 35 hatched in August and September, most of these deaths being due to starvation. A long potential breeding season, with food as the proximate factor inducing laying, is presumably what has enabled the Wood Pigeon to adapt its breeding season so successfully to man's grain harvest. Its main breeding season could well have been different in primaeval times. Indeed, it is different at the present time in London, where the birds do not depend on the grain harvest, and though the limits of the laying season are as extended as at Carlton, the main laying period comes as much as two months earlier, in May and the first half of June (S. Cramp, pers. comm.). The food situation in London has not been studied in detail to determine why May is the most favoured month there.

The clutch of the Wood Pigeon is almost invariably two, and the single eggs occasionally recorded may well be due to loss of the second. Losses of eggs were heavy, due primarily to predation by Jays, *Garrulus glandarius*, and Magpies, *Pica pica*. A watch on part of Carlton wood showed that, on the average, the area was searched by a Jay or Magpie once every 5·7 hours of daylight during the summer. Jays and Magpies do not usually take eggs from a nest on which a Wood Pigeon is sitting, and normally the eggs are covered the whole time, the female sitting from evening to morning and the male relieving her from 10.00 to 17.00 hours each day. However, the eggs are left uncovered, and so are liable to be taken by predators, when food is sparse and the incubating birds cannot obtain enough during their normal times off, also when adjacent pairs fight with each other, or when the sitting bird is frightened off by a human observer.

The nesting success of the Wood Pigeon in the two Cambridgeshire woods studied has been compared in Table 31. At Spikehall a game-keeper destroyed many Jays and Magpies, which were very scarce, but

TABLE 31

Comparison of egg and nestling losses of Wood Pigeon in two
woods, Carlton (1959–61) with heavy predation by Corvidae,
Spikehall (1961–2) with much less

Month	Carlton (10·5 hectares)			Spikehall (0·65 hectares)		
	Number of eggs laid	% Hatched	% Young flying of those hatched	Number of eggs laid	% Hatched	% Young flying of those hatched
May, June	62	19	100	58	69	88
July	153	55	92	192	66	94
Aug.	133	65	99	121	55	100
Sept.	63	56	86	123	63	92

Notes. Data from Murton and Isaacson (1964) but with the figures for Carlton in 1962 excluded (by R. K. Murton, pers. comm.) as in that year predators were shot there.

this applied only in 1962 at Carlton, where in the other years Jays and Magpies were numerous. Because of this, the proportion of eggs taken by predators was, in all, twice as high at Carlton (omitting 1962) as at Spikehall (46 per cent cf. 23 per cent). The difference was greatest in May and June, when the proportion taken was 81 per cent at Carlton and only 31 per cent at Spikehall. The high predation in this period occurred because food was short, so that Wood Pigeons sometimes left their eggs uncovered in order to feed. In August and September, the rate of predation was similar in both woods, probably because, though predators were commoner at Carlton, the density of nests was much higher at Spikehall (74 cf. 22 per hectare in 1961 and 1962), and predation tends to be higher with higher densities of nests.

This last tendency was demonstrated in an earlier study of six different localities, the proportion of eggs which gave rise to flying young being on the average 24 per cent where nests were less than 10 yards apart and 32 per cent where they were more than 10 yards apart (Murton, 1958). At Carlton, losses of eggs from predation were distinguished from other losses, and Table 32 shows that predation was higher in the years when more pairs nested, though figures for only 4 years are not enough on which to base a firm conclusion (the figures for 1962 were not comparable with those for other years, as already noted). If the rate of predation is higher at higher densities, it is probably due partly to the more frequent disputes between neighbours at higher

TABLE 32

Relation of egg predation and recruitment to density of Wood Pigeon nests at Carlton

Year	Density of nests per acre	% Eggs taken by predators	% Young fledged of eggs laid	No. of young raised per pair
1959	29	56	41	2·6
1960	25	44	50	2·8
1961	20	31	66	3·1
1962	25	18	68	3·1
1963	16	26	55	2·9

Notes. Data from Murton and Isaacson (1964). Nest predators were destroyed in 1962.

densities, so that the eggs are left uncovered more often, and partly to predators searching more intensively in areas where they find more nests. The disputes between neighbours may be regarded as a form of territorial behaviour, which helps to space out the nests and therefore makes them less conspicuous to predators. But there is no reason to think that this behaviour limits the density of nesting pairs, which varied greatly, and the defended areas are not, of course, used for feeding.

Table 32 also shows that though the proportion of eggs taken at Carlton varied in different years between 18 and 56 per cent, the number of young raised varied only between 3·1 and 2·6 per pair. This is because the birds which lose their eggs soon lay again, and as the breeding season is extended, they have several further opportunities to raise a brood. Young Wood Pigeons are rarely taken by predators, and most of the few losses were due to starvation, particularly early in the season, as already mentioned. This raises the question of whether the clutch of the Wood Pigeon is adapted to the number of young that it can raise. To test this, Murton added an extra nestling to one brood in August and to another in September. In the August brood all three young grew well, though one accidentally fell from the nest shortly before it would have flown, while in the September brood two grew well and the third extremely poorly. The results are therefore inconclusive, but in any case they refer to an artificial food supply, the grain harvest, and not to the unknown and presumably less rich conditions in which the Wood Pigeon evolved its clutch of two. One point is clear, however, that the Wood Pigeon does not modify its clutch in accordance with feeding conditions, virtually always laying two eggs, whether in April or May when food is so sparse that the nestlings often starve, or in August when grain is so plentiful that, at least on one occasion, a pair could find enough food for three young. This constancy is unusual in birds, and may possibly be linked with the fact that in the early stages the young are fed on 'pigeon milk'. Few other kinds of birds secrete food for their young.

As Wood Pigeons depend in the autumn and winter first on grain and later on clover, Murton and his team counted both the grain and the clover leaves per square foot on different types of field at Carlton, and thus obtained indices of the abundance of these foods each year. A Wood Pigeon eats about 50 grams, or 1200 grains, of wheat or barley in a day, so that the average population present at Carlton just after breeding would eat about 4.89 million grains a day. At this time there were roughly 903 million grains available which, if they disappeared solely through the activities of the Wood Pigeons, would have lasted them for some 26 weeks. But half the stubble in which the grain lies was usually ploughed up at the end of October, and from this date onward only about 239 million grains remained, enough for about another 7 weeks. The speed at which the birds pick up grain increases with its density up to about 15 grains per square foot, when they take about 30 grains a minute. At the other end of the scale, they take about 10 grains a minute at a density of 0.2 grain per square foot, below which they do not normally feed on it, presumably because it is too sparse. Wood Pigeons feeding on grain do not spend so long each day in collecting food as they do when feeding on clover in winter.

Clover leaves are the main food taken after the grain has gone, *Trifolium pratense*, the large Red Clover in the leys, being a richer source of food than *T. repens*, the small White Clover of the permanent pastures. Clover leaves reach their lowest density between late January and early March, almost certainly due to the activities of the Wood Pigeons, which throughout the study area removed on the average 46 per cent of the available leaves and in some fields in some years as much as 89 per cent. There is a little growth during the winter, and a proportion of the leaves eaten are replaced by the plant, Murton estimating that about another 36 per cent of clover leaves would have been present in the area at the end of the winter if there had been no Wood Pigeons. These figures suggest that the Wood Pigeon population is up against the limit set by food in winter. This is also suggested by the fact that, at this season, the birds spend about 95 per cent of the available daylight in active feeding, pecking at a rate of 60 to 100 times each minute, or some 34900 times in a day, taking about 44 grams dry weight of clover and 3 grams of other food in a day, and storing 10 to 14 per cent of the food taken in the crop, to be consumed during the night. An indication of the amount of clover usually taken was obtained in the severe winter of 1962–3 when, owing to thick snow, no birds could get at the clover between late December and the first week of March. At the end of this time, clover stocks were 25 per cent higher on the leys, 40 per cent higher on the pastures, and 38 per cent higher on the stubble, than in the other years, presumably due to the protection from Wood Pigeons provided by the snow. After early March, fresh clover leaves grow quickly, and the time of food shortage then ends.

The number of Wood Pigeons on the Carlton estate was counted at intervals throughout the year, and Table 33 shows the most important figures. These have been expressed not as actual numbers but as numbers per 40 hectares, because the study area was enlarged at one stage. The proportion of juveniles in the population has also been shown, this being calculated for the period just after breeding from the average

TABLE 33

Numbers of Wood Pigeons and proportion of juveniles at Carlton

	1958–9	1959–60	1960–1	1961–2	1962–3	1963–4
			Number of birds per 40 hectares			
Post-breeding (calculated)	—	171	152	129	164	101
December (maximum)	117+	62	174	51	104	41
Feb.–March (minimum)	97	34	83	64	1	33
April (maximum)	101	59	52	88	61	32
July (breeding)	74	64	51	64	41	49
			Percentages of juveniles			
Post-breeding (calculated)	—	57	58	60	61	60
February (shot sample)	35	11	46	16	24	48
			Food indices			
Grain index (average Oct.–Dec.)	—	58	335	26	255	—
Clover index (minimum Feb.–Mar.)	—	1338	1887	1676	0(1860)	1132

Notes. From Murton, Isaacson, & Westwood (1964, Table 8, extended pers. comm.). The population was not counted in December 1958 so the figure for January 1959 was used, but followed by ' + ' because it might have been a little higher in December. The bracketed clover index for 1962–63 was that under the snow.

number of young raised per pair (set out in Table 32), and measured in February on the basis of shot birds, which showed no age bias. The indices for grain in autumn and clover in winter have been added to the table. The way in which they were obtained need not concern us, since it is the comparative figures which are of special interest.

The Wood Pigeon population is normally highest just after breeding, at about the end of September. The post-breeding totals in Table 33, like those given earlier for the Great Tit (p. 58), have been assessed from the number of breeding pairs and the average number of young raised per pair, so they are somewhat higher than the number of birds actually alive at any one time, as some fledged young probably died before others left the nest. The census figures for December show that by then, in four out of five years, there was a marked reduction in numbers, probably due mainly to mortality, but perhaps also to a small number of juvenile birds moving out. In the other season there was a small increase, presumably due to a local arrival.

There was usually a further marked reduction in numbers after December, the population reaching its lowest level each year near the beginning of March. The minimum winter figures in Table 33 take no account of temporary brief absences during snow, when some birds left the Carlton estate, probably for near-by fields with brassicas, and returned in similar numbers when the snow had gone. However, the much longer and almost complete disappearance of Wood Pigeons during the prolonged cold weather from late December to early March 1962–3 was included. The next counts, in April, showed no change in numbers in two years, but an increase in three others, in 1959–60 and 1961–2 due to an arrival (or return) of juveniles, and in 1962–3 to the return of both adults and juveniles, though in much diminished numbers, after the snow. In 1960–1 there was a decrease due to poisoning by toxic chemicals on seed dressings, but these were not used in other years.

The proportion of juvenile birds in the population was about 60 per cent every year just after breeding, but thereafter it fell markedly, to between 11 and 48 per cent of the population, by February. After this it in most years stayed roughly the same until the breeding season, but in two years it increased temporarily again in April, presumably due to a passage of juveniles.

In the four years in which the grain index was measured in late autumn, the number of Wood Pigeons present in December was correlated with it. As shown in Table 33, both the number of birds present and the grain index were low in 1959–60 and 1961–2, while both figures were high in 1960-1 and intermediate in 1962–3. The proportion of juveniles in the winter population also varied in parallel, being lowest in 1959–60 and 1961–2 and highest in 1960–1, with 1962–3 intermediate.[1]

As the proportion of juveniles in the population decreased markedly between the end of the breeding season and December, the reduction in the total population in the same period was presumably due mainly to a loss of juveniles; and as the extent of this loss was correlated with the grain index, it was probably due mainly to food shortage. This view is supported by the fact that, while the adult Wood Pigeons shot in December were of similar weight in all four years, the juveniles were about 10 per cent lighter in 1959 and 1961, when grain was sparse, than in 1960 and 1962, when grain was abundant (459 cf. 514 grams, the difference being statistically significant). Juveniles, being lower than adults in the social hierarchy, tend to be displaced by adults in disputes for food. Also, though the juveniles pecked for food as often as the adults (26 cf. 23 pecks per minute), they walked a shorter distance while feeding (on the average 41 cf. 55 paces per minute), which implies that they were less selective, taking some items which adults would have rejected. These several points indicate that during the autumn juvenile Wood Pigeons succumb in competition for food with the adults, particularly when grain is sparse.

As already mentioned, there was a further reduction in the number of Wood Pigeons each year between December and early March, in the time when the birds depend on clover. The number alive at the end of this period, when food was scarcest, was highest in 1960–1, rather lower in 1961–2, much lower in 1959–60 and 1963–4 (when it was about equal), and lowest in 1962–3. The figures in Table 33 show that the clover index varied closely in parallel, and the correlation was statistically significant. There can be no reasonable doubt that the number of Wood Pigeons which survived the winter at Carlton depended on the availability of their basic food at this season.

Some further figures are set out in Table 34, which shows, in particular, that the mortality between early December and early March differed greatly in different years, being highest in 1962–3, less in 1960–1 and 1959–60, much less in 1963–4, and least in 1961–2 (when there was a small increase, presumably through immigration). These variations were not in parallel either with the clover index, or with the population density at the start of the winter. Instead, they depended

[1] Ideally, the proportion of juveniles should have been measured at the beginning of December, instead of on the basis of birds shot in February, but unbiased sampling was not possible in December, and the proportion was probably similar in December and February in three of the four winters concerned. In the other, 1962–3, the proportion was almost certainly lower in February than December, as many juveniles perished after December in the unusually cold weather.

TABLE 34

Comparison between winter losses of Wood Pigeons and the
proportion of under-nourished birds at Carlton

Year	No. alive per 40 ha. in Dec.	% Change by early March from early Dec.	% Of birds shot at less than 450 g	% Of birds shot with empty crops	Clover index
1958–9	117	− 17	2	2	—
1959–60	62	− 45	25	—	1338
1960–1	174	− 52	19	29	1887
1961–2	51	+ 25	5	5	1676
1962–3	104	− 99	36	39	0
1963–4	41	− 20	14	3	1132

Note. After Murton, Isaacson, & Westwood (*in press*).

on the difference between the number of birds which the grain supplies
permitted to survive to early December and the number of birds which
the clover supplies permitted to survive to early March. For instance,
in the winter of 1960–1 the clover index was the highest recorded, so
the number of Wood Pigeons alive in early March was the highest
recorded; but the preceding grain supplies had been good, so the
number of pigeons alive in December was also high; hence there was a
heavy mortality between then and early March. In contrast, in 1963–4
the clover index was low, so the number of Wood Pigeons alive in early
March was low, but the grain index had also been low, so the number
alive in early December had been low; hence there was only a light
mortality between then and early March.

It is reasonably certain that the mortality between early December
and early March was due primarily to starvation. Circumstantial
evidence for this is provided by other figures in Table 34. Wood Pigeons
weighing less than 450 grams are in poor condition. Also, Wood
Pigeons coming to roost with empty instead of full crops have found
feeding difficult (cf. p. 158 for the Quelea). As shown in Table 34, both
the proportion of birds weighing less than 450 grams and the proportion
roosting with empty crops differed markedly in different winters, and
the variations were closely in parallel with each other, and also with the
mortality between early December and early March each year (but not
with the clover index).

The correlation between the number of Wood Pigeons alive in early
March and the availability of clover indicates that the number of birds

remaining alive on the area keeps close to that which the declining quantity of food can support. This happens because there is direct competition for food in the feeding flocks, and one individual not infrequently displaces another from an item which it has found, with the result that some of the displaced individuals, presumably those lowest in the social hierarchy, fail to get enough food and die. Murton therefore supported the view of Lockie (1956) developed for the Rook, *Corvus frugilegus*, that, in birds which feed in flocks and have a social hierarchy, competition rapidly eliminates those lowest in the hierarchy through starvation while leaving the rest almost unaffected for the time being. Hence only a few individuals starve at any one time, even though the population may remain close to the limit set by food for several weeks or months. He further supported my view (Lack, 1954) that the behaviour patterns concerned in the social hierarchy could have been evolved through natural selection, and that there is no need to invoke Wynne-Edwards' views (1962) on group-selection to account for them. (For a further discussion of this point, see pp. 284 and 303.)

In the first 4 years at Carlton, the average breeding population was 63 per 40 hectares. As each pair produced an average of 2·4 young per year, 63 adults produced 91 fledged young, so that by the end of September, the average population was 154 per 40 hectares. This was reduced, by death and some emigration, to about 98 in December and to 70 (49 adults and 21 in their first year) in February. There was a further small decline to 44 older birds and 19 yearlings by July, when breeding got under way. On this basis, the breeding population included 30 per cent of yearlings and in a balanced population the annual adult mortality should be the same. This figure agrees fairly well with an annual adult mortality of 36 per cent estimated from ringing returns for England as a whole. Of the young birds, about 60 per cent died in their first month out of the nest, and the mortality between leaving the nest and the following February was 77 per cent, compared with only 22 per cent in the adults in the same period. Such a difference in the first year of life is characteristic of birds in general (Lack, 1954). After the winter, juveniles survived as well as adults.

As Murton and his team could not follow in the wild the survival or movements of marked individuals, their conclusion that most deaths were due to starvation rests on inference, but all the evidence is in favour of this view. It is, of course, possible that some of the birds that were short of food left the area, but if they did not return, their exodus can be regarded as equivalent to death so far as the Carlton population was concerned. There were no raptorial birds or other species preying on adult pigeons. Disease, mainly avian tuberculosis, was rare, occurring in 3·1 per cent of the birds shot and 1·6 per cent of those caught with narcotic baits. This shows, incidentally, that weakened birds were easier to shoot than healthy ones, as those caught with narcotic baits were presumably a random sample of the population. Deaths from toxic chemicals occurred only in one spring. There was heavy shooting in winter at Carlton, but this had a negligible influence on the size of the breeding population in the following year, because the number shot was always well below that which would probably have died anyway from starvation. Shooting is therefore useless, indeed wasteful, as a control measure, and the same conclusion has been reached in Holland (Doude van Troostwijk, 1964). In fact, after many years, the Ministry of Agriculture, Fisheries and Food has now withdrawn financial support for organized winter shoots of pigeons in Britain.

The only other bird which is a serious agricultural pest in Britain is the Bullfinch, *Pyrrhula pyrrhula*, one of the carardueline finches. The members of this family live mainly on seeds, and most of them feed their young on seeds, supplemented by small invertebrates. The seeds eaten by Bullfinches are of no commercial importance, but in early spring the birds eat the small centres of buds, including those of orchard fruits, notably pears, and their attacks are sometimes so heavy that no fruit is obtained, even from extensive orchards. The following account is based on work on the Wytham estate and a nearby orchard by I. Newton (D.Phil. thesis, Oxford University, also 1964, and in press).

In England, most Bullfinches breed and spend the winter in broad-leaved woods, and some in agricultural land. They nest in dense or thorny shrubs. In the spring prior to breeding, their main diet consists of buds, but they turn to fresh seeds when these become available in late April. Probably this is what determines the start of breeding in early May, because buds contain comparatively little nutriment, and seeds might well be needed before the hens can form eggs. Also when Newton provided eight hens in outdoor aviaries with seeds, six of them laid eggs in mid-April, a fortnight before he found any eggs in the near-by woods. Similarly in Sweden, the Redpoll, *Carduelis flammea*, and Siskin, *C. spinus*, have been recorded breeding two months earlier than usual in a year with a good seed crop of Spruce, *Picea abies* (Svärdson, 1957).

The date at which Bullfinches stop breeding is also determined in part by the seed crops. In Wytham, for instance, breeding ended two months later in 1962, when the last young left the nest in early October, than in 1963, when the last left in early August, and the seeds eaten at this time of year, notably those of Birch, *Betula pubescens*, and Privet, *Ligustrum vulgare*, were much more abundant in 1962 than 1963. As mentioned later, the seeds favoured by Bullfinches tend to be abundant every other year and, correspondingly, the nest records of the British Trust for Ornithology showed that late clutches were found in 1956, 1958, 1960, and 1962, but not in 1957, 1959, 1961, and 1963. Other cardueline finches also breed later than usual when the seeds on which they depend are abundant later than usual, including the Linnet, *C. cannabina*, and Goldfinch, *C. carduelis*, which feed primarily on the seeds of annual weeds and continue breeding much later than usual in fine summers, which favour the production of such seeds.

The Bullfinch usually lays 4 or 5 eggs, occasionally 3 or 6. In the nest records of the British Trust for Ornithology already mentioned, the average clutch was 4·8 in May, 4·6 in June, 4·3 in July, and 3·8 in August and September. In the years when tree seeds were plentiful, namely 1956, 1958, 1960, and 1962, the average clutch was about $\frac{1}{4}$ egg higher in May and the first half of June, and about 0·4 egg higher in the second half of June and July, than in the alternate years with fewer seeds.

Excluding losses from predation, of the nests studied in May, June, and July in 2 years in Wytham, all the hatched young flew successfully from broods of 5 or less, but only 58 per cent did so from 4 artificially produced broods of 6 or 7. Further, the proportion of hatched young retrapped alive at least 5 weeks after fledging was 62 per cent from broods of 5 or less but only 15 per cent from the 4 broods of 6 or 7 young. This suggests that broods larger than the average resulted in fewer survivors per brood than those of average size, but further data are needed to establish this, as only 4 unusually large broods were studied. It is hard to obtain sufficient figures owing to heavy losses from predation, chiefly by Jays, *Garrulus glandarius*, and Weasels, *Mustela nivalis*. Of 35 nests in woodland, 66 per cent were destroyed but of 36 in hedgerows only 39 per cent were destroyed. As in the Blackbird and Long-tailed Tit (p. 123), more were destroyed in woods than in man-made habitats, presumably because natural predators, including Jays and weasels, are commonest in woods.

Bullfinches, like most other birds, have a complete moult after breeding. In both seasons studied at Wytham, some birds started moulting in late July, but whereas in 1963 the last birds completed their moult at the end of October, in 1962 those which bred late postponed their moult, and did not finish it until the end of December.

The number of Bullfinches on 47 hectares of woodland in Wytham was estimated at intervals throughout the year by means of the capture-recapture technique modified by Leslie and Chitty (1953). In 1962, about 16 pairs bred, which had increased mainly through breeding to about 146 birds in October, there was then a progressive reduction to

98 in March, and eventually 38 pairs bred, while there were in addition some non-breeding yearling males. In September 1963, after breeding, there were about 261 birds, and the number fell steeply to about 74 in February–March, and about the same number bred in the following summer. Apart from some wandering yearling males which did not breed in the summer of 1963, there was little movement, and the increases in numbers were due mainly to reproduction and the losses to mortality. Losses were heaviest among the juveniles, as shown by the reduction in the juvenile : adult ratio in the trapped samples. In 1962–3 this ratio was 5:1 in the autumn after breeding, 3·1:1 in the winter, and 2·2:1 in the following summer. In the next year it was 3·4:1 in the autumn after breeding and fell to 1·5:1 in the winter, and to 1·1:1 in the following summer. These figures suggest that in the Bullfinch, like the Great Tit, the number of breeding pairs is not appreciably influenced by the number of young leaving the nest in the previous year, but that it is greatly affected by the mortality, particularly of the juveniles, after breeding. In the Bullfinch this mortality occurs primarily during the winter.

As predation and disease were negligible, the winter mortality was evidently due mainly to starvation, and fitting with this view, it was related to the size of the seed crops. In Wytham in winter, Bullfinches depend almost entirely on the seeds of six plants, Ash, *Fraxinus excelsior*, Birch, Privet, Bramble, *Rubus* spp., Dock, *Rumex* spp., and Nettle, *Urtica dioica*. In 1962–3, Ash was much the most important of these, and it was so abundant that only a small proportion of the available seeds was eaten by the end of the winter. Even so, a substantial proportion of other seeds was taken, perhaps because the birds require a varied diet. Like other trees discussed earlier (see p. 66), Ash tends to produce seed once every two years, and in 1963–4 there was none, while there was also extremely little privet seed and much less birch seed than in the previous year. Regular sampling of the seed crops showed that by mid-January 1964, due largely to consumption by Bullfinches, less than 1 per cent remained of the seeds of birch, nettle, and dock, though there was still 16 per cent of bramble seeds, which was reduced to 8 per cent by mid-April. It was probably due to the marked difference in the seed crops that the mortality was as high as 68 per cent in the winter of 1963–4, as compared with only 33 per cent in the winter of 1962–3. This is the more remarkable in that the winter of 1962–3 was the severest this century, and birds of many other species died in large numbers; but the seeds of ash and birch, being on the trees, were unaffected by the snow, so that Bullfinches could obtain enough od.

Newton found that the Bullfinch eats buds in the early spring primarily when seeds are scarce. In Wytham woods it takes chiefly hawthorn buds, but it prefers fruit buds where these are available. In the early spring of 1962, when there was no ash seed, Bullfinches attacked Conference pears in an orchard near Wytham, starting as early as 12 December, and they eventually destroyed every flower-bud. But in the spring of 1963, when ash seed was plentiful, Bullfinches started taking the pear buds only on 12 April and in all took less than 1 per cent. In the early spring of 1964, when there was again no ash seed, Bullfinches started taking the buds on 5 January and eventually destroyed one-third of them. Observations on aviary-fed birds showed that those given hawthorn buds in January fed almost throughout the day, taking up to thirty buds per minute, but after four days had lost so much weight that they would soon have died if they had not then been given seeds again. Birds fed on pear buds at this time also lost weight, but managed to survive for a few days. In March, when the buds were larger and the hours of daylight longer, captive Bullfinches survived on a diet of either hawthorn or pear buds, but only by consuming an immense number, and at all times they took mainly seeds when available. Hence the Bullfinch resembles the Quelea in turning to an agricultural crop primarily when its natural foods are scarce, and it is sad that this beautiful bird should obtain so little nourishment for itself in return for the great damage that it causes periodically to man.

Summarizing, the Wood Pigeon breeds in the artificial habitat of farmland, where it depends primarily on grain between the summer and the end of November and on clover from early December to the spring. Laying occurred primarily when ripe grain was available, presumably through a direct effect of food on the adults. Jays and Magpies took many eggs, especially at high nesting densities and at times when Wood Pigeons were short of food in early summer. But this predation had a negligible influence on the number of young raised, which was about the same each year, because pairs whose eggs were taken quickly laid again. The population decreased markedly each year between the end of the breeding season and the beginning of December, the losses being correlated with the availability of grain, and consisting primarily of juvenile birds in competition for food with the adults. There was further heavy mortality between early December and early March each year, its extent depending on the difference between the number of birds which the grain permitted to remain alive by early December and the number which the clover supplies permitted to remain alive by early March. There was strong circumstantial evidence that these losses, also, were due to starvation, and the number left alive by March each year was closely correlated with the availability of clover. The breeding season of the Bullfinch was linked with the availability of certain species of seeds in woods, and so, at least in two years, was the number that survived the winter. In alternate years when these seeds were sparse, Bullfinches severely damaged fruit buds.

Bullfinch eating buds.

12

THE RED GROUSE AND PTARMIGAN
IN SCOTLAND

THE Red Grouse, often given specific status as *Lagopus scoticus*, is as such the only bird species endemic to Britain, but recent authors have treated it as a subspecies of the Willow Grouse, *L. lagopus*, from which it differs especially in not assuming white plumage in winter. The Willow Grouse, known in North America as the Willow Ptarmigan, has a circumpolar range, occurring especially in the subarctic willow and birch forest and in wooded or shrubby tundra. It feeds on a variety of plants, but, as its name suggests, it depends especially on Willow, *Salix*, in winter, and in some areas, notably in parts of the U.S.S.R. and North America, the birds move from breeding grounds on open tundra to spend the winter in willow thicket (Dementiev and Gladkov, 1952; Semenov-Tyan-Shanskii 1960; Voous, 1960). This species is replaced on the bare treeless tundra farther north and higher up mountains by the related Ptarmigan, *L. mutus*, known in North America as the Rock Ptarmigan, which is discussed later in this chapter.

The relict population of the Willow Grouse in Britain lives almost exclusively on heather moors, these being extensive treeless spaces in hilly country, covered mainly in rather short heather, *Calluna vulgaris*, and the birds depend almost entirely on heather shoots, not willow, for their food. Moorland is a habitat greatly modified by man, through the clearing of trees, grazing by sheep and regular burning, and Dr. A. S

Headpiece: Red Grouse with plastic tab.

Watt informed me (pers. comm.) that previously most of what are now moors, though still dominated by heather, would have had open woodland of birch or pine, while the heather would have been more irregular, older, and taller, thus providing more cover but much less food for the Grouse, because it is especially the young shoots which the Grouse eat (cf. also Pearsall, 1950). Hence the habitat in which the British Red Grouse evolved was probably similar in general appearance to that now occupied by the nearest Willow Grouse in Scandinavia, except that in Britain the ground is covered in snow for a much shorter period each winter, which presumably accounts for the loss of the white winter plumage.

The Red Grouse is Britain's outstanding sporting bird, being regularly shot by monarchs, while the start of the shooting season on 'the Twelfth' has determined the date in August on which parliamentary commoners start their summer vacation. Because the bird has periodic declines in numbers, formerly attributed to 'grouse disease', it was the subject of one of the earliest enquiries into the fluctuations of a natural population of animals, that by Lovat et al. (1911; summarized in Lack, 1954). The chief scientists on this enquiry, R. T. Leiper and Edward Wilson, attributed the declines to the interaction between the Grouse and a parasitic nematode, *Trichostrongylus tenuis* (formerly *pergracilis*), but Lord Lovat himself, and also Macintyre (1918), suggested that food shortage might be the primary or predisposing cause.

This chapter is based on a new five-year study in Scotland by a team led by Dr. D. Jenkins on 460 hectares at 210 metres above sea level (the 'low area'), supplemented by observations on 405 hectares on an adjacent 'high area' at around 600 metres, in Glen Esk, Angus, on a flank of the Grampian mountains. The chief interest of this study has been to show the interelations between predation, disease, starvation, the state of the heather, and territorial behaviour and though the basic factors controlling numbers are still obscure, they are certainly more complex than formerly supposed. The main paper is that by Jenkins, Watson, and Miller (1963; see also Jenkins, 1963; Jenkins and Watson, 1962; Jenkins, Watson, and Miller, 1964a, b; Jenkins, Watson, Miller, and Picozzi, 1964; Jenkins, Watson, and Picozzi, 1965; Watson and Jenkins, 1964; and Watson, 1964). Both study areas consisted mainly of heather and were managed in the customary modern way, by grazing with sheep, by burning the heather, and by shooting the predators, while many Grouse were shot in August and September.

Cock Grouse started to take up territories in the autumn, at first chiefly in the early mornings, and hens associated with them, but at this season the pairings were often temporary. Other Grouse were driven off the occupied ground, some remaining in packs on parts of

194

J

the moors and others moving to less suitable feeding areas on grass or stubble fields. If there was extensive snow in winter, territories were abandoned and the birds fed in packs. But with the return of milder weather, from February onward, the cocks rather suddenly began to spend the whole day in their territories, fixed pairs were formed and the remaining birds without territories dispersed. An analysis of ringing recoveries showed that rather less than 5 per cent of both the old and the young Grouse moved more than 5 kilometres in the course of their lives, so the dispersing birds did not usually move far, chiefly to the edges of the moors, where many of them later died. Pair-formation and breeding occurred rather later on the high than the low ground.

Grouse tend to crouch when a man is near, but trained sporting dogs were used to help in counting the birds at all seasons, also in finding nests and dead birds. Many individuals were caught and marked with large plastic tabs so that they could be recognized through field-glasses, as shown in the chapter head. On the low area, the number of breeding pairs varied between rather under a pair to each two hectares in 1958 and rather more than a pair to each six hectares in 1960, while the extreme limits of numbers observed were just over 1000 (in August

TABLE 35

Numbers of Red Grouse counted alive (and shot) at Glen Esk

	1956–7	1957–8	1958–9	1959–60	1960–1
Low Area (460 hectares)					
Breeding adults and young (August)	—	991	771	358	554
shot (Autumn)	—	(476)	(134)	(56)	(86)
1st stable period October–January	488	485	406	226	351
2nd stable period February–breeding	359	390	223	158	351
Young (August)	658	361	103	388	679
High Area (405 hectares)					
Breeding adults and young (August)	—	(c.750)	647	274	541
(shot)	—	—	(100)	(20)	(50)
November–January	—	638	454	424	549
February–March	—	—	309	206	367
Breeding	—	385	185	143	367
Young (August)	—	292	100	384	666

Note. Simplified from Jenkins, Watson, and Miller (1963), Tables 4 and 5.

1961) and about 150 (in the spring of 1960). The main changes in numbers throughout the study period have been set out in Table 35.

The Grouse raises one brood a year. The young are active from hatching and take their own food, at first mainly insects, but they are accompanied by their parents. There were marked annual variations in breeding success, as shown in Table 36, the average number of juvenile birds in August being less than one per adult in 1958 and 1959, but two or more per adult in 1957, 1960, and 1961. In 1958 and 1959, but not the other three years, the heather was in poor condition in the early spring, so that the tips looked brown not green, partly due to damage by frost. Hence the poor breeding success in 1958 and 1959 may well have been due to shortage of food for the adult Grouse, but on the basis of only five years' observations, Jenkins (amplified pers. comm.) was understandably cautious on this point

The poorer production of young in 1958 and 1959 was due to losses or inadequacies at several stages in the breeding cycle. First, there was a much higher proportion of unmated cocks in these than the other years. Since Jenkins considered that many more birds of both sexes were present in February than later bred, it is not clear why a lower proportion of the hens should have found mates in these two years than the others (unless some of the hens were in too poor condition to attempt breeding).

Secondly, the average clutch was one egg smaller in 1958 and two eggs smaller in 1959 than in the other three years. As mentioned in Chapter 1 (pp. 6-7), Siivonen (1954, 1956, 1957, 1958) produced circumstantial evidence for several other species of gallinaceous birds that clutches were smaller in years when the hens were in poorer physical condition. Hence I think that the lower clutches of the Grouse at Glen Esk in 1958 and 1959 were probably due to the poorer condition of the hens resulting from the poorer state of the heather, though this needs testing for further years.[1]

Thirdly, excluding losses due to predation, 28–30 per cent of the eggs failed to hatch in 1958 and 1959, as compared with only 5–12 per cent in the other three years. Infertility accounted for a quarter of the losses in 1958 and 1959, but for none in the other three years, the rest being due to the failure of fertile eggs to hatch, mainly owing to faulty incubation. Grouse were unusually prone to desert their eggs in 1958 and 1959, when respectively 9 and 13 per cent did so after visits by the

---

[1] A less likely possibility is that, as clutches tend to be smaller later in the course of each season, the later start of breeding in 1958 and 1959 was responsible as such for the lower clutch-size. It is also possible that breeding started later because the Grouse were in poorer condition. The factors causing later breeding and smaller clutches on the high than the low area should be investigated, and so should the general decline in clutch-size later in the summer.

TABLE 36

Annual variations affecting reproductive output and summer
survival of Red Grouse on low area, Glen Esk

	1957	1958	1959	1960	1961
Breeding birds					
per 40 hectares	33	34	19	14	31
State of heather in spring	good	poor	poor	good	good
Sex ratio ♂♂ per ♀	1·2	1·35	1·5	1·1	1·0
Date of first clutch	24 May	4 June	31 May	29 May	24 May
Average clutch	7·9	6·9	6·1	8·1	7·8
Per cent of eggs predated	8	6	6	6	3
Per cent of eggs infertile,					
addled, deserted	12	28	30	5	12
Per cent of hatched					
young dying by August	46	53	73	30	46
Mean brood size in					
August	4·3	1·7	1·7	4·9	4·4
Ratio of young to old in					
August	2·0	0·9	0·4	2·3	2·0
Mean weight in grams in					
August					
of adult ♂	695	679	661	707	706
of adult ♀	612	587	578	618	614
Per cent of tabbed					
adults disappearing					
1 April–11 August	7	33	41	3	11

Notes. From Jenkins, 1963, Table 1, and Jenkins, Watson, and Miller (1963), Tables
14, 15, 19, 20, 23 (adjusted for 1959), 24 and 26. On the high area, the dates of laying
and mean clutch-size varied closely in parallel, but were later and smaller respectively.

observer, as compared with between 0 and 4 per cent in the other
three years. In addition, unusually large numbers of eggs were taken
by Carrion Crows, *Corvus corone*, in 1959, which was also attributed
to faulty incubation by the Grouse, as crows were equally numerous
in other years.

Fourthly, in 1959 many broods were attended by only one parent
instead of the usual two, even during the first three weeks after hatching.
In 1958 and 1959, also, the young from different broods sometimes
intermingled, which was not seen in the other years. In these two years,
also, only about one-twentieth of the parents gave distraction display
to a human visitor, whereas about half did so in the other years. Clearly,
parental behaviour was in several respects less efficient in 1958 and

1959 than in the other years, and presumably it was at least partly for this reason that a higher proportion of the chicks died in these two years than the others. Most losses of young occurred during the first week or two after they hatched.

Finally, the adult Grouse themselves were in poorer condition in 1958 and 1959, as those shot in August weighed, on the average, 5 per cent less than in the other years. Also, the proportion of tabbed Grouse which disappeared in the course of the summer was between one-third and two-fifths in 1958 and 1959, as compared with between 3 and 11 per cent in the other years. Jenkins and his associates did not discuss the possible reasons for these differences, but it seems possible to me that all were due to undernourishment in 1958 and 1959, resulting from the poor state of the heather.

The number of Grouse breeding on the low area showed an increase over the previous year in 1961 and 1962, no change or, if anything, a small increase in 1958, and a decrease in 1959 and 1960. Jenkins therefore concluded that successful breeding was correlated with a rise, and unsucessful breeding with a fall, in the subsequent breeding population. But since he also showed that many more young were produced each year than were needed to replace losses, I think it extremely unlikely that breeding success as such was responsible for the observed changes, and suggest instead that, if the above correlation is borne out for further years, it may mean that the factors which influence breeding success in summer continue to influence the losses in subsequent months.

In years of high numbers, about half the Grouse alive on 12 August were shot in the next few weeks, but in years of low numbers few or none were shot. The number disappearing each year between August and December was usually much greater than the number shot, while in a few areas in some years there was an increase after shooting, presumably due to immigration. Jenkins and his team therefore concluded that shooting had a negligible influence on numbers, and that it merely anticipated deaths that would have occurred soon afterwards from natural causes.[1]

The annual mortality of the Grouse was estimated from the ringing recoveries of shot birds as 67 per cent and from the observed disappearance of tabbed birds as 71 per cent. After August, the mortality rate was similar in juveniles and adults. In a balanced population, replacements should equal losses, so if two-thirds of the Grouse die each year, there should be two juveniles to each adult in the population,

---

[1] This view seems justified, but the figures in their Table 32 for the survival of tabbed birds on adjoining shot and unshot areas do not, I think, provide further support, as the numbers involved were small and the possibility of movements between the areas does not seem excluded.

and this was in fact the ratio observed in August in three of the five seasons studied. Hence these various estimates of mortality are in close agreement.

The combined loss of juvenile and adult birds between one year and the next has been as high as two-thirds in various other species studied, but in all others the losses were much higher in juveniles than adults, and in no other was the adult mortality as high as two-thirds (cf. Lack, 1954). Hence in these respects the Red Grouse appears to be exceptional, but I think that this might be due to the effects of shooting. Jenkins may be right in concluding that shooting does not alter the overall mortality rate, but I suggest that if adults are shot as readily as juveniles (and they might perhaps be shot more readily), this might well bias the juvenile:adult ratio in favour of the juveniles. In an unshot population, I would expect the juveniles to have a much higher mortality than the adults, owing to competition for food or territories, in which the adults presumably come off best, and also because this is what is known to happen in all other species so far studied. If in such a population the overall mortality were the same as that recorded by Jenkins but the adult mortality were lower and the juvenile mortality higher, the figures for the Red Grouse would be comparable with those for other species. After formulating this view, Jenkins drew my attention to the study of Choate (1963) on an unshot population of the related White-tailed Ptarmigan, *L. leucurus*, in Montana, in which the annual mortality of the adult cocks was about 20 per cent but that of the juvenile cocks in their first winter was about 69 per cent, a difference comparable with that which I suggest might hold in an unshot population of Red Grouse.

The Grouse were counted regularly on both the low and high areas at Glen Esk. On the low area, there was each year a big decrease, irrespective of shooting, in August and September, number then stayed nearly constant from October to January inclusive, decreased markedly again in February, except in one year, and then stayed nearly constant until the young hatched in midsummer. On the high area, the changes were less consistent. In August and September, there was in one year a big decrease, in another no change, despite a small number shot, and in a third a big increase, due to immigration. Numbers stayed about the same from October to January inclusive, then decreased markedly in February, and in two of the three years decreased markedly again before the birds nested. These findings have been summarized in Table 35, but to save space the numbers for successive counts during each nearly stable period have been averaged, so that the picture is oversimplified, especially for the first stable period in the late autumn and early winter, in which numbers tended to decline somewhat.

There were two main natural causes of death, predation and disease, the Grouse taken by predators usually being in good condition and the others emaciated. The remains of nearly all those killed by predators were found by the research team, because scattered feathers made them conspicuous on the ground. There were only two important predators, the Fox, *Vulpes vulpes*, and the Golden Eagle, *Aquila chrysaetus*, the latter found mainly on the high ground. In addition Hen Harriers, *Circus cyaneus*, took some Grouse on the low area in winter, and Carrion Crows took their eggs in summer. All these predators fed on a variety of other animals, the numbers of which were not studied, and none of them was primarily dependent on Grouse for food. Also, the predators were regularly shot and trapped by keepers, but apparently without appreciable effect on their numbers.

The figures by Jenkins, Watson, and Miller (1964*b*) show that on the low area about four-fifths of the birds killed by predators were found between November and March inclusive, in fairly equal numbers in each month, while most of the rest were found in April and May. As already mentioned, the numbers of Grouse on the low area decreased primarily in August–September and February, so these decreases were not caused by predation. On the high area, dead bodies were found more evenly through the year, and again their occurrence did not coincide with the observed periods of marked decrease in numbers. The figures in Table 37 show that many more Grouse were killed by predators in the winters of 1957–8 and 1958–9 than the others, these also being the two winters in which raptors were seen hunting most frequently, in which Grouse were most numerous, and in which most Grouse dispersed from the study areas. With data for only five years and with interrelated variables, it is not safe to conclude which were causally related with each other and which coincidental, and one cannot, I think, regard the figures for the high area as providing independent confirmation of those for the low, as they referred to the same years and varied in parallel. But while further confirmation is needed, Jenkins and his associates may well be right in thinking that the numbers killed by predators were related especially to the numbers of Grouse which dispersed. Supporting this view, of the Grouse marked with plastic tabs, only 6 out of 383 owners of territories were later found killed by predators, as compared with 36 out of a possible 261 marked Grouse without territories.

Grouse with territories are safer from predators than are dispersed Grouse for several reasons. The heather moorland which they occupy provides thicker cover, and cover which better matches their brown plumage, than the grass banks and stubble fields often frequented by dispersed birds. Also, the owners of territories, being more familiar

TABLE 37

Predation on Red Grouse at Glen Esk

| | Number of Red Grouse | | | |
	Present Oct.–Nov.	Dispersing	Found killed	Number of raptorial birds seen per 100 hr
	Low Area			
1956–7	341	172	44	8
1957–8	597	207	161	12
1958–9	637	414	182	10
1959–60	302	144	45	5
1960–1	468	117	87	4
	High Area			
1957–8	659	274	107	8
1958–9	541	356	92	9
1959–60	246	103	40	5
1960–1	558	191	43	5

Notes. From Jenkins, Watson, and Miller (1964b), Tables 5 and 7.

with their ground, have probably learned of better hiding places. Further, if the dispersed birds are driven out to ground less favourable for food, I presume that they have to spend longer each day in feeding, and so cannot keep so careful a watch for predators.

Jenkins and his associates considered that most of the dispersed Grouse later die anyway, and the only ones which survive to breed are those replacing dead owners of territories, including any of the latter killed by predators. They therefore concluded that predators had a negligible effect on the numbers of Grouse. Further, since shooting and trapping had a negligible influence on the numbers of the predators, they concluded that this situation would also have held in wholly natural conditions undisturbed by man. Their view is therefore that of Errington (1934, 1946; see also pp. 284–5) that predators of birds and mammals remove merely a 'doomed surplus'.

Emaciated birds were found dead chiefly between March and June inclusive, and many of them were parasitized, as shown in Table 38. Especially in earlier papers, Jenkins and his associates termed these birds 'diseased', but later (eg., their 1964 progress report) they as often called them 'starved'. As the birds were both heavily parasitized and emaciated, both terms may be justifiable. There are, however, several reasons which suggest that Lovat (1911) and Macintyre (1918) may have been right, contrary to Leiper and Wilson (in Lovat *et al.*, 1911), in

TABLE 38

Gut parasites in Red Grouse on low area, Glen Esk

	1956-7	1958	1959	1960	1961
Proportion of Grouse with tapeworms	50%	67%	76%	31%	33%
Proportion of Grouse with 1000 + trichostrongyles	47%	85%	89%	15%	22%
Mean no. trichostrongyles					
in Grouse in good condition	245	1341	4168	—	—
in Grouse in poor condition	2261	4102	7498	—	—
No. of Grouse found dead in poor condition March–June	20	55	31	3	7
No. of Grouse dispersing after January	129	95	183	68	0

Notes. From Jenkins, Watson, and Miller (1963), Tables 27, 38, 39, and Fig. 3, confirmed pers. comm. The numbers of Grouse found dead in poor condition were those classified as 'others' in their Table 27. The numbers dispersing are from my Table 36. The authors considered that the numbers dying in poor condition were about three times those found. The totals on which the percentages in the first two lines and the means in the third and fourth lines were based are given in Jenkins *et al.*, Tables 38 and 39 respectively.

considering starvation, not strongylosis, to be the basic cause of 'Grouse disease'. First, as shown in Table 38, Grouse described as in good condition sometimes carried many more trichostrongyle worms than Grouse in poor condition (compare for instance those in good condition in 1959 with those in poor condition in 1956–7). This shows that the cause of death is not simply the number of parasites present. Secondly emaciated birds were found chiefly in the first part of the spring, when heather suitable for food is presumably scarcest. Thirdly, the heather tips, which Grouse prefer, were in poor condition early in 1958 and 1959, and as shown in Table 38, many more emaciated birds were found in spring in these two years than the other three. Fourthly, Jenkins and his team found most emaciated Grouse in the grassy areas, where food is much sparser than on the heather moors. Probably, therefore, starvation is at least a predisposing cause of death, but the rate of infection perhaps plays a part as well, since the number of trichostrongyle worms present, in both healthy-looking and emaciated Grouse, was higher in 1958 and 1959, the years of heavy mortality, than in the other three years. It will be recalled that both the rate of predation in winter and the losses of young in summer were also higher in those two years than the others. With so many interrelated factors varying in parallel, it is, once again, extremely hard to be sure which were causally related. Hence great care is needed in interpretation until data are available for further years.

Jenkins (amplified in pers. comm.) considered that the basic cause of death in these emaciated birds was neither parasitic infection nor starvation, but failure to obtain a territory. That most of the emaciated birds had dispersed was shown by the high proportion found on grassland outside the main territories on moorland. Because of this, and because the owners of territories which died were replaced by dispersed birds, Jenkins concluded that deaths from disease (or starvation), like those from predation, did not appreciably affect the size of the Grouse population.

On the high area, as mentioned earlier, the seasonal decline each year in the number counted was not so concentrated into two 'steps' in August–September and February as on the low area, and there was at times a third decline after February and before breeding. I should add that a first reading of the 1963 paper suggested to me that in both areas the second period of aggression and dispersal in February was more important than that in August–September, particularly as it appeared to determine the number which would breed, but Jenkins *et al.* (1963, pp. 369, 370) Watson (1964) and Jenkins, Watson, Miller, and Picozzi (1964) have concluded that the first staking out of territories in August and September is the critical period in determining the density of breeding pairs in the following spring. Even if the precise times of year at which numbers decline on the moors need further clarification, it seems clear that each year between August and the following spring many Grouse disperse from the heather moors to marginal habitats, and that their chances of survival are small and their chances of breeding are negligible, unless they can later replace the owners of moorland territories which have died.

That the dispersal in question is a result of other individuals owning territories on the moors was tested experimentally in 1963 (Jenkins, Watson and Miller, 1964a). From August 1962 until the next breeding season, an area of 100 acres near Banchory in Kincardineshire was occupied by 14 cock Grouse with territories. After breeding 87 were present, including 57 young, but with the renewal of territorial behaviour in August 1963, the number fell to 68, which included 14 cocks with territories and 16 juvenile cocks without territories. All 14 cocks with territories were then shot. A month later, 16 cocks, 2 old and 14 juveniles, held territories on the area, but 2 of the territories were extremely small. Presumably these 16 birds held territories only because the original 14 birds had been removed, and since there were once again 14 full-sized territories, territorial behaviour evidently determined the number of resident cocks. But why should the limit have been 14–16 cocks? Watson (1964a) showed that more aggressive Grouse, as measured by the proportion of successful encounters with others, held larger territories than less aggressive cocks. But this merely raises the question of why some cocks were more aggressive than others. He also showed that territories tended to be larger where the cover was less thick, but whether because such open territories could be more easily defended and intruders more easily seen, or because they contained less food for the Grouse, or for some other reason, is not clear.

As already mentioned, Jenkins concluded that territorial behaviour rather than the mortality from predation or disease, is the basic factor limiting the density of breeding pairs in the Grouse. This behaviour presumably has an important function in pair-formation, as in many other birds. If, in addition, it limits population density, then the big annual differences in population density require explanation, and Jenkins and his group have not as yet discussed them critically in this context. They apparently favour the view that these variations are an incidental consequence of the physical condition of the birds, but they are so great that, if territorial behaviour really limits numbers, they surely ought to be adaptive.

One of the chief functions claimed for territorial behaviour in many species of birds is that it ensures an adequate food supply for the young, but this can almost certainly be ruled out for the Grouse. First, the young find food for themselves, and secondly, on this view one would have expected the adults to have claimed larger territories in the years when breeding was difficult, but as shown by Tables 35 and 36, there was no relationship between the annual variations in the density of breeding pairs and in breeding success. As already mentioned, Jenkins and Watson considered that the size of the breeding territories in spring was determined in the previous autumn, and since territories were larger in the autumns following the summers of 1958 and 1959, when the heather was in poor condition, than in the other years, it might be suggested that the birds claimed larger territories in the seasons when they had less food per unit area in autumn. But Jenkins and his group made no such claim, data are needed for further years to prove this relationship with the state of the heather, and, even if it holds good, other explanations for it are possible. Hence it is by no means certain that the annual variations in the size of the territories are adaptive. But if they are not adaptive, I would conclude, contrary to Jenkins and Watson, that the population density is not basically determined by territorial behaviour. A further difficulty is that Grouse may well be far more abundant at Glen Esk than in their presumed primaeval habitat of open woodland. According to Lovat (1911), the regular burning of heather raised shooting bags by a factor of over 20 on a Yorkshire estate, and there have been other changes beneficial to Grouse numbers under good management. It might be hard to see the true function of territorial behaviour in regulating numbers at densities far higher than those in which the behaviour in question was evolved, as argued earlier for garden Blackbirds (see p. 130).

The marked annual fluctuations in the Grouse are not sufficiently regular to be termed cyclic, but peak numbers have been reached roughly once in seven years, though with a wide scatter (Mackenzie, 1952; Moran, 1952). As, however, past records were based on shooting bags, which are greatly influenced by the production of young in the previous summer, they may not accurately reflect the annual fluctuations in the number of breeding pairs, and further measurements of the type made by Jenkins and his group are much needed. Regular fluctuations suggest a predator-prey oscillation, and the latter might be expected in the Grouse as it is virtually monophagous, though they could not be altogether regular owing to the marked annual variations in the quality of the heather already mentioned.

There are also local variations in population density. In particular there was a higher density of Grouse on a moor on diorite rock where the heather contained more protein, phosphorus, and other minerals than on another moor, also on Deeside, overlying granite, where the heather was poorer in proteins and minerals (Jenkins, Watson, Miller, and Picozzi, 1964). In the same context it is highly suggestive that regular burning of the moors greatly increased the density of Grouse (Lovat, 1911), as Jenkins and his team (Tenth Annual Report and pers. comm.) also found that the young green heather shoots encouraged by burning are much richer in proteins, phosphorus, and calcium than the old brown shoots. (Burning may also reduce the number of encysted trichostrongyle worms and hence the rate of parasitic infection.) In view of these various points I tentatively suggest that the density of the Red Grouse might, after all, be basically determined by the availability of edible heather and that a relatively simple predator-prey oscillation might be involved, with local movements due to territorial behaviour and mortality due to weather helping to keep the populations on adjacent areas more or less in phase with each other. But should this view prove to be correct, the possible functions of territorial behaviour in the Red Grouse require further evaluation, and if this behaviour really limits the breeding density, I suggest that the size of territories defended is functionally related to the state of the heather.

There has as yet been no detailed population study of the conspecific Willow Grouse (or Willow Ptarmigan), with its very different ecology.

In the Timansk area in northern U.S.S.R. east of Archangel (Dementiev and Gladkov, 1952), the birds breed on rather open tundra, taking up their territories in spring and dividing up the whole area, at a density of about 20–25 pairs per square kilometre (similar to that on the low area at Glen Esk in the sparse years). The average clutch was 11 eggs, about 3 eggs more than on Kolguev Island or in Russian Lapland, or at Glen Esk. Prior to breeding the hens weighed 600 to 700 grams, but at the end of incubation not more than 550 grams, and they then had a high infection of intestinal worms. Territories were abandoned when the young hatched and the birds moved to areas of dwarf birch and willow. About 80 per cent of the hatched young survived to the age of two months, by which time they are fully grown in the short summer season on the Timansk tundra, though they take 3 months in the more southerly steppe region in North Kazakhstan. In the Timansk area the birds depend primarily on the shoots, green leaves, and twigs of the willow for food, and they move to willow thickets for the winter. Other foods included Marsh Andromeda and various berries. Willow Grouse constitute the main food of the Gyr Falcon, *Falco rusticola*, and Snowy Owl, *Nyctea scandiaca*, in winter, and these predators migrate with the Willow Grouse to wooded tundra for the winter. A population study under these very different conditions would be of great interest. For another Russian study, see Semenov-Tyan-Shanskii (1960).

Even less has been published on the population ecology of the North American Willow Ptarmigan. In part of Alaska, numbers varied between about 5 and 25 pairs per square kilometre (Weeden, 1963). In New-foundland, the number of pairs per square kilometre was about 10 on the mainland, but as many as 175 on Brunette Island (i.e. similar to Glen Esk), and on Brunette Island the average clutch was only 6, as compared with 11 on the mainland (E. Mercer and R. McGrath, thesis at University of Wisconsin 1963, and A. T. Bergerud, pers. comm., communicated by J. J. Hickey). The causes of the marked local varia-tions in both the population density and the average clutch of the Willow Grouse would make a highly rewarding ecological study.

As mentioned at the start of this chapter, the Ptarmigan, *L. mutus*, is closely related to the Red Grouse, and in Scotland occurs above it, mainly in the arctic-alpine zone, with a small zone of overlap. The arctic-alpine zone is neither burnt nor grazed by sheep, and neither Ptarmigan nor their predators were shot by man, so the population on Derry Cairngorm studied by Watson (1965) was virtually undisturbed. On this area of 500 hectares Ptarmigan were the commonest vertebrate animal, their numbers in spring varying between 24 and 90. Since about one-third of the ground was unsuitable for them, their local density was higher and a particularly favourable area of 40

TABLE 39
Ptarmigan, *Lagopus mutus*, in the Cairngorms

	Derry Cairngorm					Whole Cairngorms	
Summer	No. of adults in spring	Ratio of cocks per hen	Number of hens with no broods	Ratio of young aged 10–12 weeks to one adult	Mean week of hatching (June)	Aver. clutch	Aver. brood (fully grown)	No. seen per 10km in summer
1945	—	—	—	0·8		(4·3)	3·0	6
1946	—	—	—	1·5		(8·0)	6·1	18
1947	—	1·3	—	0·7		(7·0)	4·1	25
1948	—	1·1	—	2·3		7·4	5·9	21
1949	—	1·2	—	2·2		7·0	6·0	35
1950	—	1·1	—	1·7		7·1	3·8	35
1951	86	1·4	19	0·3	4	5·9	3·9	40
1952	73	1·9	13	0·3	2–3	(6·0)	2·7	34
1953	—	1·7	9	0·1	3	5·0	—	32
1954	54	1·8	7	0·2	3	(4·5)	1·7	9
1955	50	1·9	4	0·4	4	(4·7)	1·2	9
1956	37	1·8	4	0·3	3	5·3	1·2	7
1957	30	2·0	1	0·7	2	5·8	2·0	5
1958	24	1·7	1	0·9	3	(5·0)	1·5	6
1959	27	1·1	0	2·0	2–3	(8·5)	—	8
1960	42	1·2	0	2·5	2	7·9	6·2	18
1961	85	1·0	1	2·1	1	7·7	4·3	30
1962	90	1·0	1	1·6	2–3	7·6	—	36
1963	89	1·1	6	0·7	1	(6·3)	2·4	30

Notes. From Watson (1965), Tables 2, 4, 5, 6 7, and Appendix 1. The Derry Cairngorm area of 500 hectares was studied only from 1951 onward. Figures for the ratio of cocks per hen 1947–50 and 1953 and of young per adult 1945–50 were based on the Cairngorms as a whole. The average clutch is placed in brackets where based on less than 5 nests.

hectares held 13 territorial cocks in good years, when some territories comprised only 2 hectares, and elsewhere as little as 1·2 hectares.

The Ptarmigan, like the Red Grouse, eats primarily plants, on the lower slopes especially heather, and above 1000 metres especially Crowberry, *Empetrum hermaphroditum*, and Whortleberry, *Vaccinium myrtillus* (Watson, 1964b). The availability of these foods was not studied. The two main predators, as for the Grouse, were the Golden

Eagle and the Fox, but Ptarmigan formed an unimportant fraction of their prey, which included Red Grouse, Mountain Hare, *Lepus timidus*, Rabbit, *Oryctolagus cuniculus*, and carrion of Red Deer, *Cervus elaphus*, also Voles, *Microtus*, in the case of the fox. No diseased or starving Ptarmigan were found.

The census on Derry Cairngorm from 1951 onward, but omitting 1953, is set out in Table 39, together with breeding data and counts for the Cairngorms as a whole. Numbers rose from 1945 to 1951, then fell until 1957-8, then rose again until 1962. The impressions of two older naturalists, Seton Gordon and Nethersole-Thompson, suggested that there were similar fluctuations in the past, with peaks shortly after 1910, 1920, 1930, and 1940, and hence a 10-year fluctuation. But the latter possibility needs further checking, as game-bags published by Mackenzie (1952) showed peaks at shorter and more irregular intervals. The latter did not, however, refer to the Cairngorms, and, as already mentioned, shooting bags do not necessarily reflect the fluctuations in the breeding population, especially as shooting parties did not visit the high ground for Ptarmigan every year. Gudmundsson (1960) reported a 10-year cycle in the Ptarmigan in Iceland, but though numbers varied markedly from year to year, Weeden (1963) saw no evidence for a 9–10 year cycle in North America.

As shown in Table 39, the average clutch in the Cairngorms varied between under 5 and over 8, usually being 7–8 eggs in the years 1946–50 and 1959–62, but only 4–6 eggs in the years 1951–8. These variations were not correlated with the time of laying, the temperature shortly before laying, or the snowfall, but were linked with the phase of the population cycle, clutches being high when the population was increasing and during the early years of high numbers, and small during the later years of high numbers and when the population was declining.

The average number of young in fully grown broods differed markedly in different years, between about 1 and 6, due primarily to variations in the mortality of the chicks in the first week or two after hatching. These variations were in parallel with those in clutch-size and hence in phase with the population cycle, but were not correlated with the date of hatching or the weather around the time of hatching. This was particularly evident in one year, when there was a marked difference in the average brood-size in two adjacent areas which experienced similar weather but in which the Ptarmigan were in a different phase of the population cycle. The proportion of unmated cocks was also higher than usual in years when the population was declining and in the later years of high numbers. The years with a high production of young were often followed by an increase in the breeding population, and the years with a low production of young by a decrease. But Watson considered that the variations in the production of young were not themselves responsible for the population changes, and that, instead, the factor responsible for the population changes also caused the variations in the production of young, which seems reasonable.

In nine seasons, the Ptarmigan on the study area were counted both in the autumn and in the following spring. The average decrease in numbers between autumn and spring was about a half, but it varied between 17 per cent in 1954–5 and just over 60 per cent in 1961–2. These variations were not in parallel with the population cycle, or with the losses of chicks in summer, but each year were such that the breeding population fluctuated in the regular way just described. Watson therefore concluded that these losses were the immediate (though not the basic) cause of the population fluctuations.

In four seasons, 1951–2, 1953–4, 1954–5, and 1955–6, with less frequent records for 1956–7, the population was counted several times between August and the following spring. In each of these years, the population was effectively constant between August and March, and then declined sharply to the number which later bred. Several points indicated that this decrease was due to dispersal, not death. First it was extremely rapid, in March one year fifty individuals disappearing in five days. Also, at this season Ptarmigan were not found dead, but they were occasionally seen in unusual habitats. Finally, the birds which vanished were primarily those without territories. Dispersal, as in the Grouse, was attributed to the aggressive behaviour of the birds with territories, and when twelve cocks with territories were killed in mid-March, all were replaced within a fortnight.

Hence this population of Ptarmigan showed many similarities to that of the Red Grouse, but there were also differences. In both species there was a big dispersal of birds without territories from the study areas, in Grouse in early autumn and again in early spring, in Ptarmigan in spring. In the Ptarmigan, unlike the Grouse, the dispersed birds did not stay near by in marginal habitats and their fate is unknown. Also, the population fluctuations were apparently more regular, and probably slower, in the Ptarmigan than the Red Grouse. In both species, it was postulated that the number of breeding pairs was determined primarily by territorial behaviour, which means that the size of territories varied in different years, by a factor of up to three or four. Watson stated that the Ptarmigan were less aggressive in the years when they settled more densely, while since the spring territories were sometimes taken up in thick snow, when hardly any vegetation protruded, he thought that the size of the territories was not influenced by the availability of food at this season. (But the size of the territories might conceivably be influenced by the food supply if Ptarmigan, like Grouse, first take up territories in autumn, abandon them in winter snow, and resume them in early spring.) Watson's further argument against food being important, that starving birds were not found, carries no weight as it is not yet known where the dispersed birds go. I suspect that food may prove to be much more important in controlling Ptarmigan numbers than yet appreciated, and conclude, as for the Red Grouse, that if territorial behaviour really limits numbers, the annual variations in the average size of the territories ought to be adaptive, presumably in relation to the food supply.

Finally, brief mention may be made of a shorter but more detailed breeding and ecological study of a third species of *Lagopus*, the White-tailed Ptarmigan, *L. leucurus*, in Montana by Choate (1963). In this species, which has a similar alpine habitat to the Scottish Ptarmigan, the average size of a territory was about one-third of a hectare in the dominant cocks but only one-tenth of a hectare in subdominant cocks, which did not obtain mates. In all, about one-third of the cocks did not obtain mates, most of these being yearlings, but yearling hens normally bred. In addition, there were latecomers of both sexes which did not breed. In 11 nests, the average clutch was just over 5 eggs, but the occasional re-nestings were smaller. About 70 per cent of the nestings were successful and 86 per cent of the eggs in them hatched. Many chicks died in their first week and, in all, over one-third but under a half died before independence. The average mortality between one summer and the next was 20 per cent in territorial cocks, but 44 per cent in breeding hens, thus accounting for the surplus of cocks in the breeding population. The losses of non-territorial cocks and non-breeding hens (mainly late arrivals) were 27 and 29 per cent respectively, while it was estimated, on the basis of a stable population, that 69 per cent of the cocks and 57 per cent of the hens died in their first winter. As already mentioned, these differences in mortality with respect to age for a natural population are very different from those for a shot population of Red Grouse.

Summarizing, in the Red Grouse and Ptarmigan in Scotland, there were marked annual differences in the proportion of unmated cocks, the average clutch-size and the survival of eggs and young. In a five-year study of Red Grouse, the two seasons of poor reproduction coincided with years when the heather was in poor condition. In a longer study of the Ptarmigan, more young were produced in years when numbers were rising and in the first years of high numbers than in the later years of high numbers and when numbers were falling. Two-thirds of both the adult and the juvenile Grouse died each year, but in an unshot population of the White-tailed Ptarmigan, adults survived much better than juveniles. Jenkins and Watson considered that in both Red Grouse and Scottish Ptarmigan the size of the breeding population was determined primarily by territorial behaviour, expelled birds being doomed except for those replacing owners of territories which died. In the Grouse, expelled birds left chiefly in early autumn or early spring, they then frequented marginal habitats, where many were killed by predators in winter and others died of starvation and/or disease in spring. In the Ptarmigan, expelled birds left in March, and their fate was not discovered. Since both species fluctuated markedly in numbers, the critical question, if territorial behaviour limited numbers, is why the birds held much smaller territories in some years than others. Jenkin-evidently considered that this was due to variations in the condition of the birds. But if territorial behaviour really limits the density, the varias tions in the size of territories are so large that they ought to be functional. For this and other reasons I suggest that the possible interaction between the birds and their main vegetable foods requires further study, and that food supplies may well be the basic factor limiting the numbers of both species, perhaps in conjunction with territorial behaviour.

Ptarmigan in winter.

13

THE WHITE STORK IN GERMANY

THE White Stork, *Ciconia ciconia*, is the most cherished of European birds. It breeds on houses and towers, also on platforms specially put up for it, and throughout its present breeding range in northern Europe it is protected not only by law but by universal sentiment, though it is sometimes shot on migration further south. People are so proud to have a Stork's nest in their village or suburb, and the bird itself is so conspicuous and places its bulky nest so prominently, that its numbers are easily and accurately counted. In Germany, in particular, amateurs in all walks of life have collaborated in annual censuses, especially from 1934 onwards, while a census of the whole province of Oldenburg has been made by Tantzen (1963) from 1928 until now. This is the longest census of any species of bird made continuously in the same area.

Each census of the White Stork has normally included not only the number of pairs with nests, but also the number of young raised in each nest. Further, many young birds have been ringed, with coded marks and ring-numbers (illustrated on p. 229) sufficiently large to be read through a telescope when the birds return to breed, so that there have been many recoveries. In addition, there have been biological studies of the breeding habits and migration routes, the latter of which will not be discussed here. The points of special interest for the present book, apart from the great length of time for which many of the censuses

Headpiece: White Storks.

have been carried out, are the variations in the number of young raised, the age of first breeding, and the influence of habitat on numbers. An unavoidable weakness is that the White Stork migrates to the southern half of Africa for the winter, so that its numbers and mortality have been little studied outside the breeding season. The basic information considered here is that collected over many years by Dr. E. Schüz and his associates, before the war at the Vogelwarte Rossitten and after it at the Vogelwarte Radolfzell (see especially Schüz, 1940, 1942, 1943, 1949, 1955, 1957, 1959, 1962, 1963; Kuhk and Schüz, 1950; Sauter and Schüz, 1954; Schüz and Szijj, 1960, 1961, 1962; Schüz et al., 1955; and the bibliography by Schüz and Zink, 1955).

The White Stork has a wide breeding range in the palaearctic, from Denmark in the north to Morocco and Algeria in the south, and from Holland and Portugal in the west to Japan in the east, but in Asia it breeds only in two widely separated and relatively small areas. Nearly all the European birds spend the winter in Africa, chiefly on the eastern side, while other individuals, mainly from Asia, winter in India. In Europe the bird is commonest in the east, fairly common in Germany, and rather sparse in Holland and Denmark. It also breeds in Spain and Portugal, but has in recent years disappeared from southern Sweden, also from Switzerland, where 140 pairs bred in 1900, and except in Alsace it does not breed regularly in France or in Italy (probably through past persecution). Britain is outside its breeding range, apart from a possible mediaeval record. In 1958, about 93000 pairs occupied nests in Europe, but there had been about double this number in 1934 and many more at the beginning of the century (Schüz and Szijj, 1962). The decline in numbers has been particularly heavy in north-western Europe. In both Denmark and Holland, for instance, the number breeding in 1958 was only about one-fifth of that in 1934, whereas in the east there has been little apparent change in numbers and in a few areas, notably Austria, a recent increase. Part, but probably only part, of the widespread decrease is attributable to human factors, especially to the drainage of damp ground where the Storks find most of their food, also to the erection of cables, into which they fly, and perhaps to the poisoning of locusts in Africa and to increased shooting of migrants around the Mediterranean and in some parts of tropical Africa. There were, however, marked fluctuations in Europe in the nineteenth century and the first part of the twentieth century (Haverschmidt, 1949), so long-term natural causes are probably involved as well.

The White Stork usually nests solitarily in traditional sites. One nest on a tower in Thuringia, still occupied in 1930, was in use in 1549, while a bill is extant for its upkeep in 1593, showing that the present high regard for the bird is centuries old. The bird also nests occasionally in trees or on rocks and, uncommonly, in small colonies of up to some thirty pairs (references in Haverschmidt, 1949). The reasons for its being colonial in a few places, including parts of Germany, Austria, and Spain, have not been studied.

The main breeding habitat in Europe is low-lying land, the bird being sparse in hilly country and absent from mountains. In the province of Oldenburg, with an area of 5416 square kilometres, the highest number of pairs per square kilometre was 5·4 in 1940 and the lowest 1·3 in 1953. But the density has varied greatly in different parts of the province, from about 21·5 in 1940 to 4·6 in 1953 in Wesermarsch (867 km²), and from 0·7 in 1940 to 0·07 in 1962 in Cloppenburg (1363 km²). In the breeding season, White Storks feed mainly on damp ground and in meadows on small vertebrates and large invertebrates, the diet varying locally and from year to year according to what is available (Haverschmidt, 1949; Hornberger, 1957; and others). The vertebrates include mice and voles, especially *Microtus arvalis* in its periodic plague years, also Moles, *Talpa europaea*, lizards, snakes, and frogs (chiefly *Rana temporaria* and only rarely *R. esculenta*, which frequents damper ground). The invertebrates include especially earthworms and larger insects such as grasshoppers and beetles. Large insects are less common in the wetter and cooler climate of north-western Europe than in the hotter and drier climate of eastern Europe, which helps to explain why the bird is sparse in Holland and Denmark and absent from Britain, and also why it has been declining in north-western Europe during the last few decades, in which the summers have in general become cooler and wetter. Several other species which feed on insects on open ground have decreased in north-western Europe in the same period, including the Red-backed Shrike, *Lanius collurio*, Roller, *Coracias garrulus*, and Hoopoe, *Upupa epops* (Kalela, 1949; Durango, 1950). On the other hand, extreme drought is also unsuitable for the White Stork, which accounts for its absence from much of Central Asia. In accordance with these conclusions, Schüz, collating the views of others, considered that a wet summer was bad for raising young Storks in north-western Europe but beneficial in the dry eastern parts of Europe.

On migration, most of the European Storks fly south-east to cross the sea at the Bosphorus, they later turn south in Asia Minor and spend the winter in the eastern part of Africa from about 14°N to the Cape Province. A small proportion fly south-west, cross the Straits of Gibraltar and spend the winter in tropical West Africa. In Africa, the number wintering in any one place depends greatly on whether rain has fallen. In the western part of the Orange Free State, for instance, there were about 80000 White Storks in one wet winter, but about one-tenth of this number in the following winter, when there was a drought (Schüz,

1959, 1962, 1963; Schüz and Szijj, 1962). In winter, White Storks feed chiefly on migratory locusts, following the swarms in large flocks, which accounts for their dependence on rain, as locusts settle to breed where it has rained.

Table 40 shows the census for the province of Oldenburg, and Table 41 the longest counts from other European areas which included a reasonably large number of pairs. To save space, the figures in some of the columns in Table 41 refer to different areas in the earlier and later years respectively, as explained in the notes, but except in the first sets of figures (above for Insterburg in East Prussia, below for Upper Silesia), one of the two areas concerned forms part of the other included in the same column. These figures are taken from the various papers by Schüz and his associates (loc. cit.), who also included a large number of censuses from other parts of Germany and elsewhere that were either shorter or involved a smaller number of pairs. Further censuses have been published by Berndt and Moeller (1958), Berndt and Rehbein (1961), and Johansen and Bjerring (1955, 1962).

The censuses in Tables 40 and 41, together with the others mentioned above, support the statement made earlier that there was a general decline in the breeding population of the White Stork between 1934 and 1958, except for a recent increase in Burgenland, Austria, while there has also been no recent decline in other parts of Austria or in Bavaria. These counts also show that, in general, the fluctuations in numbers have occurred simultaneously over a wide area, ranging from Denmark in the north to Württemberg in the south, and from Holland in the west to Upper Silesia and East Prussia in the east. For instance, in Insterburg, Oldenburg, Schleswig-Holstein, and the Neusiedlersee (Austria), numbers increased from 1934 to 1936, decreased in 1937 and 1938 and rose again in 1939. During the war, similarly, numbers fell almost steadily in Oldenburg, Stapelholm in Schleswig-Holstein, Insterburg (see Lack, 1954), Holland, and South Jutland. Between 1945 and 1953, again, the numbers continued to fall steadily in Oldenburg, Stapelholm, and South Jutland, and also in Upper Silesia except for a temporary rise in 1947 and 1948, which was likewise recorded in Baden-Württemberg. After 1953, the numbers rose again in Oldenburg, Stapelholm, and particularly Burgenland, but not in Denmark, Holland or, save between 1954 and 1955, in Baden-Württemberg. A long-continued census around Peine in Lower Saxony, but involving a much smaller number of pairs than the counts just mentioned, similarly showed a rise from 1930 to 1939, then a decline until 1944, followed by a temporary rise until 1948, somewhat irregular changes until 1955 and then a decline (Berndt and Rehbein, 1961). In this last area, the population in 1927 was only one-third of that in 1907.

TABLE 40

The White Stork, *C. ciconia*, in Oldenburg

Year	No. of pairs	Young per successful nest	% Total failures	Average number of young raised per pair
1928	123	2·8	28	2·0
1929	118	2·7	28	2·0
1930	142	3·3	20	2·6
1931	133	3·0	20	2·4
1932	169	3·6	20	2·8
1933	186	3·0	25	2·3
1934	241	2·9	16	2·5
1935	248	2·7	21	2·1
1936	249	2·7	22	2·1
1937	234	2·4	45	1·3
1938	233	2·7	54	1·2
1939	261	3·1	11	2·7
1940	274	2·8	12	2·5
1941	198	2·6	62	1·0
1942	213	2·8	40	1·7
1943	166	2·6	60	1·0
1944	171	2·5	42	1·5
1945	143	2·7	23	2·1
1946	137	3·0	23	2·3
1947	144	2·8	37	1·8
1948	124	2·7	42	1·6
1949	86	2·8	72	0·8
1950	83	3·0	29	2·1
1951	86	3·1	30	2·1
1952	81	3·5	24	2·7
1953	69	2·8	41	1·6
1954	92	3·3	34	2·2
1955	88	2·8	26	2·1
1956	92	2·9	41	1·7
1957	102	2·9	40	1·7
1958	108	2·9	37	2·0
1959	107	3·0	30	2·1
1960	113	2·7	55	1·2
1961	94	2·6	36	1·7
1962	107	2·9	7	2·7
1963	103	2·4	32	1·7

Notes. Based on Tantzen, 1963, Table 1, p. 187, in which certain printing errors (mainly in the interchange of whole columns) were pointed out in litt. by Schüz and Zink, who corrected my table. In the original, the numbers of young raised were expressed to one further decimal place.

TABLE 41

Censuses of White Storks in other areas I = Insterburg, East Prussia 1934–9, followed by U = Upper Silesia, S = all Schleswig-Holstein 1934–8, but thereafter only Stapelholm in that province, J = S. Jutland to 1953 and thereafter all Denmark, N = Netherlands, B = Württemberg 1934–9 and Baden-Württemberg from 1945, A = Austria, 1934–9 Neusiedlersee and from 1948 Burgenland

Year	Number of pairs						Percentage of pairs without young						Young per successful nest					
	I–U	S	J	N	B	A	I	S	J	N	B	A	I	S	J	N	B	A
1934	644	1748		273	49	47	20	14		12	16	26	2.4	2·8		2·9	3·2	2·6
1935	692	1935	—		39	50	30	21		21	3	18	2·1	2·7		2·7	3·1	3·0
1936	750	2111	—		47	61	15	24		21	9	33	2·7	2·5		2·8	2·2	2·7
1937	644	1969	—		43	52	59	44		36	16	48	2·0	2·5		2·8	3·2	2·9
1938	633	1892	—	—	47		43	50		51	17		2·3	2·4		2·7	3·0	
1939	693	177	151	312	49	78	13	21	13	12		10	2·2	2·4	3·0	3·0		3·4
1940		171	148	253				22	22	17				2·4	2·7	2·7		
1941		145	111	202				66	51	52				2·7	2·5	2·5		
1942		125	119	142				53	38	49				2·1	2·7	2·5		
1943		—	86	108				75	52	56				2·0	2·3	3·0		
1944		98	114	115				52	41	29				2·7	2·7	3·0		
1945	61	—	91		184		67	40	28		18		2·1	2·3	2·8		2·4	
1946	61	83	89		201		18	35	20		19		2·8	3·2	3·0		2·7	
1947	72	77	88		240		25	30	35		9		2·8	2·4	2·8		3·0	
1948	69	63	69		252	82	48	38	40		12	29	2·7	2·3	2·3		2·8	2·5
1949	58	48	40		181		72	63	72		29		2·5	2·7	2·5		3·0	—
1950	58	61	50		151	79	29	26	26		31	16	3·0	2·4	2·6		2·8	3·1
1951	46	66	45		163	108	20	20	13		12	17	3·1	3·0	3·1		3·2	3·3
1952	40	65	41		160	106	10	26	9		11	16	3·3	3·1	3·2		3·4	3·6
1953	36	56	35		128	89	36	30	30		22	39	2·7	2·5	2·7		3·0	2·8
1954		67	210		119	120		31	27		22	25		2·8	2·9		3·0	3·2
1955		72	218	57	152	124		29	14	39	22	23		2·7	2·7	2·7	3·1	3·2
1956		71	215	65	152	126		42	31	48	18	30		2·3	2·5	2·8	2·9	2·8
1957		80	196	73	154	159		40	47	32	14	32		2·8	2·7	2·9	3·0	3·0
1958		89	189	56	143	179		33	38	25	19	49		2·3	2·6	2·6	3·1	2·4
1959		87	177	51	150			31	35	22	11			2·6		2·9	3·0	

Notes. Based on Schüz (1940), Sauter and Schüz (1954), and Schüz and Szijj (1960). These workers did not publish the figures for the average number of young per successful nest for most years, but I calculated them from their overall averages of young per nest and percentages of total failures, which were always recorded. Published figures for 1953 differed in the 1954 and 1960 papers, and the more recent ones have been used. Published figures by Johansen and Bjerring (1962) for the number of pairs in Denmark 1955–9 differed slightly from those of Schüz and Szijj (1960), and I have followed the former, but have used the latter for nesting success. Zink (pers. comm.) corrected some of the figures for Baden-Württemberg.

In 1907 the White Stork was widely distributed around Peine, both in the hilly and rather dry country in the south and in the low-lying damp plains in the north. But when the population declined, it did so first in the hilly country, which provides less suitable feeding grounds than the plains, and only later in the plains. The same pattern of decrease was established by Zink (1963*a*) for the decline between 1948 and 1963 in Baden-Württemberg. In this area, as around Peine, the birds breed in two main habitats, first in the plains of the upper Rhine Valley, which provide highly favourable feeding conditions, and secondly in hilly country where marshy areas are much more restricted. The number of pairs breeding in each of these areas, designated as A (the favourable) and B (the less favourable) respectively, has been set out in Table 42. In both there was a marked decline between 1948 and 1949. In area B, there was thereafter a nearly steady decline, from 52 pairs in 1949 to only 8 in 1963, a reduction of 85 per cent, and many places were deserted entirely. In area A, on the other hand, the population was virtually the same in 1960 as in 1949, with small fluctuations in between, but there was a marked decline after 1960; but the overall decline between 1949 and 1963 was only 49 per cent, and hence much smaller than in area B.

TABLE 42

Breeding of White Stork in two habitats in Baden-Württemberg
A = favourable valleys, B = less favourable hilly ground

	Number of pairs		Young per successful nest		Percentage of pairs without young		Young raised per pair	
	A	B	A	B	A	B	A	B
1948	148	77	2·9	2·8	9	16	2·6	2·4
1949	110	52	3·0	3·0	22	40	2·3	1·8
1950	94	37	2·7	2·4	33	27	1·8	1·8
1951	102	39	3·1	3·0	12	18	2·7	2·5
1952	103	35	3·3	3·5	8	20	3·1	2·8
1953	85	25	2·9	3·1	20	24	2·3	2·4
1954	81	20	2·8	3·0	25	25	2·1	2·3
1955	99	27	3·0	3·2	21	19	2·4	2·6
1956	101	27	3·0	2·6	15	41	2·5	1·5
1957	105	26	3·0	3·0	12	19	2·6	2·4
1958	100	21	3·1	3·0	16	29	2·6	2·1
1959	107	21	2·9	3·2	9	10	2·7	2·9
1960	107	15	3·0	3·5	16	33	2·5	2·3
1961	98	11	2·7	3·0	24	45	2·0	1·6
1962	68	11	2·7	2·3	31	9	1·9	2·1
1963	56	8	2·8	2·8	18	38	2·3	1·8
Average	98	28	2·96	2·97	17	24	2·44	2·24

Note. Data from Zink (1963), extended in pers. comm.

THE WHITE STORK IN GERMANY

White Storks that have bred before tend to return to the same nest, while the young usually settle near their birthplace. Of those ringed as nestlings in Insterburg, two-thirds settled to breed within 25 km of their birthplace and over four-fifths within 50 km, but 9 per cent settled at 50–100 km, 7 per cent at 100–500 km, and 1 per cent beyond that (Schüz, 1949). The proportion settling beyond 50 km was probably a little higher than these figures indicate, as such individuals are not so often recorded as those in the home province of the observers. The proportion settling within 50 km of their birthplace was similarly about 70 per cent in the favourable habitat (A) in the Rhine valley studied by Zink. In contrast, of the young raised in the less favourable hilly country (B), only 17 per cent settled within 50 km of their birthplace and most of them moved to breed in more favourable habitats further east. There was no corresponding tendency for birds raised in area A to settle in hilly country, and those raised in area A which moved more than 50 km settled in other low-lying districts. Further, each year some sub-adult Storks occupied nests without breeding, these were nearly always in hilly or other less favourable habitats, and most of them moved again in a later year, on the average for about 20 km, to breed in more favourable areas. Hence Zink's study provides a clear instance of dispersive behaviour in birds, probably the best yet available. Moreover, it is wholly explicable in terms of natural selection, and there is no need to invoke group-selection for it (cf. Wynne-Edwards' views on pp. 302–3). Indeed, it is remarkably like the behaviour which I earlier suggested might explain the breeding dispersion of the Heron, *Ardea cinerea* (Lack, 1954, see also this book, p. 287). with sub-adult birds occupying nests without breeding, returning to breed in them in the following year if the area proved satisfactory for feeding, and moving elsewhere if not. That the Heron is colonial and the White Stork usually solitary does not affect the argument, the important point being that in both species many individuals form pairs and occupy nests without laying eggs in the first year in which they occupy breeding stations.

The gradual dispersion away from less favourable habitats recorded by Zink occurred, of course, in a declining population. With a rising population, more birds breeding for the first time would presumably settle in less favourable habitats, either because they avoid favourable habitats when they see that these are filled, or because they are expelled by the birds in occupation. But the possible means of dispersion during a period of expansion have not been studied, and it is to be hoped that Storks will again increase, so as to allow such a study to be made. Vigorous fighting is sometimes observed in the White Stork between newcomers and established pairs, which may even cause the latter to lose their eggs (Haverschmidt, 1949), but it is not clear whether this has any important role in dispersion, as the fights seem to be primarily for nests, and not for breeding territories with associated feeding areas.

Sub-adult Storks, especially those only one year old, often remain for the summer in the African wintering grounds, or return for part of the way and stay around the Mediterranean, though others return to the breeding areas (Libbert, 1954). At Insterburg in East Prussia, no Storks occupied nests when 1 or 2 years old, a few did so when 3 years old, while most did so for the first time when 4 or 5 years old and some later (Hornberger, 1954). Re-analysing Hornberger's figures (which are unsatisfactory as they stand for several reasons), Schnetter and Zink (1960) noted that 36 individuals first occupied nests at the age of 3, 85 at the age of 4, and 95 at the age of 5. It should be added that these figures refer solely to the occupation of nests, not necessarily to the laying of eggs, which was not recorded. They suggested that 17 per cent of the birds first occupied nests when aged 3, and if anything this percentage is too high, as Hornberger recorded other individuals for the first time when 6 years old or even older, but most of these had presumably been overlooked when younger. The point is important because, in contrast, Schnetter and Zink found that, of 31 Storks of known age which raised young in South Baden, 15 first did so at the age of 3, 7 at the age of 4, 5 at the age of 5, only 1 as late as 6 years old, and 3 when only 2 years old. The last constituted the first such records for Germany, though there were earlier ones for Denmark (Lange, 1954). The latest available figures for the first occupation of nests in South Baden includes 8 for birds aged 2, 51 for birds aged 3, 32 for birds aged 4, 16 for birds aged 5, and 4 for birds aged 6 (Zink, pers. comm.).

The sex of many, but not all, of the Storks occupying nests for the first term in Insterburg and in South Baden was determined by field observations. In South Baden, those aged 2 included 3 males and 3 females, among those aged 3 males predominated, and among the older age-groups the sex ratio was about equal. The figures for Insterburg included too many unidentified individuals, most of which Hornberger thought were females, for the sex ratio to be reliable. It seems, however, that in the White Stork the females do not mature before the males, and if anything, the males perhaps do so before the females.

On the views advanced earlier in this book, one would expect deferred maturity to be evolved only in species in which younger parents are less efficient than older ones in raising young. The figures provided by Hornberger (1954) strongly suggested that this was so in the White Stork, and they were re-analysed and shown to be significant by Schüz (1957), as set out in Table 43. Older parents were also shown to be more efficient than younger parents in several other species discussed in

TABLE 43

The influence of age of White Stork on breeding success in
first year of nest-occupation in Insterburg

Age of first breeding	No. of pairs studied	No. which raised young	No. of young raised	Percentage without young	Average raised in successful nests
3	17	9	16	47	1·8
4	57	34	66	40	1·9
5	68	53	120	22	2·3

Note. From Hornberger (1954) modified by Schüz (1957).

this book, but in these others the older parents had usually bred before, so that at least part of the difference may have been due, not to age as such, but to previous experience in breeding. But previous experience can be excluded in the present figures, because all the individuals analysed in Table 43 were occupying nests for the first time. This table shows that both the proportion of pairs which raised at least one young, and the average number of young in successful nests, were higher in the older than the younger parents.

These findings do not, by themselves, suggest a selective advantage for the deferment of first breeding beyond the age of 3, because the 3-year-old birds raised some young; hence if that had been all, the birds which started breeding when 3 years old should have been able to raise more young in their lives than those which first bred when older. Natural selection could favour the deferment of maturity beyond the age of three only if breeding at the age of three increases the mortality rate of the parents concerned so that, on average, they leave fewer descendants than those which first breed when older. It is not known whether breeding increases the mortality rate of adult Storks. Another point requiring study is whether those individuals which breed when 3 years old differ, for instance in hunting efficiency or habitat, from those which first breed when older. That the proportion of birds breeding when 3 years old is higher in Baden than Insterburg might mean that breeding is easier in Baden, and in this connection it is suggestive that Schnetter and Zink found that in Baden, unlike Insterburg, 3-year-old parents raised the same average number of young as older parents, at least in one year. It therefore seems possible that the deferment of breeding beyond the age of three depends only partly on hereditary factors and partly on the availability of food at the time.

My suggestion that deferred maturity has been evolved in those species of birds in which the raising of young is so difficult that it would impose undue strain on inexperienced younger individuals has been rejected by Wynne-Edwards (1962, p. 568), particularly on the grounds that, in the White Stork and other species, the age of first breeding varies. On my view, he claimed, natural selection should have resulted in a more or less fixed age of maturity. But in my view variation could be expected either if the age of first breeding can be phenotypically modified to the food situation, as suggested above, or if the advantage of starting at one particular age or a year younger were on balance almost equal. Wynne-Edwards produced no evidence for his alternative view that 'the homeostatic machinery allows only the appropriate number of individuals to breed in any given area in any one year', thus preventing over-population, and there is nothing in the published work of Schüz or others to suggest that this is what happens.

As can be seen from Tables 40, 41 and 42, each year some White Storks with nests did not raise any young. The proportion was often between 10 and 20 per cent, and Schüz reasonably concluded that at least most of these individuals were birds occupying nests for the first time. The existence of sub-adult birds which occupy nests but do not lay eggs is well established for the Common Swift, *Apus apus* (Lack, 1956b), and for various sea-birds. But it is not known how many of the Storks without young did not lay eggs; the proportion may well have been high. It can also be seen from the tables that the proportion of nests without any young varied locally, being highest in Oldenburg and Upper Silesia, next highest in Stapelholm and South Jutland, lower in Burgenland and lowest in Baden-Württemberg. It was therefore higher in the north than the south. Schüz attributed this variation to local differences in the average age at which Storks first breed and, fitting with this view, there were more nests occupied at the age of three in Baden than Insterburg, as already mentioned. The higher proportion of pairs without young in the less favourable than the favourable habitats in Baden-Württemberg has already been discussed.

In some years, which Schüz termed 'Störungsjahre', the proportion of Storks without young was much higher than usual, even up to 70 per cent, and this involved many individuals which had bred successfully in previous years. In the 26 years reviewed in Table 41, those with the highest proportion of pairs without young were 1937, 1938, 1941, 1942, 1943, 1944, 1945, 1948, 1949 and 1956.[1] As can be seen from Table

---

[1] The figures in Table 40 suggest that 1960 was another disturbed year in Oldenburg, but Tantzen (1963) recorded the behaviour of the birds as highly abnormal, and the breeding failures were perhaps due to poison put out to check a plague of the vole *Microtus arvalis*.

41 and from the figures for many other areas published by Schüz, disturbed years occurred simultaneously in many and sometimes all the areas studied, though their effect was greater in some areas than others. Their possible cause has been disputed. Schüz stated that in most of them, though not all, fewer Storks than usual returned to the breeding grounds, but I do not think that this is significant, because there has been a general decrease in numbers over the last thirty years and it does not seem to have been much more marked in the disturbed years than the rest, while there was an increase in the disturbed season of 1956. Attempts to correlate such bad years with unfavourable weather in the wintering grounds, or with trematode infections, have also failed. The one constant feature has been the unusually late return of the Storks to the breeding grounds. Hence, as suggested by Schüz, the critical factor is presumably one influencing the spring migration, but what this may be is not known. Since, however, the birds tend to return later in a cold than a warm spring (Tantzen, 1963), the weather around the time of their return may well be one factor involved.

In Holland, the commonest clutch of the White Stork is 4 eggs, but it varies between 2 and 6, while in Hungary 7 young have occasionally been raised (Haverschmidt, 1949). Owing to the difficulty of seeing into most nests, clutch-size has not been studied systematically in the White Stork, so it is not known to what extent the local, annual and seasonal differences in the number of young raised depend on differences in clutch-size and to what extent on differences in nestling mortality, but probably both factors are involved.

While White Storks commonly lay 4 eggs, the average number of young raised by the successful pairs, i.e. excluding those without any young, was rarely more than 3 per pair and occasionally as little as 2 per pair. The eggs in a clutch hatch on different days, so that the nestlings differ greatly in size and the youngest often starve. This led Schüz (1943) to postulate that the last egg or eggs form a reserve, the last young to hatch being raised only in years when food is plentiful. This is in essence the function which I later (1947, 1954) attributed to asynchronous hatching in raptorial and other birds, in which all the food goes to the first-hatched and largest nestlings until they are satisfied; if food is plentiful the youngest then receives enough, while if food is sparse it is not wasted on young that would die anyway. The position is more complex in the White Stork than in other species with asynchronous hatching because a nestling sometimes dies, not of starvation, but through being thrown out of the nest, or even killed and eaten, by one of its parents, which Schüz (1957) named 'chronism', after the titan Chronos who ate all save one of his offspring. Wynne-Edwards (1962, p. 531) considered that 'Chronism conforms with the general pattern of adaptations evolved to curb recruitment', but he provided no positive evidence for this, nor did he discuss why recruitment should need to be curbed in a population of White Storks which has been declining for many years. I wonder whether parent Storks kill primarily such nestlings as do not respond adequately to them because they are already weak from starvation, in which case the parents merely accelerate deaths that would occur anyway, and thus ensure that food will not be wasted on a dying chick. On present evidence I see no reason to change my view that the function of asynchronous hatching, in the White Stork and other species, is to bring the effective brood-size rapidly down to that which the parents can adequately feed.

The average number of young raised by pairs which raised at least one chick differed in different years, though the annual variations were less marked than those in the proportion of nests without any young. These variations tended to occur in parallel in different areas. For instance, of the areas covered in Tables 40 and 41, the high average of at least 3 young per successful pair was recorded in 4 out of the 6 areas studied in 1939, 3 out of 5 in 1946, and all 6 in 1951 and 1952. Similarly the unusually low average of 2½ or less per successful pair was recorded in 3 out of 6 areas studied in 1937, 2 out of 4 in 1941, 1942, and 1943, 3 out of 5 in 1945, and 3 out of 6 in 1948. It is suggestive that in all these latter years there was a high proportion of nests without young, while in 3 of the other 4 years of this type (1938, 1949, and 1956), an average of at most 2½ young per successful pair was raised in 2 of the areas studied.

The German workers did not discuss why the average number of young raised in successful nests should have been lower than usual in years with a high proportion of pairs without young. But Storks are known to return in spring later in the disturbed years, and it therefore occurred to me that breeding success might in general be correlated with the date of return, and hence with the date of laying. Published figures were not available by which I could test this for individual pairs, but Tantzen (1963) gave for Oldenburg the figures for the average number of birds returning in each 10-day period in each spring, which allows a comparison to be made between the average date of return and the average number of young raised each year, as set out in Table 44. This shows that both the proportion of pairs without any young, and the average number of young raised per pair in successful nests, were strongly correlated with the average date of return, breeding being in both respects more successful the earlier that the Storks returned. It may be added that of the four years listed above in which an average of at least three young was raised per successful nest in several areas, the Storks returned early to Oldenburg in 1939, 1951, and 1952, and

TABLE 44

Relation between average date of return and breeding success of
White Stork at Oldenburg

Mean date of return	Years (*36 = 1936*, etc.)	Average percentage of pairs without young	Average number of young in successful nests
5–12 April	36, 39, 40, 51, 52, 54, 62	20	3·1
14–16 April	44, 47, 50, 55, 57, 59, 63	34	2·8
18–21 April	37, 41, 42, 48, 53, 56, 58, 61	43	2·7
23 April– 3 May	38, 43, 49	62	2·7

Notes. Based on the figures for breeding success in Table 41 and the dates of arrival given by Tanzen (1963, Table 13; no data for 1943–6). Note that the dates in the left-hand column of Tantzen's table for the years 1953–63 inclusive are in the wrong order. The author informed me (per Dr. Zink) that only the dates themselves are wrong, and that the numbers of birds returning in each period in each year are in the correct order, i.e. the top line in his columns for each year refers to 1–10 March and the bottom line to 11–20 June, with the rest in between in chronological order. The average dates of return in Table 45 are very approximate, as Tantzen's figures for each year were based on small totals grouped in 10-day periods. I considered it best to exclude from the averages the very few individuals recorded as returning in June, and also the figures for 1960, as the discussion by Tantzen (1963) suggested that the high proportion of birds without young in that year was abnormal, and perhaps due to poison put out for a plague of *Microtus arvalis*. The averages for the percentage of pairs without young and the number of young in successful nests were the averages of the annual averages for the years in question in Table 40.

the date of return was not recorded in 1946; further, of the six years listed above when an average of only 2½ or fewer young was raised per pair in several areas, the Storks returned late to Oldenburg in five and the date of return was not recorded in the other. Hence this is clearly a widespread phenomenon, by no means confined to Oldenburg. It strongly suggests that the food supplies available for young Storks in Germany decrease in the course of the summer, so that those individuals which breed late have a reduced chance of raising young; but the food supplies have not been measured. Because the birds return late in years when the weather in April is cold, and because breeding is less successful when the birds start late, there has also, as noted by Tantzen (1963), been a tendency for breeding to be less successful in those years when the weather in April was unusually cold.

Schüz stated that more young Storks were raised per pair in some areas, such as Baden-Württemberg, than in others such as Oldenburg, but the figures in Tables 40 and 41 suggest that such local differences have been due primarily, if not entirely, to variations in the proportion of pairs without any young. It is surprising that, as shown in Table 42, the average number of young raised in successful nests in Baden-Württemberg was the same in the favourable area (A) and the unfavourable area (B).

The oldest wild ringed Storks so far recovered lived almost twenty years (Schüz et al., 1955). The average mortality cannot be assessed from ringing recoveries without various adjustments, partly because many first-year and second-year birds do not return to the breeding grounds (where the chances of recovery are highest), and partly because some of the older rings may wear away, while in addition many of the Rossitten records were lost in the war. The age distribution calculated by Schüz (1955) after allowing for such difficulties suggests that the annual mortality of the adults after they are two years old was about 21 per cent. On the same basis, the mortality in each of the first two years of life was possibly 30 per cent, but the true figures for this period were probably much higher.

In a stable population, the annual loss of breeding adults is equal to the recruitment of birds breeding for the first time. Hence if 21 out of every 100 breeding Storks die each year, there should be 21 newcomers. At Insterburg, most of these newcomers would be 4 or 5 years old, with a few aged 3 and a few aged 6. Supposing, to simplify the calculation, that half of them were aged 4 and the rest aged 5, and assuming that between the ages of 2 and 5 their annual mortality was 21 per cent (as for the older birds), then 21 newcomers would be the survivors from about 34 2-year-old birds. The figures in Tables 40 and 41 show that each pair of Storks produces, on the average, about 2 young a year, hence 100 adults produce 100 young, and, in a stable population, these should be reduced in 2 years to 34. If the mortality in the second year were 21 per cent, as in later years, about three-fifths of the young birds should die in their first year, while if the mortality in the second year were higher, as suggested by Schüz's figures, the mortality in the first should be rather less. These calculations were made on the assumption that most Storks first breed when aged 4 or 5, but if, as in Baden-Württemberg, about half of them first breed when 3 years old and the most of the others when 4 years old, the mortality in the early years should be proportionately higher, a little over 70 per cent from fledging to the end of the second year. All these estimates are very rough but it should, I think, be possible to calculate much more precise figures from the original data than any so far published.

While an annual adult mortality of 21 per cent appears to balance reasonably with the birth-rate and the juvenile mortality, it seems a high figure for a species in which breeding is deferred to an age of between 3 and 5 years, since the expectation of adult life is only $4\frac{1}{4}$ years, and a pair can raise an average of 2 young in a year. Hence the omission of one year's breeding would make a proportionately much greater difference to the eventual number of descendants in the Stork than in, for instance, a shearwater, which lives much longer and raises only one young a year. Presumably, however, the advantages to the Stork in not breeding when younger are sufficient to outweigh the potential loss of one or more years' offspring, and it would be interesting to know more about the nature of these advantages.

The final problem for discussion here is the regulation of numbers in the White Stork, including possible reasons for the decrease in the twentieth century. Earlier Schüz (1949) suggested that seasons when few young were produced tended to be followed by a decrease in the the number of pairs breeding 4 to 5 years later, while years of successful breeding were followed by an increase 4 to 5 years later. Similarly Berndt and Rehbein (1962) claimed that, round Peine in Lower Saxony, the average number of young raised per pair was about average in the years 1930–6 and below average in the years 1937–60 and that, correspondingly, the population rose in the years 1932–40 and decreased in the years 1941–60. I do not think, however, that the latter claim can be sustained on such scanty data, especially as long-term population trends were involved.

The much longer series of data now available for Oldenburg in Table 40 allow a more satisfactory test to be made of the relations between the reproductive output each year and the subsequent changes in numbers. The Storks in Oldenburg probably resemble those in Insterburg in first breeding mainly when 4 or 5 years old. For each year, therefore, I calculated the percentage change in the number of pairs from the previous year and compared it with the average number of young that had been produced per pair 4 and 5 years earlier. In 1935, for example, 248 pairs occupied nests, an increase of 7, or 3 per cent, on the 241 pairs present in the previous year, while the average number of young raised 4 years earlier was 2·4 and 5 years earlier 2·6 (average 2·5) per pair. When I plotted the figures thus obtained for each year on a scatter diagram, there was obviously no correlation between the percentage change in numbers each year and the average number of young produced 4 and 5 years before. There seems no point in reproducing this diagram, but the lack of relationship may be illustrated by reference to the unusually favourable and unusually unfavourable years of reproduction respectively.

The average number of young raised per pair per year in Oldenburg was between 1·9 and 2·0. There were 6 years when the average number of young raised 4 and 5 years earlier was much higher than this, between 2·4 and 2·8 per pair, namely 1935–8 inclusive, 1944, and 1956; for these 6 years the average change in numbers over the previous year was an increase of 1 per cent (the extremes being an increase of 4½ per cent and a decrease of 6 per cent). There were also 6 years when the output of young 4 and 5 years earlier was very low, between 1·2 and 1·45 per pair, namely 1942, 1946, 1947, 1948, 1953, and 1954; for these years the average change in numbers over the previous year was an increase of 2 per cent (with extremes of a 33 per cent increase and a 16 per cent decrease). Clearly, there was no average difference between the years preceded by unusually successful and unusually unsuccessful reproduction respectively, and the average change was also similar for the years in which the previous reproductive output was near to average.

No other series of data can compare in length with the 31 years available for Oldenburg, and I therefore conclude that, in the years studied here, the variations in the reproductive rate of the White Stork have had no appreciable influence on the subsequent changes in the number of breeding pairs. Obviously if the reproductive rate in any year had been extremely low, for instance if no young whatever had been produced, the breeding population four or five years later would have declined. The important point, however, is that within the limits of reproductive output actually observed, of between 0·8 and 2·8 young per pair per year, there was no apparent influence on the size of the subsequent breeding population. Hence even if, within this period, the Storks had been exercising 'prudential restraints' on breeding in Wynne-Edwards' sense, they would presumably have had no effect on their subsequent numbers. I suggest that the concept of prudential restraints in birds may be rejected, and it is pleasing that the data for rejecting this idea come from so well-known a fertility symbol as the White Stork.

If the output of young did not appreciably influence the changes in the size of the breeding population, then presumably the mortality was critical, either of the young between attaining independence and breeding, or of the adults, or of both. This almost certainly means that the critical mortality occurs in the winter in Africa, so that more cannot yet be said about it. At least, however, these findings suggest that one should seek first in Africa for the factors causing the current overall decrease in the numbers of the White Stork in Europe. But this general decrease is evidently modified by at least one factor operating during the breeding season, the dispersive behaviour demonstrated by Zink, which is presumably responsible for the present decline occurring faster in dry hilly country than moist low-lying plains, and faster in the damper and cooler climate of north-western Europe than in the drier country of eastern Europe.

Summarizing, the number of White Storks breeding in Europe has in general declined during the last thirty years, but more markedly in the cool and wet areas of north-western Europe than in the warmer and drier east, and, within Germany, more markedly in hilly than low-lying habitats. The latter difference has been due to dispersion, pairs tending to move from hilly to low-lying country. The birds first occupy nests when between two and six years old, the average number of young raised per pair in their first year of occupation being larger in the older than the younger individuals. The annual adult mortality is apparently 21 per cent, rather high for a species with deferred maturity. In many years, between 10 and 20 per cent of the pairs did not raise young, most of these presumably being sub-adults, but in a few years the proportion was much higher, up to 70 per cent, and included many individuals that had bred successfully before. Both the proportion of pairs each year without any young, and the average number of young raised in successful nests each year, were correlated with the average date of return of the Storks in spring, breeding being more successful in the years when the Storks returned earlier. The last young in a brood to hatch tend to be raised only in favourable years; further study is required to know why small young are sometimes killed by their parents. There is no good reason to think that Storks exercise 'prudential restraints', regulating their reproductive output to the size of the breeding population, and in any case the average number of young raised per pair per year had no appreciable influence on the subsequent changes in the breeding population. Hence numbers are probably regulated by the mortality in the African wintering grounds.

Stork rings large enough to be read through a telescope.

14

THE YELLOW-EYED PENGUIN

THE pioneer study of a sea-bird population, and one of the longest yet made of any bird, was that on the Yellow-eyed Penguin, *Megadyptes antipodes*, near Dunedin in New Zealand by L. E. Richdale, which appeared in a series of papers and finally in his book *A Population Study of Penguins* (1957), in which all his earlier papers were summarized. A high proportion of the birds was marked individually and special attention was paid to the effects of age on the reproductive rate, reproductive success, and the population turnover, but the birds were not studied away from the breeding area, nor was their food investigated. Apart from its results, the work was remarkable in being carried out by an amateur working single-handed in his spare time over eighteen years, from 1936–7 to 1953–4 inclusive.

Penguins are the most highly specialized of all birds for marine life. They catch all their food, mainly small fish or swimming invertebrates, in the sea, usually obtaining it near their breeding grounds, though some antarctic species have to travel long distances. Their wings are adapted as paddles, the loss of flight being made possible by the absence of land predators from their main breeding grounds in the antarctic and on remote islands, where they typically nest in large colonies in the open. But various of the species nesting on the shores of larger land

Headpiece: Yellow-eyed Penguins by their nest.

masses further north, including the Yellow-eyed Penguin, nest in small groups in burrows, often in forest. A few species migrate for a long distance, but many others, including the Yellow-eyed Penguin, are resident throughout the year near their breeding colonies.

The colony of Yellow-eyed Penguins studied by Richdale included 26 nests when first fully counted in 1938–9, but only 23 in the following year and 21 in the next, after which it rose steadily to 82 nests in 1952–3. The decrease after 1938–9 was evidently due to an unusually bad season for both reproduction and adult survival, discussed later. The subsequent rise to 82 nests was regarded by Richdale as a return to normal after a period prior to his study in which the area had been greatly disturbed by changes in human usage of the land.

In addition to the nesting pairs, there was each year in the colony a proportion of birds, on the average 38 per cent, which did not breed. These consisted primarily of sub-adults from 1 to 4 years old, together with a proportion of adult males which failed to obtain mates. No penguins bred as yearlings. Of the females, about 48 per cent first bred when 2 years old and nearly all the rest when 3 years old. Of the males, only about 8 per cent first bred when 2 years old, 35 per cent when 3 years old and another 33 per cent when 4 years old; at 5 years old probably all were mature but some still failed to obtain mates.

The recoveries of marked birds showed that established breeding adults nearly always returned to where they had bred in the previous year. About three-fifths of them retained the same mate, and most of the changes of mate were due to the death or disappearance (presumed death) of their former partner. However, in about 14 per cent of the instances in which both partners returned, they changed mates, the reasons for which are not known (but see p. 246 for the Kittiwake). As regards the new intake into the colony each year, just under half of the individuals that bred for the first time between 1939–40 and 1951–2 inclusive had been raised as young in the colony, the rest being raised elsewhere. Likewise a number of those raised as young in the colony were later found breeding in other colonies up to several miles away.

During the 18 years studied, the average date of laying each year varied only between 21 and 30 September, and in 15 of these years it fell between 22 and 26 September inclusive. This comparative constancy is common in sea-birds and is in marked contrast to what happens in small passerine birds in north temperate regions. This is presumably because the time at which the food supply increases in summer each year in temperate regions is subject to much smaller annual variations in the sea than in woods and other terrestrial habitats.

Although the average date of laying varied so little, the spread of laying within each year extended over three to four weeks and since each marked female penguin tended to lay at a similar date each year, the individual differences in laying time may well have depended on hereditary differences. It will be recalled that there was a spread of similar length in the laying period of the Great Tit each year, and that in this species the early pairs were more successful than the later in raising young. But in the Yellow-eyed Penguin, both the percentage of hatched young which left the nest, and the percentage of young leaving the nest which returned in a later year, were equal for early and late breeding pairs, so natural selection presumably favoured the earlier and later birds to about an equal extent.

The normal clutch is 2. Each egg weighs about 140 grams, and their combined weight is about 5 per cent of that of a normal female, a low proportion compared with that found in various other sea-birds. Nevertheless, the second egg rarely follows so soon as 3 days after the first, and usually after 4 and sometimes 5 days. The parent does not normally start incubation until around the time when the second egg is laid, so that the two young usually hatch on the same day. As the pairs which breed late are as successful in raising young as those which breed early, one would have supposed that there would be a great advantage in at least the early pairs laying again if they lost their eggs. But in fact no lost clutches were replaced. This, together with the long interval between the 2 eggs, imply that the formation of the eggs imposes a severe strain on the female, presumably because food is scarce at this time of year. Nearly all other species of penguins lay a clutch of 2 eggs some 4 days apart, and at least most of them do not lay again if the first clutch is lost.

Although the normal clutch is 2, 38 per cent of the females which bred when 2 years old had clutches of 1, as had 6 per cent of the 3 year olds, but only 1·5 per cent of the older birds. This difference in the clutch-size of the 2-year-olds might have been evolved by the species because, as shown later, the younger birds are less efficient parents and so cannot, like the older birds, be sure of raising 2 young; alternatively, or in addition, the strain of producing eggs might be particularly great in the 2-year-olds, before they have become fully experienced in feeding.

Incubation lasts on the average for 43·5 days and the nestling period for 106 days (usual range 97–118 days), both periods being rather long compared with those of other penguins that lay 2 eggs, though much shorter than in the King and Emperor Penguins, *Aptenodytes patagonica* and *A. forsteri*, mentioned later. Seventy-eight per cent of the eggs hatched, and 76 per cent of the hatched young successfully left the nest, so that 59 per cent of the eggs gave rise to fledglings, a fairly high figure as compared with birds in general (cf. Lack, 1954).

Omitting losses due to desertion or human disturbance, 2-year-old females hatched only 32 per cent of their eggs, 3-year-olds breeding for the first time hatched 70 per cent, 3-year-olds breeding for the second time hatched 82 per cent, 4-year-olds 87 per cent, and those aged 5–13 years 92 per cent, while there was possibly a reduction in birds older than this. Survival of the young was followed only to Christmas, that is, for about 8 of the 16 weeks that they spend on land. Using survival to this date as a criterion of success, from the broods in which at least 2 young hatched, the pairs in which one parent was 2 and the other 3 years old raised only 2 out of 6, those whose average age was 3 or 3½ years raised 42 out of 50 (84 per cent), whereas older pairs raised 89 per cent, but there were too few data for the younger parents to regard these differences as more than suggestive. Since, however, 2-year-old parents had a smaller average clutch, much higher losses of eggs, and very possibly higher losses of young than older parents, it may be marginally of advantage for them to breed at this age, and this is presumably why natural selection has resulted in only just under half of them doing so. It may be added that, while the survival of the young was followed only until half-way through the nestling period, few died in the second half. However, most of the young were not weighed, and their survival after leaving the nest was not compared for parents of different age; so the possibility remains open that the fledglings raised by younger parents survived proportionately less well than those raised by older parents after becoming independent.

Most losses of nestlings were due to starvation, and though predation occurred, it was primarily of young already weakened by starvation, as also found in the Adelie Penguin, *Pygoscelis adeliae* (Sladen, 1958), the King Penguin (Stonehouse, 1960), and the Emperor Penguin (Budd, 1961, 1962). In the Yellow-eyed Penguin, if one parent with a brood of two died, one of the nestlings usually obtained most of the food, so that the other quickly died; however, one parent working alone could raise one chick. If one parent alone cannot raise two chicks, two parents presumably could not raise four chicks, and perhaps they could not raise three, so that the normal clutch of two may well be adapted to the most efficient brood-size. But the critical test of providing parents with three young has not been made.

Yellow-eyed Penguins moult after breeding. The adults put on much fat beforehand and then come ashore and fast for about 24 days, in which they lose 45 per cent of their body-weight. Much the same happens in other penguins. The moult evidently imposes a considerable strain, and it has to be preceded by a period in which food is easily obtained.

Of the adult Yellow-eyed Penguins of 3 years old and upward marked by Richdale, about 13 per cent disappeared, presumably dying, between one year and the next, chiefly in winter, when the birds were away from the colony. This gives an expectation of further life for an adult of some 7 years. The mortality was higher in females than males, but by how much is not certain. The sex ratio was evidently about equal at hatching, and also at the yearling stage, but according to one estimate (Richdale, Table 73, p. 141) males were twice as numerous as females among the birds that survived at least 10 years, while according to another (bottom, p. 154), the average survival rate was 88·8 per cent for males and 84·2 per cent for females, which could not have produced so large a difference in the sex ratio by the end of 10 years.

The loss of juvenile penguins between the time that they left the nest and their return as yearlings could not be measured directly from ringing recoveries, as many of them dispersed to other and unvisited breeding stations; but it could be estimated. The annual adult mortality of 13 per cent, already mentioned, was presumably balanced by a recruitment of 13 per cent of new 3-year-olds. Ringing recoveries showed that the average loss in each of the second and third years of life was between 15 and 16 per cent, so that 13 newcomers aged 3 would have been derived from about $17\frac{1}{4}$ yearlings. The latter, in turn, would have been derived from the known average of 36 young raised per pair to the fledging stage by every 100 adults. Hence the average loss between fledging and return to the colony at a year old was probably about 52 per cent ($18\frac{3}{4}$ out of 36), a slightly lower figure than in various other birds (Lack, 1954).

The season of 1938–9 was extremely unsuccessful compared with the rest, as can be seen from Table 45. Only 45 per cent of the hatched young were raised to fledging, as compared with an average for all other seasons of 78 per cent, while the next lowest figure was 63 per cent. Further, the survival of the young after they fledged was evidently lower than usual, as only 22 per cent of the reared young were recovered later, and except in the following year, when the figure was only 17 per cent, it did not otherwise fall below 36 per cent, and (omitting these two years) averaged 46 per cent. After breeding, the adults started their moult unusually late and took longer than usual over it. Moreover, only 74 per cent of the adults returned to breed in the following year, as compared with an average of 86 per cent for all other years (the figure was also 74 per cent in 1939–40, but in all except one other year it was at least 80 per cent). In 1938–9, also, 42 per cent of the adults in the breeding area were unestablished and apparently wandering, as compared with 5 or 6 per cent in the two following years and hardly any in other seasons. Wandering juveniles were also commoner than usual in 1938–9, comprising 65 per cent of those seen, which was the highest

TABLE 45

Annual variations in productivity and mortality in the Yellow-eyed Penguin, *Megadyptes antipodes*

Summer of	Percentage of				
	Adult residents at least 4 years old alive next year	Eggs laid that produced fledged young	Hatched young reared (to Christmas)	Reared young recovered later	Reared young that bred later
1936–7	—	63	63	40	10
1937–8	82	62	74	51	16
1938–9	74	37	45	22	17
1939–40	74	60	73	17	17
1940–1	94	75	92	44	25
1941–2	87	55	71	37	20
1942–3	93	80	91	49	41
1943–4	94	60	83	57	45
1944–5	80	56	82	43	32
1945–6	84	49	71	36	33
1946–7	81	41	72	42	39
1947–8	91	65	75	—	23
1948–9	91	61	80	—	27
1949–50	93	62	83	—	15
1950–1	85	—	—	—	—
1951–2	76	67	79	—	—
1952–3	87	62	74	—	—
Mean	86	59	76	41	26

Note. Based on Richdale (1957), Tables 72, 67, and 29. Richdale did not publish the number of breeding pairs each year, but it decreased from 26 pairs in 1938–9 to 21 pairs in 1940–1 and then rose steadily to 82 pairs in 1952–3.

figure recorded, while the average for other years was 39 per cent.

Clearly, during the breeding season of 1938–9 and in the following winter, something was greatly amiss, presumably with the food supply, though this was not investigated. It may be added that this occurred in a year of relatively low density (26 nests) compared with the later years of the study. Also, it was followed by a decline in the number of breeding pairs in the following year, to 23 nests in 1939–40 and 21 nests in the following year, this low level being maintained until 1942–3, partly because both young and adults also survived exceptionally badly in the following winter, that of 1940 (though breeding success in the summer of 1939–40 was near average).

In contrast to 1938–9, survival was unusually good in 1940–1, 1942–3, and 1943–4; the proportion of hatched young reared (twice over 90 per cent), of reared young recovered later (once 57 per cent), and of reared young that later bred in the area (twice over 40 per cent), also the survival of adults between one breeding season and the next (93 or 94 per cent) were all unusually high, and included the highest figures recorded for any year. This high success might conceivably have been assisted by the low population density in these years, when there were respectively only 25, 26, and 32 nesting pairs, but this could n t have been the primary reason. In particular, there were only 27 nests in 1939–40, when breeding success was just below average and winter survival was as low as in the disastrous year of 1938–9; and there were only 29 nests in 1941–2, when both breeding success and winter survival were close to average.

Since epidemics were not recorded and predation was apparently negligible, except of starving young, the food supply is likely to have been the chief factor influencing both the reproductive success and the winter survival of the Yellow-eyed Penguin. In this connection, it is interesting that the summer with the lowest production of young should have been followed by the winter with the lowest survival of both adults and juveniles, while the three summers with the highest productivity were followed by the lowest winter losses. This suggests that the food situation in summer might have been related to that in the ensuing winter, but since in the intermediate years there seemed to be no correlation between breeding success and winter survival, this is by no means certain. Richdale did not consider how the population of the Yellow-eyed Penguin might be regulated.

No long-term studies have been published on the populations of other penguins, but their breeding biology is becoming well known. The antarctic Adelie Penguin carries further a trend found in other species, for the male to take the first shift on the eggs, and it fasts, in all, for two months, losing 40 per cent of its body weight (Sapin-Jaloustre, 1960). Probably it breeds farther from its main feeding grounds than other species. In the Adelie, the older young collect in crèches, and it was formerly supposed that they were then fed indiscriminately by the adults, but this has been disproven (Sladen, 1958).

The two large species of *Aptenodytes* are more remarkable. The Emperor Penguin, *A. forsteri*, breeds on stable sea-ice, often far from the open water where it feeds, it lays its single egg in the antarctic winter, and the male incubates it for the whole period, starving in all for $3\frac{1}{2}$ to 4 months and losing some 30 to 45 per cent of its weight.

Except for their periodic journeys for food, the adults live for about 10 months of each year on their breeding grounds, and then move north to moult in the pack-ice, while the young leave the colonies for the pack-ice when they weigh only between one-third and one-half of their eventual adult weight (Prévost, 1953, 1958, 1961). The summary by Budd (1961, 1962) showed that colonies vary in size between 150 and 50000 pairs, but the numbers at particular colonies have varied much less than this over the years, that at Haswell Island, for instance, having about 7000–8000 pairs in 1912 and again in 1958. That at Cape Crozier has been rather more variable, with perhaps 350 pairs in 1902 and 1500 pairs in 1963 (Caughley 1960, Stonehouse 1964). Some colonies are within a few miles of excellent feeding, even in winter, while others are 30–80 miles distant. The breeding season starts several weeks earlier in some colonies than others and breeding success varied markedly from year to year and from colony to colony, due to starvation. Hence the relationship of colony-size to the proximity of the feeding grounds, and the behavioural factors determining how many pairs settle to breed, would make as rewarding a study in this species as in the Tricolored Redwing discussed in Chapter 9.

The sub-antarctic King Penguin, *A. patagonica*, is at least as remarkable as the Emperor. It is the only sea-bird except the large albatrosses which is known to take more than a year for successful reproduction (Stonehouse, 1956, 1960). The earlier breeders have a prenuptial moult in September and October, and start laying in late November with a peak in mid-December; the young hatch in late January and survive the ensuing winter with the help of their big stores of visceral and subcutaneous fat, together with a meal from their parents once every 5 or 6 weeks, and they continue to be fed by their parents until about mid-December in the following summer. The young are dependent on their parents for between 10 and 13 months, and the whole cycle occupies the parents for between 14 and 16 months. They are then ready to be late breeders, with a peak of laying in mid-February, and their next young leave so late in the following summer that the adults cannot lay again that year. Hence the birds which breed successfully do so in 2 years out of every 3, a unique pattern in birds. But those which lose an egg or chick may start again after a shorter interval. Stonehouse considered, and I agree, that breeding takes place as rapidly as the food and other ecological conditions permit, and there is no evidence for supposing that breeding is 'restrained' to prevent overpopulation, as argued by Wynne-Edwards (1962).

Summarizing, the Yellow-eyed Penguin, like many other sea-birds, breeds at nearly the same date each year. Most females first breed when 2 or 3 years old and most males where 3 or 4, and there is suggestive evidence that the youngest parents raised fewer young than old and experienced parents. The annual adult mortality was 13 per cent. There were few losses of eggs or young in most years, but they were high in 1938–9, when the adults also survived less well than usual, and the number of breeding pairs subsequently declined. Brief mention is made of the Emperor and King Penguins, in the latter of which each adult breeds twice in 3 years.

15

THE BREEDING OF THE KITTIWAKE

T HE main interest of the study of the Kittiwake, *Rissa tridactyla*, described in this chapter is the same as in the Yellow-eyed Penguin, namely reproductive success in relation to age and experience, and in these respects there are close parallels between these two dissimilar kinds of bird. Nearly all gulls are placed in the genus *Larus*, and nearly all breed on flat ground and feed on or near the shore, except for a few freshwater species. But the Atlantic Kittiwake and the closely related Pacific species *R. brevirostris* differ in breeding on cliff ledges and in feeding far out at sea, both when breeding and in winter. The differences in breeding behaviour from other gulls associated with nesting on cliffs have been analysed by Cullen (1957), while the breeding biology of the Kittiwake has been studied in north-eastern England by Coulson and White (1956, 1958a, b, 1959, 1960, and 1961; see also Coulson 1959a, 1963a, b), from whom the following account is taken. Coulson and White studied a number of cliff colonies, some long established and others newly founded, and also a small colony where the birds nested on window-ledges on a warehouse in North Shields, Northumberland. At this last colony, the adult birds could easily be caught on their nests by slipping a wire loop through the nearly closed windows, and each was then colour-banded for individual recognition.

During the last sixty years, the Kittiwake has increased as a breeding

Headpiece: Kittiwakes nesting on warehouse.

species in England, at a rate of some 3 per cent each year. In the nineteenth century it decreased markedly through human persecution, so the increase is perhaps merely a return to its former level of abundance (Coulson, 1963a). In addition, I would suggest that feeding conditions might perhaps have improved through some incidental effect of human fishing in the North Sea, since other marine birds have increased in this area in the same period. Whatever the cause, the present increase implies that conditions are unusually favourable for the Kittiwake in England at present, though whether mainly in the breeding season or in winter, or both, is not known.

Kittiwakes, like other gulls, have deferred maturity, most females breeding for the first time when three or four years old and most males when four or five years old; younger birds at times frequent the colonies and even occupy nesting ledges, without laying eggs (Coulson, in prep.). It will be noticed that, as in the Yellow-eyed Penguin, males start breeding when older than females, and the selective factors bringing this about should be investigated.

Every year between 1954 and 1963 inclusive at the North Shields colony of Kittiwakes, the first clutch was laid in the first week of May, and the average date of laying varied in different years only between 15 and 22 May (J. C. Coulson, pers. comm.). Hence the Kittiwake resembles the Yellow-eyed Penguin and other sea-birds, and differs from the small passerine birds of north temperate regions, in having a comparatively constant breeding season. Although, however, the average date of laying was similar each year at North Shields, there was a wide spread in the dates of laying of individual birds, some starting their clutches as much as six weeks after others in the same year. (The rare late layings after loss of an earlier attempt were not included in this assessment.) Further, the average date of laying differed in different types of colony, being consistently later at small new colonies than at large and long-established ones. An example of this is shown in Table 46 for two colonies in Marsden Bay, County Durham, the large and long-established colony A and the small colony G1, where Kittiwakes first nested in 1953.

New colonies have a higher proportion of birds breeding for the first time than well-established colonies, and part, but only part, of the average difference in laying time between them is due to the fact that birds breeding for the first time lay their eggs rather later than experienced breeders. Among the individually marked birds at North Shields, those females breeding for at least the fourth time laid on the average ten days before those breeding for the first time, those breeding for the second and third times being intermediate (Coulson and White, 1960).

TABLE 46

Time of breeding of the Kittiwake at a new colony (G1) compared with a large established colony (A) of some 800 pairs at Marsden

Year	No. of pairs	Mean date of breeding (in days) after mean of colony A	Expected difference (in days) due to age composition
1952	0 (0)	—	—
1953	10 (+5)	21	6
1954	20 (+18)	17	5
1955	51 (+22)	15	4
1956	90	13	3
1957	90	13	2
1958	114	11	1

Notes. From Coulson and White (1960, Tables 1 and 4). From 1953–5 nests from an adjoining colony (G2), started in the same year, were included to give larger totals; the means did not differ between G1 and G2. The expected difference due to age arises because, in the first years after its foundation, the G1 colony consisted mainly of birds breeding for the first time, whereas colony A was well established and each year had less than 20 per cent of females breeding for the first time.

TABLE 47

Density and time of breeding of Kittiwake colonies, 1958

Colony	No. of nests	Mean density of nests per 80 ft²	Date when 50% of nests had eggs	Spread of laying (in days) for 80% of nests
Marsden A	770	8·0	23 May	30
Marsden D	271	3·8	2 June	20
Brownsman S.E.	360	3·4	31 May	19
Marsden C	144	3·3	3 June	18
Dunbar	154	3·0	1 June	20
St. Abbs	654 (part)	2·7	3 June	15
Marsden F.	44	2·4	4 June	18
Brownsman N.E.	26	1·9	4 June	14
Dunstanburgh	135	1·2	6 June	14

Notes. From Coulson and White (1960, Table 9). The colonies are on the north-east coast in the Scottish counties of East Lothian and Berwick and the English counties of Northumberland and Durham.

Table 46 shows that the average difference in the date of laying between colonies A and G1 was greater than that to be expected solely from the age of the birds; and Coulson and White found that a further factor was involved, namely the density of the nests, laying occurring earlier in denser colonies and parts of colonies. This is shown in Table 47

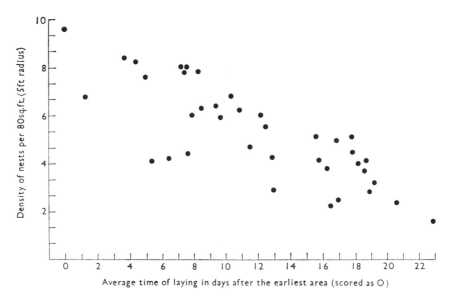

FIG. 30. Relationship between density of nests and date of laying in thirty-eight areas in seven colonies of Kittiwakes, *Rissa tridactyla*, at Marsden, Co. Durham, in 1954 (from Coulson and White, 1960, Fig. 3).

for nine separate colonies in 1958 and in Fig. 30 for thirty-eight different parts of the various colonies in Marsden Bay in 1954. A small part of the correlation with density is attributable to the nest density being higher at old colonies with more older birds than at new colonies with more younger birds, but this does not account for most of it. It recalls the effect claimed by Darling (1938) that in *Larus* gulls laying occurs earlier and is more synchronized in larger than smaller breeding colonies owing to the effects of social stimulation (cf. Lack, 1954, p. 258). As shown for the Kittiwake in Table 47, however, though laying occurred earlier in the denser colonies, the spread of laying was greater in the denser than in the less dense colonies, which is contrary to Darling's claim. Also the tendency for the Kittiwakes in denser colonies to breed earlier than the others could not have been due primarily to social stimulation in the season in question, since Coulson and White found that the birds already arrived on their ledges for the first time in spring earlier in the denser than the less dense colonies, or parts of colonies. This led them to postulate that social stimulation in one season must influence the behaviour of the birds in the following spring while they are still at sea. While this seems to me highly unlikely, I cannot suggest an alternative; conceivably age, breeding experience, or the tendency to change mates, might have some further and as yet unknown association with breeding density. Whatever may be its cause, the effect of density on the date of laying is important, since the average date differed by up to twelve days in different colonies in 1958 and by up to three weeks in different parts of the Marsden colonies in 1954, and the date of laying affects the number of eggs laid and young raised.

As already mentioned, female Kittiwakes breeding for the first time lay later than older individuals. A similar difference in the Great Tit was attributed by Perrins (p. 23) to inexperienced young females needing longer than older birds to form the necessary food reserves; this was partly on the grounds that in the Great Tit, like the Kittiwake, there must be strong selection pressure to lay as early as possible, as those which lay earliest raise most young. I wonder whether the same explanation might hold for the Kittiwake, particularly as Coulson (in prep.) found that, of the females breeding for the first time, complete newcomers laid on the average six days later than those which had frequented the colony in the previous year. The latter birds, I suggest, might have had more time for feeding prior to laying because they would already be familiar with the feeding grounds, and also with possible nesting sites.

Coulson (in prep.) also found later that the main factor modifying the date of laying in birds which had bred at least once before was not their age as such, but whether they had retained their former mates, which happened more often in older than younger birds. Eleven per cent of the females had new mates because their former mate had disappeared (presumed dead), while 26 per cent changed although their former partner was still in the colony. Excluding birds breeding for the first time, all females with new mates laid their eggs around the same date, on the average $4\frac{1}{2}$ days later than those breeding with their former mates, amongst which those which had bred together for at least six years laid particularly early, as shown in Table 49, the rest of which is discussed later. This difference suggests that newly formed pairs take longer than former mates to become adjusted psychologically and physiologically to each other, but this might not be the sole factor involved, since Coulson claimed that a change of partner somewhat retards the date of laying even in the second year of the new partnership.

The usual clutch of the Kittiwake in England is 2 eggs, but some pairs lay 3 and others only 1. At the North Shields colony, where the birds were marked, females breeding for at least the fourth time had an

243

average clutch of 2·4 eggs and 42 per cent had clutches of 3, those breeding for the second or third time had an average clutch of 1·9 eggs and 7 per cent had clutches of 3, and those breeding for the first time had an average clutch of 1·8 eggs and none had a clutch of 3. Irrespective of age, the average clutch also varied with the date of laying, for each successive week from 1–7 May onward being 2·4, 2·3, 2·1, 1·9, 1·8, and 1·5 eggs respectively, while the percentage of clutches of 3 eggs was 43, 34, 19, 5, 0, and 0 respectively in the same weeks. The effects of breeding experience and date of laying have been analysed separately in Table 48. This suggests that the average difference in clutch-size

TABLE 48

Mean clutch-size of Kittiwake in relation to breed experience and date of laying at North Shields 1952–9

Year of breeding	Date of Laying					
	1–7 May	8–14 May	15–21 May	22–28 May	29 May– 4 June	5–11 June
4th or more	(2·8)	2·4	2·3	(2·0)	(2·0)	—
2nd or 3rd	(2·5)	2·3	2·1	1·9	(1·8)	—
1st	—	(2·0)	1·9	1·8	(1·8)	(1·5)

Notes. From Coulson and White (1961, Table 3). Averages based on less than 10 clutches are bracketed.

between the earliest and most experienced breeders on the one hand, and the latest and youngest breeders on the other hand, was about one egg. Finally, there were probably hereditary differences in clutch-size, since each marked female tended to lay a clutch of similar size each year. The latter tendency has also been shown to hold in several other species (Lack, 1954, p. 28), but that the differences in question are hereditary has not been demonstrated.[1]

Coulson and White found that incubation took 27 days, that the average nestling period was 43 days, and that about 56 per cent of the eggs laid gave rise to flying young, most losses being of eggs, not chicks. From clutches of three 72 per cent of the eggs hatched, from clutches of two 69 per cent, and from clutches of one 40 per cent, but the last were laid mainly by birds breeding late and for the first time. Ninety-two

[1] A big difference in consecutive years in the average clutch (2·3 cf. 1·5 eggs) at a Murmansk colony reported by Belopolskii (1961) was attributed by Coulson and White to the fact that breeding was much earlier in one year than the other. While annual differences in the mean date of breeding are small in Northumberland, they are evidently greater in the arctic, where the ice may break up at a very different date in different years.

per cent of the hatched young were raised in broods of 1, 88 per cent in broods of 2, and 72 per cent in broods of 3. Some of the losses from broods of 3 were attributed to falls from crowded nests and others to the third chick dying because it hatched after the others. As already discussed (p. 223), I consider that asynchronous hatching is an adaptation to reduce the effective brood-size to that which the parents can raise, and its occurrence in the third egg of the Kittiwake strongly suggests to me that there are times when the parents cannot raise as many as 3 young. Also, Coulson and White found that each chick received less food per day in a brood of 3 than 2. They found, even so, that the average number of young raised from each brood of 3 was 2·2, so that if the parents with broods of 2 had raised all their young, they would still have been less productive. In fact they raised an average of only 1·8 per brood, but the comparison is somewhat misleading as these birds included many inexperienced and later breeders, whereas all broods of three were raised by experienced early breeders. That experienced breeders are more efficient than inexperienced breeders at feeding their young was shown by the fact that the average gain in weight per chick per day in broods of 2 was 16·7 grams with experienced parents but only 14·8 grams with inexperienced parents; the corresponding difference might well have been greater in broods of 3 than 2, but as all the broods of 3 were raised by experienced parents, comparison was not possible.

Hence, the commonest clutch of the Kittiwake was two, whereas the most productive brood-size was three. I do not think, however, that Coulson's findings are necessarily inconsistent with my interpretation of clutch-size, because, as just mentioned, all the broods of three were raised by experienced early breeders, which are the most successful, and these were the only individuals which laid clutches of three. It will be recalled that in the Great Tit, likewise, older parents breed earlier, have larger clutches and raise, on the average, larger broods than younger parents. In species with such phenotypic adaptative modifications in clutch-size, an analysis of survival in relation to brood-size from all broods combined will give misleading results, and for a proper evaluation it is necessary to analyse the results separately for parents of different ages and for broods hatched at different dates, which has not been done for the Kittiwake.

In 1959, Coulson (pers. comm.) added extra young Kittiwakes to make up 4 broods of 4 young each. All the young fledged, but in the one brood weighed, the average gain in weight per nestling per day was only 13·9 grams, as compared with 16·2 grams in 3 broods of 3 that year; further, only 1 of the 4 chicks showed a gain similar to that of the young in broods of 3, and 2 of them were badly underweight. This raises a further difficulty in relation to the analysis of survival with respect to brood-size in the Kittiwake, namely whether, because they weigh less at fledging, the young from larger broods might survive less well after fledging than those from smaller broods, as was found in the Great Tit, but this point has not been studied in the Kittiwake. Clearly, more allowance must be made for phenotypic variations, further experiments are needed with supplemented broods of 4, and figures are needed for the survival of the young after fledging, before the significance of clutch-size in the Kittiwake can be satisfactory evaluated. It is possible also that, as suggested by the recent increase in the breeding population, conditions are at present unusually favourable for Kittiwakes feeding young in north-eastern England.

As already mentioned, birds that retained their former mates laid earlier than those with new mates. Partly due to this, those that retained their mates also laid rather larger clutches, and since they hatched ´12 per cent more of their eggs, they raised more young, on average 0·4

TABLE 49

Effect of change of mate on breeding of Kittiwake

No. of years ♀ had bred	No. of pairs		Mean date of laying in May		Mean clutch		Mean no. of young raised	
	New mate	Same mate	New mate	Same mate	New mate	Same mate	New mate	Same mate
1	117	—	23	—	1·8	—	1·2	—
2	36	62	19	15	2·0	1·1	1·1	1·6
3, 4	58	74	19	16	2·1	2·2	1·1	1·5
5, 6	29	50	21	15	2·1	2·3	1·2	1·8
over 6	18	54	18	11	2·2	2·4	1·6	1·7

Note. From Coulson (in prep., Tables 5 and 6). Of the females breeding for the first time, 44 had spent the previous summer in the colony without breeding and these laid on the average, on 19 May, while 59 had not spent the previous summer in the colony and laid, on the average, on 25 May.

more per brood, than those with new mates, as shown in Table 49. Clearly, it is of survival value for a Kittiwake to retain its mate, and most of them do so. Moreover, of the females which had new mates although their former partner was still alive, three-quarters had failed to hatch their eggs in the previous year, and if a pairing is sterile, it is probably advantageous to change mates. However, some unsuccessful pairs re-mated and some successful pairs changed mates.

Of the adults ringed each year at the North Shields colony, 12 per

cent failed to return in a following year, and this rate of loss, all presumably due to mortality, has been confirmed by the figures for four
subsequent years (Coulson and White, 1959; Coulson, pers. comm.).
Hence the Kittiwake, like the Yellow-eyed Penguin and other sea-birds,
has a relatively low annual mortality. On the basis of this mortality,
together with the number of young raised per pair, Coulson estimated
the loss of juveniles in their first year after leaving the nest at 21 per
cent, which is lower than in most other birds so far studied (cf. Lack,
1954). The causes of mortality in the Kittiwake, and the factors influencing its numbers outside the breeding season, have not been studied.
There is no evidence for the suggestion by Wynne-Edwards (1962,
p. 334) that the visits of Kittiwakes to their colonies in the early
spring, chiefly in the early morning, are for the purpose of 'epideictic'
demonstrations.

The experiment of adding young to make up broods of above the
normal size has been carried out on an extensive scale on one other gull,
the Glaucous-winged Gull, *Larus argentatus glaucescens*, on Mandarte
Island, British Columbia, by Vermeer (1963). As in nearly all other
species of *Larus*, the normal clutch is three, but Vermeer showed that,
at least in one year, the parents were able to find enough food to raise
four, five, or even six young, and the proportion of young lost in these
large broods was similar to that in broods of three. This result seems
quite contrary to my conclusion that clutch-size is adapted to the greatest
number of young that the parents can normally raise. Possibly, however,
the present situation on Mandarte Island is unusually favourable for
the feeding of the Glaucous-winged Gull, as it is increasing rapidly,
which is attributed to the food supplies unintentionally provided by
mankind on city refuse dumps.

About ninety miles north of the area where Coulson worked in
Durham lies the Bass Rock, where a colony of Gannets, *Sula bassana*,
was studied for three years by B. Nelson (1964, and D.Phil. thesis at
Oxford). This colony, like those of the Kittiwake, is at present increasing, following persecution in the nineteenth century and subsequent
protection. The Gannet invariably lays one egg, which weighs $3\frac{1}{2}$ per
cent of the adult, and birds which lost their egg usually laid again.
Laying was normally spread over about three months each year, and
the chicks hatching at different dates survived to fledging equally well,
except that some extremely late chicks starved. Each chick spent about
ninety days in the nest and at the end often weighed half as much again
as an adult, this extra weight probably being a food reserve to enable it
to survive the period soon after it leaves the nest, when it is no longer
fed by its parents. The reason that parent Gannets no longer feed their
young after they leave the nest requires study, especially as tropical

species of *Sula* continue to feed their young at this stage. While over 90 per cent of the hatched young left the nest, Nelson estimated that about 80 per cent of the juveniles die before breeding. The annual mortality of the adults was only about 6 per cent, a lower figure than for any species of bird that I could cite in 1954, except the Royal Albatross, *Diomedea epomophora*. Most Gannets first breed when five years old, a few at the age of four. As compared with older parents, young parents were rather less efficient in incubation and the care of their young in the first few days after hatching, but they fed their young as frequently, and their young fledged at the same age. The adult Gannet undergoes a complete moult while breeding, which is highly unusual in birds, though it also occurs in the Snow Petrel, *Pagodroma nivea* (Maher, 1962). Presumably these two species find food harder to obtain outside the breeding season than when breeding, even though when breeding they also have a chick to feed.

In one year Nelson provided several pairs of Gannets with a second egg, and in such individuals the proportion of eggs which hatched was as high as in those with one egg. He then provided thirteen further pairs with a second chick of the same age as their first, and found that the proportion of young which left the nest was 83 per cent among the twins, as compared with 94 per cent among the single chicks in the same year. As the twins took only four days longer than single chicks to fledge, and weighed only about 5 per cent less at fledging, they were evidently at no appreciable disadvantage, and since, on the average, each pair with twins raised 76 per cent more young to fledging than each pair with a single chick, the normal clutch of one in this species did not correspond with the most productive brood-size, at least on the Bass Rock in the year of the experiment. Conceivably, parents feeding twins are subject to a heavier strain, and so might survive less well, than those feeding single chicks, but Nelson's observations suggested that both sets of parents had spare time and were not unduly pressed, and I agree with him in thinking that this factor is extremely unlikely to be involved. In my view the most probable explanation of these successful twinning experiments is that the food situation is unusually favourable for Gannets on the Bass Rock at the present time, as suggested by their recent increase in numbers, and that the present clutch of one was evolved under more rigorous conditions in the past in which only one chick could normally be reared. The same reason might help to explain why breeding is still deferred to the age of about five, despite the fact that individuals breeding for the first time fed their chicks as successfully as older birds, so it seems possible that, at the present time, younger birds might be able to breed successfully if they tried. This view is speculative, of course, and if it is true, it implies that the Gannet

is unable to modify its clutch-size or age of first breeding to suit unusually favourable conditions, which is surprising. It may be added
that twins were reared only if of the same age, and that if one chick was
appreciably younger than its nest-mate, it normally died almost at once.

The tropical species of *Sula* studied by Dorward (1962) on Ascension
Island provide an interesting contrast with the Gannet. While the White
(or Masked or Blue-faced) Booby, *S. dactylatra*, bred at annual intervals,
the Brown Booby, *S. leucogaster*, bred about once every eight months;
several other Ascension sea-birds also bred at a less than annual interval.
In the White Booby and probably also in the Brown, the replacement of
the primary feathers in the moult follows an unusual pattern, proceed-
ing from the innermost outward in three spaced concurrent cycles, so
that, though a whole cycle takes three years, each feather is replaced
annually. This presumably maintains the wing at high efficiency, as
two consecutive feathers are not being replaced simultaneously, as in
most other birds. In addition, the moult tends to be checked temporarily in individuals that are feeding young. Finally, though both species
of boobies regularly laid two eggs, no pair raised two young, this being
confirmed by twinning experiments; one chick persistently attacked
the other, which normally died soon after hatching. Dorward suggested
that, even so, the second egg would be of advantage as an insurance in
cases where the first failed to hatch, and that as the egg is small in
proportion to the size of the bird, the laying of a second egg would not
impose undue strain on the female; but this argument should apply
equally to the Gannet and the Red-footed Booby, *S. sula*, both of
which lay only one egg. Dorward thought it unlikely that the birds
studied by him could rear two chicks, but one instance of this was
recorded for the Brown Booby by a later visitor to Ascension, during a
period when one of its favourite foods, the fish, *Selar crumenophthalamus*,
was much more abundant inshore than when Dorward was on the island
(K. E. L. Simmons, pers. comm.). I therefore think it likely that the
White and Brown Boobies have retained a clutch of two because they
can occasionally raise two young, either in some years on Ascension, or
in other colonies.

Conforming with this last suggestion, two other species in this genus,
the Blue-footed Booby, *S. nebouxii*, and the Peruvian Booby, *S.
variegata*, usually lay two and sometimes three eggs and regularly raise
two or even three young, which Murphy (1936) considered was due to
their breeding in the abnormally rich waters of the Humboldt current
off Peru, whereas the other species breed in tropical blue waters much
poorer in food. However, Wynne-Edwards (1962, p. 536) related this
difference in clutch-size in boobies to his own views on the limitation of
reproductive rates and concluded that 'certainly it has nothing to do

with the richness or poverty of their respective habitats: this factor will govern the population-density of the adults, but it can play little or no direct part in the evolution of basic fecundity in the various species concerned'. He gave no evidence for this unusual view, and I agree with Murphy's much simpler explanation, which supports my general hypothesis that clutches are larger where, on the average, larger broods can be raised. The seemingly contrary evidence to my interpretation provided by the Gannet on the Bass Rock and the boobies on Ascension should be studied further.

Gannets with artificial twins.

Summarizing, the date of laying of the Kittiwake each year is earlier in older parents than in those breeding for the first time, earlier in those which have retained their former mates than in those which have changed mates, and earlier in crowded than sparsely settled colonies or parts of colonies. The reason for the variation with nesting density is not known. The average clutch is larger in those individuals which breed earlier in the season than in those which breed later, larger in older and more experienced breeders than in younger and less experienced breeders, and larger in those which have retained their former mates than in those of similar age with new mates. Although more individuals laid clutches of two than three, more young were raised per pair to the fledging stage from broods of three than two, while some broods of four were reared, though the young were under weight. However, as survival in relation to brood-size was not studied after the young left the nest, and as clutches of three were raised primarily by early and experienced breeders, which are also the most successful, these findings do not necessarily conflict with my view that the clutch size corresponds to that brood-size from which most young can be raised. In the Glaucous-winged Gull and Gannet, however, more young survived per brood from artificially made up broods of twice the normal size than from broods of normal size (possibly correlated with an unusually favourable situation for raising young, as the colonies are increasing). In two species of *Sula* in tropical blue waters, the clutch is two but only one chick was normally raised, but in two other species in the Humboldt current, two and at times three young were raised.

16

MUTTON-BIRDS AND THE
MANX SHEARWATER

THE main species discussed in this chapter are the two large antipodean shearwaters called mutton-birds because the heavy nestlings are collected in great numbers for food. As with other sea-birds, scientific studies have centred on their breeding biology, in which shearwaters show in extreme form the adaptations of pelagic birds. The Short-tailed or Slender-billed Shearwater, alternatively the Tasmanian or Australian Mutton-bird, *Puffinus* (or *Procellaria*) *tenuirostris*, breeds on islands in the Bass Strait and was studied by Dr. D. L. Serventy of the Commonwealth Scientific and Industrial Research Organization of Australia (Marshall and Serventy, 1956*a, b*; Serventy, 1957, 1958, 1961, 1962, 1963). The Sooty Shearwater or New Zealand Mutton-bird, *P. griseus*, has a wider breeding range in the Southern Hemisphere and was studied on an island off the South Island of New Zealand by Dr. L. E. Richdale (1963). Information has been added on the Manx Shearwater, *P. puffinus*, a smaller species, studied on Skokholm off South Wales by Dr. M. P. Harris (1966 and in prep.). The facts concerning these three species in the present chapter were obtained by the above three workers respectively if no additional citation is given.

The Short-tailed and Sooty Shearwaters migrate from the Southern

Headpiece: Australian Mutton birds on the move.

Hemisphere to far north in the Northern Hemisphere for the non-breeding season. Figure 31 shows the figure-of-eight route of the Short-tailed Shearwater, in following which it is assisted by the prevailing winds, while the winter range of the Sooty Shearwater has been reviewed by Phillips (1963). The Manx Shearwater, correspondingly, migrates to the Southern Hemisphere, mainly off Brazil, in the English winter.

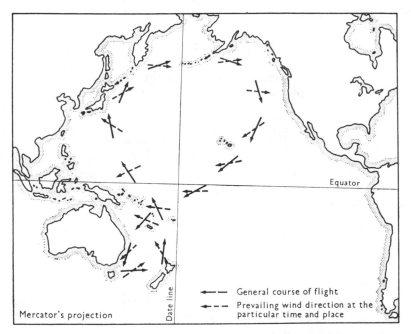

FIG. 31. Annual migration of Short-tailed Shearwater, *Procellaria tenuirostris* (from Serventy, 1958).

All three species range widely over the open sea, swimming on or under the water to catch organisms near the surface, especially squids, small fish, and euphausiid crustaceans. They nest in burrows in the soil, almost exclusively on small islands free from predatory mammals.

During eight years studied in detail, Short-tailed Shearwaters laid their eggs exclusively between 20 November and 3 December inclusive, 97 per cent of them in the last ten days of November, and over 80 per cent of them between 23 and 28 November. This is the most constant laying season known for any species of bird. It seems almost equally restricted and constant in the Sooty Shearwater, and probably also in the Great Shearwater, *P. gravis*, of Tristan da Cunha (Rowan, 1952), which is another transequatorial migrant (Voous and Wattel, 1963). In these three species, the incubation and nestling periods are so long that there seems only just time to fit them into the period between the return of the adults in spring and the need for them to migrate north again in autumn. The almost constant average date of laying, and the restricted limits of the laying season, are presumably adapted to this situation, though they will be advantageous only if, in addition, the cycle of marine foods on which the birds depend for their young is likewise relatively constant in its timing from year to year. The Manx Shearwater also has a reasonably constant average date of laying each year, but the period is much more extended, for though nearly all individuals lay their eggs in the course of about a month, a few birds lay them up to ten or eleven weeks after the first.

In the Short-tailed Shearwater, the adults of both sexes return in spring to the colonies and occupy their burrows, but they all then leave again for about a fortnight prior to laying. Although when the birds first return they already have much fat, the function of this mass departure is evidently to enable both sexes to visit the distant feeding grounds and lay up further food reserves, the female in order to form her 85-gram egg, which is about one-sixth of her own weight, and the male in order to sit on the egg for the first 12–14 days after it is laid, in which period the female again goes off to replenish her reserves, after which she sits for 10–13 days while the male goes off. The so-called 'honeymoon' prior to laying is presumable necessary because both sexes require considerable food reserves at the end of this time. A similar departure prior to laying occurs in the Snow Petrel, *Pagodroma nivea* (Maher, 1962), in the female but not the male Dove Prion, *Pachyptila desolata* (Tickell, 1962), in both sexes of the Fulmar Petrel, *Fulmarus glacialis* (Dunnett *et al.*, 1963), and almost certainly in the female Manx Shearwater. which like the Short-tailed, lays an egg of about one-sixth of its own weight. But the pre-laying departure is much less conspicuous in these last two British species, as the laying of different individuals in the same colony is much less closely synchronized than that of the Southern Hemisphere species.

All shearwaters, indeed all species in the order Procellariiformes, lay a clutch of one. If mutton-birds lose their egg, they do not lay again that year. Usually this holds also in the Manx Shearwater, though one instance has been recorded of re-laying after a month's interval, which suggests that in this species, with its extended laying season, some other late layings might also be repeats. Re-laying has also been recorded in the Giant Petrel, *Macronectes gigantea* (Warham, 1962), and more doubtfully in the British Storm Petrel, *Hydrobates pelagicus* (Davis, 1957), but it is rare in this order of birds. This is presumably because the females have difficulty in obtaining enough food to form their large eggs quickly enough, particularly in long-distance migrants like the mutton-birds, in which there would not be time for eggs laid late in the season to give rise to successful fledglings.

The above explanation is, in my view, sufficient, but Wynne-Edwards (1962, p. 489) proffered another. 'These species have, therefore, largely or completely forfeited what is otherwise a normal attribute of birds, to replace lost eggs at least once. They are all, like the Gannet, birds with relatively small eggs compared with their own large size and nutrient reserves, and the physiological cost of egg-replacement would presumably be trifling. What seems at first sight to be a lamentable and unexplained defect, however, appears in a much more reasonable light as an adaptation lowering a little bit further still the reproductive potential of the population as a whole, in very long-lived species of birds.' But while it is true that the Gannet lays a relatively small egg, it lays again if its first egg is lost, as Wynne-Edwards (p. 487) pointed out (see also this book, p. 247). On the other hand, Short-tailed and Manx Shearwaters lay an egg of one-sixth of their own weight, as just noted, and though these two figures were not known to Wynne-Edwards, those published for other species of Procellariiformes, notably Leach's Petrel, *Oceanodroma leucorrhoa*, by Heinroth (1922) were similar and among the largest ratios of egg-weight to body-weight in any birds, being equalled only by those in Kiwis, *Apteryx*, and limicoline species. Hence Wynne-Edwards was wrong to describe the eggs of Procellariiformes as 'relatively small' and he had no justification for his statement that 'the physiological cost of egg-replacement would presumably be trifling'. The available evidence strongly suggests the opposite.

The incubation period is much longer in Procellariiformes than in other birds of equivalent size, averaging 53 days in the Short-tailed Shearwater, perhaps 3 days longer in the Sooty, and about 2 days less in the Manx, and ranging between 40 days in the small storm petrels to 79 days in the Royal Albatross, *Diomedea epomophora* (Davis, 1957; Allan, 1962; Huntington, 1962; Lockley, 1942; Richdale, 1952; Warham, 1962). As already mentioned, Short-tailed Shearwaters change places on the egg once every 10 days to a fortnight, and Sooty Shearwaters after a similar period, the longest recorded interval being 16 days. But in the Manx Shearwater on Skokholm the interval is shorter, averaging only 6 days, presumably because its feeding grounds are less far from the breeding stations than are those of the two mutton-birds. In albatrosses, one bird sometimes sits for a month (Richdale, 1952; Rice and Kenyon, 1962), but the interval is only 2–9 days in storm petrels, while diving petrels, which unlike other Procellarii feed inshore, may change nightly (Richdale, 1965). Not only may shearwaters feed a long way from their breeding stations, but food is liable to be hard to obtain in stormy weather, when their prey may descend well below the sea surface. Occasionally, presumably because hungry, an incubating shearwater leaves before the return of its mate, and it is evidently for this reason that eggs of the Manx Shearwater are unusually resistant to chilling (Matthews, 1954). A similar adaptation is found for the same reason in the Swift, *Apus apus* (D. and E. Lack, 1952).

Omitting the first few days of its life, when a nestling shearwater is sometimes fed nightly, the average interval between recorded feeding visits by the parents with a big meal is 2½–3 days in the Short-tailed Shearwater, 4 days in the Sooty Shearwater, and a little under 2 days in the Manx Shearwater. (However, detailed observations on the Manx Shearwater showed that in this species the parents sometimes return at short intervals with only a little food and these meals might have been overlooked with gross weighings.) At times a chick was not fed for up to 16 days in the Short-tailed Shearwater, 25 days in the Sooty Shearwater, and a week in the Manx Shearwater. Long intervals between feeds are usually due to rough weather, and nestling shearwaters, like nestling Swifts, are adapted to withstand intermittent starvation, as they lay up large stores of fat when food is plentiful, which they draw on when food is scarce, but unlike young swifts they do not grow their feathers more slowly when food is short. Albatrosses feed their young as infrequently as shearwaters, but storm petrels and diving petrels, especially the latter, which feed inshore, bring food almost nightly (Richdale, 1952, 1965; Rice and Kenyon, 1962).

Shearwater chicks put on so much fat that for a time they weigh about half as much again as the adult. Eventually, the parents usually desert their young, which continue to grow their feathers, subsisting on their fat stores, for about another fortnight before they leave for the sea. Rarely, a Short-tailed Shearwater was fed in what would normally have been the desertion period, and this happened rather less infrequently in the Manx Shearwater. A desertion period is also found in various storm petrels (C. Huntington, pers. comm.), but not in diving petrels, prions, albatrosses, or the Fulmar (Richdale, 1954, 1964; Rice and Kenyon, 1962; Williamson, 1955). The chick of the Short-tailed Shearwater weighs about 66 grams at hatching, reaches an average maximum weight of 956 grams (highest recorded 1148 grams) and leaves at an average weight of 615 grams (highest recorded 783 grams). The corresponding average figures for Manx Shearwaters on Skokholm in 1964 were 45, 611 and 444 grams respectively, and the greatest loss recorded in the desertion period was 240 grams, from an initial 670 grams. The growth of the young Sooty Shearwater follows a similar pattern, but it stores proportionally less fat.

The young Short-tailed Shearwater remains in the nesting burrow for an average of 94 days (limits 88–108), the Sooty for 97 days (limits

86–106), and the smaller Manx Shearwater for 70 days (range 62–76). The nestling period is long in proportion to the size of bird in all Procellariiformes, being about 7 weeks in the Dove Prion, 7–8 weeks in the Fulmar, 9–10 weeks in storm petrels, 15–17 weeks in the Giant Petrel, and between 20 and 31–36 weeks in various albatrosses (Tickell, 1962; Williamson, 1952; Davis, 1957; Huntington, 1963; Allan, 1962; Warham, 1962; Rice and Kenyon, 1962; Richdale, 1952).

While the slow rate of growth of nestling Procellariiformes can readily be explained as an adaptation to a sparse and variable food supply, their long incubation periods are harder to understand, as they can scarcely be advantageous in themselves. However, there is a general correlation in birds between the lengths of the incubation and nestling periods, which suggests that the simplest way of evolving a slower rate of nestling development, as in swifts and shearwaters, may be to retard the rate of development as a whole, including that which takes place in the egg (Lack, 1948*b*); I am not very happy about this explanation, but can think of no better one. It should be added that such considerations will hold good only in species such as shearwaters and swifts which are relatively safe from nest predators. Where eggs or nestlings are liable to predation, selection will always tend to speed up the rate at which both the embryo and the nestling develop.

Wynne-Edwards (1955, 1962), who did not mention the above interpretation, argued instead that the unusually prolonged incubation and nestling periods of Procellariiformes are another means of reducing the recruitment rate and so preventing over-population: 'the conclusion cannot easily be avoided that if the incubation and fledging periods were shorter, egg and chick mortality would be less' (1955, p. 542). But this view ignores the fact that, owing to their inaccessible nesting sites, the Procellariiformes are virtually safe from nest-predation (other than that caused by man or the animals which he has introduced), since most species nest in burrows on islands, the Fulmar on cliff ledges and the albatrosses on remote islands. Moreover Wynne-Edwards provided no figures for the predation rate in any of these species to support his claim, and even if birds did reduce their reproductive rates to prevent over-population, there are far less involved ways of doing so than that of retarding embryonic and nestling development to provide longer exposure to predation.

Richdale commented that, even under favourable feeding conditions, Sooty Shearwaters have only just time to raise a chick successfully between their migrations; and while in most years most of the young survived, there were heavy losses in 1952–3. He concluded that the two parents could not raise more than one young. This, I argued earlier (1954), is the reason that Procellariiformes have evolved a clutch of one, whereas Wynne-Edwards (1955, 1962) concluded that it is essential that such long-lived birds should have only one egg in order to prevent over-population.

My interpretation of clutch-size in this group was tested experimentally for the Manx Shearwater on Skokholm in 1964 by M. P. Harris. Nine pairs provided with twins, hence initially with 18 young, successfully raised only 3 or perhaps 4 young in all (about 0·4 per pair), whereas 44 control pairs with single chicks successfully raised 42 (0·95 per pair). The comparison was complicated by the ability of a nestling shearwater to withstand considerable food shortage, and only 4 of the 18 twin young in these experiments actually died before becoming fully feathered, though most of the others were so emaciated that they could not have survived after leaving the nest. Only 3 of them, including one whose twin died early, exceeded at fledging the average weight (444 grams) of the chicks raised singly, so only these 3 were certainly raised successfully, but another which weighed 400 grams was probably successful. The others fledged at the unusually low weights (in grams) of 370, 350 (3 birds), 340, 310, 290, and 270 (3 birds), and almost certainly none of these individuals survived. Indeed, most of them were probably incapable of flight. Essentially similar results were obtained from a larger series of artificial twins in 1965.

These findings show that none of the experimental pairs was able to raise two young, and further that, for most of them, the addition of a second chick meant that they raised none at all. As two parents could not find enough food to raise two young, one parent would presumably be unable to raise one young, and this was confirmed in an earlier year at a nest where one parent died; here also the chick became fully feathered, but it was so emaciated that it almost certainly did not survive afterwards (Ralphs, 1956). Hence these findings strongly support the view that the Manx Shearwater has evolved a clutch of one because it cannot normally raise more than one chick.

An unexpected finding in these experiments was that the undernourished twins grew their feathers, including those of the wing, at about the same rate as well nourished young (in contrast, for instance, to young Swifts, *A. apus*, in which growth is retarded when food is sparse). This suggests that natural selection favours those young shearwaters which leave the island earlier, but undernourished, rather than those which leave later but well nourished. In conformity with this view, the young survive better the earlier that they leave, as shown later in Table 50.

Similar tests were carried out on the Laysan Albatross, *Diomedea immutabilis*, by Rice and Kenyon (1962). Each of 18 pairs was given 2 chicks to raise; in 15 nests both young died, and they almost certainly did so in one other instance, since on the observer's last visit both chicks were emaciated; but 1 pair raised 1 chick successfully and another pair may have raised 2 chicks. Hence 18 pairs raised at most 3 young, (0·17 per pair), whereas 18 pairs starting with a single chick raised 12 young (0·67 per pair). Supporting evidence was obtained by killing one of the 2 parents at various other nests with a young chick and, in these, only 1 out of a possible 13 young was raised. Hence in the Laysan Albatross, like the Manx Shearwater, a pair cannot normally raise 2 young, and a single parent cannot normally raise 1, so the clutch of 1 corresponds to the largest number of young that a pair can normally raise.

Similarly, when a second nestling was placed in the burrows of 23 pairs of Leach's Petrels, *Oceanodroma leucorrhoa*, by the end of 10 days the second nestling was in good condition in only 2 nests, it had died in 5, it was badly underweight in 7, while in another 9 it had disappeared, in at least 4 instances after it was badly underweight. The experiments were then stopped, but they had continued long enough to show that nearly all these parents were unable to raise 2 young (C. Huntington, pers. comm.). Again, in 2 nests of the Giant Petrel, *Macronectes giganteus*, in which 2 young hatched, 1 soon disappeared (Warham, 1962).

In mutton-birds, as already mentioned, the laying season is extremely restricted, whereas in the Manx Shearwater it is more extended, and on Skokholm young have been recorded leaving the nest at all dates between 13 August and 21 October. In the Kittiwake, as mentioned in the previous chapter, breeding is progressively less successful later in the season, and the rates of recovery of fledgling Manx Shearwaters after they leave the nest show that the same holds in this species (Perrins, in press). As can be seen from Table 50, after allowing for annual differences in recapture rates (discussed in the note to the table), the rate of recapture was nearly 13 per cent for the earliest birds to depart, nearly 9 per cent for the next earliest, rather over 6 per cent for the majority, which left between 27 August and 10 September, between 4 and 5½ per cent for those leaving in the next fortnight, and 2 per cent or less for the last to leave. As young leaving late had a comparatively poor chance of survival, it was to be expected that only a few birds would lay their eggs very late, as was the case. But since the earliest young had a much greater chance of survival than any others, it seems surprising that so few Manx Shearwaters laid their eggs very early. The only reason that can be suggested for their not breeding earlier is the same as for the Great Tit (p. 23) and Pied Flycatcher (p. 102), that the females cannot obtain enough food in spring to lay their eggs any earlier. Hence the time of breeding of the Manx Shearwater is

TABLE 50

Recapture of young Manx Shearwaters after leaving Skokholm
in relation to their date of fledging

Date of ringing (= fledging)	No. ringed	No. recaptured	Mean percentage recaptured
13–21 Aug.	612	54	12·8
22–26 Aug.	1828	142	8·8
27–31 Aug.	3513	220	6·7
1–5 Sept.	5178	297	6·8
6–10 Sept.	3253	189	6·2
11–15 Sept.	1668	101	5·6
16–20 Sept.	1054	44	3·9
21–25 Sept.	501	25	4·9
26–30 Sept.	125	3	2·1
1–14 Oct.	62	1	0·6

Note. From Perrins (in press) based on data from Skokholm Bird Observatory for young ringed 1947–1961 inclusive. The birds were ringed at night after leaving their burrows, hence the date of ringing is within a few days of their leaving the island. A few birds ringed in burrows before their departure were excluded from the analysis, as their date of departure was not recorded. As the overall recapture rate was different in different years, the percentage of recaptures from each period was analysed separately for each year, and the last column shows the means of these figures (not the overall percentage).

evidently determined primarily by the food supplies available to the adults just before laying, and not in relation to the food requirements of the nestlings later. On the other hand, the termination of laying has evidently been evolved in relation to the difficulty of raising young late in the season.

The largest of the Procellarii, the Royal Albatross and the Wandering Albatross, *Diomedea exulans*, differ from the rest in taking just over a year from the start of breeding to the successful raising of a chick, and as the birds have by then missed the next laying season and have also to moult, successful breeding occurs only once in two years (Richdale, 1952; Matthews, 1929; Carrick *et al.*, 1960; Tickell, 1960). This is due mainly to the long nestling period of 8–9 months, which extends through the bleak sub-antarctic winter, during which the nestling is fed rather intermittently like the King Penguins breeding at the same latitude (see p. 237). Pairs that lose an egg or young chick can, however, breed in the following year. I consider that these albatrosses, like the King Penguin, are breeding as fast as they can, and there is no evidence favouring Wynne-Edwards' view (1962, p. 489) that biennial breeding is yet another adaption for reducing the rate of breeding in a long-lived species to prevent overpopulation.

This biennial breeding of the large albatrosses should be distinguished from the supposed intermittent breeding of individuals of other species of Procellariiformes, postulated by Wynne-Edwards (1962, p. 564) for the Fulmar Petrel in Canada. But his evidence was indirect and is not, in my view, convincing, nor did it hold for a population of marked individuals of the same species in Scotland (Carrick and Dunnett, 1952). Neither does it hold for the Short-tailed Shearwater (D. L. Serventy, pers. comm.) nor for the Manx Shearwater. Indeed, there is no evidence for intermittent breeding of this type in any species of Procellariiformes. It is true that in many species there is a high proportion of non-breeding birds at the colonies, which in the Sooty Shearwater comprises some two-thirds of the population. But the true reason for this is that the birds do not begin to breed until they are several years old, though many sub-adults return to the colonies, form pairs and even occupy nesting holes, without laying eggs.

In the Short-tailed Shearwater, the young usually return to the colonies when 3 to 4 years old, occasionally when 2 years old, and they first breed when 5 to 8 years old. First-year birds return to neighbouring seas but without making a landfall. D. L. Serventy's figures (pers. comm.) for the age of first breeding of birds marked as chicks were (by 1963) for females: 8 aged 5, 5 aged 6, and 1 aged 7; and for males: 2 aged 5, 8 aged 6, 2 aged 7, and 1 aged 8. Hence males tend to start breeding when a little older than females, as in the Yellow-eyed Penguin (p. 231) and the Kittiwake (p. 240), perhaps correlated with a surplus of males in the population. In the Manx Shearwater, the young first return to the colonies in appreciable numbers when 2 years old, and most first breed when 5 years old, but single individuals (of unknown sex) have been recorded breeding when 3 and 4 years old. The Sooty Shearwater first breeds when about 6 years old.

No Procellariiformes are known to breed when a year old, though diving petrels do so at the age of 2 (Richdale, 1965) and one Leach's Petrel has been found with an egg when aged 3 (Gross, 1947), though probably most individuals start when older (C. Huntington, pers. comm.). At the other end of the scale, one Laysan Albatross bred when aged 7, but others not until older (Rice and Kenyon, 1962), and a female Royal Albatross first bred at the age of 9 and 2 males when aged 8 and 11 years respectively, others perhaps when yet older (Richdale, 1952). It is evidently very difficult for Procellariiformes, especially the larger species, to find enough food to raise a nestling in the time available, and I suggested (Lack, 1954) that deferred maturity has been evolved because the care and feeding of the young, and perhaps other breeding activities, would impose too severe a strain on young and inexperienced parents. Even so, it is remarkable that such species as albatrosses may not breed until 8 or 9 years old, and further study of this point is needed. It should be added that deferred maturity will be of particular value in long-lived species which lay only a single egg, like shearwaters and albatrosses, as in these the omission of a year of potential breeding will make proportionately little difference to the eventual number of offspring produced. Contrary to my view, Wynne-Edwards (1955, 1962) considered that deferred maturity is yet another means of bringing the reproductive rate low enough to prevent over-population in such long-lived birds. There is not as yet enough evidence in Procellariiformes to discuss his or my view critically.

Since in a stable population the birth-rate and death-rate are equal, it follows that, owing to their unusually low reproductive rates, the Procellariiformes should have unusually low mortality rates. The most extensive figures are those analysed by J. F. Scott (in Richdale, 1965) for the Sooty Shearwater, which has an annual adult mortality of 7 per cent, meaning that the adults have an expectation of further life of about 14 years. The mortality is similar, somewhere between 5 and 9 per cent, in the Short-tailed Shearwater (Farner, 1962). In a group of Manx Shearwaters breeding on Skokholm, 7 per cent apparently failed to return between 1963 and 1964, and only 4 per cent failed to do so between 1964 and 1965. (The figure of 7 per cent for 1963–64 may well have been too high, as some individuals were perhaps overlooked in 1964.)[1] These are lower figures than any cited for other species of birds in my earlier book (1954) except that of 3 per cent for the Royal Albatross, based on a very small sample. More recently, however, the annual mortality has been estimated at 6 per cent for rather small samples of the Fulmar (Dunnett et al., 1963) and the Gannet (see p. 248), and of 45 Storm Petrels which bred successfully on Skokholm (in two years' observation) at most three (7 per cent) failed to return in the following year (Davis, 1957).

It will be clear from the foregoing discussion that I consider the unusually low reproductive rates of shearwaters and other Procellariiformes to be the result of a series of adaptations, evolved through natural selection, enabling these birds to raise as many young as possible as quickly as possible under difficult feeding conditions. For instance, the clutch of one has been evolved because the parents can normally raise only one chick. The incapacity of mutton-birds and most other species

[1] These figures supersede earlier estimates for the Manx Shearwater by Orians (1958) and Coulson (1959b). Coulson's estimate of 18 per cent was based on the assumption that most 'adults' ringed on Skokholm were breeding birds, whereas most were really sub-adults, the mortality of which is almost certainly higher than that of breeding adults.

to replace a lost egg is due partly to the difficulty of the female in finding enough food to form a second egg, and partly to the fact that any late broods could not be raised before the onset of the autumn migration. The single brood in a year, only one in two years in large albatrosses, is all that can be raised in the time available. The unusually long nestling period is due to the relatively slow rate of growth of the young, which is an adaption to a slow feeding rate by the parents, due to the food supplies being sparse, distant and irregular, and to the consequent need for the young to build up fat reserves to allow for periods of starvation. The long incubation period has probably been evolved because the easiest way to evolve a slower rate of nestling growth is to retard the whole period of development; it is not an advantage in itself, but is of no appreciable disadvantage in birds which nest where there are no predators to take their eggs. Finally, the unusually late age of maturity is advantageous because, through the difficulties in finding food, inexperienced birds would be incapable of raising even one nestling. In contrast, Wynne-Edwards (1955, 1962) considered all these features to have been evolved in order to reduce the reproductive rate to the low annual mortality, and thus to prevent over-population, but he provided no direct evidence in favour of his views or against mine, while one of the points at issue, the significance of a brood of one, has since he wrote been subjected to experimental tests which support my interpretation.

Most birds undergo a complete moult just after breeding, and this applies to some of the Procellariiformes. But certain other species show a different timing, presumably as an adaptation to particular ecological conditions. For instance, the Snow Petrel, like the Gannet (p. 248), moults while breeding (Maher, 1962). Again the Short-tailed Shearwater moults its body feathers in summer when breeding and postpones the moult of the wing and tail feathers until it has reached its distant wintering grounds in the North Pacific, where the moult is rapid and heavy in an area with abundant food. Meinertzhagen (1956) claimed that the related Great Shearwater is temporarily flightless during the wing moult in its winter quarters, but he had no convincing evidence for this, and Serventy (pers. comm.) found that Short-tailed Shearwaters which moulted in captivity in Australia did not become flightless. Diving petrels become temporarily flightless when moulting (Murphy, 1936), but these birds, unlike other Procellarii, do not depend on their wings to find food. Swifts show variations in the timing of the moult similar to those in Procellariiformes, for instance the Alpine Swift, *Apus melba*, moulting before its autumn migration, but the Common Swift, *A. apus*, after it has reached its African wintering grounds (Lack, 1956b).

The mortality factors affecting shearwaters after they leave the nest

263

have not been studied in detail. As regards disease, Mykytowycz *et al.* (1955) found ornithosis to be common and widespread in fledgling Short-tailed Shearwaters, but supposed that under favourable conditions it did not cause important pathological changes, though it might do so if the birds were weakened by some other cause (such as food shortage). It also occurs in the Manx Shearwater on Skomer and Skokholm in South Wales, at times killing apparently well nourished fledglings (Dane, 1948; Miles and Stoker, 1948; Stoker and Miles, 1953). But in 1964, when more deaths than usual were recorded on Skokholm, only 1000 out of an estimated 26500 fledglings were killed, or about 4 per cent, so the effect on the population was negligible (Harris, 1965). Another cause of death is limey-bird disease, which may locally kill large numbers of young Short-tailed Shearwaters, though overall its effect on numbers seems negligible; it is probably not infectious (Mykytowycz, 1963). Otherwise disease has not been recorded, and as it would probably be conspicuous in the densely packed colonies of most Procellariiformes, it is probably unimportant.

On Skokholm, Great Black-backed Gulls, *Larus marinus*, kill and eat many fledgling Manx Shearwaters as they make their way from their burrows to the sea, and they also take many older birds on the surface, but these appear to be mainly non-breeding sub-adults without holes of their own. Herring and Lesser Black-backed Gulls, *L. argentatus* and *L. fuscus*, also take some Manx Shearwaters there, but are much less serious enemies. Predation by gulls or other birds is apparently negligible at the colonies of Short-tailed, Sooty, and Great Shearwaters, and the rate of predation on Manx Shearwaters on Skokholm is perhaps abnormally heavy at the present time due to a recent big increase in *Larus* gulls, which is generally attributed to their increased rate of survival in winter through feeding on the rubbish tips in coastal towns. It should be added also that, though hundreds of shearwater corpses destroyed by gulls are found each season on Skokholm, the proportion killed is probably negligible. As predation by birds is negligible in most shearwater colonies and small in the rest, it almost certainly has no important effect on the regulation of their numbers. Probably, however, the threat of such predation is an important factor causing most species of shearwaters and other petrels to return to their burrows only at night, while there is also a tendency, especially in the sub-adults, to avoid coming on moonlit nights. This conceivably reduces the frequency with which shearwaters feed their young, and probably makes it harder than it otherwise would be for the sub-adult birds to find nesting sites and to form pairs. In this connection it is interesting that on Christmas Island (Pacific Ocean), where there are no gulls or skuas, and where there were no resident land mammals, the Christmas Shearwater, *P. nativitatis*, breeds on the surface of the ground, usually under scrub (Gallagher, 1960), while in the Galapagos Audubon's Shearwater, *P. lherminieri*, and the storm petrel *Oceanodroma tethys*, fly around by day (personal observations, 1938–9; also Lévêque, 1964).

Predation, actual or potential, by rats or other mammals which can enter burrows is presumably the main reason why shearwaters and other petrels normally nest on islands which are free of them, and why they have become extinct on various islands to which rats or cats have have been accidentally introduced by man. But the primary effect of predation by mammals is to restrict the breeding sites of Procellariiformes to places where predatory mammals are absent.

This raises the question of whether shearwaters and other Procellariiformes might be limited in numbers by the availability of their nesting sites. This might perhaps be so for the Great Shearwater on Nightingale Island, in the Tristan da Cunha archipelago, where some two million pairs nest on one square mile, the whole ground is riddled with their burrows, some breed in unsuitable crevices and others lay eggs in the open (Rowan, 1952; Elliott, 1957; amplified by both in pers. comm.); but this case needs further study because, surprisingly, there is apparently much suitable but unoccupied ground on Inaccessible Island, only twenty miles away. Again, all suitable soil on Skokholm not occupied by rabbit burrows seems to be filled with the burrows of Manx Shearwaters, it is hard to believe that appreciably more pairs could find room there, and some of those that are breeding lose their eggs through repeated disturbance by other individuals in search of holes. Similarly, on the island off New Zealand studied by Richdale (1965), the Sooty Shearwater and each of the other four species of Procellarii which breed there tend to burrow at a different depth or in a different layer of the soil, so that they do not compete with each other for nesting space. Such segregation recalls Gause's principle that two species with similar ecology cannot persist in the same area (see p. 284), and suggests that there has been competition for nesting sites. This in turn suggests that the number of breeding pairs of each of these species may be limited by the availability of nesting sites; but the evidence is indirect. There are other Procellariiformes which are clearly not limited by nesting sites at the present time, such as Leach's Petrel on Kent Island, New Brunswick (C. Huntington, pers. comm.), most albatrosses, and, at least until its recent dramatic increase, the Fulmar Petrel on British cliffs. Moreover, even if there are too few nesting sites for the available pairs of shearwaters, this could not in itself regulate their total numbers, since it would merely result in a steadily increasing proportion of non-breeding birds, and this increase would presumably continue until the total population of breeding and non-breeding birds combined reached a density-dependent limit set by some other factor, such as food.

As evening falls, Manx Shearwaters collect on the sea in dense rafts near their breeding islands. Here they periodically fly up and then alight again, and the birds do not normally come in to land until well after dark. It is generally believed, as already mentioned, that they keep off-shore until dark to avoid predation by gulls, which in daylight can readily catch them on the ground, where they are clumsy. However, Wynne-Edwards (1962, p. 205) suggested a different function for these evening gatherings, that they constitute 'a mass demonstration of the whole breeding unit . . . by which the magnitude of the year's breeding effort was being conditioned and regulated'. He provided no evidence for this suggestion, and it seems highly unlikely that the whole colony takes part at one time, as he claimed, while since this behaviour continues during most of the summer, it also seems unlikely that its main function could be to regulate either breeding or total numbers, for which one would have thought that a demonstration at the start of the season would suffice. Further, even if the birds did in this way demonstrate their numbers to each other, Wynne-Edwards made no suggestion as to how they might respond to the information thus received. One must, I think, look elsewhere for the way in which the numbers of shearwaters are regulated.

Ashmole (1963a) postulated that, particularly as they do not seem to be regulated by disease, predation, or (at least in most cases) by shortage of nesting sites, the numbers of pelagic birds are most likely to be regulated in a density-dependent way by food shortage. But since outside the breeding season these birds scatter over immense areas of sea, he considered it hardly conceivable that food could, at this time, be so sparse in relation to their density that they could be in effective competition with each other for it. The only period when they reach a high density, and so might compete seriously for food, is when they are breeding, as then they are greatly concentrated by the need for safe nesting places. Ashmole continued that, as the number of breeding pairs at a colony rises, so the waters close to the colony must become depleted of food, so that the birds are forced to fly progressively farther to find it. Under these conditions he could see only one factor which could check their increase, that eventually they have to fly so far that many of them could not bring enough food to raise young. The recruitment rate would then decrease, until eventually it was about the same as the annual adult mortality, and the population would be stabilized. Under these conditions, no pair could collect sufficient food to raise more than one young, hence natural selection would favour a clutch of one, while any parents that were even slightly less experienced or less efficient than others would fail to raise any young, so natural selection would favour deferment of the age of first breeding.

Moreover, if the balance between the number of the birds and the food supply is close, as it is on this theory, any reduction in food in a particular year through extraneous causes, even a small reduction, might well cause heavy losses of nestlings from starvation. Since Ashmole wrote this, Richdale (1963) recorded such a year of heavy losses among nestlings of the Sooty Shearwater. Also Ashmole himself, whose primary interest was in tropical pelagic birds, saw heavy nestling mortality among such species in one of the years that he worked on Ascension Island, including in the Black Noddy, *Anous tenuirostris*, Wideawake Tern, *Sterna fuscata* (Ashmole 1962, 1963*b*), and Brown Booby, *Sula leucogaster* (Dorward, 1962). Further his survey of the ornithological literature revealed similar occurrences in pelagic birds in other areas, affecting the Laysan Albatross, Wideawake, Brown Noddy, *Anous stolidus*, Brown Booby, and Red-tailed Tropic Bird, *Phaethon rubricaudus* (Ashmole 1963*a*). He therefore concluded that the populations of pelagic birds might be regulated through the influence of food shortage on the mortality rate of the nestlings. In a postscript, he suggested that in tropical species the critical factor might not be the food supply itself, but its availability close to the surface of the sea, which is greatly influenced by the presence of large predatory fish, which periodically drive their prey to the surface where sea-birds can also catch them.

A critical test of Ashmole's theory might be provided by measuring what happens if the breeding adults of a pelagic species are severely reduced in numbers, since on his view food would then become more plentiful nearer to the colony, so that no, or hardly any, nestlings would starve, and eventually one might expect this to lead to a reduction in the age of first breeding and even to an increase in clutch-size. Whether clutch-size and the age of first breeding could be modified quickly, however, would presumably depend on the way in which they were evolved and the means by which they are controlled physiologically, and as the present situation may have been in existence for thousands of years, a rapid evolutionary change might not be possible. Perhaps that is why the Gannets on the Bass Rock still lay only one egg and first breed at the age of five, although they can at the present time raise twins (see p. 248). Ashmole pointed out, however, there is a marine mammal in which a dense and a sparse population can be compared, and in which the age of first breeding varies in the way expected on his theory. This is the Elephant Seal, *Mirounga leonina*, which is at present killed in large numbers by sealers at South Georgia, but not at Macquarie Island (Carrick *et al.*, 1962). At South Georgia nearly all the cows first have pups when three years old, whereas at Macquarie their average age at first breeding is six, ranging from four to seven years. This difference is correlated with a much more rapid growth of the young seals of both sexes at South Georgia than at Macquarie, which Carrick attributed to much less intense competition for food in the heavily culled population round South Georgia than in the dense and stable population round Macquarie.

One further point, not discussed by Ashmole, suggests that at least some species of shearwaters may be in competition for food during the breeding season. Bourne (1955, 1957) pointed out that in the Cape Verde, Canary, and Salvage Islands, the Little Shearwater, *P. assimilis* (*baroli*), lays its eggs in February, while the larger Cory's Shearwater, *P. diomedea*, does not start until late May or June. Similarly, the Soft-plumaged Petrel, *Bulweria mollis*, which is the same size as Cory's Shearwater, lays in December and January at about the same time as the Little Shearwater, while Bulwer's Petrel, *B. bulwerii*, which is the same size as the Little Shearwater, lays at about the same time as Cory's Shearwater. Previous authors argued that this segregation in breeding time between congeneric species was due to competition for nesting burrows and that it enabled one individual of each of the two species to alternate in the same home, like Box and Cox (Morton, 1847). But Bourne concluded that it was primarily a result of competition for food, and this seems to me the likelier explanation. Moreover he found that elsewhere, also, no two species of *Procellaria* (= *Puffinus*) or *Bulweria*, and no two species of either genus if of the same size, breed at the same time. He further showed that where, as in the Salvage Islands or Madeira, the Little and Cory's Shearwaters breed alongside a race of the Manx Shearwater, a species intermediate between them in size, the Little Shearwater has evolved a smaller race and Cory's Shearwater a larger race than usual. Such character displacement (Brown and Wilson, 1956) has presumably been evolved as a result of competition for food, each of the species concerned becoming adapted to take organisms of different size. This again suggests that there is competition for food among shearwaters in the breeding season. Some marked differences in breeding season are also found among the twelve species of Procellariiformes breeding on Gough Island in the South Pacific (Elliott, 1953, 1957; Swales, 1965), and in those of the North Pacific (Kuroda, 1960), and should be studied in relation to food supplies.

Ashmole's theory provides a stronger reason than was previously available for the evolution in shearwaters and other pelagic birds of a clutch of one, a long nestling period and the deferment of maturity, but there are two possible objections to it. First, these features might have been evolved even if the species in question were limited in numbers by food shortage or some other factor operating outside the breeding season, provided that the birds were strongly concentrated when breeding, as they are. Further the same trends, though in a lesser degree, are characteristic of inshore-feeding sea-birds such as the Yellow-eyed Penguin, which likewise have small clutches (usually 2 or 3 eggs), comparatively long nestling periods (though not so long as in shearwaters), and the deferment of maturity (to about the age of 3, instead of 4 to 7 as in shearwaters). If the trends found in inshore-feeding species are in the same direction as in pelagic birds, though less extreme, it is reasonable to suppose that they are the result of similar, but less severe, selection pressures. Most sea-birds that feed inshore when breeding also feed inshore during the winter, so their feeding grounds are probably as restricted in winter as in summer, while the increase in their numbers after breeding, and the presumed decrease in their food supplies during the winter, make it likely that their food will be sparser in winter than summer. Hence it seems most likely that the numbers of the inshore-feeding sea-birds are controlled by competition for food in winter, rather than in the breeding season. This conclusion can then be applied, by extension, to the pelagic birds.

The second difficulty concerns Ashmole's underlying assumption that, because pelagic birds range so widely outside the breeding season, they cannot at that time be limited in numbers by food shortage. The areas where food is plentiful in the surface waters of the oceans are localized at all times of year, occurring especially where there are upwellings, usually not far off land. Moreover, the Short-tailed, Sooty, Great, and Manx Shearwaters undertake long migrations into the opposite hemisphere in winter, which have presumably been evolved only because food is scarce in winter nearer to their breeding grounds. Outside the breeding season, also, their populations are larger by the previous summer's crop of young, and that in some years food may be short for them is shown, for instance, by the periodic heavy losses of Short-tailed Shearwaters on spring migration along the east coast of Australia, first-year and to a lesser extent second-year birds being mainly involved. Hence, bearing in mind that shearwaters may also range widely for food when breeding, it is at least possible that their food is as scarce in winter as summer, and that, after all, they are regulated in numbers by the food supply outside the breeding season.

More cannot be said about this problem until quantitative studies have been made of the numbers of these sea-birds in relation to their food supplies, both in and outside the breeding season. Even, however, if their numbers should prove to be limited by food supplies outside the breeding season, their large concentrations for breeding may well reduce the available food in the surrounding areas of sea, in which case the adaptations in breeding biology considered by Ashmole would still apply.

Summarizing, the Short-tailed Shearwater has a more regular and more restricted laying season than any other known bird. That of the Manx Shearwater is more extended, but those eggs laid earlier in the season are much more likely to give rise to surviving young than those laid later. The clutch of shearwaters is always one and the Manx Shearwater, like the Laysan Albatross, is unable to raise a brood of two; indeed, parents of both species provided with twins produced fewer survivors per brood than parents with single chicks. The long nestling period is considered to be an adaptation to a sparse and irregular food supply. Short-tailed Shearwaters do not breed until five to eight years old, females starting slightly earlier than males, while most Manx Shearwaters first breed when five years old. Maturity is deferred presumably because it is so difficult to raise young that inexperienced young individuals would be unable to do so. The annual mortality is about 7 per cent in the Sooty Shearwater and is also very low in the Short-tailed and Manx Shearwaters. Disease is uncommon, predation restricts breeding to islands free of carnivorous mammals and rats but otherwise seems unimportant, and nesting sites cannot limit numbers. Probably the population density is regulated by food shortage, but whether in the breeding season (Ashmole's theory) or outside it is not yet clear.

Manx Shearwater and small chick.

Benedicite
omnes
volucres

17

CONCLUSION

IN conclusion, it seems worth reviewing briefly the main new points
of general interest which the studies in preceding chapters have
revealed, and in this connection, readers may be reminded of my
appraisal of current theories of population dynamics in the Appendix.
The present book shows that there have in recent years been important
advances in our understanding of the factors influencing reproductive
rates, but that much less progress has been made on those influencing
mortality and the regulation of adult numbers. This is because the
study of breeding biology is relatively simple, whereas that of adult
numbers is much harder and requires much longer. In particular, the
proof or disproof of density-dependent regulation involves measurements over many years, both of numbers and of the mortality due to
to each main cause, and nearly all the studies reviewed here have been
carried on for too few years, while in all of them the mortality due to
one or more causes has not been measured.

As mentioned in the first chapter, the thirteen major studies reviewed
here were selected solely on the grounds of duration and sufficient
detail, and the eleven minor ones because of their relevance to the major
ones. In all, thirteen passerine species, eight other land birds and four
sea birds have been included, and they exhibit a wide diversity of feeding and breeding habits. The passerine species include insectivorous,

271

graminivorous, and frugivorous forms, and while most are monogamous and nest solitarily in territories, they also include bigamous, promiscuous, and colonial species. The other land birds, nearly all of which are territorial, include vegetarians and carnivores, nidicolous and nidifugous species, strict residents and nomads, while the sea birds, which are colonial, include both inshore and pelagic species. The most serious gap is the absence of any freshwater species, and it is surprising not to have any long-term study of a waterfowl or wader. Among the orders omitted altogether are the Anseriformes (ducks, geese, swans), Falconiformes (diurnal birds of prey), Gruiformes (cranes, rails, etc.), Psittaciformes (parrots), Coraciiformes (kingfishers, etc.) and Piciformes (woodpeckers), while the sole representatives of the big order Charadriiformes (waders, terns, etc.) are the atypical Kittiwake and Pomarine Skua.

The selection was unexpectedly biased in its geographical distribution, since of the thirteen major studies, nine were carried out in Britain, while the two tropical ones were also undertaken by British workers. But two of the birds studied in Britain were also studied elsewhere, the Pied Flycatcher in Continental Europe and the shearwaters (different species) in Australasia, and the other two major studies were carried out in Germany and New Zealand respectively. It was surprising to have no long-term population study from the United States, particularly since, as mentioned in the first chapter, four of the five major studies excluded here simply because published early enough to be in my former book were by Americans, on the Song Sparrow, House Wren, Bobwhite Quail, and Ruffed Grouse respectively, the other being on the Great Tit in Holland. Of the minor studies included here seven were undertaken in Britain, one in Germany, two in the United States, and one in Trinidad. I can only assure the reader that the strong British bias in this selection was not due to misplaced patriotism. It is sad to find that the proportion of amateur workers referred to is much lower than in my earlier book, and that out of some thirty main authors cited, only three, Dr. Campbell, Dr. Richdale, and Herr Tantzen, did their field work in spare time. On the other hand I was pleased to find that whereas my earlier book was based largely on the work of persons older than myself, two-thirds of the main authors cited here are at least ten years younger than me, so that one may confidently look forward to further advances in the subject.

In my earlier book, I suggested that the breeding seasons of single-brooded species have normally been evolved so that they lay their eggs at such a time that their young hatch in the most favourable period for raising them, usually when their food is most abundant. But the new studies reviewed here show that this idea has to be seriously modified. In the Wood Pigeon and Bullfinch there is direct evidence, and in the Great and Blue Tits, Pied Flycatcher, Common Swift, Manx Shearwater, and Cuckoo, indirect evidence that the immediate factor determining the start of breeding is the female's obtaining enough food to form eggs; and in all these species except perhaps the Wood Pigeon, at least most individuals would raise more young if they could lay their eggs earlier than they do. However, they stop laying when their food is still abundant, though it would not be abundant for young hatching from eggs laid later than this. Hence the termination of laying has evidently been evolved in relation to when young can be raised, probably modified, at least in the Bullfinch, by the need to moult while food remains plentiful.

In the Blackbird and the Swift, cold weather and sparse animal food at the time of laying may also cause a small reduction in the normal clutch for the time of year. In the Blackbird this is conceivably because cold induces the birds to lay the number appropriate earlier in the spring, but in the Swift it may well be dangerous for the birds to lay a full clutch when their reserves of food are precarious. Otherwise, there is no evidence that the food available to the hens at the time of laying influences the clutch-size of nidicolous species, though it influences the number of eggs laid in a season by the parasitic Cuckoo. In various gallinaceous birds, however, there is circumstantial evidence that clutches are larger in well-nourished than poorly nourished hens. Since these species do not feed their nidifugous young, it was to be expected that the factors influencing their clutch-size would be different from those influencing nidicolous species.

On my view that the clutch-size of nidicolous species is adapted to the largest number of young which the parents can normally raise, the addition of young to make larger broods than normal should result in fewer, not more, young surviving per brood. This expected result has been obtained in the Swift, Manx Shearwater, Laysan Albatross, Leach's Petrel, and in most years in the Great Tit. In addition, there is good evidence that the normal clutch is, or is near to, the most productive brood-size in the Starling, Quelea, Bullfinch, Wood Pigeon, and Yellow-eyed Penguin, also in the Blue Tit in most years. On the other hand, supplemented broods gave rise to more survivors than those of normal size in the Gannet and Glaucous-winged Gull, conceivably because the food situation is at present unusually favourable at the colonies concerned. An apparently similar result in the Kittiwake cannot be interpreted reliably as the survival of the young was not followed after they left the nest. The available information on survival in relation to brood-size in the Pied and Collared Flycatchers also seems contrary to my view of clutch-size, but it requires further study, with particular respect to phenotypic variations.

CONCLUSION

Phenotypic modifications in clutch-size were found in various species in which there is circumstantial evidence that they are adapted to the subsequent food requirements of the young. In the Great and Blue Tits, Pied and Collared Flycatchers, Swift, and Kittiwake, clutches tend to be largest at the start of the season and thereafter to decline, and there is evidence that these species find it harder to raise young later than earlier in the season. In the Blackbird, Song Thrush and Robin, on the other hand, clutches laid in the middle of the season are larger than those either earlier or later; correspondingly, the food available for these species in woods is most plentiful in mid-season, and this is also near to the time when the days are longest. Probably, therefore, these seasonal variations in clutch-size are such that larger clutches tend to be laid when larger broods can later be raised.

Similarly in the Great Tit, Blackbird, Yellow-eyed Penguin, and Kittiwake, older females lay rather larger clutches than those breeding for the first time and are also rather more efficient in raising young. In the Great and Coal Tits clutch-size also varies inversely with population density, presumably because it is harder for the parents to collect food for their young where the birds are crowded. Finally, in the Tawny Owl, Short-eared Owl, and Bullfinch, larger clutches are laid when their main food, woodland mice, field voles, and certain seeds respectively, is more abundant than in other years. The only observed phenotypic variation which does not seem to be adaptive is the tendency for Great and Blue Tits, Pied and Collared Flycatchers, to lay larger clutches in the years when breeding is earlier than in the the years when it is later; but the fact that this occurs in four different species in the same habitat itself suggests that an adaptation of some kind must be involved. Finally in the Tawny and Short-eared Owls, the White Stork, the Kittiwake, and the second broods of the Great Tit, the later nestlings hatch asynchronously, so that the last to hatch are the smallest and die quickly if food is short. This I regard as an adaptation to reduce brood-size rapidly to that which the food supply will support, without wasting food on chicks which would die anyway. The occasional killing of one or more of its young by the White Stork requires further study, but possibly it anticipates deaths that would occur anyway from starvation.

Most of the species considered in this book first breed when a year old, including the tits, thrushes, finches, weavers, owls, pigeons, and ptarmigan. In the Pied and Collared Flycatchers the hens and some cocks breed as yearlings, but probably about half the yearling cocks do not breed, perhaps merely through failure to obtain mates. In the Black and White Manakin and Tricolored Redwing, the hens breed when a year old, but the cocks do not assume nuptial plumage or breed until two years old. The latter is perhaps advantageous if display increases the risk of predation and if one-year-old males would in any case fail to obtain mates with the strong competition for them in promiscuous and polygynous species. Finally, in the White Stork and in those sea birds discussed here, breeding starts at an age varying between two and seven years or more, depending on the species. There is no evidence for the view of Wynne-Edwards (1955, 1962) that such deferred maturity has been evolved through group-selection in long-lived species to reduce the number of young and so prevent over-population. There is equally no proof of my alternative view that, in such species, breeding is difficult and individuals which try to breed when younger than the normal age leave, on the average, fewer not more surviving young than those which start later. My view depends on two conditions: first, that young parents are less efficient at raising young than older parents, of which there is suggestive evidence in several species, as already mentioned; and, secondly, that breeding somewhat lowers the chances of survival of young adults, of which there is as yet no evidence, though it seems not unlikely on general grounds.

In the Kittiwake, pairs that have mated in the previous year breed earlier, and so on average raise more young, than newly formed pairs. Hence there is presumably selection in favour of retaining the same mate in successive years, as Kittiwakes and other sea-birds usually do.

The annual adult mortality is about 70 per cent in a tropical estrildine finch, around 50 per cent in the Great Tit, Pied Flycatcher, Blackbird, and Song Thrush, and about 36 per cent in the Wood Pigeon. It was apparently two-thirds in a Scottish population of Red Grouse, though much lower in a natural population of the related White-tailed Ptarmigan. It is perhaps one-fifth in the White Stork, but is only a little over 10 per cent in the Black and White Manakin, Yellow-eyed Penguin and Kittiwake, and only around 6 per cent in the Gannet, Sooty, Short-tailed, and Manx Shearwaters. These figures are in general agreement with those for other species published earlier (Lack, 1954), and it is pleasing to have the first records for tropical passerine species and also to confirm that various sea birds have so low a mortality. These figures also fit my view that the higher the reproductive rate the higher the annual mortality, which I regard as a simple consequence of population balance through density-dependent regulation of the mortality. There is no evidence for Wynne-Edwards' view that the reproductive rate has been evolved through group-selection to fit the mortality.

Wynne-Edwards also claimed that birds may modify their reproductive rates to prevent over-population through 'prudential restraints' on breeding. On this view, the number of young produced each year should later have an important influence on the density of breeding pairs, but in the five longest studies reviewed here, on the Great Tit, Blue Tit, Pied Flycatcher, Tawny Owl, and White Stork, the annual variations in the number of young raised per pair have had no appreciable influence on the subsequent number of breeding pairs, and the same has evidently held in at least three other species, the Coal Tit, Wood Pigeon, and Bullfinch. Hence, even if these birds should be practising prudential restraints, they would be ineffective, at least if the variations in reproductive output are no larger than those observed. In the Great and Coal Tits the average clutch, and in the Great Tit also the survival rate of the nestlings, vary inversely with population density, but without appreciable influence on the size of the next year's breeding population. In the Ptarmigan, reproductive success is high when the population is rising but also in the first years of high numbers, and low when the population is falling, but also in the later years of high numbers, so it it evidently not responsible for the population changes.

Since the numbers of the species studied were not regulated by variations in the reproductive rate, the mortality rate was presumably critical. Potentially the most important density-dependent causes of death in wild animals are predation, disease, and starvation, to which one should perhaps add human destruction. In most of the species studied in this book predation was negligible, and though predators took many Red Grouse, these were chiefly birds without territories which would not have bred, while any owners of territories that died were quickly replaced. Disease was also unimportant, and was rarely recorded at all except in the Wood Pigeon, in the Red Grouse (mainly birds without territories which were probably short of food), and in juvenile Short-tailed and Manx Shearwaters. Many Red Grouse were shot in autumn and many Wood Pigeons in winter, but without apparent effect on the number of breeding pairs in the following spring.

If predation, disease, and human destruction were unimportant, food shortage was probably the main density-dependent mortality factor, and for this there was positive evidence in several species. In the Coal Tit and Wood Pigeon, in particular, measurements of the foods eaten and foods available through the winter showed that the number of individuals surviving at the end of each winter was proportional to the remaining food supplies. Such a close and direct relationship between bird numbers and the availability of food was probably brought about through direct competition for food and the existence of a peck-order such that the weaker individuals give way when attacked and quickly die. A peck-order is of survival value both to those higher and to those lower in the order, for those higher because they obtain food with very little fighting, and for those lower because it saves them

276

wasting time on fights which they would anyway lose, and their energies can be conserved for searching elsewhere.

Other species in which there is suggestive evidence for the limitation of numbers by food outside the breeding season are the Bullfinch, which has a marked two-year fluctuation in numbers in parallel with the seed crops which constitute its main winter foods, and the Quelea, for which seeds become very short at the end of the dry season and the beginning of the rains, when many starve. In the other tropical species studied here, the Black and White Manakin, Snow thought that its chief food, various fruits, could not be limiting, but it is hard to see what other factor could be involved. The numbers of the Red Grouse probably depend on its main food, heather, but in this connection the possible modifying influence of its territorial behaviour needs clarification. In the Great and Blue Tits, the number of juveniles surviving to the start of each winter was correlated with the beechmast crop, and though these species eat beechmast only after the start of the winter, various other seed crops fluctuate in parallel with the beech, so this correlation is presumably due in some way to the food supply. Further, the annual fluctuations in the breeding populations of the Great and Blue Tits were due mainly to the number of juveniles surviving to the start of the winter, modified in a few years by losses in severe winters, presumably through starvation. The Heron and Song Thrush are also much reduced after cold winters, presumably through starvation. Again, the fact that more food is available in winter in gardens than woods provides the readiest explanation of why Song Thrushes and Blackbirds breed at ten times as high a density in gardens as woods. There is, therefore, circumstantial evidence that food supplies outside the breeding season influence the annual fluctuations or average density of various species studied here, though more evidence is needed. There are also some unexplained fluctuations, the most striking being the apparent ten-year cycle of Scottish Ptarmigan.

There have been three valuable new findings in relation to colonial nesting. First, in the Tricolored Redwing, the size of the breeding colonies is correlated with the food situation and the flocks apparently make exploratory flights prior to settling to breed, as if assessing the food potential of the environment in relation to their numbers, but this possible means of regulating the size of the colonies requires further study. Secondly, Kittiwakes start breeding earlier, and therefore raise more young, in crowded than uncrowded colonies or parts of colonies, the main reason for which is unknown. Thirdly, in various pelagic sea birds, Ashmole suggested that crowding at the island colonies depletes the food supplies in adjoining waters, thus making it hard for the birds to raise young successfully, with the consequent evolution of clutches of one and deferred maturity; he further argued that the adult population might be limited by this process, but this I think much more doubtful.

Where White Storks are decreasing, they tend to move from less favourable to more favourable habitats to breed, sometimes after a year's failure in a poor habitat. This way of regulating the density of breeding pairs by trial and error, which I earlier postulated for the colonial Heron, would be of value especially in long-lived species which in their first breeding year may occupy nests without laying eggs. The other solitary species discussed here breed when a year old, and the density of most of them has been claimed to be regulated by territorial behaviour, but if so, territory operates very differently in different species, and the picture is highly confused.

For instance, the Bullfinch usually nests solitarily, but without territorial behaviour. Again, each pair of Wood Pigeons defends an area round its nest, and the resultant spacing probably assists conceal-ment of the nests from predators, but the birds feed in flocks, so the territory does not conserve a food supply, and there is no reason to think that it regulates numbers. A third variation is found in the Pied Flycatcher, which defends an area round its nesting hole, not a territory with a defined perimeter; however, when nesting holes are in excess of numbers, it breeds at a much higher density in rich than poor types of woods, which requires explanation. Tits also defend nesting holes and, with holes in excess, breed at a much higher density in rich than poor types of wood. Kluijver and Tinbergen (1953) argued that terri-torial behaviour set an upper limit to the numbers of the Great Tit in a favourable habitat, but this evidently did not hold in Marley wood, where the population was 60 per cent higher in one year than any other (without any corresponding change in the habitat so far as known). Again, while Coal Tits apparently claim territories in autumn, the number of breeding pairs is limited by the winter food supply. Hence, in none of the species discussed in this paragraph is there clear evidence either that territorial behaviour limits numbers, or as to how the density of pairs is regulated in relation to the nature of the habitat.

The Song Sparrow is a classical territorial species, but while the number of pairs breeding on Mandarte Island was nearly the same in three successive years, it then rose by about half as much again, a situation recalled that of the Great Tit in Marley Wood, and similarly suggesting that territorial behaviour did not limit numbers. In particu-lar, this is contrary to the idea of territory as a 'partly compressible disc'. Since, also, the birds on Mandarte feed freely outside their territories, the latter evidently do not conserve a food supply for the young. It is also hard to know why the breeding population was ten times as dense on Mandarte Island as in Ohio. Similar difficulties hold in the Blackbird and Song Thrush, which are ten times as dense in gardens as in woods. Also, the number of Blackbirds breeding each year in the Oxford Botanic Garden seemed too variable for territory to be setting a nearly fixed upper limit. Further, the birds feed freely outside their territories, both in winter and when breeding. Nevertheless, they exclude other individuals from their territories, and vacancies through death are quickly filled, so in some sense territorial behaviour influences the dispersion of the breeding pairs, but perhaps purely locally.

There are similar difficulties in regard to the role of territory in the Red Grouse and Ptarmigan, with the added point that in these species the territories could hardly help in conserving food for the young, which are active from hatching and feed themselves. But both these species exclude others of their kind from their territories, while if the owners of territories are shot they are quickly replaced by others. The chief difficulty is that both species fluctuate markedly in numbers from year to year, by a factor of five or more, the Red Grouse perhaps in relation to the heather, and it is not at all clear whether or not these variations are due to marked annual differences in territorial behaviour and, if so, whether they are advantageous. Likewise the nomadic Short-eared Owl and Pomarine Skua defend breeding territories which are much smaller in some years than others, in their case definitely correlated with the abundance of their prey, but again it is not clear whether territorial behaviour limits numbers, or merely spaces out the available pairs whose numbers have been determined in relation to food in some other way. In marked contrast is another predator on rodents, the Tawny Owl, which is strictly resident and in which the breeding density and hence the size of the territories remains nearly constant from year to year, despite big variations in the numbers of woodland mice. In this species the size of territory is not related to the food supply for the young and when mice are scarce the birds do not breed. The ownership of a territory is probably advantageous in ensuring possession of a familiar hunting ground, and territorial behaviour evidently limits adult numbers, though it permitted a slow increase from twenty to thirty pairs.

The territorial behaviour of most species of birds is generally considered to assist in pair-formation, while in many of them a wide spacing of the nests presumably assists their concealment from nest-predators; defence of a nesting site similarly ensures safe breeding for hole-nesting species. Hence there seems no need to postulate any additional function for territory. Nevertheless, in various species any owners of territories that die are rapidly replaced, so territorial behaviour plays some role in breeding dispersion. But both the nature and the functions of this role are still obscure, and the seemingly obvious view that territorial behaviour limits numbers in relation to the food supply requires more critical study than it has yet received. Further research is much needed.

In conclusion, I might add that in the light of the new studies reviewed in this book, my own ideas on population regulation remain basically those advocated in 1954, but modified in the respects mentioned in this chapter. These views are: (a) that the reproductive rates of birds have been evolved through natural selection and so are, in general, as rapid as the environment and the birds' capacities allow; (b) that mortality rates balance reproductive rates because bird populations are controlled by density-dependent mortality; (c) that starvation outside the breeding season is much the most important density-dependent factor in wild birds (but not necessarily in other animals); (d) that breeding pairs are dispersed broadly in relation to food supplies, through various types of behaviour which are as yet little understood, but which are to be explained through natural selection.

As regards the future, there is clearly need for more and longer population studies in the field, but advances in knowledge through such means are almost inevitably slow, so field experiments could be rewarding. Such experiments, like those on the supplementation of broods or the removal of territorial owners, can at times be simple, but they need to be based on sound knowledge of the natural ecology of the species concerned, as otherwise they may be badly designed or misinterpreted. Soon after writing this, I came on the presidential address to the Ecological Society of America of Professor Thomas Park (1961), and found that he emphasized the same two main points for future progress in animal ecology. The agreement is the more striking in that his personal research on laboratory populations of flour-beetles has been so different from mine on wild birds. First he stressed that 'natural history . . . is one of the prime sources of insight and knowledge for the modern ecologist. It helps him visualize a problem and ask a cogent question'. Secondly, he continued, that while 'traditionally, ecological findings are based on the observation of events which have taken place in an environment unmolested by an observer and varying according to its own natural right . . . I am persuaded that our research progress, and the validity of our interpretations, will be enhanced whenever we intelligently modify appropriate elements of the environment by predetermined plan'. This book is written in the hope that its readers will carry on from there.

APPENDIX: THE THEORETICAL CONTROVERSIES CONCERNING ANIMAL POPULATIONS

Section 1. Density-dependent regulation

SINCE my earlier book of 1954 is now out of print, it may help readers if this appendix begins with a summary of its main points, so they have been set out below successively for each chapter. It should be added that only a few key references have been cited, and for the rest the earlier book should be consulted.

Chapter 1 was purely introductory.

Chapter 2. Birds and other animals can increase in numbers extremely rapidly, as shown for instance by the Pheasant, *Phasianus colchicus*, which, when introduced to an island off north-western U.S.A., increased from 8 to 1,898 individuals in $5\frac{1}{2}$ years (Einarsen, 1945). Usually, however, animal populations fluctuate between restricted limits. In some species, such as the Heron, *Ardea cinerea*, fluctuations have been small, the highest breeding population being only double the lowest. In others, such as various insects in German conifer plantations, the highest population has been over ten thousand times the lowest, and the increase between one year and the next was up to fortyfold; but the population fell after each peak, and even the peaks were negligible hummocks compared with what repeated successful reproduction would allow if unchecked. Hence all populations except those about to become extinct are regulated, and this can come about only through density-dependent factors.

Chapter 3. In nidicolous birds the normal clutch-size is that which, on average, results in the largest number of surviving young; the young in broods of above normal size tend to be undernourished, so that fewer survive per brood than from broods of normal size. This relationship was clearest in Swifts, *A. apus*, in which undernourished young die in the nest, but was also demonstrated through ringing recoveries for the Starling, *Sturnus vulgaris*, in which most deaths occur soon after the young fly (Lack, 1948a). In various other passerine species the relationship was obscured by adaptive phenotypic modifications in clutch-size, whereby clutches tend to be larger when more young are likely to be raised. For instance, in the Nutcracker, *Nucifraga caryocatactes*, which stores nuts in autumn for young raised next spring, the clutch is three with poor nut stores, but four with good nut stores, whether due to a good natural crop or to extra nuts supplied by an experimenter (Swanberg, 1951).

Chapter 4. In various other nidicolous species there is circumstantial evidence that seasonal, annual, regional, and local variations in clutch-size are adaptive modifications to the food situation, occasionally through a direct response to food, but often through a proximate response to some other factor. In various nidicolous species with long nestling periods, such as crows, swifts, and raptors, incubation is started before the clutch is complete, so that the young hatch on different days, and when food is short the youngest and smallest die, though when food is plentiful all may be raised. This I interpreted as another adaptation for adjusting the brood-size to the food situation, and since all the food goes to the largest young until they are satisfied, food is not wasted on young which will die anyway. The reasons for the evolution of clutch-size in nidifugous species, notably ducks, which do not feed their young, were completely obscure.

Chapter 5. Litter-size in mammals presents many parallels to clutch-size in nidicolous birds, with a higher death-rate in larger litters, and also seasonal and other variations in size correlated with the food situation. The number of eggs laid by the queens of social insects depends on the number of workers and hence on the food supply. In many fish and invertebrates, the adult female probably lays as many eggs as it is physiologically capable of producing from its food reserves; but the size of the food store in the egg, and hence the number of eggs, differs greatly in different species according to the extent to which the developing embryo requires a food supply independent of its environment. Similar intraspecific modifications of the reproductive rate to the food situation occur both in the seasonal and local variations in the size and number of eggs of certain freshwater copepods, and in the hereditary differences in clutch-size of insular forms of certain lizards.

Chapter 6. The number of broods raised by a bird each year depends mainly on the length of time for which conditions are suitable for feeding young, and it may vary between populations of the same species. Most birds have a restricted breeding season, even in the tropics. In single-brooded species laying tends to be so timed that the young are raised when food is most plentiful for them (a view modified in the present book for several species, including the Great Tit, *Parus major*, and Manx Shearwater, *Puffinus puffinus*); species raising more than one brood in a year may start sufficiently before the most suitable time for two or more broods to be fitted in. While the breeding season is adapted to the ecological conditions by natural selection through 'ultimate factors', the physiological response of the bird's gonads is to 'proximate factors' which may be different, e.g. food for the young may be the ultimate factor and increasing daylength the proximate timing factor (Baker, 1938). Similar principles apply to the breeding seasons of other animals. Most birds first breed when a year old, but some species when older, probably because inexperienced birds have difficulty in finding enough food to raise young, and in addition their own chances of survival may be reduced if they breed when too young.

Chapter 7. In the Great Tit, both clutch-size and the proportion of pairs raising second broods are a little smaller when the birds are dense than sparse (Kluijver, 1951), but the difference is not great enough to be important in the regulation of numbers. When deer and certain other mammals are numerous and food is sparse, both the proportion of pregnant females and the size of litters tend to be smaller, which, combined with a heavier mortality in the young, might provide an important density-dependent check on numbers. The reduction in fecundity of experimental populations of insects when crowded is not comparable, since in nature these animals probably tend to avoid laying in crowded places.

Chapter 8. Birds show wide variations in nesting success, both between species and, within each species, between different places and different years. In passerine birds, just under half the eggs laid in open nests give rise to flying young, and in hole-nesters about two-thirds; in both types there are further losses, probably heavy, before the young become independent. In ground-nesting gallinaceous and other birds with active nidifugous young, about a quarter of the eggs laid give rise to flying young. After independence, birds in their first year still have a higher mortality than adults. The proportion of eggs laid which gives rise to breeding adults varies between 8 and 18 per cent in different species of birds but is far smaller in many fish and invertebrates.

Chapter 9. The annual adult mortality is 40–60 per cent in various passerine birds, gallinaceous birds and ducks, 30–40 per cent in various limicoline birds and gulls, about 20 per cent in certain swifts, about 10 per cent in a species of penguin, and probably much smaller still in an albatross. This rate is unaffected by age up to an age at which an extremely small proportion of the population is left alive, and wild birds usually live only a small fraction of their potential life-span. In these ways they differ markedly from animals kept in the laboratory and also from modern western man, though not from primitive man. Adult mortality-rates in the wild have been measured for only a few mammals, fish, and insects, in some of which the rate increases with increasing age. When the reproductive rate is higher, so is the mortality-rate, as shown for two separate populations of the Blue Tit, *Parus caeruleus* (Snow, 1956a), of the Wall Lizard, *Lacerta sicula* (Kramer, 1946), and of the Starling (Lack and Schifferli, 1948; now confirmed for a third population by Scheider, 1955). This does not mean that the species concerned have evolved higher reproductive rates in areas where their mortality is higher, but that, in a stable population regulated by density-dependent mortality, a higher reproductive rate inevitably results in a higher mortality rate.

Chapter 10. In birds, the sex ratio of the young is normally about equal at hatching, (and evidence that I cited for an unequal sex ratio at hatching in certain American-icterids has since been disproved by Selander, 1960). A higher mortality in adult females than adult males has been found in various ducks, gallinaceous birds, and a penguin, and the excess of males over females in many other species of birds indicates that this is widespread. In deer the sex ratio at birth is nearly equal, but females predominate among the adults.

Chapter 11. There are two main types of density-dependent regulation. Especially in certain types of limitation by food shortage, the mortality rate may vary directly and rapidly with density, but in a predator-prey interaction it may vary indirectly and in a delayed manner. A direct density-dependent relationship has been observed only in the miniature populations of nestling

APPENDIX

swifts, suckling guinea-pigs, and parasitic chalcids, also in fish fry and in barnacles settling on rocks. A delayed density-dependent effect may reasonably be inferred for the Mule Deer, *Odocoileus hemionus* of the Kaibab, U.S.A., in relation to its food supplies (Leopold *et al.*, 1947). Hence although density-dependent mortality is presumed to be widespread in nature, it has rarely been demonstrated. (I would now be extremely suspicious of two other possible cases that I suggested in 1954 on the basis of data from Errington (1945), involving respectively a direct and a delayed effect at different times of year in the Bobwhite Quail, *Colinus virginianus*. These are discussed further in Appendix, section 2.) The density-dependent losses demonstrated in experimental laboratory populations of insects have occurred under such artificial conditions that their relevance to natural populations is doubtful.

Chapter 12. The study of the food of wild birds presents various technical problems. There are seasonal and other variations in the weight of birds, in their feeding habits and their food requirements.

Chapter 13. The proportion of the available prey taken by wild birds has rarely been measured, and most of the available measurements refer to voles or caterpillars when very numerous, in the breeding seasons of the birds concerned. Four points suggest that the numbers of many birds may be limited by food. First, predation and disease can in many instances be ruled out. Secondly, birds are usually more numerous where their food is more abundant, as shown, for instance, for sea birds and certain shore birds outside the breeding season, and for the breeding birds of Finnish forests and lakes. Thirdly, related species of birds in the same area are normally separated by habitat, feeding habits or size of prey, and such isolation ('Gause's principle') has presumably been evolved because there is competition for food. A species may have a less restricted habitat or food in areas where another species that is normally present with it is absent. Many species may feed on the same type of food if it is temporarily abundant so that there is no effective competition. Fourthly, the habit of intraspecific fighting for food would not, presumably, have been evolved unless food were hard to find. The tendency for true fighting to be replaced by threat, with a resulting peck-order, has presumably been evolved because it is advantageous to both contestants, to the victor because it obtains disputed food items without hurt, and to the retreating bird because it is aware from previous encounters that it would in any case lose a fight with the individual concerned, and so is more likely to obtain food by retreating and seeking elsewhere. When the numbers of a species with a peck-order are up against the food limit, only the few individuals near the bottom of the order starve at any one time, and these quickly, so that deaths from starvation are not easily observed in nature.

Chapter 14. Predation by Sparrowhawks, *Accipter nisus*, may be heavy on certain small passerine species (Tinbergen, 1946); but if the latter are limited by food, such predation might not reduce their numbers in the long term. Most natural losses in Ruffed Grouse, *Bonasa umbellus*, are caused by predators whose chief prey is rodents, hence the numbers of the latter might influence those of the Ruffed Grouse. Errington's view (1946) that the predators of Bobwhite Quail and Muskrat, *Ondetra zibethicus*, remove surplus animals that are anyway doomed was a healthy reaction from the previous view that predators are always harmful to game, but seems based on equally little evidence. Hawks and falcons preying on other birds tend to take weakened individuals, as since confirmed by Eutermoser (1961) and Curry-Lindahl (1961).

Chapter 15. Occasional outbreaks of disease have caused heavy mortality among ducks and other birds, but their long-term influence on numbers is unknown and might be negligible. It was formerly claimed that strongylosis was responsible for the periodic declines of Red Grouse, *Lagopus scoticus* (Lovat *et al.*, 1911), but other evidence suggests that food might be the basic predisposing factor. The evidence that certain native New Zealand birds decreased through introduced diseases is purely anecdotal.

Chapter 16. After protection from hunting and the destruction of their natural predators, North American Mule Deer, White-tailed Deer, *Odocoileus virginianus*, Elk, *Cervus canadensis*, and Moose, *Alces americana*, first increased rapidly and then decreased from starvation, the latter reducing fecundity and causing deaths especially among young and aged, sometimes with secondary disease. This suggests that the numbers of these herbivores were previously limited by predators. Certain carnivorous mammals, also squirrels, seem limited by food shortage. If the predators of the muskrat remove only a doomed surplus expelled by fighting from favourable habitats, then muskrat numbers might be limited by food shortage modified by the animals' behaviour.

Chapter 17. In various edible fish, heavy fishing by man causes a marked increase in the growth-rate of the younger fish and a reduction in the age of first breeding, indicating that the populations concerned were previously limited by food shortage. Dutch Cormorants, *Phalacrocorax carbo*, took a much higher proportion of Roach, *Rutilus rutilus*, infested by a cestode, *Ligula intestinalis*, than of unparasitized fish (Van Dobben, 1952), so the effect of predation on their numbers may be complex. The wall lizard seems limited in numbers on the Italian mainland chiefly by predation and on off-shore islands by food shortage, and the resulting differences in the age structure of the populations recall those of overfished and unfished populations respectively (Kramer, 1946). Sheep Blowflies, *Lucilia* and *Chrysomyia*, are limited in a density-dependent way by food shortage. Most phytophagous insects are held in check for most of the time by insect predators or insect parasites (parasitoids), though they rarely increase to the limit set by food. The numbers of various phytophagous insect pests have been successfully and permanently reduced by introduced predators or parasitoids. But the interaction can be complex, since the introduction of a parasitic mite, *Pediculoides ventricosus*, to Fiji upset the natural balance between a hispid beetle, *Promecotheca reichei*, and its hymenopterous parasites and caused a big increase in the beetle population (Taylor, 1937).

Chapter 18. Climatic factors can produce or greatly modify density-dependent mortality. Unusual weather may cause heavy losses, but the population usually recovers quickly. Many species are changing in range, gradually because of slow climatic changes, or rapidly through alterations in the habitat by man. The species introduced to foreign lands have succeeded chiefly in cultivated land, and they have mainly been species already living in such habitats in the Old World.

Chapter 19. On the tundra, there is a 4-year cycle in the numbers of the Lemming, *Lemmus*, its predators, and Ptarmigan, *Lagopus mutus*. In the northern coniferous forest belt in America, but not Europe, there is a 10-year cycle in the numbers of the Varying Hare, *Lepus americanus*, its predators, and several species of grouse. Willow Grouse, *Lagopus lagopus* show a 4-year cycle where Lemmings are present, a 10-year cycle where the Varying Hare is present, and an irregular fluctuation in the British race where both Lemmings and Varying Hares are absent. The cyclic fluctuations in the mammalian and avian predators, the latter typically nomadic, are determined by those of their rodent prey. The causes of the rodent cycles are unknown, but are probably not extrinsic (climatic) and might be due to oscillations of predator-prey type between the rodents and their vegetable food. On this view their regularity is presumably due to the simplicity of the food chains involved, and their tendency to be synchronous in adjoining areas to movements. (This view needs somewhat modifying, however, in view of the findings of Pitelka (1957, 1958, 1959) at Point Barrow, where Brown Lemmings, *Lemmus trimucronotatus*, periodically ate out their food and thereby also their cover, thus becoming more available to predators.) Finally I suggested that the tendency for the cyclic gallinaceous birds to fluctuate synchronously with the rodents may be because the rodent-predators turn to them after the normally much more numerous rodents have crashed. (But this possibility now seems excluded, since Buckley, 1954, Hoffmann, 1958, and Keith, 1963, showed that in several areas in North America affected by the ten-year cycle, gallinaceous birds declined before, not after, the Varying Hare, while Gudmundsson (1960) found a 10-year fluctuation in the Ptarmigan in Iceland, where there are no cyclic rodents.) Since some of the cyclic game birds, including the Sharp-tailed Grouse, *Pedioecetes phasianellus*, the Willow Grouse, and perhaps the Ruffed Grouse, sometimes emigrate in large numbers after a population peak, and as I consider emigration to be an adaptation to food shortage, I now suggest that the game-bird cycles might be linked with their food supplies; at least, the latter should be examined.

Chapter 20. Mass emigrations occur at irregular intervals in birds of the taiga which depend on particular fruits or seeds which fluctuate greatly in abundance from year to year. Many more juveniles than adults participate. The ultimate factor is food shortage, the proximate response may be to food shortage or to high density. (The latter possibility is perhaps rendered unnecessary by the work of Svärdson, 1957, who showed that these irruptive species are true migrants in which a highly variable proportion of the population migrates each year, depending primarily on the food situation; for further new information see Formosov, 1960.) Nomadic movements also occur in the predators on cyclic rodents and in the marsh and water birds of the Russian steppes and Australian deserts, while comparable movements occur in various mammals and insects.

Chapter 21. Migration, a regular seasonal journey from one area to another and back again later, occurs in many birds, whales, seals, bats, fish, cuttlefish, lepidoptera, dragonflies, locusts, and probably hoverflies. Migration has been evolved where it results in a species reproducing more efficiently or dying less frequently than if it stays in one place throughout the year. Many animals of arctic or temperate regions breed only in their summer quarters, others only in their winter quarters, some in both and a few between the two. In many birds and mammals, each individual travels both ways once a year, in many fish each individual travels each way only once in its life of several years, and in many insects each individual travels only one way and the return journey is made by the next generation.

Chapter 22. The chief advantage of gregarious feeding and nesting in birds is probably an increased awareness and avoidance of, or defence against, predators. Solitary nesting assists concealment. Few territorial species feed primarily in their territories, and the question of whether territorial behaviour is important in maintaining a food supply for the young or in limiting population density remains unsettled. A few species defend winter territories.

Chapter 23. Especially in the breeding season, what I term 'dispersion' presents a remarkable and mainly unappreciated phenomenon. In a colonial species like the Heron, both the distance between colonies and their size vary markedly in relation to food supplies. Territorial species also settle more densely where their food is more plentiful. Experienced breeders tend to breed where they did before, and dispersion is probably brought about mainly by the individuals breeding for the first time, which seek through an innate response the habitat of their species, and in a colonial species an established colony, but avoid such areas when they are already crowded. The avoidance of crowded areas has survival value because young birds probably fare badly in competition with experienced adults, but how crowding is recognized is not known. Dispersion, though inconspicuous, has as great an influence on animal numbers as large-scale migrations or irruptions.

Chapter 24. In a summary of the main argument, it is stressed that the density-dependent mortality factors of food shortage, predation, and disease may interact with each other in a complex way.

Four major criticisms of the views expressed in this book have appeared since it was written. First, A. J. Nicholson's views on density-dependence, and also Gauses's principle of ecological exclusion, were rejected by Andrewartha and Birch (1954), as considered in Appendix, section 2. Secondly, various workers criticized me (while Wynne-Edwards, 1962, approved) for saying that animal populations are normally limited by food. But this is a misreading, for though I suggested that the numbers of most birds, carnivorous mammals, certain rodents, large fish where not fished, and a few insects are limited by food, I suggested that the numbers of gallinaceous birds, deer, and phytophagous insects for at least most of the time are limited by predators

APPENDIX

(including insect parasites); and it may be added that phytophagous insects comprise the great majority of the world's animal species.

Thirdly, E. M. Nicholson (1955) argued that limitation by density-dependent mortality had not been established for any bird, and that density-dependent movements provide the main checks to population density. I agree about the absence of evidence for density-dependent mortality, but attribute this to ignorance, not to this factor being unimportant. I also agree that movements are very important (my Chapters 20–23), but consider them to have been evolved as adaptations in relation to food supplies, so that their influence on population density is secondary. Nicholson also stated, in essence, the theme later developed by Wynne-Edwards (1962), which will be discussed in Appendix, section 3. Fourthly, several workers, including Wynne-Edwards, rejected my view that the reproductive rate has been evolved by natural selection to that which results in the greatest number of surviving offspring per pair, and reaffirmed an earlier theory that it is adjusted to the mortality. In addition a few minor criticisms, some of them mine, have been mentioned briefly in the foregoing summaries of Chapters 6, 10, 11, 19, and 20. In other respects, I in general adhere to what I wrote in 1954, but there have since then been many additional facts and various new and valuable ideas, the chief of which have been discussed under the species concerned in the present book.

Finally, because in the earlier book I argued that most bird populations are probably limited in numbers by their food supplies, but I could then find extremely few estimates of the proportion of their prey eaten by birds, I add here the instances of this sort published after 1952, other than those already mentioned under the particular species discussed in the present book. Nearly all of the few examples given in my earlier book referred to the breeding season, when the proportion of the available prey taken was in most cases extremely small. Confirming the latter statement, although on English moorland 75 per cent of the food brought to nestling Meadow Pipits, *Anthus pratensis*, consisted of the tipulid fly, *Tipula subnodicornis*, the birds took only 1 per cent of them (Cragg, 1961). Again, about 80 per cent of the diet of nestling Starlings, *Sturnus vulgaris*, consisted of leatherjackets, the larvae of *Tipula paludosa*, but Starlings took only about 2 per cent of those available in one summer and 7 per cent in the next (Dunnett, 1955). Again, though American warblers and other insectivorous birds feed their young largely on spruce budworm larvae, *Choristoneura fumiferana*, where these are available, at the peak of a plague, with some 8 million larvae per acre, birds took less than 1 per cent of those present (Morris *et al.*, 1958, 1963; Morris, 1963). One of the species concerned, the Bay-breasted Warbler, *Dendroica castanea*, moves into plague areas, and it increased from 10 to 120 pairs per 100 acres where the spruce budworm was particularly abundant, but even so its influence was negligible (Mook, 1963).

In winter, the situation may be very different, as shown particularly by three recent studies of American woodpeckers. These corroborate a European record cited in the earlier book (1954, p. 185) that woodpeckers destroyed up to 95 per cent of the bark-feeding larvae of a weevil where these were concentrated, though far fewer where they were scattered. In Colorado, the Engelmann Spruce, *Picea engelmanii*, is periodically devastated by the beetle *Dendroctonus engelmanni*, and three species—the Downy Woodpecker, *Dendrocopus pubescens*, the Hairy Woodpecker, *D. villosus*, and the Three-toed Woodpecker, *Picoides tridactylus*—between them removed between half and virtually all the beetles in some localities (Massey and Wygant, 1954; Knight, 1958; Baldwin, 1960). Their effectiveness was increased because they moved through the forests and stayed where beetles were abundant, as shown by Yeager (1955). Downy and Hairy Woodpeckers were similarly estimated to have removed between a half and 90 per cent of the larvae of the Codling Moth, *Carpocapsa pomonella*, from fruit orchards in Nova Scotia (MacLellan, 1958, 1959, 1961).

If birds remove so high a proportion of their main prey, they themselves are almost certainly limited in numbers by their food supply. Their effect on the numbers of the prey may, however, be complex, and will depend, in particular, on the other causes of mortality in the prey. In this connection it is interesting that of the codling moth larvae taken by the woodpeckers, 3 per cent were parasitized by the braconid *Ascogaster quadridentata*, whereas of those not taken by woodpeckers, 14 per cent were parasitized. Similarly, birds are stated to have preferred unparasitized to parasitized caterpillars of the Gypsy Moth, *Lymantria dispar* (Koroljkowa, 1956, cited by Bruns, 1960, original not seen). This is contrary to what happened in Cormorants preying on Roach, and to the general tendency for vertebrate predators to take weakened prey (see p. 285).

Some estimates are also available of predation by birds on aquatic organisms. Elson (1962) concluded that American Mergansers (Goosanders), *Mergus merganser*, and Belted Kingfishers, *Megaceryle alcyon*, especially the former, between them removed about three-quarters of the standing crop of all fish in certain Canadian rivers, and that, in particular, the average output of smolt of the Atlantic Salmon, *Salmo salar*, rose by between three and five times after the fish-eating birds had been killed. However, while these birds certainly ate many fish, their ultimate influence on the size of the fish populations was not, in my view, established by Elson, since there was effectively only one year of comparable observations before the birds were controlled (see Elson's tables, pp. 50, 52), and the low densities of fish before the bird control might, perhaps, have been due to some other factor. Secondly, Drinnan (1957) showed that in Morecambe Bay, Lancashire, in winter Edible Cockles, *Cardium edule*, were the main source of food of the Oystercatcher, *Haematopus ostralegus*. There were over 30000 Oystercatchers in the area, and one individual took, on the average, 315 cockles of 20–30 mm in length each day in January and 214 cockles of 25–35 mm in length each day in October. The influence of the Oystercatcher was not, however, important, as the total winter mortality of the cockles was 74 per cent, and only 22 per cent was attributable to Oystercatchers, the main predators probably being flat-fish. This finding did not, however, stop a Government order being issued for the destruction of the Oystercatcher. Drinnan's work, it may be added, was stimulated by that of Gibb (1956a) on the winter predation of the

APPENDIX

Rock Pipit, *Anthus spinoletta*, described in my earlier book (1954, p. 133).

Summarizing, in *The Natural Regulation of Animal Numbers* (1954) I argued that in birds the reproductive rate of each species, evolved through natural selection, is that which results in the greatest number of surviving offspring per pair, and that the population density is regulated by density-dependent mortality, in most species by food shortage outside the breeding season. I suggested however, that gallinaceous birds, deer, and most phytophagous insects are not limited by food shortage but by predators (which is probably wrong for gallinaceous birds). Records published after 1952 have been added of the proportion of the available prey eaten by birds excluding those cases discussed in earlier chapters of the present book.

Postscript

Parallels drawn between men and other animals can be dangerously misleading, but the principle found in birds, that with a larger brood each nestling receives less food, can also be demonstrated in mankind. The British National Food Survey for 1950–1 showed that among working-class people earning less than £8 per week, the average amount spent per head per week on food by a married couple was 24s. if they had no children, 19s. with one child, 16s. with two children, and 12s. with three children; correspondingly, the average amount of meat consumed by each of these groups was respectively 34, 24, 21, and 17 oz. per head per week (Mackenzie, 1954). Again, an ornithologist from western Australia sent me a cutting from a Perth newspaper, for 11 January 1957, which reported the Australian National Health and Medical Research Council as showing that the percentage of Australian families with a first-class diet was 73 per cent when there were two children, 62 per cent when there were 3 children, 38 per cent when there were 4 children, 27 per cent when there were 5 children, and only 16 per cent when there were 6 children. The first of these examples provides a straight comparison as the total amount spent per week on food was about the same in each group, but the second example was probably complicated by the fact that families tend to be larger among poorer than richer Australians.

Section 2. The attack on density-dependence

THE Distribution and Abundance of Animals by H. G. Andrewartha and L. C. Birch (1954) appeared in the same year as my *Natural Regulation of Animal Numbers*, so that the authors of neither could appraise what the other wrote, which was unfortunate as our views were so opposed. Some workers have attributed our divergence primarily to the different types of animals and of habitats with which we were concerned, Andrewartha and Birch with insect pests of cultivated land and I with wild birds in nearly natural habitats. But a difference in observational material would seem more likely, in itself, to produce a shift in emphasis than a fundamental cleavage. Moreover, the worker whose views on density-dependent control most influenced me, namely A. J. Nicholson, was, like Andrewartha and Birch, an economic entomologist. Clearly, the source of the cleavage lies deeper.

THE ATTACK ON DENSITY-DEPENDENCE

The essence of Andrewartha and Birch's views was contained in their Chapter 14, while in their previous chapter they showed by a series of examples how they analysed population changes in practice. Their chief negative point was the rejection of 'generalizations about "density-dependent factors"', which they considered (p. 649), 'have a peculiar logical status. They are not a general theory, because . . . they do not describe any substantial body of empirical facts. Nor are they usually put forward as a hypothesis to be tested by experiment and discarded if they prove inconsistent with empirical fact. On the contrary, they are usually asserted as if their truth were axiomatic. . . . These generalizations about "density-dependent factors" and competition in so far as they refer to natural populations are neither theory nor hypothesis but dogma.' They similarly consider that the expressions 'balance', 'steady-density', 'control', and 'regulation' as applied to natural populations 'stem from the dogma of "density-dependent factors", and they are allegorical'.

The substance in their criticism is that, when it was written, no instance of density-dependent mortality had been demonstrated for a natural population of animals, and this is still virtually the case ten years later. I also agree with Andrewartha and Birch, though for partly different reasons, that the results from laboratory populations cannot be applied to natural conditions, as I consider that the laboratory populations of flour-beetles, sheep blowflies and other organisms are models not experiments, and provide illustrations, not proofs, of population theories. I disagree, however, with Andrewartha and Birch's conclusion that the populations which they studied in the field were not regulated by density-dependent factors

These authors were correct in thinking that the absence of field evidence does not, and will not, make the advocates of density-dependent regulation change their minds. This is not because such views are 'allegorical' or are held as 'dogma' (to follow their misuse of two terms which have their proper meanings in different intellectual disciplines), but because, given certain assumptions about the persistence of natural populations, the existence of density-dependent regulation becomes a logical necessity. The status of this idea seems broadly similar to that of natural selection for many years after Darwin formulated it. Given that animals have hereditary differences, that large numbers die without offspring, while of the rest some leave more offspring than others, the natural selection of certain hereditary types as compared with others is a necessary consequence. The concept of natural selection was repeatedly challenged for almost a century after the *Origin of Species* appeared, partly from sheer prejudice, but partly on the correct grounds that at first hardly anything was known about genetics and that there was no proof of natural selection in the wild. Nevertheless, this concept continued to find advocates, though they had to wait nearly fifty years for the Mendelian background, some seventy years for a satisfactory mathematical formulation (Fisher, 1930), and until the last few years for a field proof (Kettlewell, 1956).

The history of the concept of density-dependence has differed from that of natural selection because it was not first enunciated in simple logical terms by an intellectual giant, and was not attached to a new theory as dramatic as that of organic evolution. Instead, it was formulated in purely mathematical terms (Lotka, 1925; Volterra, 1926), and these statements were at first overlooked by most ecologists, who would not in any case have understood them, so that their implications came to be appreciated slowly, chiefly through the advocacy of A. J. Nicholson. As Nicholson (1933) showed, the idea needed only a logical, not a mathematical, basis for its acceptance, since if an animal population continues to fluctuate in numbers over a long period between restricted limits, it follows that it is controlled by factors which tend to produce an increase after a low density and a decrease after a high density; otherwise it will either increase indefinitely or become extinct. Andrewartha and Birch rejected Nicholson's conclusion, explicitly so far as extinction is concerned (pp. 663–4), mainly on the grounds that the populations which they themselves studied were large, so that fluctuations due to factors independent of density were unlikely to produce extinction in the relatively short period of their study. But as Solomon (1957) stated in criticizing their views: 'The answer given offers us only a coincidence and a population could not persist for more than a short time without the occasional regulating assistance of a density dependent process.'

Andrewartha and Birch summarized their positive conclusions as follows (pp. 660–1): 'The numbers of animals in a natural population may be limited in three ways: (a) by shortage of material resources, such as food, places in which to make nests, etc.; (b) by inaccessibility of these material resources relative to the animals' capacities for dispersal and searching; and (c) by shortage of time when the rate of increase r is positive. Of these three ways, the first is probably the least, and the last is probably the most, important in nature. Concerning (c), the fluctuations in the value of r may be caused by weather, predators or any other component of environment which influences the rate of increase.' It should be noted that what they have termed r, the rate of increase, refers to the overall change in numbers (positive for an increase), and so takes account of both recruitment and losses, and does not mean only the recruitment or only the reproductive rate, as might be supposed. They added the important proviso that 'it is not to be supposed that the ecology of many natural populations would be so simple that their numbers would be explained neatly by any one of the principles described. . . . A large number of systems of varying complexity could be synthesized . . . from various combinations of the principles set out. . . .'

In regard to situation (a), they considered (p. 651) that limitation by nesting sites would result in a population increasing until all the sites were occupied, after which numbers would remain constant over the years. The chosen example was from bees. As mentioned in Chapter 16 of the present book, the same argument might well be applied to those pelagic birds which, owing to predation by mammals elsewhere, breed only on small islands, some of them remote, with wide areas of adjacent sea in which to feed. The argument put forward by Andrewartha and Birch implies that, under these circumstances, the number of nesting sea-birds would remain steady at that for which there was room to nest on the island. The situation cannot, however, be so simple as this, for in the absence of other and density-dependent checks, there would then be a steady and continuing increase in the number of non-breeding individuals, up to the point where they would seriously deplete the food supplies near the island, after which there would be density-dependent mortality from starvation. Temporary, but only temporary, alleviation would occur if the non-breeding surplus emigrated, but in the absence of density-dependent checks, the same situation would be repeated in the places to which they emigrated, until all possible sites were full. I suggest that similar considerations would apply to other possible instances of Andrewartha and Birch's concept of limitation by nesting sites, and that usually, if each situation were followed for long enough, density-dependent checks would be revealed.

Andrewartha and Birch's second alternative under (a), the limitation of numbers by the diminishing resource of food, results, they claimed (p. 652), in an initial increase followed by decrease to extinction locally. As stressed in their second type of limitation (b), the food must be accessible to the animals concerned, and if much of it is inaccessible, then the animals, though themselves limited by food, will not appeciably influence the density of their food supply. The proportion of the food available is, in particular, influenced by the animal's powers of dispersal, and they evidently considered (e.g. pp. 658–9) that the usual situation is local extinction followed by re-invasion from some area where the animal is temporarily abundant. To illustrate this, they cited the huge reduction and effective control in Australia of the introduced Prickly Pear, *Opuntia*, by the subsequently introduced moth *Cactoblastis cactorum*. Here the facts are not in dispute. *Opuntia* was wiped out by the moth in large areas, but it survived in local pockets, which it took time for *Cactoblastis* to colonize and eliminate, by which time further pockets of *Opuntia* had become established, and so on. While Andrewartha and Birch evidently considered that this case did not involve density-dependent regulation, Nicholson (1947) cited it as a typical example of a predator-prey oscillation, save that it was complicated by local movements, and this seems the correct view. It is revealing, however, that these workers could interpret the same set of facts so differently, which was possible because the example of *Opuntia* is historical, not experimental.

The third type of limitation (c), which Andrewartha and Birch considered the most important, was illustrated (p. 654) by the example of an animal permanently held well below the food limit by weather, predation, or some other environmental factor. After an initial increase, such a population either decreases to local extinction, which may be followed by re-invasion, or a remnant is left which may start a further increase when circumstances change and r again becomes positive. They did not, however, show convincingly how the other environmental factor held the population below the food limit and evidently attributed this to random changes, for example in weather. As already quoted from Solomon (1957), 'this offers us only a coincidence'. Also, while local movements, including recolonization after local extinction, can much complicate the situation, they cannot affect the overall summation, and they leave A. J. Nicholson's case for the operation of density-dependent checks essentially unanswered.

APPENDIX

Andrewartha and Birch's arguments were based partly on the particular population studies which they discussed in their Chapter 13. The most detailed of these was a 14-year census of the numbers of a thysanopteran insect, *Thrips imaginis*, in flowers in an Australian garden (Davidson and Andrewartha, 1948*a*, *b*; Andrewartha and Birch, 1954, pp. 568–83). The numbers of thrips were always well below what the available food and space would have permitted, but they were partly influenced by the number of flowers, which in turn depended on the weather in summer. Probably, though less certainly, survival in winter was correlated with the winter weather, and in all 78 per cent of the observed fluctuations were attributed to weather factors. They therefore concluded that 'it was not necessary to invoke "density-dependent factors"'.

This final conclusion was later criticized heavily, by Solomon (1957) as already quoted and in more detail by Nicholson (1958*b*), followed by Smith (1961), Klomp (1962), and Varley (1963), who argued that the annual fluctuations in numbers observed by Andrewartha and Birch would not have been so closely correlated with weather factors unless, in addition, there had been a density-dependent controlling factor in operation. Nicholson, for instance, after citing Andrewartha and Birch that 'not only did we fail to find a "density-dependent factor", but we also showed that there was no room for one', commented that their 'equation . . . explains only the observed variation in numbers from year to year; it gives no clue as to why the actual level about which this variation took place had the value observed. Consequently, as it is the special characteristic of a "density-dependent factor" that it adjusts population densities (i.e. actual numbers), there most certainly is room for one in the control of *T. imaginis* populations.'

The last point is of particular importance. Andrewartha and Birch were presumably correct in correlating the annual changes in the numbers of *Thrips imaginis* with climatic factors, but as stressed, for instance, by Richards (1961), this is a separate or partly separate problem from what determines the level around which the changes occur and from the density-dependent control. The factors responsible for annual changes in numbers were later termed 'key factors' by Morris (1959), followed by Varley and Gradwell (1960), who gave a simple method of testing for their existence. But these key factors, though they are responsible for the observed annual changes, and hence are usually the first to be detected by the field worker, are not, or at least need not be, density-dependent, and the density-dependent mortality may be much harder to discover.

The second population discussed by Andrewartha and Birch (pp. 583–94) was that of the Australian grasshopper *Austroicetes cruciata*, which was common and probably increasing on grazing land during the years 1935 to 1939, but which decreased very heavily indeed in 1940 owing to starvation through a severe drought. The food shortage in 1940 was due to a climatic factor, and not to the activities of the grasshopper. For a time the grasshoppers persisted in a few favoured localities where green vegetation occurred, but here, according to local residents, the birds that normally feed on these grasshoppers concentrated in great numbers and virtually ate them out. This,

as Andrewartha and Birch pointed out, is an interesting way in which predation can influence a population, in this case only when a quite different
factor had already much restricted it; further, the predators in question feed
on quite different kinds of animals during the other nine months of the year.
These conclusions seem unexceptionable so far as they go, but the study was
not continued for sufficiently long, and other possible mortality factors were
not considered in sufficient detail, to exclude the possibility that density-
dependent checks were also in operation. Birch (1957) later discussed this
case further, providing a model to illustrate how the fluctuations of weather
in relation to spatial patchiness in the animals' environment could regulate its
numbers in the sense of preventing unlimited increase and of avoiding the
certainty, though not the possibility, of extinction. He concluded that 'weather
can operate in such a way that there will be little chance of extinction provided
the fluctuations of weather are kept within limits . . . defined for each species'.
But in the discussion following this paper Nicholson (p. 216) said that 'no one
has yet given a tenable explanation as to how this mechanism could possibly
work' and considered that competition must be involved at some stage, while
Solomon (1957) commented on the same example; 'To explain why the
great irregular increases and decreases from year to year add up over a
period to approximately zero, we seem to have only two alternatives, density-
dependence at some point in the population cycle, or pure chance.'

Andrewartha and Birch made similar analyses of the population changes
of the farmland moth *Porosagrotis orthogona*, and the Spruce Budworm Moth,
Choristoneura fumiferana, of North America. In these also, certain population
changes could be correlated with climatic factors, but, at least in my view, far
too little was known of other mortality factors for the possibility of density-
dependent control to be excluded, and the complexity of the problem in the
Spruce Budworm was recently demonstrated by Morris *et al.* (1963). I would
apply a similar comment to the other invertebrate populations studied by
Andrewartha and Birch, and also to the further insect populations which
they analysed later (Andrewartha and Birch, 1960). It may be repeated that,
in all these instances, they were probably right in correlating the annual
fluctuations in numbers with climatic factors, but the question of primary
interest to Nicholson and those who followed him has been a different one,
namely what determines the level around which such fluctuations occur, and
prevents unlimited increase or decrease.

In recent years various other entomologists and workers on other
invertebrate groups have taken part in the argument, and references additional
to those already cited include Bakker (1964), Frank (1959), Huffaker (1958),
Kuenen (1958), Milne (1957a, 1957b, 1961, 1962), Nicholson (1954, 1958a, b,
1959), Rosenzweig and MacArthur (1963), Solomon (1958a, b), Thompson
(1956), Varley (1957, 1958, 1959), Varley and Gradwell (1958), and Williamson (1957), as well as the various contributors, some but not all among those
just listed, who took part in the Cold Spring Harbor Symposium devoted to
this subject (1957, No. 22), and further contributions by Andrewartha
(1959a, b, 1961), Andrewartha and Browning (1961) and Birch (1957, 1958,
1959, 1963). Reading these divergent views, the general zoologist might feel

some sympathy with Milne (1957*b*) that 'even the best field studies of the problem suffer from ecological deficiencies and statistical inadequacies which inevitably result in conclusions being matters of personal opinion and not of incontrovertible fact. This is the reason for the variety and contrariety of theories of natural control.' But while we may all agree on the inadequacy of ecological facts, the contrariety of existing theories is mainly due to a difference in basic assumptions concerning the extent to which competition is held to be important or unimportant in natural populations.

It may be added that some of the authors just cited also argued with each other at length on the proper terms to be used for density-dependent regulation, but as yet most of the new and often divergent terms proposed have not been used in detailed population studies. Perhaps the most important ideas that emerged from this discussion were, first, that even if a factor is density-dependent it may have too small an effect to regulate numbers ('density-dependent' does not necessarily mean 'controlling'), secondly, that though populations are controlled by density-dependent factors, factors which are uninfluenced by density may have profound effects on density, and, thirdly, that a density-dependent factor which in itself would not stabilize a population may do so if there is another, perhaps density-independent, factor in operation.

Finally, Andrewartha and Birch considered one bird population, that of the Bobwhite Quail, *Colinus virginianus*, studied by Errington (1945). They accepted his view that the fluctuations in the numbers of this bird were caused by heavy losses through cold winters, while in mild winters there was a 'threshold density' above which predators removed the surplus. But there were apparently changes in the level of the 'threshold' in different mild winters, and they rightly criticized Errington for attributing these to periodic 'depression phases', a term which merely conceals ignorance. They were also correct in pointing out that, if Errington was right in thinking that predation merely removes a doomed surplus, then it must operate very differently in various insects, in which the introduction of a predator or insect parasite has at times brought a pest under effective control. (As already mentioned on p. 285, Errington produced suggestive but not critical evidence to support his view of how predation works, notably in the muskrat.) Andrewartha and Birch also stated (p. 22), and I agree, that many phytophagous insects are not normally up to their food limit, while the same presumably applies to various herbivorous mammals, since, for instance, it was only after the removal of the large carnivores from the Zululand game reserves that the herbivorous big game increased to starvation levels, while the removal of small carnivores from part of the Sabi game reserve similarly resulted in a huge increase of rodents (Stevenson-Hamilton, 1947; Andrewartha and Birch, p. 502). To return to Errington's Bobwhite population, I earlier thought (1954, pp. 115–9) that the fluctuations could be accounted for by two density-dependent checks, a direct one in summer and a delayed one in winter, but now consider that not enough was recorded about this population to justify this interpretation.

The long book by Andrewartha and Birch includes much further and uncontroversial information, especially on insects, of great interest but irrelevant to the present discussion. But one further point is pertinent, namely their attack (pp. 432, 456–65) on my application to wild birds of 'Gause's concept' that two species with the same ecology cannot persist together in the same region. This, I argued, provides strong evidence that the birds in question are potential competitors for food, and hence that their numbers are limited by food. They accepted my main finding that, except in cases where food is obviously superabundant, closely related species of wild birds normally differ in geographical range, habitat, feeding habits or the kind of foods taken, but disagreed that this is a result of competition for food. 'The difficulty in this hypothesis is that, by the very nature of the case, it can hardly be proved or disproved, because we have no evidence that "competition" took place in some past epoch' (p. 463), and again: 'We are forced to conclude that his interesting results do not in any way demonstrate that "competition" between birds in nature is at all commonplace or usual. On the contrary, his results seem to show that it hardly ever occurs' (p. 464).

I fully agree with Andrewartha and Birch about the lack of direct evidence for competition, but I attribute this to competition having occurred mainly in the past, with the result that birds have evolved 'habitat selection', by which they recognize their specific habitats and hence usually avoid competing with other species. Nevertheless, such behaviour must, I consider, be maintained by natural selection at the present day, though the number of individuals of one species settling in the habitat of another may be small at any one time, and therefore hard to observe. Moreover, the circumstantial evidence for Gause's concept is extremely strong. To cite only one of the many instances which I gave in the earlier book, the European Chaffinch, *Fringilla coelebs*, is common in both broad-leaved and coniferous woodland wherever they occur in its widespread palaearctic range, except on two (but not the other) islands in the Canary archipelago, namely Gran Canaria and Tenerife, and it is only here that it occurs alongside a closely related species, the Blue Chaffinch, *F. teydea*, which replaces it in coniferous forest. Andrewartha and Birch concluded that, 'so far as the case is stated, there is no direct evidence that the two species could not live together if they were put together', to which I would comment that the range of the one comes right up to that of the other wherever the pine forest gives place to broad-leaved woodland, so they have had every opportunity to occur in each other's habitats. Referring to this same example in relation to Andrewartha and Birch's criticism, Brown and Wilson (1956) wrote: 'It is obvious that Lack's critics are not going to be satisfied by any ordinary kind of evidence.'

Andrewartha and Birch also stated (p. 432) that 'the correct inference to be drawn from these observations is that the mathematical and experimental models are quite unlike nature'. However, although Gause used mathematical equations and laboratory demonstrations, his concept does not essentially depend on them, for it is a logical consequence of natural selection: if two species have identical ecology, the chance that both are equally well adapted is negligible, so that one will inevitably replace the other where they meet. Andrewartha and Birch added (p. 457) that 'the chance that the establishment in an area of a newcomer . . . will result in the extermination of any of the old-established species must be quite small. One has to consider the wholesale dispersal of insects and other animals across the world by means of commerce during the last hundred years or so in order to appreciate this point.' But this last argument is misleading for two reasons. First, as I discussed earlier for birds (1954, pp. 201–2), the species that have become established as a result of human introduction in other lands have been largely Old World species previously adapted to cultivated land, and they have normally become established only in cultivated land, often in the absence from that habitat of native species. To this there are a few exceptions, as one might expect, but only a few. Secondly, most phytophagous insects, the group which Andrewartha and Birch had chiefly in mind, do not appear to be limited by food, in which case, of course, Gause's concept does not apply in relation to food niches. Probably the main reason for our difference of opinion on this point is that, according to Orians (1962), Andrewartha and Birch are 'functional ecologists' whereas I am an 'evolutionary ecologist', but I do not think that this difference accounts for most of the other differences between us. Since the facts about ecological isolation and Gause's concept in my earlier book were representative, the subject will not be pursued further here, except to add that Keast (1961) later provided many further illustrations in Australian birds, Kohn (1959) showed that it held in the molluscan genus *Conus*, the general principle was further considered by Hutchinson (1959) and Hardin (1960), and its importance in plants was discussed by Harper *et al.* (1961).

Two historical comments may be added. First, Gilbert *et al.* (1952) criticized my use of the term 'Gause's concept' because 'Gause makes no statement which resembles any wording of the hypothesis which has arisen bearing his name', and this criticism has since been repeated by others. Actually Gause (1934, p. 19) wrote: 'As a result of competition two similar species scarcely ever occupy similar niches, but displace each other in such a manner that each takes possession of certain peculiar kinds of foods and modes of life in which it has an advantage over its competitor.' This seems clear enough. So does 'In the light of all this evidence, one may claim that if two more nearly related species live in the field in a stable association, these species certainly possess different ecological niches' (Gause, 1939).

Secondly, Udvardy (1959) found that the principle had much earlier been stated by Joseph Grinnell, who, it may be added, anticipated various other important ideas on evolution and population ecology of the last thirty years but, for some reason, did not put out these ideas in print in a sufficiently general form to excite and stimulate other workers (except among his own students). For instance: 'Two species of approximately the same food habits are not likely to remain long evenly balanced in numbers in the same region. One will crowd out the other' (Grinnell, 1904). 'It is, of course, axiomatic that no two species regularly established in a single fauna have precisely the same niche relationships' (Grinnell, 1917). 'No two species in the same general territory can occupy for long identically the same ecologic niche. If, by chance, the vagaries of distributional movement result in introducing into a new territory the ecologic homologue of a species already endemic in that territory, competitive displacement of one of the species by the other is bound to take place. Perfect balance is inconceivable' (Grinnell, 1928). It should be added that the word 'niche' in this context is unsatisfactory because it has been used in different senses by different authors, and I agree with the criticism on this point by Ross (1957, 1958), though strongly disagreeing with his accompanying rejection of Gause's concept, for the reasons pointed out by Savage (1958).

To conclude, the marked difference in viewpoint between Andrewartha and Birch's book and my own may be attributed to three main causes. First, and least important, they studied insect pests, which normally complete at least one generation a year and the numbers of which are greatly modified by climatic variations, whereas I studied wild birds, of which the adults normally survive for more than one season and the numbers of which are much less susceptible to climatic vagaries. Secondly, Andrewartha and Birch sought primarily to account for changes in numbers between one year and the next, which seem often to be caused by climatic factors, whereas Nicholson and his followers, including myself, were primarily concerned to explain why fluctuations are comparatively restricted and occur around particular levels. Thirdly, Andrewartha and Birch considered competition unimportant, indeed they often put the word in quotation marks, whereas I followed Nicholson in regarding it as basic to the interpretation of animal numbers. Also, though Andrewartha and Birch devoted the fifth part of their book to genetic aspects of ecology, they did not seriously consider the importance of evolution in ecological theory (Orians, 1962); indeed the term 'natural selection' is not in their index, whereas I consider that the explanation of certain aspects of ecology, notably of Gause's principle that two species with similar ecology cannot persist in the same area, is to be sought in terms of natural selection.

Section 3. Animal dispersion

IN the last chapters of my book of 1954 I concluded that birds are not necessarily dispersed either randomly or uniformly over their environment, especially when breeding. Instead, they tend to breed at higher densities where their food, or the food for their young, is more plentiful. This type of distribution I termed 'dispersion', and I suggested that it was brought about mainly by the behaviour of those individuals breeding for the first time, which tend to settle more densely in the more favourable habitats only up to a certain level, after which they are more likely to raise young if they seek elsewhere, even if this means settling in a type of habitat which is less favourable except in being less crowded.

V. C. Wynne-Edwards (1959, 1960, and especially in his book *Animal Dispersion in relation to Social Behaviour* (1962)), took this concept as his starting point and elaborated it into a theory which he applied to all animals and also to many types of behaviour or distribution which I interpret in other ways. His main idea is that, while the populations of birds and other animals are ultimately limited by the availability of food, this limit, with resultant overpopulation and starvation, is not normally reached in nature, because dispersion through behaviour keeps numbers near to the 'optimum' and below the level where 'overfishing' might develop. The process of regulation he described as 'homeostatic' or self-balancing (a term of course in use in other branches of biology) and the displays and other behaviour evolved to reveal the density of populations he termed 'epideictic', which means literally the presenting of a sample. He considered that behaviour of this type must have been evolved through 'group-selection', that in addition to, and overriding, the selection of individuals and their offspring through Darwinian natural selection, whole populations of a species can be selected for, as against other populations of the same species, group-selection favouring those populations which are able to maintain themselves around 'the level at which food resources are utilized to the fullest extent possible without depletion' (p. 132). Such group-selection means that some individuals in the population, usually those lower in the social hierarchy or peck-order, must at intervals starve, or emigrate, or refrain from breeding, even though there is enough food for them at the time, if circumstances are such that their consumption of food would lead to overpopulation.

Perhaps the most critical difference between Wynne-Edwards' views and mine is his concept of the 'optimum population', which I regard as irrelevant to natural populations, though relevant to human fishing from which Wynne-Edwards derived it. In human fishing, it is desirable to preserve an economic balance between the number of fish taken and their replacement rate, since otherwise overfishing may result, meaning that fewer fish will be caught for the same expenditure of effort than at the optimum level. But human fishermen are not comparable with natural predators, as they do not essentially depend on fish for their survival or reproduction, and the owners of fishing fleets possess capital reserves, so that the analogy, for it is no more, with the interaction between a natural population of predators and their prey is not valid.

In his book, Wynne-Edwards (p. 9) wrote that 'it must be highly advantageous to survival, and thus strongly favoured by selection, for animal species (1) to control their own population densities and (2) to keep them as near as possible to the optimum level for each habitat', and he evidently envisaged the optimum level as that just above which the food resources are taken to such an extent that they are not fully replaced by reproduction. But if in the sentence just quoted 'advantageous' refers to the individuals, as it usually does in biological thinking, the optimum level (as conceived by Wynne-Edwards) need not be the most advantageous, since each predator would have a rather easier life below this level. What Wynne-Edwards presumably meant by 'advantageous' is that more individuals of the predator survive, in the long term, at this level than any other, which savours of what J. B. S. Haldane (pers. comm.) pleasantly referred to as 'Pangloss's theorem' ('all is for the best in the best of all possible worlds'), and which surely has no application to natural history.

Wynne-Edwards was particularly impressed by the apparent absence of 'overfishing' in natural populations, and this led him to postulate that predator-prey systems and ecological communities themselves evolve so as to prevent it. The idea that ecological communities evolve has also been stated or implied by other writers. There are, however, two different reasons which, between them, sufficiently explain why we do not normally observe a predatory species exterminating its prey in nature. First, as demonstrated long ago in the Lotka-Volterra equations, there is a tendency for self-regulation (homeostasis) in any system in which one species preys on another, though as shown by Gause's experiments (1934), the predator may indeed exterminate its prey under very simple ecological conditions. Secondly, only those predatory species which have not exterminated their prey survive today, hence we observe in nature only those systems which have proved sufficiently stable to persist, and many others were presumably terminated in the past by extinction. Those that persist do so as a result of historical processes, which include the evolution of the organisms concerned, but the communities or systems themselves do not 'evolve' in the biological sense of this word, but only 'change'. Organisms evolve, i.e. become modified through hereditary variations, but one should not speak of communities doing so, and the distinction between 'change' and 'evolve' is much more than purely verbal, because the use of the term 'evolution' in relation to communities brings with it implicit concepts which are strictly relevant only to organisms and their hereditary differences. For the same reason, it is incorrect to speak of the 'function' of cycles, as Leopold (1933) and Koskimies (1955) did. Cycles are a 'result' of a predator-prey interaction or some other biological process, but they are not in themselves functional and have not been evolved 'for the good of the species'.

Further, among animals that are limited by food, the fluctuations in numbers under natural conditions may be much larger than Wynne-Edwards implied. They may be particularly large where the food chains are simple, as among Brown Lemmings, *Lemmus trimucronatus*, at Point Barrow, Alaska (Pitelka, 1957). They are usually less dramatic in more complex communities (Solomon, 1949; MacArthur, 1955), one reason being that the predators concerned are able to turn to alternative prey when their main prey is scarce. But even in complex communities, the apparent absence of widespread deaths from starvation is in part illusory. As I showed in 1954 (pp. 91–94), in many species of song-birds nearly half the adults and more of the juveniles die each year, probably mainly from starvation, but nearly all these deaths pass unnoticed, despite the modern army of bird-watchers.

Wynne-Edwards (e.g. p. 11) was also wrong to consider, and was mistaken in quoting me as considering, that the vast majority of animals are limited by food. Food admittedly sets an upper limit to all animal populations, but as already pointed out, this limit seems rarely if ever to be reached under natural conditions in some of the most abundant species, notably many phytophagous insects and herbivorous mammals. The reason that such insects and mammals do not normally overeat their food supplies need not be their epideictic behaviour, as postulated by Wynne-Edwards, but simply that they are normally kept well below the food limit by predators or insect parasites. Wynne-Edwards (pp. 10–11) argued that 'external checks' such as predators and parasites are 'hopelessly undependable and fickle in their incidence' and 'would in most cases be incapable of serving to impose the ceilings found in nature', but he gave no evidence for this unusual view, which is contrary both to the Lotka-Volterra equations and to the practical experience of economic entomologists. The latter have worked on the opposite assumption, that in natural communities most phytophagous insects are kept down by their predators and insect parasites, but that many insect pests, which indeed do great damage to man's crops, have been accidentally introduced to other lands without their natural enemies, and that some of them have been successfully reduced in numbers by the later introduction of predators or insect parasites. On Wynne-Edwards' view, it is also hard to understand why the Mule Deer, *Odocoileus hemionus*, of the Kaibab plateau should have increased so drastically as to overeat their food supplies and should then have decreased heavily in numbers (see p. 285). But the story of the Mule Deer is readily intelligible given two assumptions, one that they were formerly kept well below their food limit by natural predators that were later exterminated by man, and the other that they are incapable of regulating their own density to prevent over-exploitation of their food supplies in the way postulated by Wynne-Edwards.

Hence I consider that part of the evidence produced by Wynne-Edwards for the apparent absence of 'overfishing' in nature is illusory or misconceived, while much of the genuine stability of natural populations is explicable through the density-dependent mortality factors inherent in predator-prey interactions. I fully agree, however, that dispersive behaviour may greatly modify population density, as discussed in my book of 1954, but where it does so, I consider that the behaviour in question could have been evolved by natural selection, and that there is no need to invoke group-selection for it.

Wynne-Edwards, on the other hand, attached primary importance to group-selection, as shown by the following quotations from his book: 'Where the two [group-selection and individual selection] conflict, as they do when the short-term advantage of the individual undermines the future safety of the race, group-selection is bound to win, because the race will suffer and decline, and be supplanted by another in which antisocial advancement of the individual is more rigidly inhibited' (p. 20). 'The interests of the individual are actually submerged or subordinated to those of the community as a whole' (p. 18). 'It ruthlessly suppresses the temporary interests of the rejected individual, who may be condemned to starve while food still abounds' (p. 19). There is 'great scope for selection between local groups or nuclei, in the same way as there is between allied races or species. Some prove to be better adapted socially and individually than others, and tend to outlive them, and sooner or later to spread and multiply by colonizing the ground vacated by less successful neighbouring communities' (p. 20). 'Under group-selection it is not a question of this individual or that being more successful in leaving progeny to posterity, but of whether the stock itself can survive at all' (p. 141). 'Any population whose social organization, recruitment-rate and death-rate prove incompetent and unbalanced will get into difficulties, either dwindling away, or being forced to "overfish" and consequently to starve or force itself out of its habitat: this is the normal way in which group-selection does its work' (p. 225).

In criticism of the concept of group-selection, it is in general extremely hard to see how 'altruistic' behaviour, which decreases the chances of survival of the individual concerned but increases the chances of survival of others in its group, could have a selective advantage. An obvious exception is parental behaviour, because natural selection favours those hereditary types which leave most offspring. If, for instance, those parents which defend their offspring from enemies leave, on the average, more descendants than those which do not defend them, then the habit of defending offspring will have survival value, even if a proportion of the parents concerned are themselves injured or killed when doing so. This relationship is, of course, quantitative, since if the risks involved in parental defence are too great, the parents concerned will leave fewer descendants than those which do not defend their young. Similar considerations may hold even if the other members of the group that are benefited are not the offspring of the benefactor, provided that they are closely related to it and so have many genes in common, as pointed out by Haldane (1932) and discussed further under the term 'kin selection' by Smith (1964). But selection of this type can be effective only among close relatives, and the concept of group-selection in the much broader sense used by Wynne-Edwards finds few advocates today; indeed it can probably be effective only under the highly unusual conditions of extremely small and nearly isolated populations, through the help of genetic drift (Haldane, 1932; Wright, 1945; Wynne-Edwards, 1963; Smith, 1964). Nevertheless, the existence of a theoretical argument against group-selection, however strong, may not convince naturalists, who may, not unjustifiably, consider that if new facts necessitate a seemingly unsound theory, then a satisfactory basis for it will eventually be found. In my view the most powerful argument against group selection is that it is unnecessary, because all the instances for which Wynne-Edwards invoked it can be satisfactorily explained, or seem likely so to be explained, through natural selection (including kin selection).

Perhaps the simplest example of the divergence between Wynne-Edwards' views and my own concerns our respective interpretations of the social hierarchy or peck-order in birds. Here the facts are not in dispute. Among birds such as tits and crows, which outside the breeding season feed in flocks, one individual often disputes with another for a food item, and the individual that is lower in the social hierarchy normally retreats, even if it found the item first. Lockie (1956) and I accounted for the survival value of this behaviour through natural selection in the way explained earlier (this book p. 284, summarizing 1954, pp. 151–2). But Wynne-Edwards, who did not even refer to this alternative explanation, wrote: 'If there is a shortage of food, instead of this resulting in a general and uniform debilitation of all the members of the society alike, and perhaps their ultimate extinction, the dominant animals are given a preferred chance of sustaining life and vigour throughout the period of famine. . . . Their dominance behaviour ensures that only as many as the remaining sources can sustain are allowed to partake of the food, and thus automatically the maximum number will survive; the excluded sub-ordinates either perish quickly or emigrate' (p. 139). Now Lockie and I were the first to point out that the results of such a system are as Wynne-Edwards stated, but we considered, and consider, that they are merely results, and that the evolution of the behaviour concerned is completely explicable through natural selection, as it assists the survival of both the attackir~ and the retreating individuals (see p. 284). For Wynne-Edwards, however, 'it is not difficult to see that the hierarchy itself, and the conventional standards of mutual appraisal . . . are group-characters' (p. 140). In my view there is no need to introduce group-selection into this example.

Similarly, with respect to the periodic spectacular irruptions into western Europe of such birds from the taiga as the Crossbill, *Loxia curvirostra*, Waxwing, *Bombycilla garrulus*, and Nutcracker, *Nucifraga caryocatactes*, Wynne-Edwards wrote (p. 471) that 'students who have not recognized the overriding power of group-selection have sometimes wondered why, since so many of the emigrants usually succumb, selection has not long ago elimi-nated the inclination to emigrate', and he considered it 'an automatic social guillotine', reducing numbers locally to what the food supply will support, though he also supposed that it assisted pioneers of the species to colonize new areas. Cloudsley-Thompson (1957) also thought that emigration could be explained only through group-selection. But in 1954 (pp. 227–38, this book p. 286), I provided a different and simpler explanation of this behaviour which Wynne-Edwards nowhere discussed, that it is advantageous for most of these birds, and especially for the juveniles, to emigrate in times of food shortage because if, when food is very sparse, they stay to compete for it with experienced adults, they will almost certainly perish, whereas if they emigrate they will at least have a chance of surviving elsewhere and returning to their natural home later. I also reviewed evidence indicating that, in several irruptive species, return flights have in fact been observed, and Wynne-Edwards provided no evidence that 'so many of the emigrants usually suc-cumb'. My explanation has received confirmation, and partial modification, in the later findings of Svärdson (1957; see also p. 286), who showed that the species concerned are much more like true migrants than formerly supposed. Once again, therefore, the facts are explicable in terms of natural selection, and while the result might be 'an automatic guillotine', the reason that this irruptive behaviour has been evolved is that it is on balance advantageous to the individuals which participate.

Territorial behaviour, likewise, is explicable in terms of orthodox natural selection. Whether, in fact, breeding pairs of birds defend exclusive territories of such a size as to ensure a food supply for their young is arguable, as discussed earlier in this book, but if behaviour of this type occurs, it is of such obvious advantage to the territorial owners and their young that one need not invoke group-selection to account for it, especially if, as I suggested earlier (1954), it is also advantageous to newcomers seeking territories to avoid crowded areas.

Again, among birds which nest in colonies, Wynne-Edwards considered (p. 159) that 'there seems to be no serious obstacle to accepting, as a working hypothesis, the idea . . . that colonies of birds . . . are capable of discharging the important dispersive function of limiting the number of breeders, and of limiting it also to a maximum consistent with the conservation of the available resources of food'. But he provided no positive evidence that colonial birds in fact exclude others or, in the case of those with deferred maturity, that they prevent the younger individuals from breeding, nor did he suggest how they might do these things. Did he mean that the existing members of a colony make combined attacks on newcomers? There is no published evidence that they do so. And how, in the case of various sea-birds for instance, might they prevent younger individuals which have acquired nesting sites in the colony from actually laying eggs? Further, he once again ignored an alternative explanation put forward earlier by me (1954, p. 272) that in colonial birds, such as the Swift, *Apus apus*, and Heron, *Ardea cinerea*, the experienced breeders return to where they bred in the previous year, while the yearlings settle provisionally in some existing colony but without breeding, staying that season and returning to breed in the next if they find suitable conditions, including enough food, and leaving for another colony if they do not. By this latter means, a true dispersion in relation to the food supply can be achieved with respect to both the size and spacing of breeding colonies, and as such behaviour is advantageous for the yearlings themselves, it could have been evolved by natural selection, and there is no need to invoke group-selection for the benefit of the colony as such.

In my view Wynne-Edwards partly misinterpreted even his first example (p. 3), based on Jespersen (1929), that the density of sea-birds in the North Atlantic varies according to the density of their food. I earlier cited the same example (1954, p. 145) to suggest that food might be limiting numbers, and I agree with Wynne-Edwards (p. 3) that 'this is a dispersion that the birds must have brought about by their own efforts'. If he had meant by this that they merely search until they find food I would agree, but instead he (p. 27) postulated that the function of the rising and falling flight of shearwaters and other sea-birds 'could well be "dispersive"', providing the individual with a frequency sample of visual recognition contacts, which could be integrated with the current abundance of food, and result in compensatory movements and the adjustment of density. Without some such adaptive mechanism . . . it would clearly be impossible to achieve the high correlation between density and food-supply that has been shown to exist.' But over great areas of the Atlantic, Jespersen recorded only one individual bird (of all species) per day, and it is almost impossible, and also unnecessary, to suppose that the birds deliberately avoid each other's company at these low densities. Moreover, it is well established that many sea-birds, so far from avoiding each other's company, feed by 'enhancement' (Hinde, 1961), joining individuals seen actively feeding, and Wynne-Edwards did not discuss this view.

According to Wynne-Edwards, most other birds have much more refined ways than sea birds of achieving homeostatic dispersion, namely through 'epideictic displays'. The latter form 'a tremendously important and hitherto completely unexplained component of social behaviour . . . especially evolved to provide the necessary feed-back when the balance of population is about to be restored, or may need to be shifted. . . . They generally involve conventions . . . and have come to assume a highly symbolic quality' (p. 16). Under the heading of epideictic behaviour Wynne-Edwards included almost all forms of social behaviour in which birds participate in groups, such as the courtship leks of Blackcock, *Lyrurus tetrix*, and other promiscuous species, the 'panic flights' of nesting terns, the mass roosting and mass displays before roosting of Starlings, *Sturnus vulgaris*, the aggregations of sea birds in colonies and their return to the ledges several weeks before laying, the mass gatherings on the sea of Manx Shearwaters, *Puffinus puffinus*, even the 'moult migrations' of Shelducks, *Tadorna tadorna*, and at least in part the clumping of Swifts, *A. apus*, in cold weather, also to take two examples from outside birds, the flashing of fireflies, and the nocturnal ascent of the plankton.

But most of the above phenomena had been previously, and in my view adequately, explained in other ways, and in no instance has Wynne-Edwards provided positive evidence for his views. For instance, lek displays have probably been evolved because, in the species concerned, males which display in groups attract more females than males which display solitarily (Lack, 1939), and Wynne-Edwards (1962, pp. 215–16) provided no evidence for his view that the lek has a 'dispersive function' or that the males regulate the number of females fecundated (see also the discussion in Chapter 10, pp. 172–3). Again, the 'panic flights' of terns and some other colonial species are presumably what their name implies, a means of escape from falcons or other aerial predators by flying low in a mass, and such flights are also seen in flocks of terns resting temporarily on migration, when it is even more unlikely that they should have an epideictic function in relation to the food supply than in the breeding season. Wynne-Edwards provided no good evidence refuting this alternative explanation, and that some such flights have no apparent cause may be either because the birds saw a predator overlooked by the human observer, or because one individual bird made a mistake in identification and the behaviour spread quickly through the colony (because it is advantageous, if a predator is approaching, for all individuals to react quickly). Again, the habit of forming large roosts for sleeping has probably been evolved through considerations of safety, and despite the detailed studies of roosting Starlings by several observers, including Wynne-Edwards himself, he presented no positive evidence for his view (pp. 298–9) that 'the primary function of the roost is to bring members of the population-unit together, so that whenever prevailing conditions demand it they can hold an epideictic demonstration. The practical result of this is to stimulate the adjustment of population density through emigration, when the economic and social pressure proves to be sufficiently high'. Further, synchronized flights prior to entering the roost, which Wynne-Edwards considered epideictic, are identical with the behaviour of Starlings when a falcon attacks (Tinbergen, 1951), so are presumably a form of behaviour evolved to confuse birds of prey, to which otherwise the assembling Starlings might be specially vulnerable.

Again, the aggregation of sea-birds into nesting colonies seems adequately accounted for through the limitation of suitable sites safe from predators, combined with the fact that in general a newcomer will have a greater chance of selecting a safe site if it joins an established colony (as the latter would not be there unless it had been safe in the previous year) rather than if it selects an empty cliff (which might be empty because it had proved dangerous to former occupants) (Lack, 1954). Further, the return of sea birds to their nesting ledges several weeks before laying is probably to ensure a site and assist pair-formation, and there is no reason to think that a colony assesses its density by this means. The mass gatherings of Manx Shearwaters can also be otherwise explained, and there is no evidence to support Wynne-Edwards' view (see p. 266).

Wynne-Edwards likewise wrote of the moult-migration of the Shelduck and other duck (p. 320) that 'no very acceptable explanation has hitherto suggested itself' and 'it seems not improbable that . . . it has evolved, at least locally, into a significant occasion for massing together and submitting to the pressure of accumulated numbers. If so, it presumably serves to promote the regulation of population-density in the species'. But since this behaviour occurs after breeding, usually in an area remote from where the birds bred, and since it involves only the adults, not the young, and in some other species of ducks only the males, any epideictic function seems wildly improbable. On the other hand, as ducks become flightless when moulting, their habit of seeking remote and safe places in which to do so is readily and sufficiently explained on these grounds alone. Similarly, alternative explanations are available for many other aspects of social behaviour which Wynne-Edwards claimed, without any positive evidence, as epideictic. To mention only one more, would any marine zoologists concede an epideictic function for the nocturnal ascent of the plankton?

Wynne-Edwards also claimed that group-selection is necessary to account for the alarm calls and white scuts or rumps of social mammals and birds, but these could well have been evolved through the need for the young of these species to follow and be warned by their own parents, i.e. through natural selection (or kin selection if this term is to be used for members of a family). Again, Wynne-Edwards wrote (p. 574) that 'on the old hypothesis that natural selection must always favour the genes that enable the individual to leave the largest legacy of offspring to posterity, it would be expected that perennation [i.e. the adults breeding in successive years] would have a clear advantage over monotely [breeding once and then dying] . . . That monotely is so common . . . is additional illustration of the inadequacy of the hypothesis.' But natural selection could well favour the evolution of monotely when the chances of the adult surviving from one breeding season to the next are small and when, in addition, relief of the female from the need to maintain its own body after breeding means that it can produce many more eggs than would otherwise be the case. Yet again, Wynne-Edwards considered (p. 276) that the evolution of sterile caste in social insects 'can only have been effected by selection at the group level' since 'no agency can select in favour of sterility among organisms competing in status as individuals'. But sterile workers are products of the queens, and hence there could be natural selection between queens in regard to their production of sterile workers, if the latter also affect, as they clearly may, the number of fertile descendants produced. While much further research is needed to explain the difficult problem of how sterile castes were evolved, there is on present evidence no necessity to invoke group-selection, and the Williamses (1957) showed how kin selection might be involved. Finally, Wynne-Edwards discussed tribal behaviour in man, but man is so influenced by tradition that any parallel with the social behaviour of animals is highly dangerous.

Another important section of Wynne-Edwards' book was concerned with reproductive rates, and he returned to the view, advocated by various earlier workers and some modern ones (e.g. Cloudsley-Thompson, 1957), that the recruitment rate of a species, which includes its clutch-size, number of broods and the age of first breeding, has been evolved to balance the mortality rate, so that overpopulation is avoided. He wrote (p. 485) of my alternative view that clutch-size is a product of natural selection that 'this argument contemplates selection as acting at the level of the individual, relentlessly discriminating against those that leave fewer than the maximum possible number of progeny or posterity. It leaves entirely out of account the over-riding effect of group-selection, that occurs between one population or society and another, and normally results in fixing the optimum breeding rate for the population as a whole.' The omission of the concept of group-selection from my argument was, of course, deliberate, since I held, and hold, that natural selection must favour that genotype which results in most surviving offspring; this indeed is what one means by natural selection, and I cannot conceive of any effective way in which group-selection could under normal conditions restrict the reproductive rate of an animal below that which natural selection would permit. Moreover, natural selection provides a satisfactory explanation of the known facts relating to clutch-size.

In this connection, Wynne-Edwards did not discuss in his book my earlier figures showing that in the Starling, the Swift, and usually the Great Tit (Lack, 1948a, 1954; et al. 1957) the most frequent clutch-size is the same as that brood-size from which, on average, most young are raised per brood. The more recent experiments on Swifts and various Procellariiformes des-cribed in the present book provide much stronger support for my hypothesis and Wynne-Edwards' later attempt (1964) to re-interpret the findings for the Swift are unconvincing (Lack, 1964a). Again, he produced no evidence in support of his view that the low reproductive rates of Procellariiformes are an adaptation to their low annual mortality, and as discussed at length in Chapter 16, all the features concerned can be interpreted on the view that these species are reproducing as fast as possible (including their clutch of one, their failure to replace a lost egg, their long incubation and nestling periods, their single brood in a year, in large albatrosses one brood in two years, and their long deferment of maturity, though the last point is much harder to explain than the rest). Wynne-Edwards' view on clutch-size in boobies, *Sula*, was also criticized earlier (p. 250).

The only serious evidence that Wynne-Edwards (1962) brought forward to support his interpretation is the tendency for larger birds to live longer and to lay smaller clutches than smaller birds. But there are such striking

308

exceptions that this is clearly not a general rule. Thus the smallest of all birds, the humming-birds, normally lay two eggs, while the largest, the Ostrich, *Struthio camelus*, lays 15–20 eggs (McLachlan and Liversidge, 1957); or if a flightless bird be disallowed, all the species of storm petrels lay a single egg, whereas many ducks and gallinaceous birds of much larger size lay clutches of ten eggs and some of fifteen eggs or more. However, the tendency holds broadly within certain orders or families of birds.

In raptorial birds, for instance, various of the large eagles and vultures lay only one egg, many buzzards and small eagles lay two or three eggs, and various small falcons and hawks usually lay four or five eggs, and the larger species probably live longer than the smaller ones. But this relationship need not be due to an adjustment of clutch-size to the mortality rate. I suggest, instead, that the large prey on which large raptors depend are in general much sparser than the small prey on which small raptors depend, and that their respective clutch-sizes have been adapted to the availability of food for their young. The same view was taken for the raptors laying only one egg by Amadon (1964). That the clutch-size of each raptorial species is in fact close to the greatest number of young for which the parents can find enough food is strongly suggested by the frequency with which, in such species, one or more of the brood die in the nest, presumably from food shortage.

This last interpretation was also rejected by Wynne-Edwards (1962, pp. 531–4), who cited Ingram (1959) that in many raptors a larger nestling often attacks and kills a smaller nest-mate. It is not clear from the vague descriptions reviewed by Ingram how often the smaller nestling is actually killed by its sibling, as distinct from dying of starvation in competition for food, and I suspect that it may be less frequently than Ingram supposed. However, such 'cainism' was observed in the Lesser Spotted Eagle, *Aquila pomarina*, by Wendland (1958), who also cited records in other raptors. But even when the attacks of a nest-mate are the immediate cause of death, it is clear from these authors' evidence that the predisposing cause of death is food shortage among the nestlings, since a well-fed older chick does not attack its nest-mate. In essence, therefore, Wendland's and Ingram's interpretation agrees with mine (Lack, 1947, 1954, see also p. 282), that asynchronous hatching is a valuable adaptation because it results in the nestlings being of very different size, with the result that, when food is short, as it often is, all of it goes to the larger chicks, while the younger chick or chicks quickly die. As a result, the brood-size is rapidly reduced to that which the food supply can sustain, virtually none is wasted on young chicks that will starve anyway, and the surviving nestlings are almost as well nourished as they would have been if the younger ones had never hatched. On the other hand, when food is plentiful all the brood is raised.

Wynne-Edwards omitted to discuss my interpretation of this point, as well as the precise study of Lockie (1955a) of how asynchronous hatching operates in relation to food shortage in nestling Jackdaws, *Corvus monedula*, in which, incidentally, 'cainism' is absent. Instead, Wynne-Edwards commented (p. 534) that 'our explanation would differ from Ingram's only in one important respect, namely that there is certain to be a conventional mechanism that governs the intervention of the parents', while later he concluded (p. 537) that 'it is highly probable that the parents are protected in the normal way by social conventions from over-exploiting the food supply, and thus jeopardizing future resources, merely in order to meet the short-term demands of their nestlings: the question is not one of compulsory or inevitable starvation leading to mortality, but rather of the exercise of prudential restraint in terms of present and future economic conditions.' But to my thinking it is inconceivable that parent birds would withhold food from their own young in order to avert a threat of future famine to the population as a whole, and all the available facts are satisfactorily explained on the view that the parents are finding as much food, and raising as large a brood as they are capable of doing at the time in question. This was also the view of Owen (1960) on the function of asynchronous hatching in the Heron, *Ardea cinerea*, in which, as in the Jackdaw, 'cainism' has not been observed. Wynne-Edwards provided no facts to support his alternative view of 'prudential restraint', nor did he suggest how the parent birds might diagnose the need for it. Similar considerations apply to the White Stork, *C. ciconia*, in which a parent may even kill one of its chicks, but this has already been discussed in Chapter 13 (p. 223).

Wynne-Edwards' view that the reproductive rate of each species is adapted to its mortality presumably involves both long-term evolutionary trends and immediate adjustments. As an example of the former, he would presumably argue that all Procellariiformes have evolved a clutch of one because they always live a long time. But such long-term adaptations would not avail to produce population balance without immediate density-dependent adjustments as well, and if such adjustments are effective, then the annual variations in the number of young raised should significantly influence the intake of new adults and hence the fluctuations in the breeding population. But as summarized in Chapter 17, in the five population studies continued for longest, on the Great and Blue Tits, Pied Flycatcher, Tawny Owl, and White Stork, marked annual variations in the number of young produced had no appreciable influence on the subsequent changes in the breeding population. Hence even if these species had been practising 'prudential restraints' they would have been ineffective. Moreover, though this point is crucial to his theory, Wynne-Edwards did not produce contrary evidence for any species that variations in the reproductive rate affected the subsequent density of breeding pairs. On my view, however, this lack of correlation was to be expected, because I consider that the primary factor influencing adult numbers is density-dependent mortality outside the breeding season.

Undoubtedly the most difficult point in the present discussion is the interpretation of deferred maturity. There is no evidence for Wynne-Edwards' view that it has been evolved in relation to the mortality rate of the species, but also very little evidence as yet to support my view that the attempt to breed at too early an age would be both ineffective and dangerous. I have summarized the main points brought out by the population studies considered in this book in Chapter 17, and do not think that anything further can usefully be said without further facts.

Wynne-Edwards' book received both highly favourable and highly unfavourable reviews (for the former, e.g. Anon., 1962 and Nicholson, 1962; and for the latter, e.g. Braestrup, 1963 and Elton 1963). It may be asked why, if what I have said is correct, his views should have gained such strong support in certain quarters. One reason is that some of the views in question have been current for a long time, though usually implicitly rather than explicitly, and they have never previously received anything like such comprehensive treatment. Apart from this, and the lucid style, the two main reasons were given by Anon. (1962): 'Any biologist is bound to be attracted by two very general aspects of this thesis: first, . . . the universality and the underlying reason for social life; and second, that the theory finds a place in animal populations for the phenomenon that biologists call homeostasis—the regulation of activity at an appropriate level. Homeostatic mechanisms . . . have long been familiar to physiologists. In recent years comparable devices have been found to reign within individual cells, and in the innermost working mechanisms of heredity. It would be surprising if so widespread and indeed characteristic a feature of life did not also work to regulate the life of animals *en masse*.' The first reason was put to me in conversation somewhat differently by another biologist, that the book drew attention to the existence of many remarkable social displays in birds and other animals which are not to be explained through sexual selection.

Both these reasons rest on ignorance by other biologists of what ecologists have already discovered. First, various ornithologists have long been aware of many displays and other social behaviour in birds which are not to be explained in terms of sexual selection; but, rightly in my view, they have ascribed various different functions to them and not a single overriding one (epideictic). However, the general reader might not be aware of this from Wynne-Edwards' book, as he did not usually discuss the earlier interpretations of the phenomena which he considered to be epideictic. Secondly, it is of course true that natural populations could not be regulated without homeostasis, and though a few workers like Andrewartha and Birch have claimed that natural populations are not regulated, most modern workers agree with A. J. Nicholson that they are, primarily through density-dependent mortality factors, though dispersive behaviour plays an important secondary role. Ecologists have not used the term homeostasis, but the idea of self-balancing populations has been widely accepted by them at least since the paper by A. J. Nicholson (1933).

To summarize, there is indeed a phenomon of dispersion, whereby birds and other animals modify their population density in relation to the food supply through movements and in other ways, especially when breeding, but this phenomenon is not nearly so extensive as Wynne-Edwards claimed. Also at least most of the behaviour considered epideictic by Wynne-Edwards can be satisfactorily interpreted in other ways, and no positive evidence has been presented for an epideictic function. Further there is no reason to suppose that reproductive rates have been evolved to balance mortality rates; reproductive rates are explicable through natural selection, and the balance between birth-rates and death-rates can be attributed to density-dependent mortality. Finally, not only low reproductive rates, but also the types of behaviour discussed by Wynne-Edwards, including those which genuinely involve dispersion, are explicable through natural selection and there is no need to invoke group-selection. It may be added that the discussion here has been concerned primarily with birds because Wynne-Edwards himself took his most numerous and most striking examples from birds and based his theory upon them, but similar criticisms could be made of his views on other animals.

BIBLIOGRAPHY

ALLAN, R. G. 1962. The Madeiran Storm Petrel, *Oceanodroma castro*. *Ibis* 103b: 274–95.

AMADON, D. 1964. The evolution of low reproductive rates in birds. *Evolution* 18: 105–10.

ANDERSEN, T. 1961. (A population of Tawny Owl (*Strix aluco L.*) in Northern Zealand, studied in the breeding season) *Dansk. orn. Foren. Tidsskr.* 55: 1–55 (English summary 46–53).

ANDREWARTHA, H. G. 1959a. Density-dependent factors in ecology. *Nature, Lond.* 183: 200.

— 1959b. Self-regulatory mechanisms in animal populations. *Aust. J. Sci.* 22: 200–5.

ANDREWARTHA, H. G., & BIRCH, L. C. 1954. *The Distribution and Abundance of Animals* (Chicago).

ANDREWARTHA, H. G., & BIRCH, L. C. 1960. Some recent contributions to the study of the distribution and abundance of insects. *A. Rev. Ent.* 5: 219–42.

ANDREWARTHA, H. G., & BROWNING, T. O. 1961. An analysis of the idea of 'resources' in animal ecology. *J. theor. Biol.* 1: 83–97.

ANON. 1962. The nature of social life. *Times Lit. Suppl.*, 14 December 1962.

ASHMOLE, N. P. 1962. The Black Noddy, *Anous tenuirostris*, on Ascension Island. Part 1. General Biology. *Ibis* 103b: 235–73.

— 1963a. The regulation of numbers of tropical oceanic birds. *Ibis* 103b: 458–73.

— 1963b. The biology of the Wideawake or Sooty Tern, *Sterna fuscata*, on Ascension Island. *Ibis* 103b: 297–364.

BAKER, J. R. 1938. The evolution of breeding seasons. *'Evolution' Essays present to E. S. Goodrich* (Oxford), pp. 161–77.

BAKKER, K. 1964. Backgrounds of controversies about population theories and their terminologies. *Z. angew. Ent.* 53: 187–208.

BALDWIN, P. H. 1960. Overwintering of woodpeckers in bark beetle-infested spruce-fir forests of Colorado. *Proc. Int. orn. Congr.* 12: 71–84.

BECKER, K. 1958. Die Populationsentwicklung von Feldmäusen (*Microtus arvalis*) im Spiegel der Nahrung von Schleiereulen (*Tyto alba*). *Z. angew. Zool.* 45: 403–31.

BELOPOL'SKII, L. O. 1961 (1957). *Ecology of Sea Colony Birds of the Barents Sea* (transl. from Russian 1957) (Jerusalem).

BENT, A. C. 1932. Life histories of North American gallinaceous birds. *U.S. natn. Mus. Bull.* 162.

BERNDT, R. 1960. Zur Dispersion der Weibchen von *Ficedula hypoleuca* im nördlichen Deutschland. *Proc. Int. orn. Congr.* 12: 85–96.

BERNDT, R., & MOELLER, J. 1958. Bestandsentwicklung des Weissstorchs (*Ciconia c. ciconia*) im Regierungsbezirk Hildesheim von 1907 bis 1953. *Vogelring* 27: 39–47.

BERNDT, R., & REHBEIN, F. 1961. Ein halbes Jahrhundert Brutstatistik vom Weissstorch (*Ciconia c. ciconia*) im Kreis Peine. *Vogelwarte* 21: 128–36.

BERNDT, R., & STERNBERG, H. 1963. Ist die Mortalitätsrate adulter *Ficedula hypoleuca* wirklich unabhängig vom Lebensalter? *Proc. Int. orn. Congr.* 13: 675–84.

313

BIBLIOGRAPHY

BETTS, M. M. 1954. Experiments with an artificial nestling. *Br. Birds* **47**: 229–31.
— 1955. The food of titmice in oak woodland. *J. Anim. Ecol.* **24**: 282–323.
— 1956. Further experiments with an artificial nestling gape. *Br. Birds* **49**: 213–15.
— 1958. Notes on the life history of *Ernarmonia conicolana* (Heyl.) (Lep., Eucosmidae). *Ent. mon. Mag.* **94**: 134–7.
BEVEN, G. 1963. Population changes in a Surrey oakwood during fifteen years. *Br. Birds* **56**: 307–23.
BIRCH, L. C. 1957. The meanings of competition. *Am. Nat.* **91**: 5–18.
— 1958. The role of weather in determining the distribution and abundance of animals. *Cold Spring Harb. Symp. quant. Biol.* **22**: 203–18.
— 1960. Stability and instability in natural populations. *N. Z. Sci. Rev.* **20**: 9–14.
— 1963. Population ecology and the control of pests. *Bull. Wld Hlth Org.* **29** (Suppl.): 141–6.
BOURNE, W. R. P. 1955. The birds of the Cape Verde Islands. *Ibis* **97**: 508–56.
— 1957. Additional notes on the birds of the Cape Verde islands, with particular reference to *Bulweria mollis* and *Fregata magnificens*. *Ibis* **99**: 182–90.
BRAESTRUP, F. W. 1963. Special review (of V. C. Wynne-Edwards on 'Animal dispersion in relation to social behaviour'). *Oikos* **14**: 113–20.
BRERETON, J. LE G. 1962. Evolved regulatory mechanisms of population control. Evolution of living organisms. *Symp. R. Soc. Vict.* **8**: 81–93.
BROWN, W. L., & WILSON, E. O. 1956. Character displacement. *Syst. Zool.* **5**: 49–64.
BRUNS, H. 1960. The economic importance of birds in forests. *Bird Study* **7**: 193–208.
BUCKLEY, J. L. 1954. Animal population fluctuations in Alaska—A history. *Trans. N. Am. Wildl. Conf.* **19**: 338–57.
BUDD, G. M. 1961. The biotopes of Emperor Penguin rookeries. *Emu* **61**: 171–89.
— 1962. Population studies in rookeries of the Emperor Penguin, *Aptenodytes forsteri*. *Proc. zool. Soc. Lond.* **139**: 365–88.
BUMP, G., DARROW, R. W., EDMINSTER, F. C., & CRISSEY, W. F. 1947. *The Ruffed Grouse. Life History, Propagation, Management* (New York).
CAMPBELL, B. 1954–5. The breeding distribution and habitats of the Pied Flycatcher (*Muscicapa hypoleuca*) in Britain. *Bird Study* **1**: 81–101; **2**: 24–32, 179–91.
— 1955. A population of Pied Flycatchers (*Muscicapa hypoleuca*). *Proc. Int. orn. Congr.* **11**: 428–34.
— 1959. Attachment of Pied Flycatchers *Muscicapa hypoleuca* to nest-sites. *Ibis* **101**: 445–8.
CARRICK, R., CSORDAS, S. E., & INGRAM, S. E. 1962. Studies on the Southern Elephant Seal, *Mirounga leonina* (L.). IV. Breeding and development. *C.S.I.R.O. Wildl. Res.* **7**: 161–97.
CARRICK, R., & DUNNET, G. M. 1952. Breeding of the Fulmar, *Fulmarus glacialis*. *Ibis* **96**: 356–70.
CARRICK, R., KEITH, K., & GWYNN, A. M. 1960. Fact and fiction on the breeding of the Wandering Albatross. *Nature, Lond.* **188**: 112–4.
CAUGHLEY, G. 1960. The Cape Crozier Emperor Penguin rookery. *Rec. Dom. Mus., Wellington* **3**: 251–62.

BIBLIOGRAPHY

CHAPMAN, F. M. 1935. The courtship of Gould's Manakin (*Manacus vitellinus vitellinus*) on Barro Colorado Island, Canal Zone. *Bull. Am. Mus. nat. Hist.* **68**: 471–525.

CHOATE, T. S. 1963. Habitat and population dynamics of White-tailed Ptarmigan in Montana. *J. Wildl. Mgmt.* **27**: 684–99.

CLOUDSLEY-THOMPSON, J. L. 1957. Some comments on the natural control of animal populations with especial reference to insects. *Entomologist* **90**: 195–203

COULSON, J. C. 1959a. The plumage and leg colour of the Kittiwake and comments on the non-breeding population. *Br. Birds* **52**: 189–96.

— 1959b. The adult mortality of the Manx Shearwater on Skokholm. *Skokholm Bird Observatory Report* 1959, pp. 24–6.

— 1961. The post-fledging mortality of the Blackbird in Great Britain. *Bird Study* **8**: 89–97.

— 1963a. The status of the Kittiwake in the British Isles. *Bird Study* **10**: 147–79.

— 1963b. Egg size and shape in the Kittiwake (*Rissa tridactyla*) and their use in estimating age composition of populations. *Proc. zool. Soc. Lond.* **140**: 211–27.

COULSON, J. C., & WHITE, E. 1956. A study of colonies of the Kittiwake, *Rissa tridactyla* (L.). *Ibis* **98**: 63–79.

COULSON, J. C., & WHITE, E. 1958a. The effect of age on the breeding biology of the Kittiwake, *Rissa tridactyla*. *Ibis* **100**: 40–51.

COULSON, J. C., & WHITE, E. 1958b. Observations on the breeding of the Kittiwake. *Bird Study* **5**: 74–83.

COULSON, J. C., & WHITE, E. 1959. The post-fledging mortality of the Kittiwake. *Bird Study* **6**: 97–102.

COULSON, J. C., & WHITE, E. 1960. The effect of age and density of breeding birds on the time of breeding of the Kittiwake, *Rissa tridactyla*. *Ibis* **102**: 71–86.

COULSON, J. C., & WHITE, E. 1961. An analysis of the factors influencing the clutch size of the Kittiwake. *Proc. zool. Soc. Lond.* **136**: 207–17.

CRAGG, J. B. 1961. Some aspects of the ecology of moorland animals. *J. Anim. Ecol.* **30** 205–34.

CRAMP, S., PETTET, A., & SHARROCK, J. T. R. 1960. The irruption of tits in autumn 1957. *Br. Birds* **53**: 49–77, 99–117, 176–92.

CREUTZ, G. 1955. Der Trauerschnäpper (*Muscicapa hypoleuca* (Pallas)). *J. Orn., Lpz.* **96**: 241–326.

CROOK, J. H. 1960. Studies on the social behaviour of *Quelea q. quelea* (Linn.) in French West Africa. *Behaviour* **16**: 1–55.

— 1962. The adaptive significance of pair formation types in weaver-birds. *Symp. zool. Soc. Lond.* **8**: 57–70.

— 1963. Monogamy, polygamy and food supply. *Discovery* (1963); pp. 35–41.

— 1964. The evolution of social organization and visual communication in the weaver-birds (Ploceinae). *Behaviour*, Suppl. X.

CULLEN, E. 1957. Adaptations in the Kittiwake to cliff-nesting. *Ibis* **99**: 275–302.

CURIO, E. 1958. Geburtsortstreue und Lebenserwartung junger Trauerschnäpper (*Muscicapa h. hypoleuca* Pallas). *Vogelwelt* **79**: 135–48.

— 1959a. Verhaltensstudien am Trauerschnäpper. *Z. Tierpsychol.* Suppl. 3, pp. 1–118.

— 1959b. Beiträge zur Populationsökologie des Trauerschnäppers (*Ficedula h. hypoleuca* Pallas). *zool. Jb.* **87**: 185–230.

BIBLIOGRAPHY

CURIO, E. 1960. Lebenserwartung und Brutgrösse beim Trauerschnäpper (*Muscicapa h. hypoleuca* Pallas). *Proc. Int. orn. Congr.* **12**: 158–61.

CURRY-LINDAHL, K. 1961. Conservation and predation problems of birds of prey in Sweden. *Br. Birds* **54**: 297–306.

DANE, D. S. 1948. A disease of Manx Shearwaters (*Puffinus puffinus*). *J. Anim. Ecol.* **17**: 158–64.

DANE, D. S., MILES, J. A. R., & STOKER, M. G. P. 1953. A disease of Manx Shearwaters. Further observations in the field. *J. Anim. Ecol.* **22**: 123–33.

DARLING, F. F. 1938. *Bird Flocks and the Breeding Cycle* (Cambridge).

DAVIDSON, J., & ANDREWARTHA, H. G. 1958a. Annual trends in a natural population of *Thrips imaginis* (Thysanoptera). *J. Anim. Ecol.* **17**: 193–9.

DAVIDSON, J., & ANDREWARTHA, H. G. 1948b. The influence of rainfall, evaporation and atmospheric temperature on fluctuations in the size of a natural population of *Thrips imaginis* (Thysanoptera). *J. Anim. Ecol.* **17**: 200–22.

DAVIES, P. W., & SNOW, D. W. 1965. Territory and food of the Song-Thrush. *Br. Birds* **58**: 161–75.

DAVIS, P. 1957. The breeding of the Storm Petrel. *Br. Birds* **50**: 85–101, 371–84.

DEMENTIEV, G. P., & GLADKOV, N. A. 1952. *Birds of the Soviet Union* (Moscow), vol. 4, pp. 15–23.

DISNEY, H. J. DE S., & HAYLOCK, J. W. 1956. The distribution and breeding behaviour of the Sudan Dioch (*Quelea q. aethiopica*) in Tanganyika. *East Afr. agric. J.* **21**: 141–7.

DISNEY, H. J. DE S., & MARSHALL, A. J. 1956. A contribution to the breeding biology of the weaver-finch *Quelea quelea* (Linnaeus) in East Africa. *Proc. zool. Soc. Lond.* **127**: 379–87.

DORWARD, D. F. 1962. Comparative biology of the White Booby and the Brown Booby *Sula* spp. at Ascension. *Ibis* **103**b: 174–220.

DOUDE VAN TROOSTWIJK, W. J. 1964. Some aspects of the Woodpigeon population in the Netherlands. *Ardea*, **52**: 13–29.

DRINNAN, R. E. 1957. The winter feeding of the Oyster Catcher (*Haematopus ostralegus*) on the Edible Cockle (*Cardium edule*). *J. Anim. Ecol.* **26**: 441–69.

DUNNET, G. M. 1955. The breeding of the Starling *Sturnus vulgaris* in relation to its food supply. *Ibis* **97**: 619–62.

DUNNET, G. M., ANDERSON, A., & CORMACK, R. M. 1963. A study of survival of adult Fulmars with observations on the pre-laying exodus. *Br. Birds* **56**: 2–18.

DURANGO, S. 1950. Om klimatets inverkan på tornskatans (*Lanius collurio* L.) utbredning och levnadsmöjligheter. *Fauna Flora, Upps.* **45**: 49–78.

EDBERG, R. 1958. Winter mortality of Tawny Owls (*Strix a. aluco*) in Central Sweden. *Fågelv.* **17**: 273–80 (with English summary).

EINARSEN, A. S. 1945. Some factors affecting Ring-necked Pheasant population density. *Murrelet* **26**: 39–44.

ELGOOD, J. H., and WARD, P. 1963. A snake attack upon a weaver-bird colony. Possible significance of synchronous breeding activity. *Bull. Br. orn. Club* **83**: 71–73.

ELLIOTT, H. F. I. 1953. The fauna of Tristan da Cunha. *Oryx* **2**: 41–53.

— 1957. A contribution to the ornithology of the Tristan da Cunha group. *Ibis* **99**: 545–86.

ELSON, P. F. 1962. Predator-prey relationships between fish-eating birds and Atlantic Salmon. *Fish. Res. Bd. Can. Bull.* **133**: 1–87.

BIBLIOGRAPHY

ELTON, C. S. 1963. Self-regulation of animal populations. *Nature, Lond.* **197**: 634.

ERRINGTON, P. L. 1934. Vulnerability of Bob-white populations to predation. *Ecology* **15**: 110–27.

— 1945. Some contributions of a fifteen-year local study of the Northern Bobwhite to a knowledge of population phenomena *Ecol. Monogr.* **15**: 1–34.

— 1946. Predation and vertebrate populations. *Q. Rev. Biol.* **21**: 144–77, 221–45.

ERZ, W. 1964. Populationsökologische Untersuchungen an der Avifauna zweier nordwestdeutcher Grossstädte. *Z. wiss. Zool.* **170**: 1–111.

EUTERMOSER, A. 1961. Schlagen Beizfalken bevorzugt kranke Krähen? *Vogelwelt* **82**: 101–4.

FARNER, D. S. (based on SERVENTY, D. L.) 1962. In *Handbook of North American Birds*, ed. R. S. PALMER, (New Haven) vol. 1, p. 184.

FISHER, R. A. 1930. *The Genetical Theory of Natural Selection* (Oxford).

FORMOSOV, A. N. 1960. La production de graines dans les forêts de conifères de la taiga de l'U.R.S.S. et l'envahissement de l'Europe occidentale par certaines espèces d'oiseaux. *Proc. Int. orn. Congr.* **12**: 216–29.

FRANK, P. W. 1959. Ecology and demography, from *The Study of Population* by P. M. HAUSER, & O. D. DUNCAN (Chicago, 1959), pp. 652–77.

FRITH, H. J. 1956. Breeding habits in the family Megapodiidae. *Ibis* **98**: 620–40.

— 1959. Breeding of the Mallee Fowl, *Leipoa ocellata* Gould (Megapodiidae). *C.S.I.R.O. Wildl. Res.* **4**: 31–60.

GALLAGHER, M. D. 1960. Bird notes from Christmas Island, Pacific Ocean. *Ibis* **102**: 489–502.

GAUSE, G. F. 1934. *The Struggle for Existence* (Baltimore).

— 1939. In discussion of PARK, T. Analytical population studies in relation to general ecology. *Am. Midl. Nat.* **21**: 255.

GIBB, J. 1950. The breeding biology of the Great and Blue Titmice. *Ibis* **92**: 507–39.

— 1954a. Population changes of titmice, 1947–51. *Bird Study* **1**: 40–48.

— 1954b. Feeding ecology of tits, with notes on the Treecreeper and Goldcrest. *Ibis* **96**: 513–43.

— 1955. Feeding rates of Great Tits. *Br. Birds* **48**: 49–58.

— 1956a. Food, feeding habits and territory of the Rock Pipit, *Anthus spinoletta*. *Ibis* **98**: 506–30.

— 1956b. Territory in the genus *Parus*. *Ibis* **98**: 420–9.

— 1957. Food requirements and other observations on captive tits. *Bird Study* **4**: 207–15.

— 1958. Predation by tits and squirrels on the eucosmid *Ernarmonia conicolana* (Heyl.). *J. Anim. Ecol.* **27**: 375–96.

— 1960. Populations of tits and Goldcrests and their food supply in pine plantations. *Ibis* **102**: 163–208.

— 1962a. Tits and their food supply in English pine woods: a problem in applied ornithology. *Festschr. Vogelschutzwarte Hessen, Rheinland-Pfalz und Saarland*, pp. 58–66.

— 1962b. L. Tinbergen's hypothesis of the role of specific search images. *Ibis* **104**: 106–11.

GIBB, J. 1962c. The importance of territory and food supply in the natural control of a population of birds. *Sci. Rev.* **20**: 20–21.

317

BIBLIOGRAPHY

GIBB, J. A., & BETTS, M. M. 1963. Food and food supply of nestling tits (*Paridae*) in Breckland pine. *J. Anim. Ecol.* 32: 489–533.

GILBERT, O., REYNOLDSON, T. B., & HOBART, J. 1952. Gause's hypothesis: An examination. *J. Anim. Ecol.* 21: 310–12.

GILLIARD, E. T., 1959. Notes on the courtship behavior of the Blue-backed Manakin (*Chiroxiphia pareola*). *Am. Mus. Novit.* 1942: 1–19.

GOODBODY, I. M. 1952. The post-fledging dispersal of juvenile titmice. *Br. Birds* 45: 279–85.

GRACZYK, R. 1959. (Forschungen über das Auftreten und den quantitativen Stand der Amsel (*Turdus merula* L.) in Polen.) *Ekol. pol.* A 7: 55–82.

— 1961. Die Untersuchungen über Variabilität, Biologie und wirtschaftliche Bedeutung der Amsel. *Ekol. pol.* A 9: 453–85.

GRIMSHAW, H. M., OVINGTON, J. D., BETTS, M. M., & GIBB, J. A. 1958. The mineral content of birds and insects in plantations of *Pinus sylvestris* L. *Oikos* 9: 26–34.

GRINNELL, J. 1904. The origin and distribution of the Chestnut-backed Chickadee. *Auk* 21: 364–82.

— 1917. The niche-relationships of the California thrasher. *Auk* 34: 427–33.

— 1928. Presence and absence of animals. *Univ. Calif. Chron.* 30: 429–50 (reprinted 1943, Joseph Grinnell's *Philosophy of Nature* (Berkeley)).

GROSS, A. O. 1947. Recoveries of banded Leach's Petrels. *Bird-Banding* 18: 117–26.

GUDMUNDSSON, F. 1960. Some reflections on Ptarmigan cycles in Iceland. *Proc. Int. orn. Congr.* 12: 259–65.

GURR, L. 1954. A study of the Blackbird *Turdus merula* in New Zealand. *Ibis* 96: 225–61.

HAARTMAN, L. VON. 1949. Der Trauerfliegenschnäpper 1. Ortstreue und Rassenbildung. *Acta zool. fenn.* 56: 1–104.

— 1951a. Der Trauerfliegenschnäpper II. Populationsprobleme. *Acta zool. fenn.* 67: 1–60.

— 1951b. Successive polygamy. *Behaviour* 3: 256–74.

— 1954. Der Trauerfliegenschnäpper III. Nahrungsbiologie. *Acta zool. fenn.* 83: 1–92.

— 1955. Clutch size in polygamous species. *Proc. Int. orn. Congr.* 11: 450–3.

— 1956a. Territory in the Pied Flycatcher, *Muscicapa hypoleuca*. *Ibis* 98: 460–75.

— 1956b. (The phenological research work organized by the Societas Scientiarium Fennica.) *Soc. Sci. Fenn. Årsbok* 33: 1–23.

— 1957. Adaptation in hole-nesting birds. *Evolution* 11: 339–47.

— 1958. The incubation rhythm of the female Pied Flycatcher (*Ficedula hypoleuca*) in the presence and absence of the male. *Ornis fenn.* 35: 71–76.

— 1960. The *Ortstreue* of the Pied Flycatcher. *Proc. Int. orn. Congr.* 12: 266–73.

HALDANE, J. B. S. 1932. *The Causes of Evolution* (London), pp. 207–10.

HARDIN, G. 1960. The competitive exclusion principle. *Science* 131: 1292–8.

HARPER, J. L. *et al.* 1961. The evolution and ecology of closely related species living in the same area. *Evolution* 15: 209–27.

HARRIS, M. P. 1965. Puffinosis on Skokholm. *Br. Birds* 58: 426–33

— 1966 The breeding biology of the Manx Shearwater. *Ibis* 108: 17–33

HARRISON, C. J. O. 1960. The food of some urban Tawny Owls. *Bird Study* 7: 236–40.

HARTLEY, P. H. T. 1953. An ecological study of the feeding habits of the English titmice. *J. Anim. Ecol.* 22: 261–88.

BIBLIOGRAPHY

HAVERSCHMIDT, Fr. 1949. *The Life of the White Stork* (Leiden).

HAVLIN, J. 1962a. Environmental requirements in the Blackbird, *Turdus merula* L. *Pr. brn. Zake.čsl. Akad. Věd.* **34**: 1–48.

— 1962b. Variability of somatic characters in the European Blackbird, *Turdus merula merula* Linné, 1758. *Zool. Listy* **11**: 1–14.

— 1962c. Age structure and mortality rate in Blackbird populations. *Zool. Listy* **11**: 279–85.

— 1963a. (Breeding density in the Blackbird *Turdus merula* Linn.) *Zool. Listy* **12**: 1–17.

— 1963b. (Reproduction in the Blackbird (*Turdus merula* L.). *Zool. Listy* **12**: 195–216.

HAYLOCK, J. W. 1959. Investigations on the habits of Quelea birds and their control. Dept. Agric. Kenya, p. 16.

HEINROTH, O. 1922. Die Beziehungen zwischen Vogelgewicht, Eigewicht, Gelegegewicht und Brutdauer. *J. orn., Lpz.* **70**: 172–285.

HEYDER, R. 1955. Hundert Jahre Gartenamsel. *Beitr. Vogelk.* **4**: 64–81.

HINDE, R. A. 1961. Behaviour in '*Biology and Comparative Physiology of Birds*' (New York and London), Vol. 2, p. 394.

HOFFMANN, R. S. 1958. The role of predators in 'cyclic' declines of grouse populations. *J. Wildl. Mgmt.* **22**: 317–19.

HONER, M. R. 1963. Observations on the Barn Owl (*Tyto alba guttata*) in the Netherlands in relation to its ecology and population fluctuations. *Ardea* **51**: 158–95.

HORNBERGER, F. 1954. Reifealter und Ansiedlung beim Weissen Storch. *Vogelwarte* **17**: 114–49.

— 1957. Der Weisse Storch in seinem Nahrungsrevier. *Mitt. Ver. Math. Naturw. Ulm* **25**: 373–410.

HUNTINGTON, C. E. 1962. In *Handbook of North American Birds*, ed. R. S. PALMER (New Haven), vol. 1, pp. 232–3.

— 1963. Population dynamics of Leach's Petrel, *Oceanodroma leucorrhoa*. *Proc. Int. orn. Congr.* **13**: 701–5.

HUFFAKER, C. B. 1958. The concept of balance in nature. *Proc. Int. Congr. Ent.* **10**(2): 625–36.

HUTCHINSON, G. E. 1959. Homage to Santa Rosalia. *Am. Nat.* **93**: 145–59.

HUXLEY, J. S. 1934. A natural experiment on the territorial instinct. *Br. Birds* **27**: 270–7.

INGRAM, C. 1959. The importance of juvenile cannibalism in the breeding biology of certain birds of prey. *Auk* **76**: 218–26.

JENKINS, D. 1963. Population control in Red Grouse (*Lagopus lagopus scoticus*) *Proc. Int. orn. Congr.* **13**: 690–700.

JENKINS, D., & WATSON, A. 1962. Fluctuations in a Red Grouse, *Lagopus scoticus* (Lath.) population 1956–9. *The Exploitation of Natural Animal Populations*, eds. E. D. LE CREN and M. W. HOLDGATE (Oxford), pp. 96–117.

JENKINS, D , WATSON, A., & MILLER, G. R. 1963. Population studies on Red Grouse, *Lagopus lagopus scoticus* (Lath.) (in north-east Scotland. *J. Anim. Ecol.* **32**: 317–76.

JENKINS, D., WATSON, A., & MILLER, G. R. 1964a. Current research on Red Grouse in Scotland. *Scott. Birds* **3**: 3–13.

JENKINS, D. WATSON, A., & MILLER, G. R. 1964b. Predation and Red Grouse populations. *J. appl. Ecol.* **1**: 183–95.

BIBLIOGRAPHY

JENKINS, D., WATSON, A., MILLER, G. R., & PICOZZI, N. 1964. Unit of grouse and moorland ecology. *Rep. Nat. Conserv.* 1964: 95–98.

JENKINS, D., WATSON, A., & PICOZZI, N. The Grouse chick survival in captivity and in the wild. *Proc. Congr. Int. Union Game Biol.* 6 (in press).

JESPERSEN, P. 1929. On the frequency of birds over the high Atlantic Ocean. *Verh. Int. orn. Kongr.* 6: 163–72.

JOHANSEN, H., & BJERRING, A. 1955. Bestanden af Stork (*Ciconia ciconia* (L.)) i Danmark 1952–4. *Dansk. orn. Foren. Tidsskr* 49: 114–26.

JOHANSEN, H., & BJERRING, A. 1962. Bestanden af Stork (*Ciconia ciconia* (L.)) i Danmark 1955–60. *Dansk. orn. Foren. Tidsskr.* 56: 40–55.

KALELA, O. 1949. Changes in geographic ranges in the avifauna of northern and and central Europe in relation to recent changes in climate. *Bird-Banding* 20: 77–103.

KEAST, A. 1961. Bird speciation on the Australian continent. *Bull. Mus. comp. zool. Harv.* 123: 305–495 (esp. 445–9).

KEITH, L. B. 1963. *Wildlife's Ten-Year Cycle* (Madison).

KENDEIGH, S. C. 1941. Territorial and mating behavior of the House Wren. *Illinois biol. Monogr.* 18: 1–120.

KETTLEWELL, H. B. D. 1956. Further selection experiments on industrial melanism in the Lepidoptera. *Heredity* 10: 287–301.

KLOMP, H. 1962. The influence of climate and weather on the mean density level, the fluctuations and the regulation of animal populations. *Archs. néerl. zool.* 15: 68–109.

KLUYVER, H. N. 1951. The population ecology of the Great Tit, *Parus m. major* L. *Ardea* 39: 1–135.

— 1952. Notes on body weight and time of breeding in the Great Tit, *Parus m. major* L. *Ardea* 40: 123–41.

— 1963. The determination of reproductive rates in Paridae. *Proc. Int. orn. Congr.* 13: 706–16.

KLUYVER, H. N., & TINBERGEN, L. 1953. Territory and the regulation of density in titmice. *Archs. néerl. zool.* 10: 265–89.

KNIGHT, F. B. 1958. The effects of woodpeckers on populations of the Engelmann spruce beetle. *J. econ. Ent.* 51: 603–7.

KOHN, A. J. 1959. The ecology of *Conus* in Hawaii. *Ecol. Monogr.* 29: 47–90.

KOSKIMIES, J. 1955. Ultimate causes of cyclic fluctuations in numbers in animal populations. Pap. Game Res. (Finnish Game Foundation), *Riistat. Julk.* 15: 1–29.

KRAMER, G. 1946. Veränderung von Nachkommenziffer und Nachkommengrösse sowie der Altersverteilung von Inseleidechsen. *Z. Naturf.* 1: 700–10.

KUENEN, D. J. 1958. Some sources of misunderstanding in the theories of regulation of animal numbers. *Archs. néel. zool.* 13 Suppl. 1: 335–41.

KUHK, R. and SCHÜZ, E. 1950. 1949 wieder ein Störungsjahr im Bestand des Weiss-Storchs, *Ciconia ciconia*. *Orn. Beob.* 47: 93–97.

KURODA, N. 1960. Remarks on the breeding seasons in the *Tubinares*, particularly of the North Pacific. *Proc. Int. orn. Congr.* 12: 445–9.

— 1963. Adaptive parental feeding as a factor influencing the reproductive rate in the Grey Starling. *Res. Popul. Ecol.* 5: 1–10.

LACK, D. 1939. The display of the Blackcock. *Br. Birds* 32: 290–303.

— 1940. Courtship feeding in birds. *Auk* 57: 169–78.

— 1942–3. The breeding birds of Orkney. *Ibis* 84: 461–84; 85: 1–27.

— 1943–4. The problem of partial migration. *Br. Birds.* 37: 122–30, 143–50.

— 1947. The significance of clutch-size. *Ibis* 89: 302–52.

BIBLIOGRAPHY

LACK, D. 1948*a*. Natural selection and family size in the Starling. *Evolution* **2**: 95–110.

— 1948*b*. The significance of clutch-size Part III. Some interspecific comparisons. *Ibis* **90**: 25–45.

— 1954*a*. *The Natural Regulation of Animal Numbers* (Oxford).

— 1954*b*. Two Robin populations. *Bird Study*, **1**: 14–17.

— 1955. British tits (*Parus* spp.) in nesting boxes. *Ardea* **43**: 50–84.

— 1956*a*. Further notes on the breeding biology of the Swift, *Apus apus*. *Ibis* **98**: 606–19.

— 1956*b*. Swifts in a Tower (London).

— 1958. A quantitative breeding study of British tits. *Ardea* **46**: 91–124.

— 1963. Cuckoo hosts in England. *Bird Study* **10**: 185–202.

— 1964*a*. Significance of clutch-size in Swift and Grouse. *Nature, Lond.* **203**: 98–99.

— 1964*b*. A long-term study of the Great Tit (*Parus major*). *J. Anim. Ecol.* **33** (Jubilee Suppl.): 159–73.

LACK, D., & E. 1952. The breeding behaviour of the Swift. *Br. Birds* **45**: 186–215.

LACK, D., & E. 1958. The nesting of the Long-tailed Tit. *Bird Study* **5**: 1–19.

LACK, D., GIBB, J., & OWEN, D. F. 1957. Survival in relation to brood-size in tits. *Proc. zool. Soc. Lond.* **128**: 313–26.

LACK, D., & SCHIFFERLI, A. 1948. Die Lebensdauer des Stares. *Orn. Beob.* **45**: 107–14.

LANGE, H. 1954. Gibt es zweijährige Brüter und alte Nichtbrüter beim Weissen Storch? *Vogelwarte* **17**: 150–8.

LEES, J. 1946. All the year breeding of the Rock-Dove. *Br. Birds* **39**: 136–41.

LEOPOLD, A. 1933. *Game Management* (New York), p. 69.

LEOPOLD, A., SOWLS, L. K., & SPENCER, D. L. 1947. A survey of over-populated deer ranges in the United States. *J. Wildl. Mgnt.* **11**: 162–77.

LESLIE, P. H., CHITTY, D., & CHITTY, H. 1953. The estimation of population parameters from data obtained by means of the capture–recapture method. *Biometrika* **40**: 137–69.

LÉVÊQUE, R. 1964. Notes sur la reproduction des oiseaux aux Iles Galapagos. *Alauda* **32**: 7–44.

LIBBERT, W. 1954. Wo verbleiben die Weissstörche aller Altersstufen in den Brutmonaten? *Vogelwarte* **17**: 100–13.

LICHATSHEV, G. N. 1955. The Pied Flycatcher (*Muscicapa hypoleuca* Pall.) and its connection with the breeding area (translated title). *Pap. Ringing Bureau Moscow* **8**: 123–56.

LOCKIE, J. D. 1955*a*. The breeding and feeding of Jackdaws and Rooks, with notes on Carrion Crows and other Corvidae. *Ibis* **97**: 341–369.

— 1955*b*. The breeding habits and food of Short-eared Owls after a vole plague. *Bird Study* **2**: 53–69.

— 1956. Winter fighting in feeding flocks of Rooks, Jackdaws and Carrion Crows. *Bird Study* **3**: 180–90.

LOCKLEY, R. M. 1942. *Shearwaters* (London).

LÖHRL, H. 1949. Polygynie, Sprengung der Ehegemeinschaft und Adoption beim Halsbandfliegenschnäpper (*Mucicapa a. albicollis*). *Vogelwarte* **15**: 94–100.

— 1957. Populationsökologische Untersuchungen beim Halsbandschnäpper (*Ficedula albicollis*). *Bonn. zool. Beitr.* **2**: 130–77.

BIBLIOGRAPHY

Löhrl, H. 1959. Weitere Fälle von Polygynie und Adoption beim Halsband-schnäpper (*Ficedula albicollis*). *Vogelwarte* **20**: 33–34.

Lotka, A. J. 1925. *Elements of Physical Biology* (Baltimore).

Lovat, Lord. 1911. *Moor management*. In *The Grouse in Health and in Disease*, ed. Lovat (London), pp. 372–91.

MacArthur, R. 1955. Fluctuations of animal populations, and a measure of community stability. *Ecology* **36**: 533–6.

MacIntyre, D. 1918. Heather and grouse disease. *Br. Birds* **12**: 53–60.

MacKenzie, J. M. D. 1952. Fluctuations in the numbers of British tetraonids. *J. Anim. Ecol.* **21**: 128–53.

MacKenzie, N. 1954. Low wages and large families. *New Statesman and Nation*, 26 June: 823.

MacLellan, C. R. 1958. Role of woodpeckers in control of the Codling Moth in Nova Scotia. *Can. Ent.* **90**: 18–22.

— 1959. Woodpeckers as predators of the Codling Moth in Nova Scotia. *Can. Ent.* **91**: 673–80.

— 1961. Woodpecker control of the Codling Moth in Nova Scotia orchards. *Atlant. Nat.* **16**: 17–25.

Maher, W. J. 1962. Breeding biology of the Snow Petrel near Cape Hallett, Antarctica. *Condor* **64**: 488–99.

Marchant, S. 1960. The breeding of some S.W. Ecuadorian birds. *Ibis* **102**: 349–82, 584–99.

Marshall, A. J. 1949. Weather factors and spermatogenesis in birds. *Proc. zool. Soc. Lond.* **119**: 711–16.

Marshall, A. J., & Disney, H. J. de S. 1957. Experimental induction of the breeding season in a xerophilous bird. *Nature, Lond.* **180**: 647–9.

Marshall, A. J., & Serventy, D. L. 1956a. The breeding cycle of the Short-tailed Shearwater, *Puffinus tenuirostris* (Temminck), in relation to trans-equatorial migration and its environment. *Proc. zool. Soc. Lond.* **127**: 489–510.

Marshall, A. J., & Serventy, D. L. 1956b. Moult adaptation in relation to long-distance migration in petrels. *Nature, Lond.* **177**: 943.

Massey, C. L., & Wygant, N. D. 1954. Biology and control of the Engelmann Spruce Beetle in Colorado. *U.S. Dep. Agric. Circ.* 944.

Matthews, G. V. T. 1954. Some aspects of incubation in the Manx Shear-water, *Procellaria puffinus*, with particular reference to chilling resistance in the embryo. *Ibis* **96**: 432–40.

Matthews, L. H. 1929. The birds of South Georgia. *Discovery* Rep. 1: 561–92.

Mayer-Gross, H., & Perrins, C. M. 1962. Blackbirds rearing five broods in one season. *Br. Birds* **55**: 189–90.

McLachlan, G. R., & Liversidge, R. 1958. *Roberts' Birds of South Africa* (Cape Town).

Meidell, O. 1961. Life history of the Pied Flycatcher and the Redstart in Norwegian mountain area (rewritten by L. von Haartman). *Nyt Mag. zool.* **10**: 5–48.

Meinertzhagen, R. M. 1956. Birds in Greenland. *Bull. Br. orn. Club* **76**: 17–22.

Merikallio, E. 1946. Über regionale Verbreitung und Anzahl der Landvögel in Süd und Mittelfinland, etc. *Annls. zool. Soc. Bot. fenn. Vanamo* **12**: esp. pp. 34–36.

Milne, A. 1957a. The natural control of insect populations. *Can. Ent.* **89**: 193–213.

BIBLIOGRAPHY

MILNE, A. 1957b. Theories of natural control of insect populations. *Cold Spring Harb. Symp. quant. Biol.* **22**: 253–71.

— 1961. Definition of competition among animals. *Symp. Soc. exp. Biol.* **15**: 40–61.

— 1962. On a theory of natural control of insect population. *J. theoret. Biol.* **3**: 19–50.

MOOK, L. J. 1963. Birds and the spruce budworm, in *Dynamics of Epidemic Spruce Budworm Populations*, ed. R. F. MORRIS. *Mem. ent. Soc. Can.* **31**: 268–71.

MORAN, P. A. P. 1952. The statistical analysis of game-bird records. *J. Anim. Ecol.* **21**: 154–8.

MOREAU, R. E. 1950. The breeding seasons of African birds—I. Land birds. *Ibis* **92**: 223–67.

MOREL, G., & BOURLIÈRE, F. 1955. Recherches écologiques sur *Quelea quelea quelea* (L.) de la basse vallée du Sénégal. 1. Données quantitatives sur le cycle annuel. *Bull. Inst. fr. Afr. noire* **17** (A): 618–63.

MOREL, G., & BOURLIÈRE, F. 1956. Recherches écologiques sur les *Quelea quelea quelea* (L.) de la basse vallée du Sénégal. 11. La Reproduction. *Alauda* **24**: 97–122.

MOREL, G., MOREL, M.-Y., & BOURLIÈRE, F. 1957. The Black-faced Weaver-bird or Dioch in West Africa. *J. Bombay nat. Hist. Soc.* **54**: 811–25.

MOREL, M.-Y. 1964. Natalité et mortalité dans une population naturelle d'un passereau tropical, le *Lagonosticta senegala*. *Terre Vie* **111**: 436–51.

MORRIS, D. 1954. The snail-eating behaviour of Thrushes and Blackbirds. *Br. Birds* **47**: 33–49.

MORRIS, R. F. 1959. Single-factor analysis in population dynamics. *Ecology* **40**: 580–8.

— 1963. Predation and the spruce budworm in *Dynamics of Epidemic Spruce Budworm Populations*, ed. R. F. MORRIS. *Mem. ent. Soc. Can.* **31**: 244–8.

MORRIS, R. F., CHESHIRE, W. F., MILLER, C. A., & MOTT, D. G. 1958. The numerical response of avian and mammalian predators during a gradation of the spruce budworm. *Ecology* **39**: 487–94.

MORTON, J. M. 1847. *Box and Cox* (London).

MURPHY, R. C. 1936. *Oceanic Birds of South America* (New York).

MURTON, R. K. 1958. The breeding of Woodpigeon populations. *Bird Study* **5**: 157–83.

— 1961. Some survival estimates for the Woodpigeon. *Bird Study* **8**: 165–73.

MURTON, R. K., & ISAACSON, A. J. 1962. The functional basis of some behaviour in the Woodpigeon *Columba palumbus*. *Ibis* **104**: 503–21.

MURTON, R. K., ISAACSON, A. J., & WESTWOOD, N. J. 1963a. The food and growth of nestling Woodpigeons in relation to the breeding season. *Proc. zool. Soc. Lond.* **141** 747–81.

MURTON, R. K., ISAACSON, A. J., & WESTWOOD, N. J. 1963b. The feeding ecology of the Woodpigeon. *Br. Birds* **56**: 345–75.

MURTON, R. K., & ISAACSON, A. J. 1964. Productivity and egg predation in the Woodpigeon. *Ardea* **52**: 30–47.

MURTON, R. K., WESTWOOD, N. J., & ISAACSON, A. J. 1964. A preliminary investigation of the factors regulating population size in the Woodpigeon *Columba palumbus*. *Ibis* **106**: 482–507.

MYKYTOWYCZ, R. 1963. 'Limey-bird disease' in chicks of the Tasmanian Mutton-bird (*Puffinus tenuirostris*). *C.S.I.R.O. Res. Org.* **7**: 67–79

BIBLIOGRAPHY

MYKYTOWYCZ, R., DANE, D. S., & BEECH, M. 1955. Orthinosis in the petrel, *Puffinus tenuirostris* (Temminck). *Aust. J. exp. Biol. med. Sci.* **33**: 629–36.

MYRES, M. T. 1955. The breeding of Blackbird, Song Thrush and Mistle Thrush in Great Britain. Part I. Breeding seasons. *Bird Study* **2**: 2–24.

NELSON, J. B. 1964. Factors influencing clutch-size and chick growth in the North Atlantic Gannet, *Sula bassana*. *Ibis* **106**: 63–77.

NEWTON, A. 1874. Rev. enlarged 4th ed. of W. YARRELL, *A History of British Birds* (London), vol. 1, p. 491.

NEWTON, I. 1964. Bud-eating by Bullfinches in relation to the natural food-supply. *J. appl. Ecol.* **1**: 265–79.

NICE, M. M. 1937. Studies in the life history of the Song Sparrow, vol. 1. *Trans. Linn. Soc. N. Y.* **4**: 1–247.

— 1953. The question of ten-day incubation periods. *Wilson Bull.* **65**: 81–93.

NICHOLSON, A. J. 1933. The balance of animal populations. *J. Anim. Ecol.* **2**: 132–78.

— 1947. Fluctuations of animal populations. *Aust. N. Z. Ass. Advmt. Sci.*, 1947, pp. 1–14.

— 1954. An outline of the dynamics of animal populations. *Aust. J. zool.* **2**: 9–65.

— 1958a. The self-adjustment of populations to change. *Cold Spring Harb. Symp. quant. Biol.* **22**: 153–73.

— 1958b. Dynamics of insect populations. *A. Rev. Ent.* **3**: 107–36.

— 1959. Density-dependent factors in ecology. *Nature, Lond.* **183**: 911–12.

NICHOLSON, E. M. 1955. Special review. Lack on the natural regulation of animal numbers. *Br. Birds* **48**: 38–42.

— 1962. Special review. *Ibis* **104**: 570–1.

OLSSON, V. 1958. Dispersal, migration, longevity and death causes of *Strix aluco*, *Buteo buteo*, *Ardea cinerea* and *Larus argentatus*. *Acta vertebr.* **1**: 81–189.

ORIANS, G. H. 1958. A capture-recapture analysis of a shearwater population. *J. Anim. Ecol.* **27**: 71–86.

— 1960. Autumnal breeding in the Tricolored Blackbird. *Auk* **77**: 379–98.

— 1961a. Social stimulation within blackbird colonies. *Condor* **63**: 330–7.

— 1961b. The ecology of blackbird (*Agelaius*) social systems. *Ecol. Monogr.* **31**: 285–312.

— 1962. Natural selection and ecological theory. *Am. Nat.* **96**: 257–63.

OWEN, D. F. 1960. The nesting success of the Heron *Ardea cinerea* in relation to the availability of food. *Proc. zool. Soc. Lond.* **133**: 597–617.

PARK, T. 1961. An ecologist's view. *Bull. ecol. Soc. Am.* **42**: 4–10.

PEARSALL, W. H. 1950. *Mountains and Moorlands* (London), esp. pp. 143–7.

PERRINS, C. M. 1963. Survival in the Great Tit, *Parus major*. *Proc. Int. orn. Congr.* **13**: 717–28.

— 1964. Survival of young Swifts in relation to brood-size. *Nature, Lond.* **201**: 1147–8.

— 1965. Population fluctuations and clutch-size in the Great Tit, *Parus major*. *J. Anim. Ecol.* **34**: 601–47

PHILLIPS, J. H. 1963. The pelagic distribution of the Sooty Shearwater *Procellaria grisea*. *Ibis* **105**: 340–53.

PIECHOCKI, R. 1960. Über die Winterverluste der Schleiereule (*Tyto alba*). *Vogelwarte* **20**: 274–80.

— 1961. Über die Grossgefieder-Mauser von Schleiereule und Waldkauz. *J. orn., Lpz.* **102**: 220–5.

BIBLIOGRAPHY

PITELKA, F. A. 1957. Some characteristics of microtine cycles in the arctic. *Arctic Biology*, ed. H. P. HANSEN. *18th Ann. Biol. Colloq.*, pp. 73–88.

— 1958. Some aspects of population structure in the short-term cycle of the Brown Lemming in northern Alaska. *Cold Spring Harb. Symp. quant. Biol.* (1957) **22**: 237–51.

— 1959. Population studies of Lemmings and Lemming predators in northern Alaska. *Int. Congr. zool.* **15**: 757–9.

PITELKA, F. A., TOMICH, P. Q., & TREICHEL, G. W. 1955a. Ecological relations of jaegers and owls as lemming predators near Barrow, Alaska. *Ecol. Monogr.* **25**: 85–117.

PITELKA, F. A., TOMICH, P. Q., & TREICHEL, G. W. 1955b. Breeding behavior of jaegers and owls near Barrow. Alaska. *Condor* **57**: 3–18.

PRÉVOST, J. 1953. Formation des couples, ponte et incubation chez le Manchot Empereur. *Alauda* **21**: 141–56.

— 1958. Étude comparative de la mortalité à la colonie de Manchots empereurs de Pointe-Geologie pendant les années 1952 et 1956. *Oiseau* **28**: 99–111.

— 1961. *Écologie du Manchot Empereur* (Paris).

RALPHS, P. 1956. Notes on Manx Shearwater, 1956. *Skokholm Bird Observatory Report 1956*, pp. 19–22.

RICE, D. W., & KENYON, K. W. 1962. Breeding cycles and behavior of Laysan and Black-footed Albatrosses. *Auk* **79**: 517–67.

RICHARDS, O. W. 1961. The theoretical and practical study of natural insect populations. *A. Rev. Ent.* **6**: 147–62.

RICHDALE, L. E. 1952. Post-egg period in albatrosses. *Biol. Monogr.* No. 4, *Nuffield Publ.* No. 1 (Dunedin).

RICHDALE, L. E. 1954. The starvation theory in albatrosses. *Auk* **71**: 239–52.

— 1957. A Population Study of Penguins (Oxford).

— 1963. Biology of the Sooty Shearwater *Puffinus griseus*. *Proc. zool. Soc. Lond.* **141**: 1–117.

ROSENZWEIG, M. L., & MACARTHUR, R. H. 1963. Graphical representation and stability conditions of predator-prey interactions. *Am. Nat.* **97**: 209–23.

ROSS, H. H. 1957. Principles of natural coexistence indicated by leafhopper populations. *Evolution* **11**: 113–29.

— 1958. Further comments on niches and natural coexistence. *Evolution* **12**: 112–13.

ROWAN, M. K. 1952. The Greater Shearwater *Puffinus gravis* at its breeding grounds. *Ibis* **94**: 97–121.

SAPIN-JALOUSTRE, J. 1960. *Écologie du Manchot Adélie* (Paris).

SAUTER, U. 1956. Beiträge zur Ökologie der Schleiereule (*Tyto alba*) nach den Ringfunden. *Vogelwarte* **18**: 109–51.

SAUTER, U., & SCHÜZ, E. 1954. Bestandsveränderungen beim Weissstorch: Dritte Übersicht, 1939–53. *Vogelwarte* **17**: 81–100.

SAVAGE, J. M. 1958. The concept of ecologic niche, with reference to the theory of natural coexistence. *Evolution* **12**: 111–12.

SCHEIDER, W. 1955. Die Lebensdauer und Brutgrösse beim mitteldeutschen Star. *Proc. Int. orn. Congr.* **11**: 516–21.

SCHIFFERLI, A. 1957. Alter und Sterblichkeit bei Waldkauz (*Strix aluco*) und Schleiereule (*Tyto alba*) in der Schweiz. *Orn. Beob.* **54**: 50–56.

SCHMAUS, A. 1938. Der Einfluss der Mäusejahre auf das Brutgeschäft unserer Raubvögel und Eulen. *Beitr. Fortpfl Biol. Vögel* **14**: 181–4.

SCHNETTER, W., & ZINK, G. 1960. Zur Frage des Brutreifealters südwestdeutscher Weiss-Störche (*C. ciconia*). *Proc. Int. orn. Congr.* **12**: 662–6.

BIBLIOGRAPHY

Schüz, E. 1940. Bewegungen im Bestand des Weissen Storches seit 1934. *Orn. Mber.* **48**: 1–14.

— 1942. Bestandsregelnde Einflüsse in der Umwelt des Weissen Storchs (*C. ciconia*). *Zool. Jb. (Systematik)* **75**: 103–20.

— 1943. Über die Jungenaufzucht des Weissen Storches (*C. ciconia*). *Z. Morph. Ökol. Tiere* **40**: 181–237.

— 1949. Reifung, Ansiedlung und Bestandswechsel beim Weissen Storch (*C. ciconia*). *Ornithologie als biologische Wissenschaft*, ed. E. Mayr & E. Schüz (Heidelberg), pp. 217–28.

— 1955. Über den Altersaufbau von Weissstorch-Populationen. *Proc. Int. orn. Congr.* **11**: 522–28.

— 1957. Das Verschlingen eigener Junger ('Kronismus') bei Vögeln und seine Bedeutung. *Vogelwarte* **19**: 1–15.

— 1959. Problems about the White Stork *Ciconia ciconia* in Africa seen from a European viewpoint. *Proc. First Pan-Afr. orn. Congr. Ostrich Suppl.* **3**: 333–41.

— 1962. Über die nordwestlich Zugscheide des Weissen Storchs. *Vogelwarte* **21**: 269–90.

— 1963. Über die Zugscheiden des Weissstorchs in Afrika, Ukraine und Asien. *Vogelwarte* **22**: 65–70.

Schüz, E., & Szijj, J. 1960. Vorläufiger Bericht über die Internationale Bestandsaufnahme des Weissstorchs 1958; Bestandsveränderungen beim Weissstorch: Vierte Übersicht, 1954 bis 1958. *Vogelwarte* **20**: 253–73.

Schüz, E., & Szijj, J. 1961. Vom Weissstorchbestand in Deutschland 1934 bis 1958. *J. orn. Lpz.* **102**: 28–33.

Schüz, E., & Szijj, J. 1962. Report on the international census of the White Stork 1958. *Bull. int. Comm. Bird Preserv.* Tokio, 1962. **8**: 86–98.

Schüz, E., & Zink, G. 1955. Bibliographie der Weissstorch—Untersuchungen der Vogelwarten Rossitten—Radolfzell und Helgoland. *Vogelwarte* **18** (suppl.): 81–85.

Schüz, E. *et al.* 1955. Hohe Lebensalter bei Störchen. *Vogelwarte* **18**: 21–22.

Selander, R. K. 1960. Sex ratio of nestlings and clutch size in the Boat-tailed Grackle. *Condor* **62**: 34–44.

Semenov-Tyan-Shanskii, O. I. 1960. *The Ecology of Tetraonidae* (English summary pp. 301–9 of book in Russian, Moscow, 1960).

Serventy, D. L. 1957. Duration of immaturity in the Short-tailed Shearwater *Puffinus tenuirostris* (Temminck). *C.S.I.R.O. Wildl. Res.* **2**: 60–62.

— 1958. Recent studies on the Tasmanian Mutton-Bird. *Aust. Mus. Mag.* **12**: 327-32.

— 1961. The banding programme on *Puffinus tenuirostris* (Temminck). *C.S.I.R.O. Wildl. Res.* **6**: 42–55.

— 1962. In *Handbook of North American Birds*, ed. R. S. Palmer (New Haven), vol. 1, pp. 182–4.

— 1963. Egg-laying timetable of the Slender-billed Shearwater *Puffinus tenuirostris. Proc. Int. orn. Congr.* **13**: 338–43.

Siivonen, L. 1954. On the short-term fluctuations in numbers of tetraonids Pap. Game Res. (Finnish Foundation for Game Preservation), *Riistat. Julk.* **13**: 1–10

— 1956. The correlation between the fluctuations of Partridge and European Hare populations and the climatic conditions of winters in South-West Finland during the last thirty years. Pap. Game Res. (Finnish Game Foundation), *Riistat. Julk.* **17**: 1–30.

BIBLIOGRAPHY

Siivonen, L. 1957. The problems of the short-term fluctuations in numbers of tetraonids in Europe. Pap. Game Res. (Finnish Game Foundation), *Riistat. Julk.* **19**: 1–44.

— 1958. Basic reasons for tetraonid lows and the application of the results obtained. *Suom. Riista* **12**: 43–54.

Skutch, A. F. 1949. Do tropical birds rear as many young as they can nourish? *Ibis* **91**: 430–55.

— 1953. Delayed reproductive maturity in birds. *Ibis* **95**: 153–4.

— 1961. Helpers among birds. *Condor* **63**: 198–226.

Sladen, W. J. L. 1958. The pygoscelid penguins. 1. methods of study. 2. the Adélie Penguin *Pygoscelis adeliae* (Hombron & Jacquinot). *Scient. Rep. Falkld Isl. Depend. Surv.* **17**: 1–97.

Smith, F. E. 1961. Density dependence in the Australian Thrips. *Ecology* **42**: 403–7.

Smith, J. M. 1964. Group selection and kin selection. *Nature, Lond.* **201**: 1145–7.

Snow, D. W. 1955a. The breeding of the Blackbird, Song Thrush, and Mistle Thrush in Great Britain. Part 2. Clutch-size. *Bird Study* **2**: 72–84.

— 1955b. The breeding of Blackbird, Song Thrush, and Mistle Thrush in Great Britain Part 3. Nesting success. *Bird Study* **2**: 169–78.

— 1956a. The annual mortality of the Blue Tit in different parts of its range. *Br. Birds* **49**: 174–7.

— 1956b. Territory in the Blackbird, *Turdus merula*. *Ibis* **98**: 438–47.

— 1958a. *A Study of Blackbirds* (London).

— 1958b. The breeding of the Blackbird, *Turdus merula*, at Oxford. *Ibis* **100**: 1–30.

— 1961. The natural history of the Oilbird, *Steatornis caripensis*, in Trinidad, W.I. Pt. 1. General behaviour and breeding habits. *Zoologica* **46**: 27–48.

— 1962a. A field study of the Black and White Manakin, *Manacus manacus*, in Trinidad. *Zoologica* **47**: 65–104.

— 1962b. A field study of the Golden-headed Manakin, *Pipra erythrocephala*, in Trinidad, W.I. *Zoologica* **47**: 183–98.

— 1962c. The natural history of the Oilbird, *Steatornis caripensis*, in Trinidad, W.I. Pt. 2. Population, breeding ecology and food. *Zoologica* **47**: 199–221.

Solomon, M. E. 1949. The natural control of animal populations. *J. Anim. Ecol.* **18**: 1–35.

— 1957. Dynamics of insect populations. *A. Rev. Ent.* **2**: 121–42.

— 1958a. Meaning of density-dependence and related terms in population dynamics. *Nature, Lond.* **181**: 1778–80.

— 1958b. Perfect and imperfect density dependence in population dynamics. *Nature, Lond.* **182**: 1251–2.

— 1959. The meaning of density-dependence and related concepts. *Proc. Fifteenth Int. Congr. zool.*, London, 1958, pp. 784–7.

Southern, H. N. 1954. Tawny Owls and their prey. *Ibis* **96**: 384–410.

— 1959. Mortality and population control. *Ibis* **101**: 429–36.

Southern, H. N., Vaughan, R., & Muir, R. C. 1954. The behaviour of young Tawny Owls after fledging. *Bird Study* **1**: 101–10.

Steinbacher, G. 1953. Zur Biologie der Amsel (*Turdus merula* L.). *Biol. Abh.* **5**

Stevenson-Hamilton, J. 1937. *South African Eden* (London), esp. p. 259.

Stoker, M. G. P., & Miles, J. A. R. 1953. Studies on the causative agent of an epizootic amongst Manx Shearwaters. *J. Hyg., Camb.* **51**: 195–202.

BIBLIOGRAPHY

STONEHOUSE, B. 1956. The King Penguin of South Georgia. *Nature, Lond.* **178**: 1424–6.

— 1960. The King Penguin *Aptenodytes patagonica* of South Georgia. 1. Breeding behaviour and development. *Scient. Rep. Falkld Isl. Depend. Surv.* **23**: 1–81.

— 1964. Emperor Penguins at Cape Crozier. *Nature, Lond.* **203**: 849–51.

SUOMALAINEN, H. 1937. The effect of temperature on the sexual activity of non-migratory birds, stimulated by artificial lighting. *Ornis fenn.* **14**: 108–12.

SVÄRDSON, G. 1957. The 'invasion' type of bird migration. *Br. Birds* **50**: 314–43.

SWALES, M. K. 1965. The sea-birds of Gough Island. *Ibis* **107**: 17–42, 215–29.

SWANBERG, P. O. 1951. Food storage, territory and song in the Thick-billed Nutcracker. *Proc. Int. orn. Congr.* **10**: 545–54.

TANTZEN, R. 1962. Der Weisse Storch *Ciconia ciconia* (L.) im Lande Oldenburg. *Oldenburger Jahrbücher* **61**: 105–213.

TAYLOR, T. H. C. 1937. *The Biological Control of an Insect in Fiji* (London).

THOMPSON, W. R. 1956. The fundamental theory of natural and biological control. *A. Rev. Ent.* **1**: 379–402.

TICEHURST, N. F., & WITHERBY, H. F. 1940. Report on the effect of the severe winter of 1939–40 on bird-life in the British Isles. *Br. Birds* **34**: 118–32, 142–55.

TICEHURST, N. F., & HARTLEY, P. H. T. 1948. Report on the effect of the severe winter of 1946–7 on bird-life. *Br. Birds* **41**: 322–34.

TICKELL, W. L. N. 1960. Chick-feeding in the Wandering Albatross *Diomedea exulans* Linnaeus. *Nature, Lond.* **185**: 116–17.

— 1962. The Dove Prion, *Pachyptila desolata* Gmelin. *Scient. Rep. Falkld Isl. Depnd. Surv.* **33**: 1–55.

TINBERGEN, L. 1946. De Sperwer als roofvijand van zangvogels. *Ardea* **34**: 1–213.

— 1949. Bosvogels en insecten. *Nederl. Bosch Tijdschr.* **4**: 91–105.

TINBERGEN, L. *et al.* 1960. The dynamics of insect and bird populations in pine woods. *Archs. néerl. zool.* **13**: 259–472.

TINBERGEN, N. 1951. *The Study of Instinct* (Oxford), p. 170.

— 1957. The functions of territory. *Bird Study* **4**: 14–27.

TOLLENAAR, D. 1922. Legperioden en eierproductie bij eenige wilde vogelsoorten, vergeleken met die bij hoenderrassen. *Meded. Landbouwhoogeschool Wageningen* 23 verh. 2.

TOMPA, F. S. 1962. Territorial behavior: the main controlling factor of a local Song Sparrow population. *Auk* **79**: 687–97.

— 1963. Behavioral response of Song Sparrows to different environmental conditions. *Proc. Int. orn. Congr.* **13**: 729–39.

— 1964. Factors determining the numbers of Song Sparrows *Melospiza melodia* (Wilson), on Mandarte Island, B.C., Canada. *Acta zool. fenn.* **109**: 1–68.

TRETTAU, W. 1952. Planberingung des Trauerfliegenschnäppers (*Muscicapa hypoleuca*) in Hessen. *Vogelwarte* **16**: 89–95.

TRETTAU, W., & MERKEL, F. 1943. Ergebnisse einer Planberingung des Trauerfliegenfängers (*Muscicapa hypoleuca* Pallas) in Schlesien. *Vogelzug* **14**: 77–90.

UDVARDY, M. F. D. 1959. Notes on the ecological concepts of habitat, biotope and niche. *Ecology* **40**: 725–8.

BIBLIOGRAPHY

ULFSTRAND, S. 1962. On the nonbreeding ecology and migratory movements of the Great Tit (*Parus major*) and the Blue Tit (*Parus caeruleus*) in southern Sweden. *Fågelv.* Suppl. 3, p. 145.

VALVERDE, J. A. 1960. La population d'Aigles Impériaux (*Aquila heliaca adalberti*) des marismas du Guadalquivir; son évolution depuis un siècle. *Alauda* **28**: 20–26.

VAN DOBBEN, W. H. 1952. The food of the Cormorant in the Netherlands. *Ardea* **40**: 1–63.

VARLEY, G. C. 1957. Ecology as an experimental science. *J. Ecol.* **45**: 639–48.

— 1958. Meaning of density-dependence and related terms in population dynamics. *Nature, Lond.* **181**: 1778–81.

— 1959. Density-dependent factors in ecology. *Nature, Lond.* **183**: 911.

— 1963. The interpretation of change and stability in insect populations. *Proc. R. ent. Soc. Lond.* C. **27**: 52–57.

VARLEY, G. C., & GRADWELL, G. R. 1958. Balance in insect populations. *Proc. Int. Congr. Ent.* **10** (2): 619–24.

VARLEY, G. C., & GRADWELL, G. R. 1960. Key factors in population studies. *J. Anim. Ecol.* **29**: 399–401.

VENABLES, L. S. V., & U. M. 1952. The Blackbird in Shetland. *Ibis* **94**: 636–53.

VERMEER, K. 1963. The breeding ecology of the Glaucous-winged Gull (*Larus glaucescens*) on Mandarte Island, B.C. *Occ. Pap. Br. Columb. prov. Mus.* 13, p. 90.

VESEY-FITZGERALD, D. F. 1958. Notes on breeding colonies of the Red-billed Quelea in S. W. Tanganyika. *Ibis* **100**: 167–74.

VOLTERRA, V. 1926. Variazioni e fluttuzaioni del numero d'individui in specie animali conviventi. *Atti Accad. naz. Lincei. Memorie* (6) **2**: 31–113.

VOOUS, K. H. 1960. *Atlas of European Birds* (London), esp. pp. 79, 230.

VOOUS, K. H., & WATTEL, J. 1963. Distribution and migration of the Greater Shearwater. *Ardea* **51**: 143–57.

WAGNER, H. O. 1957. Variation in clutch size at different latitudes. *Auk* **74**: 243–50.

— 1960. Beziehungen zwischen Umweltfaktoren und der Brutzeit, Zahl der Gelege sowie ihrer Grösse. *Zool. Anz.* **164**: 161–72.

WARD, P. 1963. Contributions to the ecology of the weaver-bird *Quelea quelea*, Linnaeus, in Nigeria (thesis, University College, Ibadan).

— 1965. Feeding ecology of the Black-faced Dioch, *Quelea quelea*, in Nigeria. *Ibis* **107**: 173–214. See also Ibis **107**: 326–49.

WARHAM, J. 1962. The biology of the Giant Petrel *Macronectes giganteus*. *Auk* **79**: 139–60.

WATSON, A. 1957. The behaviour, breeding, and food-ecology of the Snowy Owl *Nyctea scandiaca*. *Ibis* **99**: 419–62.

— 1964a. Aggression and population regulation in Red Grouse. *Nature, Lond.* **202**: 506–7.

— 1964b. The food of Ptarmigan (*Lagopus mutus*) in Scotland. *Scott. Nat.* **71**: 60–66.

— 1965. A population study of Ptarmigan (*Lagopus mutus*) in Scotland. *J. Anim. Ecol.* **34**: 135–72.

WATSON, A., & JENKINS, D. 1964. Notes on the behaviour of the Red Grouse. *Br. Birds* **57**: 137–70.

WEEDEN, R. B. 1963. Management of Ptarmigan in North America. *J. Wildl. Mgmt.* **27**: 673–83.

BIBLIOGRAPHY

WEITNAUER, E., & LACK, D. 1955. Daten zur Fortpflanzungsbiologie des Mauerseglers (*Apus apus*) in Oltingen und Oxford. *Orn. Beob.* **52**: 137-41.

WENDLAND, V. 1958. Zum Problem des vorzeitigen Sterbens von jungen Greifvögeln und Eulen. *Vogelwarte* **19**: 186–91.

— 1963. Fünfjährige Beobachtungen an einer Population des Waldkauzes (*Strix aluco*) im Berliner Grunewald. *J. orn., Lpz.* **104**: 23–57.

WILLIAMS, G. C., & D. C. 1957. Natural selection of individually harmful social adaptations among sibs with special reference to social insects. *Evolution* **11**: 32–39.

WILLIAMS, J. G. 1954. The Quelea threat to Africa's grain crops. *East Afr. agric. J.* **19**: 133–6.

WILLIAMSON, K. 1952. The incubation rhythm of the Fulmar. *Scott. Nat.* **64**: 138–147.

— 1959. Changes of mating within a colony of Arctic Skuas. *Bird Study* **6**: 51–60.

WILLIAMSON, M. H. 1957. An elementary theory of interspecific competition. *Nature, Lond.* **180**: 422–5.

WILSON, C. E. 1947. The Sudan Dioch in grain-growing areas. *Sudan Notes Rec.* **28**: 151–6.

WRIGHT, S. 1945. Tempo and mode in evolution: a critical review. *Ecology* **26**: 415–19.

WYNNE-EDWARDS, V. C. 1955. Low reproductive rates in birds, especially sea-birds. *Proc. Int. orn. Congr.* **11**: 540–7.

— 1959. The control of population-density through social behaviour: a hypothesis. *Ibis* **101**: 436–41.

— 1960. The overfishing principle applied to natural populations and their food-resources: and a theory of natural conservation. *Proc. Int. orn. Congr.* **12**: 790–4.

— 1962. *Animal Dispersion in Relation to Social Behaviour* (Edinburgh).

— 1963. Intergroup selection in the evolution of social systems. *Nature, Lond.* **200**: 623–6.

— 1964. Significance of clutch-size in swift and Grouse. *Nature, Lond.* **203**: 99.

YEAGER, L. E. 1955. Two woodpecker populations in relation to environmental change. *Condor* **57**: 148–53.

YOUNG, H. 1951. Territorial behavior in the Eastern Robin *Proc. Linn. Soc. N. Y.* **58-62**: 1–37.

— 1956. Territorial activities of the American Robin *Turdus migratorius*. *Ibis* **98**: 448–52.

ZINK, G. 1963a. Populationsuntersuchungen am Weissen Storch (*Ciconia ciconia*) in S. W. Deutschland. *Proc. Int. orn. Congr.* **13**: 812–18.

— 1963b. Der Weissstorch-Bestand in Baden-Württemberg 1960–1962, *Beitr. naturk. Forsch. SüdwDtl.* **22**: 89–96.

INDEX

(*Note:* All birds are indexed under the vernacular group name followed by the specific name, and are also listed under the genus followed by the species, cross-referring to the vernacular name. The same procedure has usually been followed for other organisms, but some of them have been indexed under both vernacular and scientific names where simpler.)

INDEX